MW01195812

JOURNAL FOR THE STUDY OF THE OLD TESTAMENT
SUPPLEMENT SERIES

381

Editors
David J.A. Clines
Philip R. Davies

Executive Editor
Andrew Mein

Editorial Board
Richard J. Coggins, Alan Cooper, J. Cheryl Exum,
John Goldingay, Robert P. Gordon, Norman K. Gottwald,
John Jarick, Andrew D.H. Mayes, Carol Meyers,
Patrick D. Miller

COPENHAGEN INTERNATIONAL SEMINAR

13

General Editors
Thomas L. Thompson
Niels Peter Lemche

Associate Editors
Modens Müller
Hakan Ulfgard

Jerusalem
in Ancient History
and Tradition

edited by

Thomas L. Thompson

with the collaboration of
Salma Khadra Jayyusi

 T&T CLARK INTERNATIONAL
A Continuum imprint
LONDON • NEW YORK

Copyright © 2003 T&T Clark International
A Continuum imprint

Published by T&T Clark International
The Tower Building, 11 York Road, London SE1 7NX
15 East 26th Street, Suite 1703, New York, NY 10010

www.tandtclark.com

All rights reserved. No part of this publication may be reproduced or transmitted in
any form or by any means, electronic or mechanical, including photocopying,
recording or any information storage or retrieval system, without permission in
writing from the publishers.

British Library Cataloguing-in-Publication Data
A catalogue record for this book is available from the British Library

Typeset and edited for Continuum by Forthcoming Publications Ltd
www.forthcomingpublications.com

Printed   in Great Britain by The Cromwell Press,
Trowbridge, Wiltshire.

ISBN 0-8264-6664-8 (hardback)
       0-5670-8360-8 (paperback)

CONTENTS

Foreword   vii
Preface   xiii
Acknowledgments   xvi
Abbreviations   xviii
List of Contributors   xxi

THOMAS L. THOMPSON
An Introduction: Can a History of Ancient Jerusalem
and Palestine be Written?   1

MICHAEL PRIOR
A Moral Reading of the Bible in Jerusalem   16

NIELS PETER LEMCHE
'House of David': The Tel Dan Inscription(s)   46

MARGREET STEINER
Expanding Borders: The Development of Jerusalem
in the Iron Age   68

SARA MANDELL
Rome, Syria and the Jerusalem High Priest:
The International Bases of the High Priest's Rule
of the Jerusalem City-State: 175–63 BCE   80

JOHN STRANGE
Herod and Jerusalem: The Hellenization of an Oriental City   97

FIRAS SAWAH
Jerusalem in the Time of the Kingdom of Judah   114

LESTER L. GRABBE
Ethnic Groups in Jerusalem   145

PHILIP R. DAVIES
From Zion to Zion: Jerusalem in the Dead Sea Scrolls   164

THOMAS M. BOLIN
The Making of the Holy City: On the Foundations
of Jerusalem in the Hebrew Bible   171

INGRID HJELM
Brothers Fighting Brothers: Jewish and Samaritan
Ethnocentrism in Tradition and History   197

THOMAS L. THOMPSON
Holy War at the Center of Biblical Theology:
Shalom and the Cleansing of Jerusalem   223

DAVID M. GUNN
'Next Year in Jerusalem': Bible, Identity and Myth
on the Web   258

KEITH W. WHITELAM
Imagining Jerusalem   272

Index of References   290
Index of Authors   0

The hijacking of commercial airplanes and their use in the destruction of New York's *World Trade Center* on 11 September 2001 created much uncertainty about plans to have a small conference in Jordan on 12-14 October on the theme of Jerusalem in ancient history and tradition. Three members of the biblical institute at the University of Copenhagen were to take part and the present writer had been responsible for planning the conference together with Dr Salma Khadra Jayyusi. Altogether twelve historians, archaeologists and biblical scholars from six different countries were to meet for two days in Amman to discuss new perspectives on the history of ancient Jerusalem and its relationship to biblical tradition. The audience was to include teachers and scholars from universities in Jordan, Palestine and Syria.

In spite of the uncertain political situation, we decided to hold the conference. For myself, this included accepting a long-standing invitation to visit Riyadh. Accordingly, on 6 October, I flew to that hyper-modern Phoenix-like, big-city of the desert to give a lecture at the King Faisal Islamic research center on the history of Palestine. My hosts were taken up with the task of reassuring their American–Danish guest in a rapidly deteriorating political situation. Within a day of my arrival, the Americans had decided to begin bombing Afghanistan rather than consider negotiations, which would be brokered by either Pakistan or Saudi Arabia. The Saudis expressed understanding for the American need to avenge the horrible and murderous attack on innocent people in New York, but they were also aware of the thousands of innocent Afghanis who would die in a military action that perhaps might be avoided. It was inevitable that my visit was taken up with many long theological discussions about 'holy war' (to be fought only by God) and revenge (which belongs only to God). We also struggled with the fine distinctions of journalists between Islamic terror and American bombing and—central to all our discussions—about the relationship between Palestinians and Israelis which is at the core of any peaceful development in the Middle East. The academic study of religion and freedom of discussion were defended. So also, the misuse of religious language to manipulate society through fundamentalism and uncritical theology was viewed as extremely dangerous. In all these discussions was the awareness that we were on the threshold of just such a dangerous world of competing fundamentalisms. As the bombing in Afghanistan continued as I flew to Amman on 12 October, disjointed thoughts of discussing Jerusalem's ancient past evoked a surrealistic giddiness that replaced my earlier sense of vulnerability with nausea.

I was unhappy that the theme of the conference, *'Jerusalem in ancient history and tradition'* did not seem as tame and comfortable in Amman in October 2001 as it had in Copenhagen the previous summer when we planned it. It quickly became clear that many of my colleagues had re-written their talks after 11 September. History and tradition had become two palpably distinct realities that competed with each other; not just now, but also in the ancient past. The meeting began where many of us already were in our own private thoughts, as the opening speaker, Michael Prior, bluntly demanded that we distinguish between the good and the bad in religious traditions. In doing so he argued for a view of the Bible as a means of oppression as well as that our scholarship be ethically responsible in recognizing its relationship to modern politics. His illustrations with the biblical traditions of the Promised Land and of David's eternal covenant were not less significant for their Palestinian audience. Prior's lecture set a question for the conference, to which each speaker in turn attempted to contribute.

Niels Peter Lemche presented a computer-driven discussion on the 'House of David' inscription fragments from the eighth century, which had been found at Tell el-Qadi, an Iron Age ruin at the headwaters of the Jordan. This inscription has been the center of a decade-long debate among biblical archaeologists and historians. Claimed by some to be direct historical evidence for the Bible's kingdom of David, other scholars have given the fragments a wide range of readings and interpretations, dating them from as early as the ninth to late in the eighth century. Some have suggested that the fragments come from more than a single inscription and a few have raised the possibility that the texts show signs of being forgeries. Modern political concerns have encouraged charges of bias, dishonesty and even anti-Semitism, sprinkled freely wherever the issue has been discussed. While Lemche's demonstration showed that the possibility that we are dealing with a forgery is substantial, his decision not to give a decisive judgment on the issue was frustrating for some. His lecture was followed by Margreet Steiner's presentation of Kathleen Kenyon's 40-year-old excavation of Jerusalem's absent strata from the tenth century.

Steiner, nevertheless, refused to interpret this as unambiguous evidence that Jerusalem had not existed during this period, which the Bible presents as the time of David's great kingdom. She rather—like Lemche—preferred uncertainty in her conclusions and spoke of the likely existence of a town and perhaps a small 'chieftainship' in her historical reconstruction. The reader will also face a similar frustration with two of the papers included in this volume, which could not be presented at the meeting in Amman. Sara Mandell's article discusses the international character of Jerusalem's politics during the second and first centuries. This historian's understanding of the 'Hellenization' of Jerusalem and Palestine disagrees considerably with the understanding implicit in the archaeologist John Strange's paper, which places the development of Hellenization much later. Strange's paper on the policies of Herod the Great during the last half of the first century BCE, moreover, reinterprets the 'Wailing Wall' as a retaining wall for an agora, rather than as a wall belonging to a temple. Both papers significantly change our understanding of Jerusalem at this period, without being reconcilable with each other.

Such implicit disharmony between the various presentations, and between the speakers and the audience, can also be noticed in Firas Sawah's comprehensive presentation of Palestine's history during the first half of the first millennium BCE. This survey was not only based on the Kenyon excavations that Steiner discusses, but also substantially disagrees with Steiner's understanding of Jerusalem's tenth century. An even greater difference can be seen in Sawah's presentation of the seventh-century reign of Josiah, especially in his effort to integrate biblical and historical information, and the understanding of this period as it is discussed in Ingrid Hjelm's paper. Here, a dominant Samaria had not ceased to exist as an integral part of Palestine's political life at this time. One of the conference's most successful results, in my view, has been the recognition and acceptance of the necessity of the freedom and independence for each scholar to draw conclusions based on very limited historical evidence for the past, whatever political interests might dictate. The distinction between tradition and history's distinct views of the past as comprising two separate realities, which could be harmonized with only the greatest caution, was the invaluable and unanimous gain of the congress's open discussions. The disagreements support understanding and keep the discussion open.

While most of the differences in our interpretations of historical events, contexts and periods dealt with major issues that are in fact irreconcilable, no disagreements were so extreme or so far-reaching as those presented on the theme of ethnicity. The disagreement regarding the understanding of an Israelite ethnicity presented in Lester Grabbe's paper, and that of a new Israel's critique of ethnicity in my own contribution, is a long-standing disagreement that is expected to continue. It was, however, critically sharpened by Hjelm's distinction between competing Samaritan and Jewish voices in the biblical tradition. Philip Davies' paper also gave some new focus on the issue. He took up second-century attitudes towards Jerusalem as expressed in texts from Qumran, which led him to further questions about the development of a spiritual Judaism in competition with an expanding Jewish nationalism. The interest in the theme of ethnicity and nationalism at the conference was an unexpected bonus for the conference's second day, as it gave the conference a central focus of great importance. In one way or another, it is the central research question of more than half of the present volume. It is taken up in the papers contributed by Thomas Bolin and David Gunn, who also were unable to come to Amman. Much in line with the more historically oriented discussions of Hjelm and Davies, Bolin surveys the Bible's variant stories about the foundation of Jerusalem and understands them as interactive stories created during the Hellenistic period. He argues that these narratives were used by competing Jewish groups, each of which lay claim to their own understanding of Jerusalem. Gunn's paper moves this discussion into a modern context of political persuasion by taking up the theme of the exile's 'longing for Jerusalem' and its function in building identity between the modern state of Israel and Judaism internationally. A final paper by Keith Whitelam addresses issues, raised by most of the conference members, regarding the voice of modern scholarship in its unsuccessful efforts to create a past for Jerusalem by trying to make archaeological evidence fit the Bible's story of David.

In putting this volume together for publication I have not been unhappy with the clash of interpretations presented. One of a scholar's first tasks is to diminish distortions that have been created by efforts to own history and use it for purposes never intended. I hope that these few selected critical essays on Jerusalem's history and traditions might add some clarity to the debates about the heritage of this city and its traditions. That professional scholars disagree about the past, which is their task and duty to present critically, is a mark of progress in a field that has too often been dominated by religious and political agendas. Altogether, five of the papers included here were not presented in Amman; yet, each of them adds its singular voice and supports the discussion begun there. What cannot be included here are the discussions that surrounded these papers: not only the discussion among the various presenters—some of that can be read between the lines—but more importantly the many comments, critiques and issues of debate that were raised by those who were with us. Nor can this book give voice to the open and critical atmosphere, encouraging honest intellectual discussion at a most difficult time, that our hosts in Amman and our colleagues from Jordanian, Palestinian and Syrian universities provided us with.

The long habit of archaeologists, historians and biblical scholars to view the Bible as history and, at the same time, to understand it as a religiously privileged intellectual tradition basic to Judaism, Christianity and Islam, has created an authority for the professional scholar that is beyond reason. First of all, the Bible makes bad history. What we know about that history and what we can reconstruct from archaeological evidence, shows a history of southern Syria that is very different from the biblical stories. The Bible's stories and songs do not tell us what happened in Jerusalem or Palestine at any period, but rather they tell us about how people in this region thought and wrote. The questions of history writing need to be based on evidence, from the periods we describe, and they need to be based on a critical reading of our biblical texts. However, the interests of this book are not limited to the writing of good history about Jerusalem. They also relate to those religiously privileged traditions about Jerusalem that are not history. The Bible's story of Jerusalem is filled with parable and example story: it is theology before it is history. Equally important as the question of history in trying to understand the Jerusalem of the past are questions about the writing and reading of a tradition and about a past that gives understanding and which writers have created with purpose.

This Bible is Samaria and Jerusalem's voice in the ancient world; it is ancient Palestine's voice; at times it is the voice of those living in the land. It is also the voice of those speaking with the loss that is exile's estrangement. Historically, this religious and philosophical product of the late Persian or Hellenistic world of the mid-fifth to mid-second century BCE is the spiritual ancestor of the Samaritan, Jewish, Christian and Islamic faiths. Each in their turn adopted different forms of this frequently rewritten Bible as their foundation document.

Thomas L. Thompson
2 April 2002
Copenhagen

To strive to be a citizen of the world is a difficult endeavor particularly in an age haunted by narrow nationalisms, ethnic obsession and fervid fundamentalism. Yet no one who is capable of experiencing this, even for a few moments, can view with indifference the infliction of injustice on any part of humanity. It was, I think, the American poet Stanley Kunitz who said something to the following effect: Whatever bruises life in one particular place, is, at the same time, stealing something substantial from the dignity of human beings everywhere.

Until the sense of mutual concern and human solidarity prevails among all races and cultures, civilization will remain retarded. As a Palestinian fed on anguish and grief in an endless diaspora, I have sharply felt the enormous injustice inflicted on my people for the sake of a dream itself half steeped in anguish. Can the agony of one people really be sufficient reason to create, in an attempt to assuage it, a new agony for another, innocent people? In this case, though, a further, specific factor has entered the equation. The dream was half steeped not just in anguish, but also in an antiquated pietism totally at odds with an age of modernism and scientific thrust. Nor was that all. The dream clearly harbored, behind its biblical claims, a political design of major dimension.

The suffering of the Jews in history is beyond question. There have, until very recent times, been only a few enlightened periods marked by normalcy and respect; and outstanding among these, it should be said, was the greater part of the 800 years or so of Islamic rule in al-Andalus, in southern Spain, where Jews were even at times appointed ministers of state. As for the political aspect of the present-day situation, this has been subject to extensive analysis and interpretation. It was the religious aspect that remained the more perturbing, by virtue of its essential vagueness, being lodged more in metaphysics than substantiated by historical evidence, notably with regard to Jerusalem and the Temple. Any close-ended, petrified, unchangeable view of religious texts (and I am not speaking here just of Judaism), where questioning becomes blasphemy and inquiry a descent from grace, would stand as a constant deterrent to logic and scientific conclusion. Constant repetitions over the centuries have confirmed its inflexible dictum, entrenching it in a cumulative memory that relies on the absolute power of the religious and its unwavering outlook. The story of the Jews embodies a heartbreaking aspiration to a physical place held intangibly in the memory. All is perceived through legend; all is conveyed on an elegiac note.

When I confronted this issue, I found myself assailed by a mass of questions for which I could find no full answer in scientific terms. I am not a historian, let alone a historian of the Bible or of ancient Palestine or Israel. Such fields are the subject of lifelong study, clearly incompatible with the work of a literary historian and critic like myself. Nevertheless, I felt a profound need to know and to have others know, in more precise terms, what the metaphysical claims truly amounted to; for there are numerous human beings now living, or still to be born, who will pay for all this with their shattered families, their homes, their land and livelihood, even their very lives.

No cultivated person should presume to reject the truth of history, insofar as this can be set forth in lucid and scientific terms. And of one thing I was already fully aware: the tragedy of my country and people had been born out of an exaggerated emphasis directly contrary to such a spirit. I came to view with dismay the way the historical view of Palestinian life was portrayed for the sake of a grand design, how it was made to bend and stretch this way and that, how it was wilfully camouflaged or eclipsed, eradicating human roots, and obscuring the facts of history. It was clear to me, too, that the design in question had power to convince only those either ignorant or wilfully biased, and was therefore bound to know only a temporary triumph before the elaborate deception was at last brought out into the light. The human mind and spirit will not endure permanent delusion, nurtured in strategy and issuing in violence and duress. At this very moment, honest minds are emerging on all sides prepared to defy a rhetoric fed to a gullible or indifferent world.

In searching out historical truth, one can only pray to stay on the side of balance and tolerance, to keep one's humanity alive. But I have been disturbed to note what even intelligent minds can accept without question: the dominance of myth over the human mind, the artful recreation of a history decked with contrived imagery and deliberate misrepresentations of past and present. However, the Palestinian distorted present could, I felt, be corrected easily enough where good will and honesty prevail; it was in the stories of the remote past, portrayed eloquently and often with great poetic power, that the dangers and difficulties lay.

It was therefore with considerable enthusiasm that I began reading the notably courageous and dispassionate studies by a number of Western biblical scholars and archeologists of the Holy Land. I also began eagerly reading the history of Palestine, and especially of Jerusalem, the city of my youth. The tragic narrative was, I found, disturbing, even alarming, to the spirit. Here is the story of two peoples brought together by a political design whose outcome could never have been foreseen; constrained to breathe the same air, love the same nature, walk on the same roads and therefore subjected to the anger of the fallen and the unholy wrath of the aggressor, both eventually losers and victims.

Countless disasters have mushroomed from the forced conjunction of a remote past impinging on the present. What we have today is a political scheme wrapped in the garb of a religious authority frozen in history, fed from one generation to the next like some magic potion. This scheme imposes a pietism on a vast world in which many millions exist who could never believe in or see any logic in its religious claims.

However, now, at last, the judicious conclusions of numerous historians and archeologists, some from Israel itself, are bringing the truth to light.

So much hinges in the end on scientific data derived from the excavation of ruins and the reading of ancient texts. My fortuitous contact with Professor Thomas Thompson, whose biblical studies are well known, led to this book, which was produced, thanks to his unmatched discipline and authority and to the enthusiastic cooperation of the other eminent biblical and archeological scholars who took part, in less than 14 months. I should like to thank them all profoundly for one of the most cordial associations I have ever known in assembling a major book.

Salma Khadra Jayyusi

ACKNOWLEDGMENTS

This is one of a number of works prepared by East–West Nexus/PROTA (Project of Translation from Arabic)/Al-Manara, on the issue of Jerusalem. Such a broad project has naturally attracted various enthusiastic and patriotic sponsors who are happy to subsidize the work and lend it their moral support. They all share a refined appreciation of high-level scholarship and the truthful, enlightened transmission of knowledge, together with a true commitment to do their utmost to save what they can of this beleaguered city from Israel's systematic erosion of its integrity and Arab identity.

Among those generous sponsors who have prominently contributed in both areas of support, my heartfelt thanks go to

Mr Haseeb Sabbagh

and Mr Sabeeh al-Masri

whose generous and spontaneous contribution towards the preparation of this book enabled us to bring it to fruition in English.

I should also like to add my thanks to Dr Basil Aql for bringing the idea of helping compile scholarly work on Jerusalem to the attention of such a great patriot and philanthropist as Mr Sabbagh.

The memorable symposium we held in October 2001 in Amman, Jordan, in which the many contributors for the various Jerusalem projects participated, saw stern and rigorous discussion among the scholars invited from various parts of the world, and from quite a number of Jordanian intellectuals; and these discussions were complemented, in the evenings, by Arab hospitality and friendliness. My heartfelt thanks go to Mrs Subhiyya K. al-Ma'ani for her great generosity and elegant hospitality, which was matched only by the equally splendid generosity and hospitality of Mrs Na'ila al-Wa'ri. The magnificent reception provided by Dr Raouf Abu Jaber and his wife Mireille merits very special thanks, as do the receptions supplied by Dr Hisham Qaddoumi, by Dr Faisal Kamal and his wife Nawal, by Mrs Laila al-Khalidi al-Husaini, and by my brother Faisal al-Khadra and his wife Nuha.

My gratitude goes, too, to Mr Samer al-Majali, President and CEO of Royal Jordanian Airlines, for facilitating the journeys of symposium participants from Europe and America, through the medium of the expert service for which Royal Jordanian Airlines are famous. Some of those thanked above are members of Al-Manara, our project's branch in Jordan, and these deserve my added gratitude for the considerable help they extended in that capacity. In this respect my heartfelt thanks go to Dr Subhi Ghosheh, the Vice-President of Al-Manara, for his unostentatious but tireless help behind the scenes, and to members of his staff at the Yaum al-Quds offices in Amman. The smooth success of the meeting in Amman was made possible by various other members: Laila al-Khalidi al-Husaini, the President of Al-Manara, and Na'ila al-Wa'ri, Nawal Hashisho Kamal and Dr Nuha al-Khadra. Special thanks go to my assistant, Mahdi al-Rawadieh, for his constant vigilance and for his intelligent and untiring help.

Salma Khadra Jayyusi
Director, East–West Nexus/PROTA/Al-Manara
Cambridge, London, Jordan

ABBREVIATIONS

ABD	David Noel Freedman (ed.), *The Anchor Bible Dictionary* (New York: Doubleday, 1992)
AfO	*Archiv for Orientforschung*
AGJU	Arbeiten zur Geschichte des antiken Judentums und des Urchristentums
ANET	James B. Pritchard (ed.), *Ancient Near Eastern Texts Relating to the Old Testament* (Princeton: Princeton University Press, 1950) (2nd edn = 1955)
AOAT	Alter Orient und Altes Testament
ATANT	Abhandlungen zur Theologie des Alten und Neuen Testaments
BA	*Biblical Archaeologist*
BARev	*Biblical Archaeology Review*
BASOR	*Bulletin of the American Schools of Oriental Research*
BBB	Bonner biblische Beiträge
Bib	*Biblica*
BMP	British Museum Publications
BN	*Biblische Notizen*
BR	*Bible Review*
BWANT	Beiträge zur Wissenschaft vom Alten und Neuen Testament
BZAW	Beihefte zur *ZAW*
CAH	Cambridge Ancient History
CANE	Jack M. Sasson (ed.), *Civilizations of the Ancient Near East* (5 vols.; New York: Charles Scribner's Sons, 1995)
CBQ	*Catholic Biblical Quarterly*
CIS	*Corpus inscriptionum semiticarum*
DDD	K. van der Toorn, B. Becking and P.W. van der Horst (eds.), *Dictionary of Deities and Demons in the Bible* (Leiden: E.J. Brill, 2nd rev. edn, 1999)
DTT	*Dansk Teologisk Tidsskrift*
EA	El-Amarna Tablets
ESHM	European Seminar in Historical Methodology
FRLANT	Forschungen zur Religion und Literatur des Alten und Neuen Testaments
HAT	Handbuch zum Alten Testament
IEJ	*Israel Exploration Journal*

IES	Israel Exploration Society
JBL	*Journal of Biblical Literature*
JSOT	*Journal for the Study of the Old Testament*
JSOTSup	*Journal for the Study of the Old Testament*, Supplement Series
JSP	*Journal for the Study of the Pseudepigrapha*
KTU	M. Dietrich, M. Loretz and J. Sanmartín, *The Cuneiform Alphabetic Texts from Ugarit* (Münster: Ugarit-Verlag, 1995)
LXX	Septuaginta
MB	Mitteilungen und Beiträge
NEAEHL	E. Stern (ed.), *The New Encyclopedia of Archaeological Excavations in the Holy Land* (4 vols.; Jerusalem: Israel Exploration Society, 1993)
NS	New Series
NTOA	Novum Testamentum et orbis antiquus
OCD	*Oxford Classical Dictionary*
OTL	Old Testament Library
OTS	Oudtestamentische Studiën
PEFA	Palestine Exploration Fund Annual
PEQ	*Palestine Exploration Quarterly*
RB	*Revue Biblique*
SBL	Society of Biblical Literature
SBLDS	SBL Dissertation Series
SEG	Supplementum Epigraphicum Graecum
SJOT	*Scandinavian Journal of the Old Testament*
SPB	Studia postbiblica
TDOT	G.J. Botterweck and H. Ringgren (eds.), *Theological Dictionary of the Old Testament*
UF	*Ugarit-Forschungen*
UN	United Nations
VT	*Vetus Testamentum*
VTSup	*Vetus Testamentum*, Supplements
ZAH	*Zeitschrift für Althebraistik*
ZAW	*Zeitschrift für die alttestamentliche Wissenschaft*
ZDMG	*Zeitschrift der deutschen morgenländischen Gesellschaft*

LIST OF CONTRIBUTORS

Thomas M. Bolin
Associate Professor, St Norbert College, De Pere, WI, USA

Philip R. Davies
Professor emeritus, Department of Biblical Studies, University of Sheffield, UK

Lester L. Grabbe
Professor, Department of Theology, University of Hull, UK

David M. Gunn
Professor, Religion Department, Texas Christian University, Fort Worth, TX, USA

Ingrid Hjelm
Research Associate, Carsten Niebuhr Institute, University of Copenhagen, Denmark

Salma Khadra Jayyusi
Director, East–West Nexus/PROTA/Al-Manara, Cambridge, London, Jordan

Niels Peter Lemche
Professor, Faculty of Theology, University of Copenhagen, Denmark

Sarah Mandell
Professor, Department of Religious Studies, University of South Florida, Tampa Bay, FL, USA

Michael Prior
Chair of Holy Land Research Project, School of Theology, Philosophy and History, St Mary's College, University of Surrey, UK

Firas Sawah
Independent Scholar, Homs, Syria

Margreet Steiner
Independent Scholar, Leiden, the Netherlands

John Strange
Docent emeritus, Faculty of Theology, University of Copenhagen, Denmark

Thomas L. Thompson
Professor, Faculty of Theology, University of Copenhagen, Denmark

Keith W. Whitelam
Professor, Department of Biblical Studies, University of Sheffield, UK

AN INTRODUCTION:
CAN A HISTORY OF ANCIENT JERUSALEM AND PALESTINE BE WRITTEN?

Thomas L. Thompson

In the history writing of Western scholarship, the history of Palestine has ever been dominated by interest in the Bible and its origins within ancient Israel and Judah. Until the last 25 years, even the history of the Bronze Age (3000–1200 BCE) was largely written in terms of Hebrew beginnings and as a prelude to the history of Israel. Particularly since 1967, the clear development of a Palestinian nationalism in the wake of the conquest and occupation of the West Bank by Israel, has brought with it a much greater independence of archaeology and historical writings from both biblical studies and the question of Jewish roots. The debate about the nature of Jerusalem and Palestine's history for both the Bronze Age and especially for the Iron Age (1200–600 BCE) has grown in intensity and sharpness to the degree that it has touched upon questions of origin, and especially on issues of religious continuity and ethnicity. The writing of a history of Israel based on the traditions of the Bible has been cast seriously in doubt, and the question of whether such a history can be written at all has been seriously entertained by historians.[1] The difficulties in historical methods related to this question about whether we can write a history of Israel in the Iron Age—given that the topic has its roots in biblical literature—is matched only by the more secular face of what is in fact the same question. Can a history of Palestine, and, within such a history, the history of Jerusalem be written—given that its roots lie *apart* from the tradition?

The Janus-faced character of our historical problem becomes apparent as soon as we begin asking about the history of this region in the archaeological and historical sources. Problems of describing the population groups within Palestine as early as 1200 BCE become critically overloaded with anachronistic questions of ethnic origins from later periods. The

---

1.   L.L. Grabbe, *Can a 'History of Israel' be Written?* (JSOTSup, 245; ESHM, 1; Sheffield: Sheffield Academic Press, 1997).

biblically competitive roles of Samaria and Jerusalem of the late Persian and Hellenistic periods not only distract us from the Iron Age history of the region as a whole, it makes it most difficult to interpret the historical knowledge we have of this early period even as it relates directly to these cities. In an effort to clarify these problems, I will identify some of the historical problems surrounding the definition of Israelite ethnicity and how they have been influenced by the intellectual developments of the Assyrian and Persian empires and their influence on the development of biblical tradition. In this way, I hope to be able to re-open the question of a history of Palestine, of which Jerusalem and Israel's histories form a small part.

Shifting the historical focus of Jerusalem and Palestine's Iron Age away from the Bible as origin story of Judaism and Christianity takes us away from what has been essentially a theological task of identity creation. Looking instead at Palestine's early past, as a history of a particular geographic region, breaks the continuity of our historical account with what we have long understood as its future in the history of religions. The question of history's ownership is thus exposed by quick imaginations offering alternative trajectories. While contemporary interests might conjure possible new contexts within histories of pre-diaspora, pre-Christian or pre-Islamic Palestines, I prefer to hold myself to the limitations of the Iron Age and to a pre-biblical Jerusalem, if only to salvage some vestige of antiquity's independence from its future. I do not do this in order to give up history's role as origin story. I wish to emphasize that all the more, that I might more clearly identify the role that Iron Age Jerusalem and its contemporary Palestine did play in our world's history, rather than the biblical roles of an anachronistic vintage, which is put to the service of modern political purposes.

The first problem demanding critical attention lies in our description of a large number of new settlements which developed as a result of the collapse of Bronze Age towns and of international trade, which had been supported by Egypt's control of the region between 1300 and 1100 BCE. As historians, we have been so preoccupied with whether our history agrees with the Bible that we have allowed a naive reading of the Bible to select the archaeological information available to us, even as we try to interpret it critically. So, although we have broad agreement that new settlement in the highlands resulted from a migration of the population from the lowlands, we have largely limited ourselves to the settlements in the region between Ramallah and Jenin. This has allowed us to readjust our story of Israel's origins, but it also has seduced us into keeping as much of that story as we possibly can. Can we refocus on a history of Palestine when energies are wasted in debates about the Israelite ethnicity during the three centuries prior to the rise of the state known variously as 'Bit Humri' and 'Israel' with its center in Samaria? Is the question about whether we have sufficient reason to speak of a city in tenth-century Jerusalem—and with it, justification to speak of the 'United Monarchy' of Saul, David and Solomon of biblical lore—a historical question?

I am not convinced that the debates have been very productive for our history writing, where our questions lie elsewhere. New settlements begin already towards the end of the Late Bronze Age, especially in the coastal plain, and they continue in the early part of the Iron Age. They are spread widely throughout the Upper and Lower Galilee, the Jezreel, the Beth-shean and Jordan valleys, the northern Negev and throughout the whole of the Transjordan plateau. Once the great extent of new settlement and diffusion of Palestine's population is sufficiently realized, the question about identity and ethnicity is much simpler. Given that the population of these new villages is identifiable as indigenous to the region of greater Palestine and derives from both the agricultural and pastoral economies of the earlier Bronze Age, new ethnic groups should hardly yet play a role in our descriptions of this early settlement. If ethnic groups did develop in the course of Iron Age Palestine and Jerusalem, they must have been products of some development later than this initial settlement.

Only in the settlement of the coast and in areas of the central valleys is there evidence of newcomers in texts which allow us to associate immediate origins from Egypt, the Anatolian coast and the Aegean. In the regions bordering the southern and eastern steppes, associations with Arabs and early pastoralists of the Syrian steppe need also to be considered. Where there is evidence of newcomers to Palestine, this is linked with evidence of integration with indigenous populations. Discussions about Philistines and even Arabs as ethnic entities within Palestine at this early period are too quick and too anachronistic.[2] It is true that the biblical name 'Philistines' has its origin in the Egyptian name *peleset*, a name used for bands of sea-farers that raided the Egyptian Delta in the thirteenth century. The root name takes on different meanings over time. It is later used by the Assyrians in the form of *palashtu* as a general geographically oriented term

2. See the related discussion on the 'Philistines' in G.W. Ahlström (with a contribution by Gary O. Rollefson), *The History of Ancient Palestine* (ed. D.V. Edelman; JSOTSup, 146; Sheffield: JSOT Press, 1993).

for southern Palestine,[3] and much later by the fifth-century Greek writer Herodotus. Later still it is used by the Romans, in the form *Palæstina*, often for the whole of southern Syria. The existence of such a specific ethnic group of Philistines is unlikely, given that many other groups from the Aegean and Anatolia show themselves on Palestine's coast, such as the *Tjekker* and *Denyen*. It is only the much later heroic stories of the Bible's Samson, Saul and David that present Philistines in these tales as a single 'people', living along the southern coastal plain (Judg. 13–16; 1–2 Samuel).

On Israel as a Name and a People

The name 'Israel' on the famous Egyptian stele of Pharaoh Merneptah at the end of the thirteenth century does not refer to a particular ethnic group among other distinct groups within Palestine, though the text does use the hieroglyphic sign for 'people' in writing the name. Much more interestingly, this text gives us the earliest known use of a patriarch 'Israel' as a literary metaphor, as the father and patron of Palestine's people. The metaphor's function is similar to the figure of the biblical Jacob, who, after wrestling with God, is given a new name, 'Israel', that he might represent Palestine's people (Gen. 32.29; see esp. the song in Gen. 49). In related stories, Israel's twelve sons, themselves the 'fathers' of twelve tribes, are to inherit the whole of Palestine, only later to have that inheritance taken from them because of their failure to obey the Torah (Josh. 22.19-24). In the much earlier Egyptian stele's poem, Israel is paired with the woman Hurru (a personification of the land) as his widow.[4] 'Israel's seed is no more' declaims the text, and the pharaoh, as Hurru's new husband and patron, takes the land as his bride. The family role of the children of Hurru is given to the towns over which Merneptah claims patronage (Gaza, Ashkelon, Gezer and Yenoam, cities, which also in biblical tradition continue to be identified as belonging to the Egyptians and Philistines).

---

3.   In an inscription of Adad-Nirari's (810–753) campaign, *Pa-la-as-tu* occurs together with Tyre, Sidon, Israel and Edom (*ANET*, pp. 281-82), perhaps indicating the south of Palestine (and conceivably the coastal region); however, in the Saba'a inscription of Adad-Nirari's fifth year, Adad-Nirari marches his army against *Pa-la-ash-tu*, where only the town of Damascus is mentioned (*ANET*, p. 282). In later inscriptions, Judah seems to be distinquished from coastal towns such as Ashkelon and Gaza.

4.   I. Hjelm and T.L. Thompson, 'The Victory Song of Merneptah, Israel and the People of Palestine', *JSOT* 27.1 (2002), pp. 3-18.

In this first reference to the name Israel in history, the name occurs as a metaphor of myth, not a name of any historical people. The name itself might well have come from the name of the Late Bronze region of Asher (used for both a region of Palestine and as a 'son of Israel' in the Bible). It is also possible that the name draws on a pun with the poem's phrase 'Israel's seed is no more'—the name might be that of Palestine's fertile Jezreel valley.

The many new village/pastoral settlements of the Iron I period (1200–900 BCE) show little identifiable distribution as peoples in Palestine before the tenth century. It is only in the course of the tenth century that settlements are organized around the larger towns in the lowlands and along the coast. The great towns of Byblos, Sidon and Arvad,[5] on the Lebanese coast, appear as early as the twelfth century in Assyrian texts. It is only from the tenth-century Egyptian campaign of Sheshonk I that lowland towns in the Jezreel valley such as Beth-shean, Megiddo and Taanach, and the hill country towns of Gibeon, Rehob and Ayyalon show themselves as playing significant roles as political centers.[6] It is likewise first from the ninth century and mid-eighth century that evidence begins to accumulate from Assyrian texts that Palestine has become organized in a series of petty states, forming stable political regions. Some of these are Aram, Israel, Bit-Ammon, Moab, Edom and Judah, which form military and economic coalitions with the older town centers of the lowlands like Byblos, Tyre and Sidon, Ashkelon and Gaza.[7] It is first at this period that we can possibly speak of 'ethnic' or 'national' formations, defined by their geographical regions, having names such as Edom, Moab, Ammon and Aram, as well as Israel and even Judah. By the mid-ninth or mid-eighth century, the settlements of each of these regions had long since been continuously economically interrelated, so that the development of stable political identities is certainly possible.

But, even so, there are problems that should make us hesitate to give such names the significance of coherent and mutually exclusive, ethnic groups. The dominant, patron–client, political structure of the time,[8] which orients both region and state in pyramids of personal ties of loyalty, perceived in metaphors of the family, is reflected in the names of three of

5. *ANET*, pp. 274-76.
6. *ANET*, pp. 263-64.
7. *ANET*, pp. 278-80, with references to Aram and Israel; see further, pp. 281-82.
8. M. Liverani, *Power and Propaganda* (Copenhagen: Tusculanum, 1979), and *Prestige and Interest* (Padua: Carocci, 1990).

these new states: Bit Ammon, Bit Humri (Israel) and possibly Beytdwd (Jerusalem? or Judah?). An Ammonite, Israelite or Judean is identifiable as belonging to such a group of people, not because of birth, but by personal bonds of loyalty to the king.[9] The association with specific patron deities is in accord with these political divisions (the god Chemosh for Moab, Hadad for Aram, Yahweh for Israel and Qa'os for Edom). Religion, however, seems first of all tied to the political allegiance of a specific ruler to his god as patron, than with what one might describe as the faith of a people.[10] While languages throughout the region are closely associated, recognition of dialect distinctions is instructive. For instance, a 'core Canaanite' language can be recognized by associating the several dialects of Israelite with Phoenician. Judean, however, shows itself far more closely tied with what has been called 'fringe Canaanite', as we find Judean inscriptions more closely linked to the fringe dialects of Ammonite, Moabite and Judean than to Israelite.[11]

Regional distinctions in the character of the earliest of the settlements of the Iron Age had become apparent already from the very beginning of the twelfth century. These help us distinguish the economies of the settlements of the Galilee from the coast, the Jezreel, the central highlands, the northern Negev and the Transjordan. These distinctions also force us to see the geographical separation of Palestine's population as quite significant for the emergence of different peoples, each with their own distinct history of development.[12] The population of the Judean hills, where new settlement does not begin until much later than it does in the regions to the north of Jerusalem, is associated with the sedentarization of pastoralists during the eleventh and tenth centuries.[13] The region has a history of development quite different from, for example, the central hills of Israel. The settlement in Judea, on the other hand, had a natural symbiotic rela-

---

9. See, e.g., 'The Vassal Treaties of Esarhaddon', *ANET*, pp. 534-41.

10. So, for example, in the Mesha stele, the king Mesha introduces himself as 'the son of Chemosh'. When he speaks of Israel having previously conquered the territory, he speaks of Omri and his son who dwelt in the land, because the god Chemosh was angry at the land (*ANET*, pp. 320-21).

11. E.A. Knauf, 'War biblisch-Hebräisch eine Sprache?', *ZAH* 3 (1990), pp. 11-23; E.A. Knauf with S. Maani, 'On the Phonemes of Fringe Canaanite', *UF* 19 (1987), pp. 91-94; T.L. Thompson, *The Early History of the Israelite People* (Leiden: E.J. Brill, 3rd edn, 2000 [1992]), pp. 334-39.

12. I. Finkelstein, *The Archaeology of the Israelite Settlement* (Jerusalem: Israel Exploration Society, 1988); and esp. Thompson, *Early History*, pp. 215-309.

13. Thompson, *Early History*, pp. 288-90.

tionship with pastoralists along Palestine's southern rim, much as did the Negev towns of Beersheva, Khirbet el-Meshash and Tell Jemmeh. Moreover, the early major towns of the Judean hills were Hebron, Khirbet Rabud and Lachish, while Jerusalem's dominance over the region is clearly indicated only much later. We know little of tenth-century Jerusalem, where we have only the remains of a retaining wall clearly dated to this period.[14] During the ninth and perhaps still through much of the eighth century, Jerusalem is a small town at the head of the Ayyalon valley. Only with the entrance of Assyrian interests into the region of southern Palestine late in the eighth century, does Jerusalem become a significant town dominating the hill country of southern Palestine.

In the ninth century, when Assyria begins to expand its influence into the southern Levant, we have a number of small regional states in Palestine which develop distinct peoples, identifiable through their distinctive histories, dialects and geographical borders, each with competitive political and religious allegiances. Early examples of such regional competition, prior to Assyria's expansion, can be seen already in the Iron I period, with marked Phoenician influence on olive production in the settlements of the western Galilee in contrast to other settlements in the south. In the ninth century, the issue of political control of the Jezreel and Beth-shean valleys created a long and indecisive competition between Tyre, Damascus and Samaria. From the mid-ninth-century Mesha inscription from Jordan, we learn of a struggle between Samaria and Moab over the region of Madeba and Mt Nebo.[15] Such conflicts can be expected to intensify the ethnic identity of the core regions of conflict, while at the same time dispersing such identity in areas of the periphery. In a comparable way, when the Assyrians first entered the region, political pressures to create coalitions in opposition to the armies of the great king[16] would weaken local competitions, and, accordingly, ethno-religious identification.

During this period, Israel (or Bit Humri) was certainly the greater power of the highlands. In contrast, the Judean hills were sparsely populated, relatively poor and not obviously centralized.[17] If Jerusalem, and not

14. M.L. Steiner, *Excavations in Jerusalem 1961–1967*. III. *The Settlement in the Bronze and Iron Ages* (Copenhagen International Seminar, 9; Sheffield: Sheffield Academic Press, 2001).

15. *ANET*, pp. 320-21.

16. For examples of the make-up of such coalitions, see the anthology of texts in *ANET*, pp. 276-300.

17. For a recent description of this region, cf. T.L. Thompson, *The Bible in History: How Writers Create a Past* (London: Jonathan Cape, 1999–2000), pp. 161-67;

Lachish, had dominated the Judean hills in the tenth and ninth centuries—and evidence for this is very limited—they did so in the form of a small chieftainship, economically dominated by Israel's Samaria. A common religious patronage under the God Yahweh—shared also with the region of Seir, closely tied with Edom—is the only unifying association that can be historically confirmed.

In the course of the eighth century, the Assyrian empire absorbed first Aram and then Israel, with their capitals in Damascus and Samaria. It went on to extend its influence to the coastal towns of Phoenicia and Palestine. Many regions of Palestine suffered imperial policies of mass deportations, involving the transference of large numbers of people both into and out of Palestine. The leadership of the society was either subordinated to the Assyrians or deported; young men were taken into military service and skilled laborers were transported to Assyria's cities. At times, whole villages and towns were uprooted and resettled in distant regions of the empire, as others were brought into the land from as far away as Afghanistan and Arabia to replace them.[18] Local rule and its indigenous patronage were subordinated to the empire's provincial administration. The local society was transformed. Both political independence and ethnic loyalties were intentionally undermined and destroyed in the course of many successive deportations.[19] Citizens of empire were created in their stead.[20]

The purpose of such social experimentation was to control and integrate the society, not to destroy it. The regions in Palestine most seriously affected by such policy were the lower Galilee and Phoenicia, the southern coastal area and the hills of Judea, as well as Samaria itself, but not the population of the surrounding hills.[21] From the period following Samaria's fall in 722 there is considerable archaeological evidence of cultural and economic continuity in the population of the former state of Israel. Both

N. Silberman and I. Finkelstein, *The Bible Unearthed: Archaeology's New Vision of Ancient Israel and the Origin of its Sacred Texts* (New York: Free Press, 2001), pp. 169-95.

18.	B. Oded, *Mass Deportation and Deportees in the Neo-Assyrian Empire* (Wiesbaden: Otto Harrassowitz, 1979; S. Irvine, *Isaiah, Ahaz and the Syro-Ephraimite Crisis* (SBLDS, 123; Atlanta: SBL, 1990); Thompson, *Early History*, pp. 339-51.

19.	Thompson, *Early History*, pp. 340-41.

20.	H.W. Saggs, 'Assyrian Prisoners of War and the Right to Live', *AfO* 19 (1982), pp. 85-93; Thompson, *Early History*, p. 340.

21.	Oded, *Mass Deportations*. See the lists of towns on pp. 116-35 and the map that accompanies the volume.

the indigenous material culture, and the language and religion of the region were maintained. The town of Samaria, itself, clearly, continued to play its dominating role over the region of northern Palestine, but it did so now as part of the Assyrian Empire.[22] The history of northern Palestine after 722 has yet to be written, hidden as it has been by Western scholarship's biblically oriented history. The central highlands and valleys of northern Palestine continued to support the greater part of Palestine's population during the entire period of empire under successive Assyrian, Babylonian, Persian and Greek administrations. This dominance continued for more than five centuries, until the revolt of the Hasmoneans in Jerusalem against the Seleucids in the Hellenistic period. In my *Early History* of 1992, I had argued that 'by the end of the sixth century, Jerusalem and Judah of the Assyrian period had ceased to exist as thoroughly as had Samaria and Israel of the eighth century'. However, the population of Israel outside of Samaria had in fact been affected by deportation far less than had that of Judea. The tradition of the 'lost tribes' and the 'empty land' are essentially Jewish traditions, anachronistically reading Judea's past for the whole of the hill country.[23]

On Writing the Tradition

Because the biblical story of Samaria and Jerusalem's destruction was written from the much later perspective of Jerusalem, that later perspective from the south needs to be understood. Neither Israel nor Samaria, as functioning parts of the Assyrian Empire, were of any interest to later writers in Jerusalem. Those who had been deported under the Assyrians had no place in the centuries-later theological story that the Bible tells about Jerusalem and its God. Whether they were from Samaria and the Jezreel, from Galilee and Phoenicia or from the coastal region as far south as Gaza, these people and their fate have been silenced. Especially those Sennacherib deported when he razed Lachish to the ground, and those he expelled from the villages of Judea in 701, were displaced by the biblical story. They have disappeared from history. During the five centuries following the fall of Samaria the Bible says nothing about the existence of the greater part of Palestine's population. To be sure, after the wars the

---

22. Further on this, see I. Hjelm, *Jerusalem's Rise to Sovereignty in Tradition and History* (London/New York: T&T Clark International, forthcoming [2004]).

23. Thompson, *Early History*, p. 415.

population had picked up the rhythm of their lives once again, in their towns and on their farms in Palestine. Yet, their history is hidden because historians have followed the silence of the 'lost tribes' and 'empty land' of the biblical story.

This silence, however, is now undermined by the abundant archaeological and written evidence we possess. This material now allows us to write their history. The critical scholar must ask, with Keith Whitelam,[24] why we have followed such silence when it has not been necessary. I am not inclined to evoke Zionist plots or to follow any kind of conspiracy theory to explain away the historian's deadly sins of anachronism and sloth. It is far easier, I think, for us as teachers to repeat what we have learned and thought we understood than to do anything else. We were taught silence by our teachers and, as dutiful students, we have silenced the history it is our duty to write.

What Whitelam has described as 'the silencing of Palestinian history' begins with the Bible's story. Lest this also be misunderstood, we must consider that when our biblical author lived and took up his narrative of Jerusalem's destruction in a yet more distant past, the destruction of that past was already nearly complete. Samaria's historical continuity with the past is ignored by the biblical author. With it, the language, customs, memories and traditions, which Samaria had maintained through centuries following its loss of political independence, were ignored. The author did not interest himself in such continuity, because it did not fit the role that Samaria played within his story. In the Bible, all lines of continuity are drawn from that future and lead back to old Israel only as one theme within a theological drama that centers in Jerusalem. It is essential to the balance of this Jerusalem narrative that Samaria and its people take the role exemplifying punishment past, an unmistakable warning of Jerusalem's destruction to come. Samaria is given the tragic role of the woman, Rachel, a mother weeping for her children who are no more, while Jerusalem stars in the role of harlot. Once Yahweh's beloved, Jerusalem heedlessly and faithlessly exposes her beauty and riches to her lover in Babylon.

This tale of Jerusalem past, as offered by the author of the book of Isaiah, writing from the city of the late Persian or early Hellenistic period,[25]

---

24. K.W. Whitelam, *The Invention of Ancient Israel* (London: Routledge, 1996); for a response, see T.L. Thompson, 'Defining History and Ethnicity in the South Levant', in Grabbe (ed.), *Can a 'History of Israel' be Written?*, pp. 166-87.

25. N.P. Lemche, 'The Old Testament—A Hellenistic Book?', *SJOT* 7 (1993), pp. 163-93; Thompson, *Early History*, p. 356 n. 10.

features Jerusalem as a figure of piety. Jerusalem is the 'repentant remnant' which has learned from the past, pregnant with a righteousness which will transform the future.[26] That is the meaningful context of the heroic story of the late eighth-century King Hezekiah's Jerusalem, the last and fragile remnant of a great past, resisting the Assyrian Sennacherib's hubris and blasphemy with humble tears and simple trust in Yahweh. It is a story that draws its closure in the destruction, in the dawn's early light, of the greatest army on earth—185,000 strong struck down by Yahweh's plague. The context in which this story is to be understood is not 701 BCE, but lies in a future drawn from a Jerusalem yet to be realized. The prophet Isaiah does not tell a continuous narrative from Samaria to Jerusalem's fall. He places his story of Hezekiah's resistance to the Assyrians more dramatically, immediately before his great song of return, a song which centers his book on the theme of Yahweh's mercy that ends Jerusalem's exile in Babylon nearly two centuries in the future. It is Yahweh who addresses this lyrical *aria* to his prophet: 'Comfort, O comfort my people; speak tenderly to Jerusalem and tell her that her enslavement is over: her crime is paid for' (Isa. 40.1).

In this context, the Hezekiah narrative reads as an example story epitomizing divine mercy; it is a story of what could have been. After his army is destroyed by Yahweh, Sennacherib retreats and returns to Nineveh to pray—as Hezekiah had prayed to Yahweh in the temple in Jerusalem—to the god of Assyria in *his* temple. As in a Greek play, the great man, who had mocked the divine in hubris, meets his appropriate fate. Prayers to an empty god empty him, as he is assassinated in the temple by his own son (Isa. 37.35-38). The scene shifts back to Jerusalem and is given a contrasting doublet. Not Sennacherib, but Hezekiah is sick and the one who is to die; he—like Sennacherib—turns in humble prayer to Yahweh. Yahweh, however, hears his prayers and sees his tears. As proof to the audience that Yahweh is a god whose promises give strength, he gives a sign that defines him as the Lord of History. The past could have been otherwise, Isaiah's theology argues. For although we cannot change the past, only survive as a remnant in repentance, Yahweh is a god with power over the past. Like the sun in Gibeon's sky and the moon in Ayyalon's valley (Josh. 10.12-13), the shadow of Hezekiah's sundial not only has stopped; it has gone backwards. Fifteen years are given to Hezekiah to live again.

---

26. Isa. 37–39; reused in slightly revised form in 2 Kgs 18–20 in the stories of the last kings of Jerusalem. For the entire discussion of the Hezekiah story in Isaiah, see Hjelm, *Jerusalem's Rise to Sovereignty*.

The lesson, however, is for the generations of the future. In the story's final scene, Isaiah trims Hezekiah to humanity's measure. As soon as he is out of danger, he receives an envoy from the future. The Babylonians comes and are shown all of Jerusalem's beauty and wealth (Isa. 39). A doomsday-directed irony, playing on Hezekiah's fickle, human trust in the great powers of empire, is exposed as the curtain comes down on this evocation of Jerusalem's coming destruction. It is this scene, immediately before Yahweh sings his song of comfort, ending Jerusalem's exile in the Persian period, which allows Isaiah to argue that Yahweh, as the Lord of History, erases the past. Divine mercy is evoked in radical metaphors; not only can sins be forgiven, the past can be altered. The faithless Jerusalem sent in exile becomes a new Israel, yet to be created: to be contrasted to the past as its faithful remnant.

Isaiah's story is taken up in the stories of Israel's kings (2 Kgs 18–20), when Samaria has already been destroyed and the story turns to tie Jerusalem's fate with that of Samaria. The narrator reminds his readers that in the eyes of God, neither Samaria nor Jerusalem has any special meaning.[27] While even in Sodom had been found the good family of Lot, not a single righteous man was to be found in Jerusalem.[28] As such, another city of ordinary men, Jerusalem, even more than Sodom, will soon lie in ruins, when God is with them in his wrath. However, the harsh tones of the black and white morality of the story is problematic, as this author also struggles to present this story of divine judgment as coming from a god of mercy. But first the old Jerusalem must be silenced and the past rejected. It is not enough that Samaria and its people no longer exist, Jerusalem's ties with the past must also be cut if it is to succeed to Samaria's role in the form of a new Israel. As suffering leads to understanding, exile holds the promise of divine mercy. This is the figure for those who survive captivity. Theirs is a destiny as a new and faithful Israel. Three times, the entire population is taken into exile; even so, all who remained, fled to Egypt. The glory of a Jerusalem past no longer exists in this narrative. A small remnant lives as prisoners with their 'king' in Babylon while the curtain closes on the past. This empty Jerusalem echoes the prophet Jeremiah's vision of an ignorant Jerusalem in the nothingness before creation. The city has been razed and turned into a desert, a world before creation: a world, formless and empty, a heaven without light, as the mountains shook and the heights quaked. There was no humanity; the birds of the sky had fled' (Jer. 4.23-26). This 'myth of the empty land' tears Jerusalem from its historical past and casts its future with the exiles in Babylon. The reader awaits the return of a repentant remnant in the stories of Nehemiah and Ezra set in the Persian period. It is a never-ending story, in which they too set out to build a city and a temple (cf. Gen. 11.1-9).

In contrast to the Samaritans, who have traditions of continuity with the Iron Age kingdom of Israel, the writers of the Bible have created a rejected past which contrasts with an ideal future yet to come. While Samaria's historical continuities with the past after 722 BCE have been ignored by the biblical authors in favor of another story, the past as a whole has no saving grace within the Bible's story. Jerusalem and Judah's history is also ignored after it falls under Babylonian patronage in 587, even as our archaeological evidence speaks against this 'myth of the empty land' as an historical account of Jerusalem and Judah's past.[29] Historical and cultural continuities are well attested and not only provide a basis for Jerusalem and Palestine's history in the sixth century, but they are fundamental to understanding the Persian period, which does not begin historically with an empty Jerusalem, whatever Nehemiah's narrative needs might be. Nor do we have evidence for an organized return of people from Mesopotamia to Jerusalem in the early Persian period. Transportation of West Semites from Mesopotamia did take place, but there was also clear continuity between Judea's earlier Iron Age culture and that of the Persian period.

The silencing of Samaria's history after 722 and that of Jerusalem's after 587 in favor of historicizing the narratives of the Bible, involves a remarkable silence in the history writing of other regions in Palestine, especially of the Galilee, the coast and the Transjordan. Historians have been misled by the Bible's story to reconstruct *the beginnings* of the small province of Jehud within a *rebuilt Jerusalem*. Such disorientation and un-critical method have led to great confusion in the effort of biblical studies to identify the voices of our texts in some 'new', 'post-exilic' Jerusalem as if that were a historical rather than a theological context.

This confusion in scholar's historical perspective is pervasive today and needs to be resolved if we are to proceed. To what extent is the acceptance of the Samaritan Bible in such a 'post-exilic' Jerusalem a critical aspect of

29. H.M. Barstad, *The Myth of the Empty Land: A Study in the History and Archae-ology of Judah during the 'Exilic' Period* (Symbolae Osloenses fasc. supplet., 28 Oslo: Scandinavian University Press, 1996).

its claim to supersede Samaria as a 'new Israel'?[30] Samaritans claim this same tradition in an assertion of continuity with its past.[31] But is either claim historical? Are their asserted contexts legitimate? We must be cautious about identifying utopian visions of founding a 'new Jerusalem' from returning exiles, illustrated in the stories in the books of Ezra and Nehemiah, as if they were historical contexts and not a continuation of the Bible's story world. At least the book of Ezra continues the Bible's never-ending story of flawed humanity's search for the path of righteousness and closes its story of Ezra's 'brave new Jerusalem' with a closing scene of the people of Jerusalem ridding themselves of their own future. This is not history but moral lesson.

Apart from the very brief period of Hasmonean rule during the Hellenistic period, no single group or people ever successfully gains control of both political power in Palestine and the production of its traditions. During the limited period that the Hasmoneans played a role in the development of this complex tradition of the Bible, they never came to control it and they never found full acceptance within it. 'Judaism' meant many different things during the Hellenistic period and is hardly to be simply equated with some form of ethnicity.[32] Far more appropriate is a description of Judaism as a religion, a philosophy, or perhaps even more comprehensively, an intellectual trend, reflecting the intellectual life of different peoples and groups within Palestine at a specific time. In the self-understanding of its ancient authors, Judaism's Bible is so identified with the whole of Palestine that it has created a tradition of many voices. The biblical tradition expresses much of early Palestine's great diversity, even as Western scholarship has often silenced the diversity of these cultivated voices, in its effort to create a coherent account of its tradition.

Can a history of Iron Age Jerusalem and Palestine be written? I do not think it can be done as long as our historical perspectives remain captive within a historicized Bible. I am very much aware that those who have tried to stand critically apart from the tradition—whether as historians, archaeologists or biblical scholars—have for too long been seduced by the

30. E. Nodet, *A Search for the Origins of Judaism: From Joshua to the Mishnah* (JSOTSup, 248; Sheffield: Sheffield Academic Press, 1997).

31. I. Hjelm, *The Samaritans and Early Judaism: A Literary Analysis* (JSOTSup, 303; Sheffield: Sheffield Academic Press, 2000).

32. T.L. Thompson, 'Hidden Histories and the Problem of Ethnicity in Palestine', in M. Prior (ed.), *Western Scholarship and the History of Palestine* (London: Melisinde, 1998), pp. 23-40.

tradition's all-embracing theological metaphors. I think a history of Palestine in the Iron Age—or for that matter, a history of Israel of this same period—can be undertaken with some hope of success, if we continue to develop the independence of our archaeological and historical disciplines. We must learn to read the codes of the tradition in order to understand what it has done in transforming the past and where it has other interests than our historical ones. I am much less sanguine about this field's all too many voices of national and religious self-interest that have contributed to this discussion. Efforts to write Palestine's history as if it were an introduction to, or worse a justification for the Bible's use of war and social dislocation as metaphors for its theological discussions have had disastrous effects on both our society and its understanding of biblical literature.[33]

33. See, e.g., M. Prior, *The Bible and Colonialism: A Moral Critique* (The Biblical Seminar, 48; Sheffield: Sheffield Academic Press, 1997), and esp. *idem, Zionism and the State of Israel: A Moral Inquiry* (London: Routledge, 1999); R.M. Schwartz, *The Curse of Cain: The Violent Legacy of Monotheism* (Chicago: University of Chicago Press, 1997).

A MORAL READING OF THE BIBLE IN JERUSALEM

Michael Prior

The attacks in the USA on 11 September 2001, and the multitude of commentary since, add a certain urgency to the subject that I have pursued over many years: the co-existence of a potential for good and for evil in many of the religious traditions of the world. Christianity has both Jesus' Teaching on the Mount (Mt. 5–7), an abundance of social activity directed towards improving the lots of the poor, as well as a long record of complicity in the exploitation of the natives in regions colonized by Western nations. Judaism has a litany of prophetic pronouncements against exploitation of the poor, as well as a foundational document that confers rights the assumption of which demands the disadvantage of others, whether Canaanites in the past or Palestinians today. While President Bush, Prime Minister Blair and a host of others, religious and political, protest that Islam is a peaceful religion, Osama Bin Laden and associates rejoice in the destruction of the lives of the thousands killed on 11 September and promote militarism in the name of Islam. While virtually all religions can point to their ennobling qualities, few can boast of being untainted by imperialist and exploitative aspirations and achievements.

Studying the Bible in Jerusalem has made me particularly sensitive to the place of the reader and has encouraged me to develop what might be called a 'Moral Reading of the Bible'. Over the last 20 years I have confronted some of the morally problematic traditions of the Bible, in the Old Testament/Hebrew Scriptures in particular, and the deployment of these traditions in ideological support of projects that have caused devastation in several regions in the past. The spoliation continues in the Middle East, where we are left with an ongoing, unresolved problem between Israel and the Palestinian Arabs, the perdurance of which, in the estimation of many, is a contributory factor to the tragic circumstances which relate to 11 September, and expressed themselves most recently in the British-assisted US invasion of Iraq.

My reading of the Bible in Jerusalem has led me to reflect upon not only the deployment of the Bible as an agent of oppression, but also on the public nature of the discipline of Biblical Studies, pointing to the necessity of its practitioners exercising a public responsibility and an ethical accountability. My exegetical interests might have taken a different direction had I not undertaken significant portions of my postgraduate biblical studies in the land of the Bible. Studying in Jerusalem, more precisely in East Jerusalem, has been one of the biggest catalysts for change in my own life. Things would have been different had I confined myself to study in biblical institutes and libraries in Dublin, Rome or London.

The Location of Exegesis

The biblical discourse in the West is currently in the control of the university departments of biblical studies—as it was in Church and Synagogue circles previously—who decide upon which questions are important and the appropriate training required of its practitioners. From the beginning, however, liberation theologians in Latin America drew attention to the primacy of the context of one's theological reflections (*lugar teológico*). Western interpretation, they insist, will always be distorted, since the Bible's central message is that God is on the side of the oppressed, while interpreters from North America and Europe do not know the experience of being subject to economic, personal, or institutional oppression, and interpret the Bible from their positions of power.[1] Virtually all Western biblical scholars live in comfort and guaranteed security, and are respected members of prestigious academic institutions. Such circumstances, one learns, become an obstacle to an authentic reading of the text. Doubtless, a different dynamic operates in circles influenced by Liberation Theology

In Brazil, for example, the concerns of the poor and exploited predominate, and the reading of the Bible proceeds from their perspectives. Such is the lack of confidence in the methods and concerns of Western biblical

---

1.   See, e.g., Elsa Tamez, *Bible of the Oppressed* (Maryknoll, NY: Orbis Books, 1982), and the works of R.S. Sugirtharajah: *idem* (ed.), *Voices from the Margin: Interpreting the Bible in the Third World* (London: SPCK, 1991); *idem* (ed.), *The Postcolonial Bible* (The Bible and Postcolonialism, 1; Sheffield: Sheffield Academic Press, 1998); *idem, The Bible and the Third World: Precolonial, Colonial, and Postcolonial Encounters* (Cambridge: Cambridge University Press, 2001); and *idem, Asian Biblical Hermeneutics and Postcolonialism: Contesting the Interpretations* (The Biblical Seminar, 64; Sheffield: Sheffield Academic Press, 1999).

studies that the biblical scholars brought up in them are allowed to enter the so-called Contextual Bible Study process only as servants, and participate only when they are invited by the people. Rather than being perceived as teachers with an enviable repository of wisdom, gained through expertise in the historical-critical methods of Bible study, biblical scholars are admitted only if they commit themselves to begin with the social reality as perceived, and to engage in socio-political transformation through Bible reading.[2]

For Ignacio Ellacuría, President of the University of Central America in San Salvador, authentic theology incorporates three elements: reflection, ethical option and praxis. Authentic Christian Theology involves a reflection from Christian faith, the object of which is the reign of God. Because it arises from being immersed in 'the historical reality' of the people of God—the concrete situation of people—such a theology introduces a fundamental ethical option: one which properly leads to action (praxis). The three elements, however, ought not to be considered as separate and in temporal sequence, but rather as completely integrated and almost simultaneously present in a dynamic tension in the richness of encountering the weight of reality.[3]

Ellacuría insists that the context of theological reflection is vital to the discipline. His context was that of being among the poor people of Latin America,[4] whom he considered to be crucified on the cross of Latin America.[5] Just as Ignatius of Loyola, the founder of the Jesuits, exhorted his disciples to go on their knees at the foot of the cross and ask, 'What have I done, what am I doing, what will I do for Christ crucified?', so Christians today, Ellacuría urged, should reflect on the condition of the poor and ask, 'What have I done, what am I doing for the people on the cross, and what will I do to uncrucify them, and have them raised?'[6] For Ellacuría, then,

2.   Thus Leif E. Vaage, 'Text, Context, Conquest, Quest: The Bible and Social Struggle in Latin America', in Eugene H. Lovering Jr (ed.), *Society of Biblical Literature 1991 Seminar Papers* (SBLSP, 30; Atlanta: Scholars Press, 1991), pp. 357-65.

3.   On the richness of the historical context of reflection see Ignacio Ellacuría, *Filosofía de la realidad histórica* (Madrid: Editorial Trotta, 1990).

4.   Ignacio Ellacuría, 'Los pobres, "lugar teológico" en America Latina', *Misión Abierta* 4–5 (1981), pp. 225-40.

5.   Ignacio Ellacuría, 'El Pueblo crucificado. Ensayo de soterología histórico', *Revista Latinoamerica de Teología* 18 (1989), pp. 305-33.

6.   Ignacio Ellacuría, 'Las Iglesias latinoamericanas interpelan a la Iglesia de España', *Sal Terra* 826 (1982), pp. 219-30 (230).

living among the crucified people was the pre-eminent place of theology.[7] It might also exact a price.

Father Ellacuría, striving to bring the poor down from the cross was put up there himself in a dramatic expression of his commitment to theological reflection and praxis. On 16 November 1989, government soldiers murdered him and five other Jesuits of the university, together with a seminary cook and her daughter. Jon Sobrino, another Jesuit of the university would have been murdered also on that night had he not been out of the country at the time. For Sobrino, too, the task of theology is to bring the poor of Latin America off the cross.[8] Both Fathers Ellacuría and Sobrino were theological advisors to Archbishop Oscar Romero, also murdered on 24 March 1980, while he was celebrating Mass. Theologizing, in some contexts, then, can be a matter of life and death.

The Transforming Power of Experience

Although the focus of my own engagement with the Holy Land was 'the biblical past', I could not avoid the modern social context of the region. My experiences in 'the land of the Bible', supplemented by substantial reading down the years, have changed not only my perception of the modern politics of the region, but, although not realizing it along the way, have altered radically also my understanding of the task of a biblical scholar. Indeed, as well as being an absorbing academic pursuit, my engagement with the Holy Land, and with moral issues involved in the subject of the Israel–Palestine conflict, have absorbed much of my scholastic energy for some time and have assumed a sense of personal responsibility of the quality of a moral imperative. My studying the Bible in the land of the Bible, then, provoked perspectives that scarcely would have arisen elsewhere. A word of explanation is called for.

7.   See Kevin Burke's study of Ellacuría's theology, *The Ground Beneath the Cross: The Theology of Ignacio Ellacuría* (Washington, DC: Georgetown University Press, 2000).

8.   Jon Sobrino, 'The Crucified Peoples: Yahweh's Suffering Servant Today', in Leonardo Boff and Virgil Elizondo (eds.), *1492–1992: The Voice of the Victims* (London: SCM Press; Valley Forge, PA: Trinity Press International, 1990), pp. 120-29 (= *Concilium* 6). See also Sobrino's 'Human Rights and Oppressed Peoples: Historical-Theological Reflections', in Michael Hayes and David Tombs (eds.), *Truth and Memory: The Church and Human Rights in El Salvador and Guatemala* (Leominster: Gracewing, 2001), pp. 134-58.

Experiences can change people, and my own changing circumstances as a reader of the Bible required me to revise my perceptions continually. My encounters with the Holy Land have brought about changes in me, to only the most significant of which I allude here.[9] While, in general, I am suspicious of appeal to personal experience as a basis for academic argument, the practice can be redeemed. The kind of people we are influences to a large extent how we absorb experiences—modern literary criticism pays particular attention to the standpoint of the reader, almost to the point in some extreme cases of ignoring altogether that of the author.[10] Moreover, according to the Irish poet, Patrick Kavanagh, 'the self serves only as an example', while W.B. Yeats insists that, 'If we understand our own minds, and the things that are striving to utter themselves through our minds, we move others. Not because we have understood or thought about those others, but because all life has the same root' (in *Samhain* 5 [1905]).

People of my religious and personal dispositions—a Christian and a Catholic priest—naturally approach the Bible with a sense of awe. The biblical readings within the Christian liturgy always conclude with the sentence 'This is the Word of the Lord', to which the hearers respond, 'Thanks be to God'. The opening verses of the New Testament Letter to the Hebrews sum up a Christian attitude to God and his engagement with human history:

> In many and various ways God spoke of old to our fathers by the prophets; but in these last days he has spoken to us by a Son, whom he appointed the heir of all things, through whom also he created the world. He reflects the glory of God and bears the very stamp of his nature, upholding the universe by his word of power. (Heb. 1.1-3)

9.   In my article 'Studying the Bible in the Holy Land' (which appears in Michael Prior [ed.], *They Came and they Saw: Western Christian Experiences of the Holy Land* [London: Melisende, 2000], pp. 104-27) I have laid out the genesis of my engagement and the different stages of the development of my views in the light of my experience in the Holy Land. See also my 'Confronting the Bible's Ethnic Cleansing in Palestine', in *The Link (Americans for Middle East Understanding)* 33 (2000), pp. 1-12.

10.   A phrase in medieval philosophy, *quidquid recipitur in modo recipientis recipitur* ('whatever is received is received according to the mode of the receiver', that is, not that of the giver), serves as a helpful analogy to the process of understanding an (ancient) text. When the contents of a jug is poured into glasses of different shapes it assumes the configurations of the receiving glasses, not that of the jug! The analogy is somewhat crude, of course, since people, unlike glasses, cannot force every new experience into their own preformed configuration; indeed, their very configuration not infrequently is altered significantly.

The revered place of the Bible within Christian spirituality and theology is reflected also in an abundance of commentary from all periods of the 2000 years of Christian reflection. Consider just one assessment, contained in the fifteenth-century Irish manuscript, *Leabhar Breac*.[11]

> One of the noble gifts of the Holy Spirit is the Divine Scriptures. Whereby every ignorance is enlightened, and whereby every earthly sadness is comforted, whereby every spiritual light is kindled, whereby every weakness is strengthened, for it is through the Holy Scriptures that heresy and schisms are cast forth from the Church, that every quarrel and dissent is pacified. In it is found perfect counsel, and fitting instruction by each and every degree in the Church. By it the snares of the devil and vices are expelled from every faithful one in the Church. For the divine Scripture is a mother and a gentle nurse (*máthair agus buime*) to all the faithful ones who meditate and consider it, and who are nurtured until they are chosen sons of God through its counsel. For wisdom gives generously to her sons, the many savours of the sweet liquor and the pleasures of the spiritual food whereby they are ever inebriated and gladdened.

More recently, at the Second Vatican Council (1961–65), several of these attitudes were reiterated. According to its Constitution on Divine Revelation (*Dei Verbum*, the Word of God), the Scriptures enlighten the mind, strengthen the will, and fire the human heart with the love of God (para. 23). All preaching and all religion should be nourished and ruled by the Sacred Scripture, because in the Sacred Scriptures one finds strength for faith, food for the soul and a pure and lasting fount of spiritual life (paras. 21-23). The study of the sacred page should be the very soul of theology. The faithful should engage in frequent reading of the Scriptures, a reading which ought to be accompanied by prayer. And, quoting St Jerome, it notes that 'Ignorance of the Scriptures is ignorance of Christ' (paras. 23-25). In practice also, the biblical text is at the heart of the Christian life, and plays a significant part in all formal prayers of the Church.

---

11. *Leabhar Breac* (Speckled Book) is now in the library of the Royal Irish Academy, Dublin (MS 23 P 16). Murchadh Riabhach O'Cuindlis is the scribe who compiled the massive text (1408–11). See Kathleen Mulchrone *et al.*, *Catalogue of Irish Manuscripts in the Royal Irish Academy* (Dublin: n.p., 1926–70), No. 1230, pp. 379-404. A facsimile edition (*Leabhar Breac* [*The Speckled Book*], otherwise styled *Leabhar Mór Dúna Doighre* [*The Great Book of Dun Doighre*]) was published in Dublin in 1876.

Conventional Biblical Scholarship

In addition to being a Christian believer, however, I am a biblical scholar, trained in postgraduate biblical academies in Dublin, Rome, London and Jerusalem. In all four I learned the skills of the discipline, which, in the main, transported the scholar into the imagined world of biblical antiquity in order to understand the different periods of the past that produced the various books of the Bible—the so-called historical-critical method of the discipline. At University College Dublin I acquired a better grasp of the languages necessary for biblical studies: Hebrew, Greek, Syriac (and German). The Pontifical Biblical Institute in Rome offered more language study, intensive engagement with the biblical texts and with the necessary ancillary disciplines (geography, archaeology, biblical history, etc.), as well as a superb library and a thriving Academy of significant biblical scholars. In King's College, London, I completed my study of the Second Letter of Paul to Timothy, which had been the major focus of my study while in the *École Biblique et Archeologique de Jérusalem* (1983–84). That year-long stay in Jerusalem was followed in the late 1980s and throughout the 1990s by annual visits for the purposes of study, and by a year as Visiting Professor of Theology in Bethlehem University and Scholar-in-Residence in Tantur Ecumenical Institute for Theology (1996–97).

Even my first visit, in Spring 1972, was significant. Prior to it, I shared views about the politics of the region that were typical of young people of my generation. I remember as a six-year child my profound admiration at the establishment of the State of Israel in 1948, just one year before my own country, the then Irish Free State, broke from the Commonwealth and declared itself a republic. I shared my teachers' enthusiasms for the Israeli success in revivifying Hebrew and establishing it as the vernacular, a determination which could serve as a model for the Irish nation as its aspiration to restore Gaelic as the language of the people was languishing.

The intensive training programme in spirituality within the Vincentian Community, which I joined in 1960 in the hope of becoming a Catholic priest, prided itself on its detachment from 'secular affairs'. Already in seventeenth-century France, our founder, St Vincent de Paul, being aware of the divisiveness of political preferences among his disciples in different nation states, cautioned against engaging in 'the affairs of princes'. In any case, much of my time was taken up with the study of Experimental Physics and Mathematics at the university (1961–65).

In the seminary, piety and theology were portrayed as being of a some-what metahistorical order, above any set of particular social or political circumstances. However, I was excited by Pope Paul VI's encyclical *Populorum Progressio*, with its bold analysis of contemporary polity, its criticism of nationalism and its advocacy of a trans-national world-order. While Liberation Theology was gestating in the womb of Latin America, what passed for a distinctive Irish Theology operated within a static ideo-logical framework, reposing in the jaded marriage between a triumphalist and self-assured Irish Catholicism and a revolutionary nationalism, which by then had become totally 'routinized'. All the while, social unrest was simmering in 'the Six Counties' of Northern Ireland, but I had not been 'up north' up to that time.

My courses on the Old Testament first sensitized me to the social and political context of theological reflection, albeit concerning only the past. We enquired into the real-life situations of the Hebrew Prophets, and considered the contexts of the Wisdom Literature. Beyond the narratives of Genesis 1–11, with its stories about the creation and the flood and the stories of Israel's exodus from Egypt, however, I do not recall much engagement with the books of Moses, the entire Torah for the Samaritans and the foundation for the Jewish Bible. Its mandate to commit the geno-cide of the inhabitants of Canaan rather escaped my attention. Moreover, the atrocities recorded in the following biblical book, Joshua, made no particular impression on me. The stories about the monarchy got a gener-ous airing, noting the link between religious perspectives and changing political circumstances. Nevertheless, my study of the Old Testament introduced me to a historiography, which from fragmentary evidence attempted to portray 'the past'. Just as I was not sensitive at that stage to the fact that Irish nationalist historiography had imposed a rigid nationalist framework on everything that preceded the advent of interest in the nation state, it never crossed my mind that the biblical narrative also might be a fabrication of a past, reflecting the distinctive perspectives of its later authors.

The Six-Day War

Right in the middle of my four years of study of theology, the war of 5-11 June 1967 broke out. In addition to stimulating my first curiosity in the Israeli–Arab conflict, Israel's conquest of the West Bank, the Golan Heights, the Gaza Strip and Sinai brought me 'face to face', via TV, with wider international political realities. I recall rushing through the seminary supper each evening to see how diminutive, innocent Israel was faring against its rapacious Arab predators. None of the reporting had any sympathy for the Arab position. All my sources of information, of course, projected it as a classic conflict between virtuous David and despicable Goliath. The startling, speedy and comprehensive victory of diminutive Israel produced surges of delight in me. And I had no reason to question the mellifluous mendacity of Israel's Foreign Minister, Abba Eban, in a speech delivered at the United Nations in that urbanity and self-assurance characteristic of Western diplomats however fraudulent, claiming that Israel was an innocent victim of Egyptian aggression.[12]

Later that summer in London, I was intrigued by billboards in Golders Green, with quotations from the Hebrew prophets, assuring readers that those who trusted in biblical prophecy could not be surprised by Israel's victory. Up to then I had never encountered an association between contemporary events and biblical prophecy. Biblical prophecy, the biblical Academy insisted, related to the period of the prophet and was not about predicting the future. The prophets were 'forth-tellers' for God, rather than foretellers of future events. I was intrigued that others thought differently.

I was to learn later, in the 1980s and 1990s, that the 1967 war inaugurated a new phase in the Zionist conquest of Mandated Palestine, one which brought theological assertions and biblical interpretations to the very heart of the ideology which propelled the Israeli conquest and set the pattern for Jewish settlement. After two more years of theology, ordination and three years of postgraduate biblical studies, I made my first visit to Israel–Palestine at Easter 1972, with a party of postgraduate students from the Pontifical Biblical Institute, Rome.

Seeing and Believing

Albeit one inquiring virtually exclusively into the archaeological remains of ancient civilisations, the visit offered the first challenge to my favourable predispositions towards Israel. I was disturbed immediately by the ubiquitous signs of the oppression of the Arabs, whom later I learnt to call

12. The Israeli representative misled the emergency meeting of the UN Security Council (the morning of 5 June) with fabricated details that Egypt had initiated the conflict with the shelling of Israeli villages and the bombing of towns (UN Doc. S/PV 1347). International media repeated the false information, and on the following day the Israeli Foreign Minister, Abba Eban, a party to the cabinet decision to launch a pre-emptive attack on Egypt, repeated the deceit (UN Doc. S/PV 1348).

Palestinians. I was witnessing some kind of 'institutionalized oppression'—I cannot recall whether 'apartheid' was part of my vocabulary at the time. The experience must have been profound since, when the Yom Kippur War broke out in October 1973, my support for Israel did not match my enthusiasm of 1967. I had no particular interest in the area for the remainder of the 1970s, but I recall watching on TV the visit of Egypt's President Sadat to the Israeli Knesset in November 1977, an initiative which would culminate in a formal peace agreement between Egypt and Israel in Camp David in 1979. Things changed for me in the 1980s.

In 1981 I went with a party from my university to visit Bir Zeit University in the Israeli-occupied West Bank. Because the campus was closed by the military just before our arrival, carefully planned programs had to yield to Palestinian '*ad-hoc*ery'. Bir Zeit put a bus at our disposal, and equal numbers of its and our students constituted a university on wheels. I was profoundly shocked when I began to see from the inside the reality of land expropriation and the on-going Jewish settlement of the West Bank. I began to question the prevailing view that the Israeli occupation was for security reasons, but even with such obvious evidence I could not bring myself to abandon it. There were, of course, many other instances of social repression in the world, but my experience up to that time had not brought me to those other regions.

Although I was researching the Pauline Epistles during my sabbatical year in the *École Biblique* in 1983–84, day-to-day life in Jerusalem sharpened my sensitivities. I was beginning to suspect that the Israeli occupation was not after all for security reasons, but was an expansion towards the achievement of 'Greater Israel', which, I was to learn later, was the goal of even mainstream Zionism—the 'Revisionists' of the Likud party had wanted the east bank of the Jordan also. The silence of the cloister was broken several times each day with sonic booms from military aircraft flying north to Lebanon or Syria. During that period, I was certain that Israel would attack Syria, if only to unify the Israelis, who, it seemed to me, were showing signs of serious social disharmony. In the event I was proved wrong. But what had all of this to do with reading the Bible in Jerusalem?

One incident in particular alerted me to the religious dimension of the conflict. On a spring morning in 1984, the Voice of Israel radio reported that during the night a Jewish terrorist group had been caught attempting to blow up the Dome of the Rock and the Al-Aqsa Mosque on the Haram al-Sharif (The Noble Sanctuary, which Jews refer to as the Temple Mount), only a few hundred meters south of the *École Biblique*. Subsequently the newspapers published pictures of some of those convicted of the offence, wearing the typical dress of the religious Jewish settler movement *Gush Emunim*. The report recorded that one was reading from the book of Psalms as the judge read out the verdict. That an attempted act of such international and inter-faith significance sprang from religious fervour shocked me. Settler Jews performed other acts of terror during that year, and the name of the overtly racist Rabbi Meir Kahane, who claimed to derive his ideology from the Law of Moses, was seldom off the headlines, further underlining the link between aggressive settlement activity and biblical piety.

I can date to that period also voicing my first displeasure at my perception that the land traditions of the Bible appeared to mandate the genocide of the indigenes of 'Canaan'. At the end of his Public Lecture in Tantur, I suggested to Marc H. Ellis, a young Jewish theologian who was developing a Jewish Theology of Liberation with strong dependence on the Hebrew Prophets,[13] that it would be no more difficult to construct a Theology of Oppression on the basis of other biblical traditions, especially those dealing with Israelite origins that demanded the destruction of other peoples.

However, I had more pressing academic demands when I returned to London after my sabbatical, but I did record some reflections on my year in *Scripture Bulletin*, the journal of the Catholic Biblical Association of Great Britain, of which I was then editor.[14] In 1985 I led a study tour to Israel and the Occupied Territories, and led a group of priests on a 'Retreat through Pilgrimage' in 1987[15] and made other visits in 1990 and 1991. In 1991, I participated in an International Peace Walk from Jerusalem to Amman, and although I did not reach the destination, I gained the acquaintance of several groups of Israeli soldiers and police, enjoyed detention twice and faced what appeared to be an inevitable spell in prison for trespassing on arbitrarily declared 'closed military zones'.

It took some time for my experiences to acquire an ideological framework. Gradually I read more of the modern history of the region and had formal meetings with some prominent Palestinians, churchpeople and

13. Subsequently published as Marc H. Ellis, *Toward a Jewish Theology of Liberation* (Maryknoll, NY: Orbis Books, 1987).

14. Michael Prior, 'Israel: Library, Land and Peoples', *Scripture Bulletin* 15 (1984), pp. 6-11.

15. Michael Prior, 'Living Stones: A Retreat with Palestinian Christians', *New Blackfriars* 70 (1989), pp. 119-23.

others. I made three visits in 1993: one at Easter to prepare the Cumberland Lodge Conference on Christians in the Holy Land,[16] one for study in August and the third to bring a group of students. Although my academic concentration in that period was on the scene of Jesus in the synagogue in Nazareth (Lk. 4.16-30), my growing unease about the link between biblical spirituality and oppression stimulated me to examine the land traditions of the Bible, and so I began to read the narrative systematically with that theme in mind. Already I had written a number of articles on the Holy Land.[17] With my manuscript on Luke 4 completed on 22 July 1994,[18] I could give my whole attention to the land traditions of the Bible in the *École Biblique* in August.

Yahweh and Ethnic Cleansing

What struck me most about the biblical narrative was that the divine promise of land was integrally linked with the mandate to exterminate the indigenous peoples, and I had to wrestle with my perception that those traditions were inherently oppressive and morally reprehensible. Even the Exodus narrative was problematic. While it portrays Yahweh as having compassion on the misery of his people and as willing to deliver them from the Egyptians and bring them to a land flowing with milk and honey (Exod. 3.7-8), that was only part of the picture. Although the reading of Exodus 3, both in the Christian liturgy and in the classical texts of liberation theologies, halts abruptly in the middle of v. 8 at the description of the land as one 'flowing with milk and honey',[19] the biblical text itself

16. See Michael Prior and William Taylor (eds.), *Christians in the Holy Land* (London: World of Islam Festival Trust, 1994).

17. Michael Prior, 'A Christian Perspective on the *Intifada*', *The Month* 23 (1990), pp. 478-85; 'Living Stones: Christians in the Holy Land', *Doctrine and Life* 42 (1993), pp. 128-34; 'Palestinian Christians and the Liberation of Theology', *The Month* 26 (1992), pp. 482-90; 'Christian Presence in the Occupied Territories', *Living Stones Magazine* 9 (1993), pp. 3-4; 'Living or Dead Stones? The Future of Christians in the Holy Land', *Living Stones Magazine* 9 (1993), pp. 4-6; and 'The Vatican–Israel Fundamental Agreement', *Living Stones Magazine* 10 (1994), pp. 2-4.

18. Michael Prior, *Jesus the Liberator: Nazareth Liberation Theology (Luke 4.16-30)* (The Biblical Seminar, 26; Sheffield: Sheffield Academic Press, 1995).

19. E.g. Sobrino, 'Human Rights and Oppressed Peoples', p. 137; for examples from Gustavo Gutiérrez, Philip Berryman *et al.*, see Michael Prior, *The Bible and Colonialism: A Moral Critique* (The Biblical Seminar, 48; Sheffield: Sheffield Academic Press, 1997), pp. 278-84.

continues, 'to the country of the Canaanites, the Hittites, the Amorites, the Perizzites, the Hivites, and the Jebusites'. Manifestly, the Promised Land, flowing with milk and honey, had no lack of indigenous peoples, and, according to the narrative, would soon flow with blood:

> 'When my angel goes in front of you, and brings you to the Amorites, the Hittites, the Perizzites, the Canaanites, the Hivites and the Jebusites, and I blot them out, you shall not bow down to their gods, or worship them, or follow their practices, but you shall utterly demolish them and break their pillars in pieces.' (Exod. 23.23-24)

Matters got worse in the narrative of the book of Deuteronomy. After the king of Heshbon refused passage to the Israelites, Yahweh gave him over to the Israelites who captured and utterly destroyed all the cities, killing all the men, women and children (Deut. 2.33-34). The fate of the king of Bashan was no better (3.3). Yahweh's role was central:

> 'When Yahweh your God brings you into the land that you are about to enter and occupy, and he clears away many nations before you—the Hittites, the Girgashites, the Amorites, the Canaanites, the Perizzites, the Hivites...and when Yahweh your God gives them over to you...you must utterly destroy them... Show them no mercy... For you are a people holy to Yahweh your God; Yahweh your God has chosen you out of all the peoples on earth to be his people, his treasured possession.' (Deut. 7.1-11; see also 9.1-5; 11.8-9, 23, 31-32)

And again, from the mouth of Moses:

> 'But as for the towns of these peoples that Yahweh your God is giving you as an inheritance, you must not let anything that breathes remain alive. You shall annihilate them—the Hittites and the Amorites, the Canaanites and the Perizzites, the Hivites and the Jebusites—just as Yahweh your God has commanded, so that they may not teach you to do all the abhorrent things that they do for their gods and you thus sin against Yahweh your God.' (Deut. 20.16-18)

It was some shock to realize that the narrative presents 'ethnic cleansing' as not only legitimate, but as required by the deity. The book of Deuteronomy ends with Moses' sight of the Promised Land before he dies (34.1-3). Although Moses was unequalled in his deeds, he left a worthy successor, Joshua, who, after Moses had lain his hands on him, was full of the spirit of wisdom (34.4-12). So much for the preparation for entry into the Promised Land.

The first part of the book of Joshua (2.1–12.24) describes the conquest of a few key cities and their fate in accordance with the laws of Holy War.

Even while the Gibeonites were to be spared, the Israelite elders complained at the lapse in fidelity to the mandate to destroy all the inhabitants of the land (9.21-27). Joshua took Makkedah, utterly destroying every person in it (10.28). A similar fate befell other cities (10.29-39): everything that breathed was destroyed as Yahweh commanded (10.40-43). Joshua utterly destroyed the inhabitants of the cities of the north as well (11.1-23). Yahweh gave to Israel all the land that he swore to their ancestors he would give them (21.43-45). These legendary achievements of Yahweh through the agencies of Moses, Aaron and Joshua are kept before the Israelites even in their prayers: 'You brought a vine out of Egypt; you drove out the nations and planted it' (Ps. 80.8; see also 78.54-55; 105.44).

By modern standards of international law and human rights, what these biblical narratives mandate, of course, are 'war-crimes' and 'crimes against humanity'. To respond by insisting that we ought not to judge earlier centuries by the standards obtaining at a later time is not sufficient,[20] since we who are the readers are living in our own time, not in the past. Biblical critics might seek refuge also in the claim that the problem lies with the predispositions of the modern reader, rather than with the text itself, but one cannot escape so easily. One must acknowledge that much of the Books of Moses, and the book of Deuteronomy in particular, contains menacing ideologies and racist, xenophobic and militaristic tendencies. Clearly, the implications of the existence of such dubious moral dispositions, presented as mandated by the divinity, within a book which is canonized as Sacred Scripture, invited the most serious investigation. Was there a way of reading the traditions, which could rescue the Bible from being a blunt instrument of oppression and acquit God of the charge of being the Great Ethnic-Cleanser?

In that August of 1994, the *École Biblique* library had just received a Festschrift consisting of studies in the book of Deuteronomy. In addition to articles covering the customary source-, historical-critical and literary discussions, it contained one by F.E. Deist, with the intriguing title, 'The Dangers of Deuteronomy', which discussed the role of that book in support of apartheid.[21] It dealt with the text from the perspective of its

20. Such an attitude reflects typical nineteenth-century confidence in the ever-evolving nature of society which reaches its climax in Western democracies, ignoring, of course, the atrocities committed in the period after the Enlightenment, not least the twentieth century, which surpass anything committed earlier.

21. F.E. Deist, 'The Dangers of Deuteronomy: A Page from the Reception History of the Book', in F. García Martínez, A. Hilhorst, J.T.A.G.M. van Ruiten and A.S. van

reception history, especially within the ideology of an emerging Afrikaner nationalism. During that month I also read A.G. Lamadrid's discussion of the role of the Bible and Christian Theology in the Iberian conquest of Latin America.[22] The problem, then, went beyond academic reflection on the interpretation of ancient documents of dubious morality.

The Bible as Instrument of Oppression

It was becoming very clear to me that some biblical narratives had contributed to the suffering of countless indigenous people. The traditions of Deuteronomy had provided intellectual and moral authority for the Iberian devastation of 'Latin America' in the late mediaeval period, for the Afrikaner exploitation of non-whites in southern Africa right up to the 1990s and was continuing to do so in the ongoing Zionist exspoliation of the Arabs of Palestine. Not only did these narratives have the capacity to infuse exploitative tendencies in their readers, then, but my research was confirming how in practice they had fuelled virtually every form of militant colonialism emanating from Europe, by providing allegedly divine legitimization for Western colonizers in their zeal to implant 'outposts of progress' in 'the heart of darkness', to adapt the language of Joseph Conrad. This was not to pretend, of course, that those engaged in imperialist adventures took their cue from the biblical narrative—invariably their motivation was economic gain—but merely to indicate how these narratives, with their predilection for the 'chosen', could provide moral legitimacy of the highest order for those who positioned themselves among the 'elect' of God.

When I got back to England, I wrote an article, 'The Bible as Instrument of Oppression', giving the three case studies of Latin America, southern Africa and Palestine.[23] Apart from the surprise at seeing my photo and a synopsis of my message appearing in the *Catholic Times*, there was little sign that my 15 minutes of fame was about to descend on me. The subject,

der Woud (eds.), *Studies in Deuteronomy: In Honour of C.J. Labuschagne on the Occasion of his 65th Birthday* (Leiden: E.J. Brill, 1994), pp. 13-29.

22. A.G. Lamadrid, 'Canaán y América. La Biblia y la Teologia medieval ante la Conquista de la Tierra', in R. Aguirre and F. Garcia Lopez (eds.), *Escritos de Biblia y Oriente, Bibliotheca Salmanticensis Estudios* 38 (Salamanca: Universidad Pontificia, 1981), pp. 329-46.

23. Michael Prior, 'The Bible as Instrument of Oppression', *Scripture Bulletin* 25 (1995), pp. 2-14.

I judged, deserved fuller investigation, but before embarking on a more substantial monograph, it would be prudent to examine the situation in Old Testament scholarship.

Western Scholarship and the Holy Land

Somebody must have addressed the moral question before, I presumed. Back in Jerusalem for August 1995, I realized that this was not the case. Even though Gerhard von Rad lamented in 1943 that no thorough investigation of 'the land' had been made up to that point,[24] in fact no serious study of the topic was undertaken for another three decades. But surely W.D. Davies' seminal studies had compensated for the neglect hitherto![25] Davies acknowledged later that he had written his seminal *The Gospel and the Land* at the request of friends in Jerusalem, who, just before the war in 1967, urged his support for the cause of Israel.[26] Moreover, he wrote *The Territorial Dimensions of Judaism* under the direct impact of that war and its updated version, because of the mounting need to understand the theme in the light of events in the Middle East, culminating in the Gulf War and its aftermath.[27] I was intrigued by the frankness with which Davies publicized his hermeneutical key: 'Here I have concentrated on what in my judgement must be the beginning for an understanding of this conflict: the sympathetic attempt to comprehend the Jewish tradition'.[28]

While Davies considers 'the land' from virtually every other conceivable perspective, little attention is given to broadly moral and human rights issues. In particular, he excludes from his concern, 'What happens when the understanding of the Promised Land in Judaism conflicts with the claims of the traditions and occupancy of its other peoples?' He excused himself by saying that to engage that issue would demand another

24. Gerhard von Rad, 'The Promised Land and Yahweh's Land in the Hexateuch', in *idem, The Problem of the Hexateuch and Other Essays* (London: SCM; Philadelphia: Fortress Press, 1966 [repr. 1984]), pp. 79-93 (79).

25. W.D. Davies, *The Gospel and the Land: Early Christianity and Jewish Territorial Doctrine* (Berkeley: University of California Press, 1974); *The Territorial Dimensions of Judaism* (Berkeley: University of California Press, 1982); *The Territorial Dimensions of Judaism: With a Symposium and Further Reflections* (Minneapolis: Fortress Press, 1991).

26. Davies, *Territorial Dimensions* (1982), p. xiii.

27. Davies, *Territorial Dimensions* (1991), p. xiii.

28. Davies, *Territorial Dimensions* (1982), pp. xiii-xiv.

volume,[29] without indicating his intention of embarking upon such an enterprise. I wondered whether Davies would have been equally sanguine had white, Anglo-Saxon Protestants, or even white Catholics of European provenance, been among the displaced people who paid the price for the prize of Zionism. Reflecting a somewhat elastic moral sense, Davies, although perturbed by the aftermath of the 1967 conquest, took the establishment of the State of Israel in his stride. Showing no concern for the foundational injustice done to the Palestinians in 1948—80 per cent driven from their homes, and over 400 villages destroyed so that they could not return, etc.—Davies wrote as if there were later a moral equivalence between the dispossessed Palestinians and the dispossessor Zionists. The rights of the aggressor and the victim were finely balanced, although clearly his scales tilted rather towards the dispossessors.

Walter Brueggemann's *The Land* brought me no further.[30] While he saw land as perhaps 'the central theme' of biblical faith, he bypassed the treatment to be meted out to the indigenous inhabitants, affirming, 'What is asked is not courage to destroy enemies, but courage to keep Torah [the Law of Moses]', and thereby avoiding the fact that 'keeping the Torah' in this context demanded accepting its xenophobic and destructive militarism.[31] By 1994, however, Brueggemann was less sanguine, noting that while the scholastic community had provided 'rich and suggestive studies on the 'land theme' in the Bible…they characteristically stop before they get to the hard part, contemporary issues of land in the Holy Land'.[32]

It was beginning to dawn on me that much biblical investigation—especially that concentration on the past which is typical of the historical-critical method—was quite indifferent to moral considerations. Indeed, it was becoming clear that the discipline of Biblical Studies over the last hundred years reflected the Eurocentric perspectives of virtually all Western historiography and had contributed significantly to the oppression of native peoples. The benevolent interpretation of biblical traditions, which advocate atrocities and war crimes, had given solace to those bent on the exploitation of new lands at the expense of native peoples. While the

29. Davies, *Territorial Dimensions* (1991), p. xv.

30. Walter Brueggemann, *The Land: Place as Gift, Promise, and Challenge in Biblical Faith* (Philadelphia: Fortress Press, 1977).

31. Brueggemann, *The Land*, pp. 3, 48, 60.

32. Walter Brueggemann, in W. Eugene March (with a Foreword by Walter Brueggemann), *Israel and the Politics of Land: A Theological Case Study* (Louisville, KY: Westminster/John Knox Press, 1994).

behaviour of communities and nation states is complex and is never the result of one element of motivation, there is clear evidence that in several regions of imperialist and colonialist expansion the Bible has been and still is, for some, *the idea* that *redeems the conquest of the earth*.[33] This was particularly true in the case of the Arabs of Palestine, in whose country I had reached these conclusions as I studied the Bible.

Having had my moral being sensitized by the biblical mandate to commit genocide, I was amazed that scholars had a high esteem for even the book of Deuteronomy. Indeed, commentators conventionally assess it to be a theological book *par excellence* and the focal point of the religious history of the Old Testament. In the 1995 Lattey Lecture in Cambridge University (14 November), Professor Norbert Lohfink argued that the book of Deuteronomy provides a model of an utopian society in which there would be no poor.[34] In my role as the formal proposer of a vote of thanks—I was the Chairperson of the Catholic Biblical Association of Great Britain—I invited him to consider whether, in the light of that book's insistence on a mandate to commit genocide, the utopian society would be possible only after the invading Israelites had wiped out the indigenous inhabitants. The protocol of the Lattey Lecture left the last word with me, and subsequently I was given a second word, being invited to deliver the 1997 Lattey Lecture, for which I chose the title, *A Land Flowing with Milk, Honey, and People*.[35]

By the Autumn of 1995, I was well into a book on the subject. In the university mid-term in November I went to discuss with Sheffield Academic Press my draft manuscript on 'The Bible and Zionism'. The editor, apprehensive at my concentration on Zionism, persuaded me to use three case studies. The task ahead, then, would require further immersion in the histories of Latin America, South Africa and Israel, as well as a more detailed study of the biblical narrative and its interpretation in the hands of the biblical Academy. While I got much of this work done in the course of that academic year, I had not managed to finish the manuscript before embarking for Bethlehem to take up my position as Visiting Professor.

33. See Michael Prior, 'The Bible and the Redeeming Idea of Colonialism', *Studies in World Christianity* 5.2 (1999), pp. 129-55.

34. Norbert Lohfink, 'The Laws of Deuteronomy: Project for a World Without Any Poor', *Scripture Bulletin* 26 (1996), pp. 2-19.

35. Michael Prior, *A Land Flowing with Milk, Honey, and People* (Cambridge: Von Hügel Institute, 1997); also published in *Scripture Bulletin* 28 (1998), pp. 2-17.

Working against a background of bullet fire and in the shadow of tanks added a certain intensity to my research. Several bullets landed on the flat roof of Tantur Ecumenical Institute on 25-26 September 1996. Two Palestinians, one a graduate of the university, were killed in Bethlehem and many more, Palestinians and Israeli soldiers, were killed in the disturbances elsewhere in the West Bank. However, with no bullets flying in Jerusalem on 26 September, I was able to deliver my advertised Public Lecture in the Swedish Christian Study Centre, entitled 'Does the God of the Bible Sanction Ethnic Cleansing?' By mid-December I was able to send the manuscript of *The Bible and Colonialism* to Sheffield Academic Press.

Later that same year I preached at the Christmas Midnight Mass in Bethlehem University, presided over by Monsignor Montezemolo, the Holy See's Apostolic Delegate, a key player in the signing of the Fundamental Agreement between the Holy See and the State of Israel on 30 December 1993.[36] I reflected with the congregation that, not withstanding the Christmas rhetoric about God's glory in the Highest Heaven and peace on earth, the reality of Bethlehem brought one down to earth rather quickly. I assured them that passing by the checkpoint between Bethlehem and Jerusalem twice a day made me boil with anger at the humiliation which the colonizing enterprise of Zionism had inflicted on the people of the region.

The proofs of *The Bible and Colonialism* arrived on Good Friday 1997 and I got my first taste of teargas in the vicinity of Rachel's Tomb on my way to Easter Sunday Mass at St Catherine's in Bethlehem. On 3 April, I delivered the Tantur Public Lecture, 'The Moral Problem of the Bible's Land Traditions', followed by questions both appreciative and hostile. In dealing with a trilogy of hostile questions, I used the opportunity to say that I considered Zionism to be one of the most pernicious ideologies of the twentieth century, particularly evil because of its essential link between oppression and religious values.

The Bible and Colonialism was launched in London in December 1997,[37] by which time the English papers of the 1996 Amman *Yom al-Quds* Conference were also published.[38] I had promised in *The Bible and Colonial-*

---

36. Someone thought it worthwhile to post my sermon on the internet. Go to <http://www.jerusalemites.org/jerusalem/christianity/5.htm>.

37. See n. 19 above for publication details.

38. Michael Prior (ed.), *Western Scholarship and the History of Palestine* (London: Melisende, 1998).

ism (p. 259 n. 2) that I would discuss elsewhere the more theological aspects of Zionism and, while still in Jerusalem in 1997, I had laid out my plans for writing the book I had really wanted to write some years earlier. I submitted a draft manuscript to a distinguished publisher in November 1997 and even though the anonymous reader found it to be 'a brilliant book which must be published', the press declined because, I was informed orally, the press had 'a very strong Jewish list' and could not offend its Jewish contributors and readers. While an American publishing company judged it to be 'a prodigious achievement of historical and theological investigation' and 'a very important work', it deemed that it would not really suit its publishing program. Routledge 'bit the bullet', publishing it under the title *Zionism and the State of Israel: A Moral Inquiry*.[39]

A Moral Reading of the Bible

From being a biblical scholar reflecting the biblical Academy's emphasis on the historical-critical methods of the discipline, since the early 1980s, in response to carrying out substantial parts of my studies in the Holy Land, I have begun to probe issues of the Reception History and the Moral Exegesis of the biblical text, with especial relevance to the realities of people's lives in that region. The urgency of the task is suggested by the enormity of the tragedy of the region and its alleged moral and theological legitimization. Salman H. Abu-Sitta's description of the Palestinian tragedy holds the problematic in sharp relief:

> The Palestinian Nakba is unsurpassed in history. For a country to be occupied by a foreign minority, emptied almost entirely of its people, its physical and cultural landmarks obliterated, its destruction hailed as a miraculous act of God and a victory for freedom and civilised values, all done according to a premeditated plan, meticulously executed, financially and politically supported from abroad and still maintained today, is no doubt unique.[40]

Zionism, however one estimates its value to international Jewry, is responsible for the dispossession, dispersion and humiliation of the indigenous

---

39. Michael Prior, *Zionism and the State of Israel: A Moral Inquiry* (London: Routledge, 1999).

40. Salman H. Abu-Sitta, *The Palestinian Nakba 1948: The Register of Depopulated Localities in Palestine (with accompanying Map, Palestine 1948: 50 Years after Al Nakba—The Towns and Villages Depopulated by the Zionist Invasion of 1948)* (Occasional Studies Series [Palestinian Return Centre], 4; London: The Palestine Return Centre, 1998), p. 5.

Arab population of Mandated Palestine over the last 55 years. While such devastation is not unique in the history of human civilisation, it does have distinctive features. Most alarmingly from a moral perspective, the injustice to the indigenous population is passed over in most Western discourse, including biblical and theological scholarship and in some religious circles is even clothed in the garment of piety. Mainstream Christian theological commentary on Israel–Palestine, however, is driven by guilt feelings concerning the treatment of Jews in the past and is characterized by a detachment from the political context of Zionism, by naïveté or misinformation concerning the realities of its conquest of and rule over Palestine and by a certain paralysis of conscience regarding the unjust treatment of the indigenous population.[41]

The cost to the indigenous population of the Zionist achievement in 1948–49 and 1967 casts a dark cloud over the aspirations of the ethnocentric dream of nineteenth-century Zionist nationalist colonialists. The sacral discourse of the achievement of Zionism, which since 1967 has been transposed from the secular aspiration to create a state for Jews to the apocalyptic one of redeeming *Eretz Yisrael*, is undermined by the reality of the catastrophe for the indigenous population. Redemption of *Eretz Yisrael* has required 'the spilling of the blood' of the indigenous Palestinian population. Spilling the blood of the Other, however, is described more appropriately as atrocity rather than redemption.

All too frequently the ideological underpinning for European colonialism availed of the biblical paradigms of 'ethnic cleansing' and 'belligerent settler colonialism', the legitimization of which has the authority of Sacred Scripture.[42] With even more authority, the Jewish claim to 'return' relies on the Bible, which is a *sine qua non* for alleged moral legitimacy. The Bible read at face value, then, provides a moral framework, which metamorphoses Zionist colonialist settlement in our own day into a divinely sanctioned polity.[43] The taking possession of the Promised Land and the forcible expulsion of the indigenous population in 1948–49, then, derives

41. See Michael Prior, 'Speaking Truth in the Jewish–Christian Dialogue', in David Thomas and Clare Amos (eds.), *A Faithful Presence: Essays for Kenneth Cragg* (London: Melisende), pp. 329-49.

42. See further Michael Prior, 'Ethnic Cleansing and the Bible: A Moral Critique', *Holy Land Studies: A Multidisciplinary Journal* 1 (2002), pp. 37-59.

43. See Michael Prior, 'The Right to Expel: The Bible and Ethnic Cleansing', in Naseer Aruri (ed.), *Palestinian Refugees and their Right of Return* (London/Sterling, VA: Pluto Press, 2001), pp. 9-35.

its alleged legitimacy primarily from the biblical mandate, whether viewed as the repository of Israel's sacred history or as one of the cornerstones of its national mythology. The biblical narrative functioned as the objective historical account of Jews' title to the land, a claim allegedly borne out by archaeological findings, even for secular nationalists uninterested in the Bible as the repository of a theological claim to Palestine.[44]

What is most distressing from a moral and religious perspective, is that, since 1967 in particular, the major ideological support for Zionist imperialism and the principal obstacle to treating the indigenous people with respect come from religious circles for whom the biblical narratives of land, understood in a literalist fashion, are normative. From a religious perspective, the 'transfer' of the indigenous population, which the Zionist enterprise required, was a small price to pay for 'scaling the wall', and shortening the delay before the coming of the Messiah. It is a matter of concern that most religious Jews have little regard for the indigenes who have paid the price for the establishment of Israel. But then, neither did Joshua in the biblical narrative.

My reading of the history of Zionism, using the published findings of researchers into the Zionist and other archives, has confirmed that the 'transfer' of the Arab population was promoted by virtually the whole pantheon of Zionist ideologues, albeit mostly in secret—a conclusion which comprehensively unmasks the myth of the benevolent and peaceful intentions of Zionism. I have seen also that Israeli appeal to an exclusively 'defensive ethos' is merely a public relations device, as well as an exercise in conscious self-deception, assuaging both world opinion and the consciences of Zionists. This led to the conclusion that the consistency with which the State of Israel is excused from having to conform to Inter-

44. While the Bible is not the only provider of alleged moral legitimacy for Zionism it is the most powerful moral one, without which the Zionist conquest would be no more legitimate than any other enterprise of colonial plunder. The Bible read at face value provides not only a moral framework which transposes Jewish claims into a divinely sanctioned legitimacy, it postulates the taking possession of the Promised Land and the forcible expulsion of the indigenous population as the fulfilment of a biblical mandate (see Michael Prior, 'Zionist Ethnic Cleansing: The Fulfilment of Biblical Prophecy?', *Epworth Review* 27.2 [2000], pp. 49-60). However, the appeal to the Bible is mainly to those traditions which portray Yahweh as a promoter of an ethnic and xenophobic 'nationalism', premised on attitudes of racial dominance and exclusion. While these attitudes accord with those of nineteenth-century European colonialism, they do not advance the goal of other traditions within Judaism, such as that inviting the Jewish community to be 'a light to the nations'.

national Law and decent behaviour is one of the great eccentricities of modern political ethics.

Given the 'international community's' general disdain for ethnic cleansing, it is surprising that Christian reflection on the Holy Land has not gone much further than reflect predictable conformity with political realities as they develop. At best, one detects in the attitudes within the Churches an adherence to 'the fallacy of balance'—the assumption that, in this unique situation of conflict, there is an equality of rights, an equality of pain, an equality of sacrifice, and so on, as if 'the rights of the rapist and the victim' were finely balanced.

It is disappointing that in an age in which apologizing for misdeeds and omissions is part of the landscape, there is little sign of perturbation within the biblical Academy concerning the profusion of evils arising from particular understandings of the biblical text. The exspoliation of the indigenous population of Palestine at the hands of Zionists, with an obvious reliance on the biblical narrative, appears to leave the Academy untouched. Indeed the very attempt to raise the issue for consideration is perceived to be scandalous. The modern penchant for moral distress and apology, it appears, is restricted to events of the past for which moderns have no responsibility and costs nothing. Such a disposition is consistent with obduracy concerning matters in which one has a clear responsibility. The imperative seems to be to own up to only those things for which one has no responsibility.

Conclusion

Researching the Bible in a city under military occupation and in a land from which the majority of its indigenous Arab population had been expelled—with the Bible allegedly supplying moral legitimization of divine provenance—provided a unique context for developing a hermeneutic, which involved an ethical and theological evaluation of my context, and pointed to a reassessment of the nature of the discipline of Biblical Studies itself. While struggling to make sense of my context and my task, of course, I had no sense of establishing a novel methodology, such as might later be classified as a political, or public paradigm for biblical interpretation. In 1984 I had no sense of embarking upon what subsequently would be called a 'post-colonial' study—or, to use a not altogether elegant term 'Contemporizing Interpretation'[45]—of the biblical narrative. Nor had I a

---

45. See Heikki Räisänen, *Beyond New Testament Theology: A Story and a Programme* (London: SCM Press, 2000), pp. 203-209.

sense of engaging in a discourse that might later be designated a 'Moral Exegesis of the Bible'.

Because of the tragic social consequence of the polities obtaining in the region during my stays in the land of the Bible, I had particular reason to be concerned about the public responsibility of Biblical Studies; that is, one that embraces the need to construct a publicly accessible, and not just an academic or theological–religious discourse that attends to moral questions. My concerns began with questions as to how to deal with the fact that the Bible was used in that region to protect a hegemonic political system of oppression, and how to respond to that situation as a scholar, aware of how such matters appeared to be of no concern to the biblical Academy, either that *in situ* in the Holy Land or anywhere else in the world.

Western support for the Zionist enterprise was particularly striking from a moral perspective. Whereas elsewhere the perpetrators of colonial plunder were objects of opprobrium, the Zionist conquest was widely judged to be a just and appropriate accomplishment, with even unique religious significance. Much of the rationale for that evaluation derived from literalist interpretations of particular traditions of the Bible: the Zionist prize was no more than what the Jewish people deserved in virtue of God's promises as outlined in the biblical narrative. But the impact of the deployment of the text was more widespread.

When I discovered in 1994 that appeal to the biblical narrative was a critical ideological element 'legitimizing' apartheid in South Africa, as well as being a determining element in the theological underpinning for the colonization of 'Latin America', I wrote my first comparative study on the role of the Bible in the oppression of people.[46] This was an arresting assertion in a context in which the Bible was conventionally used as an instrument of liberation within Liberation Theology.

This development in my perceptions suggested the necessity of considering the perspective of the victims of various colonial enterprises, an endeavour analogous to reading the biblical text 'with the eyes of the Canaanites'; that is, with a sensitivity to the moral question of the impact which colonizing enterprises and the Zionist conquest and settlement in Palestine in particular, have had on the indigenous populations. The Academy, of course, does not read the biblical narrative 'with the eyes of the Canaanites'. Rather, it broadly accepts the perspectives of the biblical authors, who make it clear that the claim of the divine promise of land is

---

46. Prior, 'The Bible as Instrument of Oppression'.

integrally linked with the alleged divine mandate to exterminate its indigenous people. But even if the narrative of the biblical books from Genesis
to Joshua did correspond to what actually happened—the view that its
literary genre is history runs in the face of all serious scholarly comment—
it should not escape an evaluation based on criteria of morality. It was
clear to me that these land traditions posed fundamental moral questions,
relating to one's understanding of God's nature and dealings with humankind and of human behaviour, especially in the light of the use to which
they had been put in fuelling imperialist genocidal enterprises in a wide
variety of contexts for close on 2000 years. The communities that have
preserved and promulgated these biblical narratives—including the biblical Academy—should shoulder some of the responsibility for what has
been done in conformity with their values.

The neglect of the moral dimension in biblical scholarship has many
explanations. While practitioners of the historical-critical method strive
assiduously to discover whatever can be ascertained about the social, religious and political context of each of the biblical writings, they are less
sensitive to their own social, religious and political contexts, and the
impact that these might have on their interpretation of the biblical texts.
Few appear to see it as a necessary task of the discipline to evaluate the
biblical texts in terms of modern ethical criteria or display any inclination
to involve their scholarship in any processes of social transformation.[47]
Their task is complete once they have illuminated their segment of the
past. There is no question of seeing themselves as being called to be
critical transformative intellectuals, with a responsibility of delineating
models for the overthrow of systems of domination and oppression on the

47. Thus, for example, Jan Botha adjudicated South African New Testament
scholarship in the 1970s and 1980s, with its exclusive interests in the contexts of the
first century, to be irrelevant to the social turmoil obtaining in the country as it shook
off apartheid ('Aspects of the Rhetoric of South African New Testament Scholarship
Anno 1992', *Scriptura* 46 [1993], pp. 80-99 [93]). In Elisabeth Schüssler Fiorenza's
estimation, the conventional biblical Academy distinguishes itself by detachment from
issues of contemporary ferment, operating as if in a political vacuum and being
accountable only to its 'in-house' fraternity of scholars, who pay no attention to their
own social locations or to how the discipline serves political functions. Thus, in a 40-
year period, no President of the SBL has used his presidential address to consider the
political context of his scholarship. Since 1947, no presidential address alluded to any
aspect of world or national politics, such as the civil rights movement, liberation
struggles, Martin Luther King, the Shoah, and so on (*Rhetoric and Ethic: The Politics
of Biblical Studies* [Minneapolis: Fortress Press, 1999], p. 23).

world scale. Other factors also add to the neglect in the area of the land of the Bible.

Much Biblical Studies has been propelled by the search for ancient Israel as the taproot of Western civilisation and the antecedent of Christianity. Consequently the history of the entire region of the biblical narrative has been merely a backdrop to the history of Israel, Judah and Second Temple Judaism, with the Bible centre stage and all other evidence in its service.[48] The biblical narrative's presentation of the genocide preceding the establishment of biblical Israel required no apologia, since, in addition to being in conformity with the alleged divine mandate, the biblical culture reached its evolutionary zenith in the form of Western Christendom. Thus, even William Foxwell Albright, the doyen of biblical archaeologists, had no qualms about the plunder attendant upon Joshua's enterprise, which he understood in a largely historically reliable way.[49] An analogous indulgence obtains in the modern period also in the benign Western assessment of the Zionist enterprise.

The Reception History of the biblical text concerns itself with the history of the effects of texts, rather than simply inquiring into their literary

48. The wider history of the region has been written out—there is urgent need to construct a 'secular history' of the region or a 'history without the Bible'. See Keith W. Whitelam, *The Invention of Ancient Israel: The Silencing of Palestinian History* (London: Routledge, 1996).

49. 'From the impartial standpoint of a philosopher of history, it often seems necessary that a people of markedly inferior type should vanish before a people of superior potentialities, since there is a point beyond which racial mixture cannot go without disaster... Thus the Canaanites, with their orgiastic nature worship, their cult of fertility in the form of serpent symbols and sensuous nudity and their gross mythology, were replaced by Israel, with its pastoral simplicity and purity of life, its lofty monotheism and its severe code of ethics' (William Foxwell Albright, *From the Stone Age to Christianity: Monotheism and the Historical Process* [New York: Doubleday, 1957], pp. 280-81). Prior to Keith Whitelam's critique (*The Invention of Ancient Israel*, p. 88), no commentator had drawn attention to Albright's undisguised racist attitudes, which were typical of virtually every Western colonial enterprise that predicated that the 'superior' peoples of the West had the right to exploit, and in some cases exterminate, the 'natives'. In a similar vein, George E. Wright, another distinguished American biblical scholar, justified the genocide of the narrative of Joshua in terms of the inferiority of the indigenous culture (in George E. Wright and R.H. Fuller [eds.], *The Book of the Acts of God: Christian Scholarship Interprets the Bible* [London: Gerald Duckworth, 1960], p. 109). Reflecting these conventional values, Albright also judged that through Zionism Jews would bring to the Near East all the benefits of European civilization ('Why the Near East Needs the Jews', *New Palestine* 32 [1942], pp. 12-13).

origins.[50] It is my contention that the Academy responsible for the exegesis of the texts of the Bible has a responsibility also to comment on how these texts have been deployed in each generation over the millennia since the period of their composition. While behind much of the imperialist expansion of the Western world's past lies the Bible and its reception in Christian ideology, and while it may be plain to modern readers of the Bible that its mega-narratives have played a huge part in the imperializing impulse, it seldom seems to bother biblical scholars to the point of critical opposition.

I have investigated the deployment of the Bible in a way that attempts to respect the complexity of the social and political conditions in each region examined. The complexity of my research subject required discussion of the Bible and modern biblical hermeneutics, post-biblical Jewish and Christian cultures, the colonization by Europeans of Latin America, South Africa and the Middle East, the history and development of Zionism, the international law of war and of occupation and human rights, and so on. If the task of dealing competently with virtually every aspect of the problem is so formidable as to intimidate even the most versatile and gifted academic, the concerned individual nevertheless is left with the moral imperative of deciding on the matter. Responsibility for moral judgment and action rests with the individual and cannot be shifted even to others more gifted, learned and morally upright than oneself.

It is gratifying to learn more recently that, after a long period of silence, the need for a Moral Exegesis of the biblical text is being recognized by some. Heikki Räisänen insists that 'a moral evaluation of biblical texts and

---

50. Ulrich Luz spoke of *Wirkungsgeschichtliche Exegese* ('Wirkungsgeschichtliche Exegese. Ein programmatischer Arbeitsbericht mit Beispielen aus der Bergpredigtexegese', *Berliner Theologische Zeitschrift* 2 [1985], pp. 18-32). The historical understanding of a text can never be exhausted by enquiring only into the prehistory of the text and the circumstances obtaining at the time of composition, with its inevitable concentration on the intention of the author. Just as texts have histories before their final form of composition, they also have histories within the experience of different generations of interpreters after the time of composition. Scripture must be seen to be a living voice in each era. While it is conceded nowadays that the horizon of the reader of a text as well as that of the author must be brought into the discussion, and a certain interaction and perhaps even fusion take place, the interpretative process must also engage the tradition of investigation of the text (see the discussion in Mark S. Burrows and Paul Rorem [eds.], *Biblical Hermeneutics in Historical Perspective: Studies in Honour of Karlfried Froehlich on his Sixtieth Birthday* [Grand Rapids: Eerdmans, 1991]).

of their interpretation is indispensable today' and applauds my application of a moral critique to the Zionist enterprise.[51] Peter Miano criticizes the biblical Academy for virtually ignoring the moral dimensions of the biblical texts and real life contexts. He suggests that when the values and moral standards of biblical passages go unrecognized, they are susceptible to being misappropriated and misapplied, sometimes with damaging consequences. Taking his cue from my Moral Critique, Miano proposes a 'Value Critique', 'the deliberate examination of the value systems presumed by and expressed in the stories of the Bible'.[52]

Still, the area of Israel–Palestine, as against those of Feminist, or Fundamentalist Exegesis, remains a safe haven against such probings, as in the case of Elisabeth Schüssler Fiorenza's programme for an 'ethics of accountability' in Biblical Studies.[53] The claim in our own age that the biblical narrative, however repulsive its deployment as part of the ideological support for colonialism in the past, legitimizes the 'ethnic cleansing' of the Palestinian Arabs is not challenged within the biblical Academy. Although sensitive to those biblical texts which have been adduced to legitimize war, nurture anti-Judaism and misogyny, justify slavery, and promote colonial dehumanization, and so on, Schüssler Fiorenza does not rise to the challenge of facing one of the most blatant uses of the Bible as a charter for oppression, and one for which the domestic politics in, and foreign policy of, the United States has a particular responsibility. Perhaps it is her own 'social location' that prevents her from facing what is one of the great scandals of the international biblical community—namely, its silence in the face of Political Zionism's cynical embrace of the biblical narrative as an integral element of the ideological justification for its programme. This constitutes a dereliction of responsibility from which the next generation of biblical scholars surely will wish to extricate itself.

Biblical scholars, one would hope, should be obliged to protest against outrages being perpetrated in the name of fidelity to the biblical covenant. Yet I am virtually alone within the biblical Academy in having violated the unique 'no-fly-zone' of Israel–Palestine. I have drawn attention to the 'orientalist' presuppositions of much of the biblical Academy and have demonstrated that the major biblical works on 'land' were indifferent to the rights of the indigenous people and, in some instances at least, were

51. Räisänen, *Beyond New Testament Theology*, p. 207.
52. Peter J. Miano, *The Word of God and the World of the Bible: An Introduction to the Cultural Backgrounds of the New Testament* (London: Melisende, 2001), p. 12.
53. See Schüssler Fiorenza, *Rhetoric and Ethic*.

politically compromised. The view that the Bible provides the title-deed for the establishment of the State of Israel and for its policies since 1948 is so pervasive even within mainstream Christian Theology and university-based Biblical Studies, that the very attempt to raise the issue is sure to elicit opposition. The disfavour usually takes the form of personal abuse and the intimidation of publishers.

I am happy to allow my research activity to be judged on whether I have pursued significant truth-questions, with a sensitivity to, and moral concern for, the social consequences of the use of the biblical narrative as an instrument of oppression. I have engaged in biblical research with the spirit of what Schüssler Fiorenza calls an 'ethics of accountability'—that is, with a concern for exposing 'the ethical consequences of the biblical text and its meanings', especially when these have promoted various forms of oppression, not least through 'colonial dehumanization' and for making their findings known to a wider public.[54] Because of the moral seriousness of the debate I do not apologize for trespassing upon the domain of the emotionally detached, intellectually dispassionate and rationally value-neutral disposition considered by some to be the appropriate one for biblical scholars.[55]

There is perhaps a therapeutic aspect to my Moral Exegesis. As I now understand the discipline, biblical exegesis, in addition to probing into the circumstances of the composition of the biblical narratives, should concern itself with the real conditions of people's lives, and not satisfy itself with comfortable survival in an academic or ecclesial ghetto. My academic work addresses aspects of biblical hermeneutics and informs a wider public on issues that have implications for human wellbeing, as well as for allegiance to God. While such a venture might be regarded as an instructive academic contribution by any competent scholar, to assume responsibility for doing so is for me, who has witnessed the dispossession, dispersion and humiliation of one victimized people in particular, of the order of a moral imperative. It is high time that biblical scholars, Church people and Western intellectuals read the biblical narratives of the promise of

54. Schüssler Fiorenza, *Rhetoric and Ethic*, pp. 28-29. John Riches (*The Bible: A Very Short Introduction* [Very Short Introductions; Oxford: Oxford University Press, 2000], p. 6), referring to my *The Bible and Colonialism*, points his readers to 'An excellent guide to the use of the Bible in the colonial period is provided by Michael Prior, etc.'

55. See, for instance, the 1945 presidential address to the SBL given by Morton S. Enslin (later published as 'The Future of Biblical Studies', *JBL* 65 [1946], pp. 1-12).

land 'with the eyes of the Canaanites', and deal with the consequences of their Reception History.

Much of my work is an exploration into terrain virtually devoid of enquirers and is an attempt to map out some of the contours of that terrain. It does not pretend to have all the answers, but it does reflect my dissatisfaction with the prevailing scholastic assessments of the matter, especially the most common ones, which prefer the security of silence to risking the opprobrium of speaking out.[56] It is, I trust, consistent with the concerns of St Vincent de Paul, whose interpretation of the Scriptures was significantly influenced by his encounter with the marginalized and the exploited. My study of the Bible in the land of the Bible in particular introduced me to a context of wide international and interfaith significance in which the biblical narrative is appealed to as an instrument of oppression. Thus, as a direct result of studying in Jerusalem, my historical-critical reading gave way to a Moral Reading of the Bible.

Studying in Jerusalem gave me what liberation theologians call 'primary experience', without which an argument is not rooted in reality and does not find an appropriate direction. 'Being there', relying on some first-, rather than merely second-hand experience, has no substitute. Witnessing the reality of the victims—as a non-Palestinian foreigner, it is not possible to be altogether within the reality—not only adds authority to one's perceptions, but imposes an obligation to respond to that reality to the extent one's moral generosity allows.

56. See further Michael Prior, 'The State of the Art: Biblical Scholarship and the Holy Land', *Holy Land Studies: A Multidisciplinary Journal* 1.2 (2003), pp. 65-92.

'HOUSE OF DAVID': THE TEL DAN INSCRIPTION(S)[*]

Niels Peter Lemche

This article is a revised version of an illustrated presentation on the Tel Dan inscriptions that I delivered at a seminar at the University of Copenhagen in August 2000. Since then I have continued working with the subject and produced a revision which includes slides and text. A Danish version was presented at my department in December 2000.

The aims of this study are:

1. To present the most discussed inscription(s) among Old Testament scholars in the last decade.
2. To discuss the question: One or more inscriptions?
3. To discuss the problem of dating the inscription(s).
4. To discuss the various interpretations that have been proposed for the inscription(s)—especially the enigmatic term ביתדוד, which it contains.
5. To discuss whether the inscription(s) is/are genuine or fake.
6. To discuss the importance of this/these inscription(s) for the history of historical Israel in ancient times.

Presenting the Inscription(s)

In 1993, during his excavations at the site of ancient Dan, which is situated in the most northern part of the modern state of Israel, the Israeli biblical archaeologist Avraham Biran discovered the fragment of an inscription (Fig. 1), soon to become the focus of a heated debate among biblical scholars because this inscription might be of decisive importance for answering a long-running question: Is King David really a historical person? (Biran and Naveh 1993). The reason that the fragment roused such interest is the fact that it mentions (in l. 9) the form, apparently a name,

---

[*] In memory of Frederick H. Cryer.

ביתדוד, *bytdwd* (Fig. 2). Most scholars and certainly almost every lay-person reckon this to be a reference to 'the House of David', alias the Kingdom of Judah.

Figure 1. *The Tel Dan Inscription(s) Fragment A (from BARev [March/April 1994], p. 27)* [1]

Figure 2. bytdwd *(Excerpt from Fragment A)*

The excavations at Tel Dan, which is the modern Israeli name for a site that earlier maps list as Tell el-Qadi (in English 'the Tell of the Judge'), had uncovered a major, fortified city, originating back in the Bronze Age. (Tel Dan/Tell el-Qadi is now a popular visitor attraction because of its situation at the sources of the Jordan River and its almost tropical park.)

In the Old Testament, the city of Dan appears in Judges 18 as Laish, a city that changed its name after the settlement in this place of the tribe of

1.   This photograph is the 'base image' used in Figs. 2, 11, 12, 13, 14 and 15.

Dan. This tribe founded a Levite shrine here. Apart from this there are few references to Dan in the Old Testament, except when it—in elliptical summaries of the territory of the Land of Israel—is reckoned to be at the opposite end of Beersheba. In 1 Kings 12, King Jeroboam places one of his golden calves in the sanctuary of Dan.

Years before Avraham Biran found his first fragment, archaeology had shown that Dan in the Iron Age was placed in the battle zone between the Kingdom of Israel—in those times better known as Samaria or the 'House of Omri'—and the Aramaeans of Damascus. As far as we can see, Dan may have become part of the Aramaean kingdom in connection with Hazael's attack on Israel (c. 800 BCE). The greatness of Damascus was, however, not to last for long, as the Aramaeans in the course of the eighth century BCE had to yield to Assyrian power. This history has played an important role in connection with the interpretation of inscribed fragments from the Tel Dan inscription.

Or we should perhaps say 'inscriptions', as two more fragments were found in 1995 (Biran and Naveh 1995) (see Figs. 3 and 4). These new fragments may be from the same inscription as the first, found two years earlier. Today it is normal to refer to the three fragments as fragment A, B1 and B2, respectively.

Figure 3. *Tel Dan Fragment B1*
(from IEJ *45 [1995], p. 5)*

Figure 4. *Tel Dan Fragment B2*
(from IEJ *45 [1995], p. 8)*

The fragments were not found *in situ* as far as their original position is concerned. All three had been reused as fill material in walls during the rebuilding of Dan. The first fragment, fragment A, was found close to the southern city-gate. Unfortunately, some confusion arose as to the exact findspot of fragment A. The first published photo of the location (in monochrome) raised doubts in the minds of some that the site had been reconstructed for the benefit of the camera and that the photograph (see Fig. 5) did not in fact show the true findspot (Biran and Naveh 1993):

Figure 5. *Original Photo of the Place Where Fragment A was Found*
(from IEJ *43 [1993], p. 82)*

Figure 6. *Inverted Photo of the Original Place of Fragment A*
(from BARev *[March/April 1994], p. 38)*

Soon a new photograph was produced—this time in colour—which in a more precise way showed where fragment A had been found (Fig. 6). Regrettably, however, this photograph was printed in mirror image(!) and the controversy continued (Anonymous 1994: 38). Such misunderstandings became important when some scholars began to doubt the authenticity of the inscription. A number of scholars formed the opinion that no pictorial record of the inscription's findspot existed, and that the pictures made available were actually reconstructions of the site. They argued that, instead of producing a correct picture of the inscription *in situ*, the archaeologists had tried to (re)construct the scene only after they realized the potential importance of their find.

However, further analysis of the two photos has now disproved the theory, and shows that the original photos were, in fact, correct. A comparison of the photos tells us that there is agreement between the first (black and white) photograph and the later, colour one. The two photos were found to show the same scene, but from different angles. There should be no doubt that the location depicted in the two photos is the place where fragment A was really found.

The fragments B1 and B2 were discovered about 8 m from fragment A.

The largest of the three fragments, fragment A, includes the broken remains of 13 lines; fragments B1 and B2 introduce another eight.

Here I offer the text of Fragment A along with a translation:

[ ] . מר⌈⌉[ ] 1
[°°[ ] אבי . יס⌉ 2
[וישכב . אבי . יהך . אל⌉ 3
[ראל . קדם . בארק ⌈. אבי⌉[ ] 4
[אנה . ויהך . הדד . קדמי⌈[⌉ 5
י . מלכי . ואקתל ⌈. מל⌉⌈ך . מר⌉ 6
[כב . ואלפי . פרש ⌉. 7
⌈מלך . ישראל . ⌈ה⌉קת⌈⌉ 8
ך . ביתדוד . ואשם 9
ית . ארק . הם . ל. 10
[אחרן . ולה⌉ 11
[לך . על . ⌈ש⌉[⌉ 12
[⌈מ⌉צר . ע⌈ל⌉ל⌉[ ] 13

1   [ ] ... [   ]
2   [ ] my father [   ]
3   and my father died. He went to [*Is-*]
4   rael was already in the land of my father [ ]
5   I, and Hadad went before me [   ]
6   my king and I killed kin[g *cha-*]
7   riots and thousands of horse[men   ]
8   king of Israel, and killed [   ]
9   *Betdawd,* and I put [   ]
10   their country was [   ]
11   other and [   ]
12   over [   ]
13   siege of [   ]

The following is the text of fragments B1 and B2, again with a translation:

[ ]וגז⌈ר⌉[°] 1
[ ]°לחמה . בא⌉ 2
[ ]⌈ה⌉ו . יעל . מלב⌈י⌉⌉ 3
[ ]⌈המלך . הדד⌉ 4
[ ]אפק . מ⌈ן . ב⌉ 5
[ ]⌈נ⌉[⌉.א⌈סרי . א⌉ 6
[ ]רם . בר .⌉ 7
[ ]⌈י⌉⌈הו . בר⌉ 8

1   [ ] and cut [   ]
2   [w]ar in [   ]
3   [ ] and my king rose [ ]
4   [ ] Hadad made king [ ]
5   and I went fr[om] [   ]
6   [ ] prisoners [   ]
7   [ ]rm son [   ]
8   [ ]yhw son [   ]

The text of the fragments is in a kind of Aramaic which Frederick Cryer has described as 'pidgin-Aramaic' (Cryer 1994). Some problems remain concerning the spelling of a number words that are atypical of Iron Age Aramaic—among these are the use of *plene* בית ('house'). Further, some linguistic characteristics of Aramaic appear to be missing from the fragments—such as the *status emphaticus*, the Aramaic equivalent to the substantive with the article in Biblical Hebrew.

One Inscription?

The most recent photographs of the fragments appear to show that all three belong to one and the same inscription:

Figure 7. *The Usual Arrangement of the Tel Dan Fragments*
(from BARev *[July/August 1997], p. 34)*

The argument is that direct 'joins' can be made between A and B1/B2. Unfortunately, it is has not been possible for me to inspect the fragments, which are currently on display at the Israel Museum in Jerusalem, and to ascertain first-hand whether joins can be made. However, a leading Israeli archaeologist told me a few years ago that he had had the opportunity to inspect the fragments before they were placed on display in the museum, and there were no such joins. Thus, it seems that talk of joins may well be wishful thinking on the part of the original publishers of the inscription. Besides, an examination of the photographs makes it apparent that the lines of fragment A do not absolutely match the ones of fragment B1.

On the other hand, there can be no doubt that fragments B1 and B2 belong together and that joins exist between the two fragments. The three fragments may therefore belong to one and the same inscription or derive from two different inscriptions.

All three fragments are made of the same dark grey basalt, and writing on them appears to show a good degree of similarity. That is not to say that the forms are identical—differences can be found between individual letters, especially in the lower portions of the letters ⊃ and ⊅.

In a doctoral dissertation submitted to the University of Sydney, which was recently published by Sheffield Academic Press, the Australian scholar George Athas presents a new, innovative and well-argued theory about the Tel Dan Fragments (Athas 2003). According to Athas, fragments A and B1/B2 belong to one and the same inscription, though the extant portions were some distance apart in the unbroken original. Performing a hands-on experiment in which he reconstructed the conditions under which the inscription would have been created—Athas proposes that an ancient scribe would have chalked his words on the stone surface before a skilled mason carved them—Athas was able to demonstrate that the variations in line orientation are quite in keeping with an inscription made on a large piece of stone:

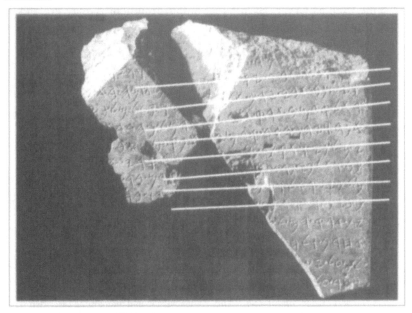

Figure 8. *'Lining-Up' the Lines of Fragments A, B1 and B2*
(Base Image from IEJ *45 [1995], p. 10)*

If Athas is correct—and in my view his approach is quite brilliant—all earlier reconstructions of this text and its interpretation are rendered obsolete, since most of them are based on theories involving the non-existent joins.

The Date of the Inscription(s)

How old is/are this/these inscription(s)? The original editors dated the inscription to the middle of the ninth century BCE. According to their reconstruction of the common text, the Israelite kings Ahaziah and Joram are mentioned. However, in a comprehensive study of the fragment A published in 1994, Frederick Cryer pointed—on the basis of a paleographic investigation—at a much later date, for example, 700 BCE (Cryer 1994).

Now, paleography is not a very precise method of dating texts, something that is made obvious by recent discussion about the date of the Dead Sea Scrolls. Accordingly, neither the first nor the second date of these fragments rests on what we may call 'exact science'. It is more or less based on the personal opinion of the scholars involved. As an alternative to Cryer's dating, we may refer to the work of the German scholar, Joseph Tropper, who published a study of the fragment A (Tropper 1993) around the same time as Cryer. By his reckoning, fragment A may go back to c. 800 BCE.

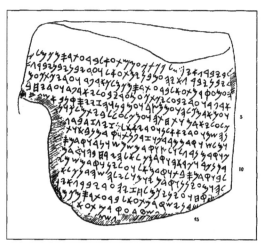

Figure 9. *The Sfire Inscription from Syria*
(from Herbert Donner and Walter Röllig, Kanaanäische und aramäische Inscriften III
[Wiesbaden: Otto Harrassowitz, 1964], Plate XV)

In general, specialists concentrate on the date 800 BCE as the most likely date of the composition of this inscription, although, admittedly, just as much may be said in favour of Cryer's date, if we compare the shape of the individual letters in the Tel Dan inscription with, say, the Aramaic inscriptions from Sfire in Syria from c. 725 BCE (Fig. 9).

A comparison of the forms of the letters מ and כ may be especially relevant in this connection.

The date will of course be very important for the interpretation of the content and situation of these inscriptions. A subject to which I now turn.

The Interpretation of the Inscription(s)

The interpretation of the Tel Dan fragments is dependent on the decision about whether to view all three fragments as parts of one and the same inscription or as belonging to two separate inscriptions. It is also extremely important if we accept the joins between all three fragments presented by the original editors, Avraham Biran and Joseph Naveh, when they published fragments B1 and B2 in 1995.

This is the reconstruction of Biran and Naveh:

```
 1   [ ]וגזר[.].ע[.מר]
 2   [.-]-א.בא.תלחמה[בה.עלוה.יסקן].אבי.[ ]
 3   [ש]וישכב.אבי.יהך.אל[.אבהו]ה.ויעל.מלבי[ש]
 4   [.יתי][.ן]ראל.קדם.בארק.אבי.ן[.ו]המלך.הדד[.]אן
 5   [---]אנה.ויהך.הדד.קדמי[ן.ו]אפק.מן.שבע[ת.]
 6   [ר]י.מלהי.ואקתל.מל[ן]כ.שב[ען.אסרי.אן]לפי.ר
 7   [.אחאב]כב.ואלפי.פרש.[.קתלת.איח.יהו]רם.בר.
 8   [מל]מלך.ישראל.ותל[ת.איח.אחז]יהו.בר[.]יהורם.מל
 9   [א.ואהפך][ד.ביתדוד.ואשם.[.]אית.קרית.הם.חרבת.
10   [ ]ישמ[ן]ית.ארק.הם.ל
11   [אחרן.]ולה[-.]ויהוה.מ[
12   [.]לך.על.יש[ראל.ואשם.
13   [ ].מצר.עלן]
```

Their translation of the reconstrcuted text reads thus:

1   [...   ...] and cut [...   ]
2   [...] my father went up [against him when] he fought at [...]
3   And my father lay down, he went to his [ancestors]. And the king of I[s-]
4   rael entered previously in my father's land. [And] Hadad made me king.
5   And Hadad went in front of me, [and] I departed from [the] seven [...]
6   s of my kingdom, and I slew [seve]nty kin[gs], who harnessed thou[sands of cha-]
7   riots and thousand of horsemen. [I killed Jeho-ram son af [Ahab]

8   king of Israel, and [I] killed [Ahaz]iahu son of [Jehoram kin-]
9   g of the House of David. And I set [their towns into ruins and turned]
10   their land into [desolation ...   ]
11   other [...   and Jehu ru-]
12   led over Is[rael ...   and I laid]
13   siege upon [...   ]

It should be noted that King Ahab's name has been inserted into the inscription without much ado in this way:

כב.ואלפי.פרש...]אחאב.[

It is, however, well known among oriental scholars that the lacuna is probably the most dynamic element when reconstructing the meaning of a fragmentary inscription. The lacuna may contain all the important information needed to prove a case!

Another excellent—or perhaps bad—example of the extent of reconstruction might be found in ll. 9-10:

...ואשם.]אית.קרית.הם.חרבת.ואהפך.]א
ית.ארק.הם.ל]ישמן.[...

which can be translated as:

...and I reduced [their cities to ruins and made] their country a [wilderness]...

While this translation might *appear* biblical and might be considered a plausible reconstruction of the text, it is still no more than a reconstruction that restores more than 60 per cent of the extant inscription.

In order to illustrate the wide-ranging possibilities of different readings of this text I introduce here the reconstruction made by the Dutch scholar Jan Wim Wesselius which he published in 1999 (Wesselius 1999). The reconstructed text reads:

1   ]אה.יהא.השי]ת[.]שר.ע]בדי.מלחא.]וגזר[.דינה [
2   ]וחז]האל.אבי.יס]פה.בה]תל]חמה.בא]י `
3   וישחב.אבי.יהח.א]ן.בית]ה.שיאל.מלכ]ש [
4   ראל.קדם.בארק.אבי]ן.ו]ן]המלך.הדד]א[.]א]יתי [
5   אנה.שיהך.הדד.קדמ]ן.ו[אפק.מ--בע] [
6   י.מלכי.ואקתל.מל]כ]ן.ש]רן.אסרי.א]לפי.ר [
7   חב.ואלפי.פרש.]קתלת.אית.יו]רם.בר.]אחאב. [
8   מלך.ישראל.וקתל]ת.אית.אחז]יהו.בר]יהורם.מל [
9   ך.ביתדוד.ואשם.] [.[
10   ית.ארק.הם.ל]ן [
11   אחרן.ולה]י[ם][
12   לך.על.יש]ראל [
13   מצר.על]ן [

Wesselius offers the following translation:

1 [I was] the commander of the se[vants of the king, and his] jud[ge.]
2 [Haza]el, my father, afflic[ted him when h]e fought against [my] fa[ther]
3 and he lay down (sick). My father went to his [city (again)] And the king of I[s-]
4 rael had previously entered my father's land, [and] Hadad made m[e] king,
5 (indeed) me, and Hadad went in front of me, [and] I left...[ ]
6 ...of my kingdom, and I killed [tw]o ki[ngs], who harnessed th[ousands of cha-]
7 riots and thousand of hoses: [I killed Jo]ram son of [Ahab]
8 king of Israel, and I kill[ed Akaz]iahu son of [Joram ki-]
9 ng of the House of David, and I put [ ]
10 their land to [ ]
11 another and ... [ki-]
12 ng over Is[rael]
13 siege upon [   ]

The Author

It is obvious that the restoration of the content of the lacunae is all-important for the interpretation of the text. According to the reconstruction by Biran and Naveh, the text was composed and placed at Dan by the king of Aram, Hazael, who boasts of having killed King Joram of Israel and Ahaziah of the 'House of David'. However, according to Wesselius it is King Jehu of Israel who speaks to us in this inscription. Neither the name Hazael nor Jehu appears in the fragments found until this date. Wesselius' thesis has accordingly been refuted by another Dutch scholar, Bob Becking from the University of Utrecht (Becking 1999). Becking disputes the idea that we should talk about only one inscription. Now, finally, Gershon Galil has proposed Bar-Hadad, son of Hazael, to be the author (Galil 2001). The discussion looks set to continue for many years to come as we—the scholars—take advantage of the plethora of lacunae in the text, lacunae that allow us to make extensive use of our powers of fantasy.

David or 'House of David'?

However this may be, the most important questions remains: Is King David of Israel mentioned by this text? In this connection only ll. 8-9 of fragment A are relevant. Let us review these lines without any reconstruct-tion of the content of the lacunae:

מלך . ישראל.ו]קח[ן]
ך . ביתדוד . ואשם] [

The king of Israel is mentioned in l. 8; in l. 9 follows *bytdwd*. The first impression is without doubt that this should be seen as a reference to the Kingdom of Judah known from the Old Testament. This explains why most contributors to the discussion of the text have reconstructed the lacuna before ביתדוד in this way: [מל]ך. Thus the kings of Israel and Judah seem to appear in the same context.

Maybe one would like to ask the question: Why write '(the) house of David' (in one word)? Why not simply Judah?

Israel, or in the terminology of modern scholars, the Northern Kingdom, most regularly appears in contemporary inscriptions as either the 'House of Omri' (Akkadian *Bît Ḫumriya*, in Hebrew it would be בית עמרי) or Samaria (or Samarina, Hebrew שמרן) following the name of the capital of the kingdom. The phrase 'House of Omri' is never used as the name of the state of Israel in the Old Testament. The Old Testament uses as the name of this kingdom either 'Israel' for Samaria or 'Ephraim'—the latter name never used outside the Old Testament.

The Mesha inscription from ancient Moab dating from the ninth century BCE seems to use 'Omri' in two different ways—as a personal name and as the name of the kingdom of Israel in this context:

> Omri conquered all the land of Madeba, and he stayed there in his time and half of his son's time, altogether 40 years. (ll. 7-8).

This line is usually taken to refer to Omri, king of Israel. However, if the reference to 'Omri' is to the *person*, how could he stay in Madeba 'half of his son's time'? It is obvious that Omri is to be understood as the apical name of the kingdom and not the person Omri, who is intended in the last part of the passage in question.

In normal conditions the regular parallel in ll. 8 and 9 in the Tel Dan inscription would be

> ...king of Israel...king of Judah...

or else

> ...the king of the House of Omri... The king of the House of David...

The way in which 'House of David' is written in the Tel Dan fragment creates another problem. In the Old Testament 'the House of David'—בית דוד—always appears as two words, not as one word as at Tel Dan.

Neither do we have any evidence in the Old Testament or in ancient Near Eastern inscriptions attesting the title 'king of the House of X'. Accordingly, we never find the word-pair in the Old Testament: 'king of the House of Omri'//'king of the House of David'. Whenever the 'House of David' is mentioned in the Old Testament, it always functions as the dynastic name of the Kingdom of Judah (or Jerusalem), in exactly the same way as the 'House of Omri' in ancient inscriptions indicates the Kingdom of Israel. The state gets its name from the name of its ruling royal family or from the name of the founding family of the state (whether real or mythical).

Thus, Jehu is in an Assyrian inscription referred to as the 'son of Omri', which he of course was not. In the ancient Near East of the Iron Age such dynastic names appear with a certain frequency. This practice includes the Aramaean states of Syria and Mesopotamia, such as *Bit Adana, Bit Gusi*, among others. These names are always written in two words in Akkadian, as in Aramaic inscriptions including a word divider (.). Only place names may occasionally appear as one word, as does, for instance, Bethel. (I owe this observation to the German scholar Axel Knauf.)

The appearance of the *single* word, *bytdwd*, has induced some scholars—including Thomas Thompson and myself—to ask the question: Does the Tel Dan inscription at all speak about 'the House of David'? (Lemche and Thompson 1994). May *bytdwd* be nothing more or less than a reference to a locality and function as a toponym of a place, for example, in the vicinity of Dan? Or might it be the name of an object of some sort? We might, for instance, think of *bytdwd* as the name of a temple devoted to a deity, *Dwd*—something that earlier scholars such as Gösta Ahlström believed could be identified on the basis of Hebrew personal names (Ahlström 1959). Other scholars have referred to a passage in the aforementioned Mesha inscription (1. 12), in which King Mesha boasts of having removed something called אראל דודה from is sacred place at Atarot. In most translations, the passage is rendered along the lines of 'and I removed its DWD-altar(?) from its place...' We do not, however, know for sure if this is a special altar constructed according to a DWD-model, or whether it was an altar devoted to a deity called DWD. However, this passage in the Mesha inscription may indicate that not every inscription bearing the element *dwd*/דוד might include a reference to biblical King David. It might not be the House of King David which is mentioned in the Tel Dan inscription.

It would, however, be a mistake to say that many people—except for a few specialists—have accepted any interpretation of the phrase *bytdwd* according to which the *bytdwd* is not the House of King David of the Old Testament. This is easy to understand when, on the one hand, we consider the closeness between the expression *bytdwd* in l. 9 and the mentioning of Israel in l. 8, and, on the other hand, we remember that it is part of human nature to look for confirmation of one's own preferences. I will return to this subject in my closing remarks.

Is this/Are these Inscription(s) Genuine?

A few years ago, many Old Testament scholars were seriously disturbed when some of the colleagues began to question the authenticity of this inscription. Two scholars in particular placed themselves in the centre of this discussion: on one side was Fred Cryer, and on the other the Italian orientalist Giovanni Garbini, who, since the publication of his 1988 volume on *History and Ideology in Ancient Israel*, has often been considered a maverick in biblical studies. We should, however, not forget that Garbini is an extremely competent specialist in North-West Semitic languages, including Aramaic.

Garbini is certain that the Tel Dan inscription is a fake (Garbini 1994). Though his argumentation is complex, among his most pertinent observation we find—apart from the physical state of preservation of the text, which is literarily better preserved than any other inscription from its alleged time of origin (it almost seems a newly written text)—'common language' between the Tel Dan inscription and other Aramaic inscriptions from the Iron Age. That is to say, the Tel Dan inscription contains words and phrases already known for a long time from other Aramaic inscriptions. In other words, the Tel Dan text could have been composed on the basis of previously known inscriptions.

As a matter of fact, we find a thematic similarity between the Mesha inscription and the Tel Dan inscription, which may indicate that the person who composed the Tel Dan inscription also knew the Mesha inscription and, so-to-speak, copied parts of the Mesha inscription when he constructed his fragment of the Tel Dan inscription. Thus Garbini has 'produced' the following extract from the Mesha inscription, which physically matches the Tel Dan fragment A:

Mesha	Tel Dan
...	...
...I from all...	...My father...
I *king of Israel* and subdu[ed]...	And my father died. Han went to...
...and his son followed him...	[Is]rael was before in the land of my father...
but *I made my triumph* and house and I[srael]...	I, and Hadad went in front of me...
Madeba and lived in...	...My king *and I killed*...
Qiryatan and the man in Gad...	*Chariots and thousands of horsem[en]*...
[I]srael Atarot...	*king of Israel*, and killed...
the city, a view for Ke[mosh]...	...*Betdawd*, and I put...
went in front of it...	Their country was...
Maharat and...	Other and...
walked...	...over...
...siege of...	

If we compare this extract with Fragment A from Tel Dan we find a striking and disturbing similarity.

Frederick Cryer formulated his theory of the spuriousness of the Tel Dan inscription on the basis of his own inspection of the fragments in the Israel Museum, the findings of which he presented in oral form at a seminar in Copenhagen some years ago. Here he distributed copies of photos taken by an American colleague, Russell Gmirkin (cf. Gmirkin 2002), in the Israel Museum in Jerusalem, showing the broken side of Fragment A. These photos revealed marks from the chisel used by the person who carved the inscription into the stone. These marks, however, sometimes continue from the front side down the broken side!

When putting the present study together, I, unfortunately, had no access to these photos. However, even an inspection of some of the widely published photos of the inscription may yield some disturbing substance to Cryer's argument. I have produced the following samples to illustrate some of the 'criminal' spots (Fig. 10 [next page]). If Cryer's observation is correct, they might prove that the text of fragment A has been placed on the stone slab *after* it had obtained its present form. Then there would be no support of the assumption that the inscription is old. It would be a forgery from recent times, something somebody 'salted' into the excavations of Avraham Biran, something Biran was supposed to find and believe to be genuine.

Figure 10. *Fragment A with Indication of 'Criminal' Spots (from* IEJ *43 [1993], p. 89)*

Figure 11. *Excerpt from Fragment A (Top)*

Figure 12. *Excerpt from Fragment A (End of l. 8)*

Let me present as my first example a case from the first preserved line of fragment A (Fig. 11). The letter in question is usually believed to represent an *m*: in its palaeo-Hebrew form written 𝕐. It is remarkable how the vertical stroke of this *m* continues down the broken side, while at the same time the left part of the letter seems to be much less obvious.

My second example concerns the *q* at the breaking point at the end of l. 8 (Fig. 12). It is clear from the photograph that the stone has been damaged near the centre of the *q*; it appears, however, as if the *q* continues right down into the broken part, where traces of it would not be expected.

If we try to find the middle point of the text based on the extent of the written surface of the slab, we observe something approaching a 'grid' formation (indicated on the photograph by crossing lines). The centre is situated in the lower part of the inscription, leaving the 'Beth David' close to the point of the crossing lines (Fig. 13). A third line of reference makes it clearer that both 'King of Israel' and 'House of David' are some way removed from the centre established in this way.

Figure 13. *Fragment A: Diagonal Lines Showing Physical Centre of the Inscription* *('King of Israel' = upper horizontal; 'House of David' = lower horizontal)*

If, as an experiment, we try to establish the natural centre of the inscription, that is the point of focus when looking at the inscription, as illustrated again using guide lines, we find both 'King of Israel' and 'House of David' almost in the centre (Fig. 14). On this diagram I have removed the non-written part of the slab. Only the inscribed surface of the stone has been preserved.

Figure 14. *Fragment A: A Re-Arrangement of Diagonal Lines*
Showing Optical Centre of the Inscription
('King of Israel' = upper horizontal; 'House of David' = lower horizontal)

Now, when a new set of lines, marking the vertical and horizontal axes, are superimposed on the text, it is quite striking that the all-important phrases 'King of Israel' and 'House of David' can be found exactly at the point of focus, the place that catches the attention of the onlooker (Fig. 15). It is impossible not to spot the presence of these phrases which are, so-to-speak, exactly at the centre of the fragment—as we now have it.

Figure 15. *Fragment A, with Vertical and Horizontal Lines*
Showing the Centre of the Inscription
('King of Israel' = upper [short] horizontal;
'House of David' = lower [short] horizontal)

All of this may be coincidental, but I would argue that this inscription includes probably too many coincidences. All this evokes one's suspicion; it is almost too good to be true.

I, however, also have to admit, having inspected the fragments personally at the Israel Museum on three separate occasions, that anyone wishing to detect post-break chisel marks on the fragments will find features that they can interpret in this way. And yet, these 'chisel marks' are hardly so characteristic that one is compelled to view them as wilfully inserted chisel strokes, rather than naturally occurring features in/on the stone. As such, it might simply be the case that the mark on the broken surface close to the *m* on fragment A's top edge (discussed above) resulted from the violent blow that in ancient times shattered the Tel Dan inscription.

Conclusions

Even if my observations about the almost uncanny prominence of the terms 'King of Israel' and 'House of David' are not accepted, I have to admit that the arguments in favour of seeing the Tel Dan fragments as fake need to be much more forceful—certainly stronger than I have been able to show in this survey—if they are to prove beyond doubt that the inscription is the work of a forger. Although arguments can be found (e.g. Garbini's study), these are hardly strong enough to win over the person—scholar or layperson—who does not want to be convinced.

The same has to be said about the interpretation of ביתדוד in l. 9. If a person is set on understand this term as a reference to the 'House of David, extremely strong arguments are needed if a change of opinion is going to be brought about. And it is true to say that as yet we have not found such strong arguments. The arguments we possess may be good enough to convince a person who would like to be convinced, but hardly anybody else.

At the end of the day, is the Tel Dan inscription important for the study of the history of Israel in Antiquity?

Of course is important—*if* it is genuine. And, until the opposite has been proven, we have to reckon it to be genuine. The fragments from Tel Dan certainly include important historical information because they refer to a warlike situation, most likely between the Aramaeans of Damascus and the Kingdom of Israel. However, the identity of the composer of the inscription as well as those of the kings referred to in the inscription look set to remain topics of discussion.

The crucially important matter is, however: Does this inscription prove that King David has ever existed? Does this inscription really mention the king of all of Israel, the very same that we find in the Old Testament? Again, it is likely that a sizeable majority of the lay population would say that the inscription contains a reference to the biblical King David, although they are hardly bothered by the fact—as are a few supposed 'specialists'—that the reference contains a serious categorical mistake: a house is not a person. The 'House of David' can never be David the king (or anybody carrying the name of David)—whether one chooses to interpret 'house' as a reference to a real house or to a family or dynasty, or to something or someone else who is named after a putative apical ancestor.

We may say that an inscription dating from between c. 850 and 700 that mentions the 'House of David'—especially if it is from the ninth century BCE—makes it a little more likely that the King David of the Bible has a historical background, but it cannot prove that he is a historical person. We may think of many other possibilities of how to understand the meaning of the three radicals *dwd*/דוד in the inscribed fragment from Tel Dan, and some of them might be of importance when we are discussing the historical David, and whether he was a human king, a heroic figure from a distant and foggy past, or a deity, eventually adopted by a ruling dynasty as its apical ancestor.

I will stop at this point and go no further on the question of the history of Israel/Palestine in the tenth century BCE. There is no reason to expand on this history today, a history about which scholars have never reached any kind of agreement.

Bibliography

Ahlström, Gösta W.
  1959   *Psalm 89: Eine Liturgie aus dem Ritual des leidenden Königs* (Lund: C.W.K. Gleerup): 163-73.
Anonymous
  1994   '"David" Found at Dan', *BARev* (March/April): 26-39.
Athas, George
  2003   *The Tell Dan Inscription* (JSOTSup, 360; Copenhagen International Seminar, 12; Sheffield: Sheffield Academic Press).
Becking, Bob
  1999   'Did Jehu Write the Tel Dan Inscription?', *SJOT* 13: 187-201.
Biran, Avraham, and Joseh Naveh
  1993   'An Aramaic Stele Fragment from Tel Dan', *IEJ* 43: 81-98.
  1995   'The Tel Dan Inscription: A New Fragment', *IEJ* 45: 1-18.
Cryer, Frederick H.
  1994   'On the Recently-Discovered "House of David Inscription" ', *SJOT* 8: 3-19.
Galil, Gershon
  2001   'A Re-Arrangement of the Fragments of the Tel Dan Inscription and the Relations between Israel and Aram', *PEQ* (January–June): n.p.
Garbini, Giovanni
  1988   *History and Ideology in Ancient Israel* (London: SCM Press).
  1994   'L'iscrizione aramaica di Tel Dan', *Atti della Accademia Nazionale dei Lincei* 391: 461-71.
Gmirkin, Russell
  2002   'Tool Slippage and the Tel Dan Inscription', *SJOT* 16: 293-302.
Lemche, Niels Peter, and Thomas L. Thompson
  1994   'Did Biran Kill David? The Bible in the Light of Archaeology', *JSOT* 64: 3-22.
Tropper, Josef
  1993   'Eine altaramäische Steleninschrift aus Dan', *UF* 25: 395-406.
Wesselius, Jan-Wim
  1999   'The First Royal Inscription from Ancient Israel: The Tel Dan Inscription Reconsidered', *SJOT* 13: 163-86.

EXPANDING BORDERS:
THE DEVELOPMENT OF JERUSALEM IN THE IRON AGE

Margreet Steiner

Introduction

In 1952, Father J. Simons published his famous book *Jerusalem in the Old Testament*,[1] which contained a compilation of all biblical and archaeological studies concerning ancient Jerusalem until World War II. After its publication, Simons' book became the 'Jerusalem Bible' for historians, biblical scholars and archaeologist alike. It was only in 1961, when the British archaeologist Kathleen Kenyon, together with A.D. Tushingham and Père de Vaux started to excavate in Jerusalem that new information on ancient Jerusalem became available. Kenyon described her reason for focusing her work on Jerusalem as follows:

> When the British School of Archaeology in Jerusalem completed its excavations at Jericho in 1958, it had the not very easy task of deciding what should be the next site it would tackle. Jericho had been such a success that there was a risk that work at any other place would be bathos. Jerusalem seemed to be the only other site that in importance could compete with Jericho.[2]

Kenyon's idea was to apply the Wheeler-Kenyon method of careful stratigraphical research, which had been so successful at Jericho to Jerusalem's complicated situation. She was confident that it would be thereby possible to answer every unsolved riddle once and for all. These riddles concerned such unrelated problems as why the entrance to Jerusalem's ancient water shaft was located outside the contemporary city walls; the chronology of the fortifications on the southeastern hill and the dating of the extension of the ancient town over the western hill.[3] She therefore dug in small squares in areas all over the city.

1. J. Simons, *Jerusalem in the Old Testament* (Leiden: E.J. Brill, 1952).
2. K.M. Kenyon, 'Biblical Jerusalem', *Expedition* (Fall 1962), pp. 30-37 (32).
3. K.M. Kenyon, *Digging Up Jerusalem* (London: Ernest Benn, 1974), pp. 47-54.

Unlike the researchers before her, Kenyon was not a 'biblical archaeologist'; that is, someone who conducted archaeological research as part of Bible studies. For her, the archaeology of Palestine was a branch of general world archaeology, and its task, therefore, was to enrich our knowledge of the ancient world by systematic research and the strict application of scientific methods. Kenyon's objectives were not specifically biblical, but rather historical in a broad sense.

Unfortunately, these excavations, which continued until 1967, did not end the controversies. Although some problems had been satisfactory resolved, the debate went on as before. The weaknesses of Kenyon's way of digging in separate small squares, with little attention to architectural units and her constant use of the *pars-pro-toto* principle ('If I don't find it in this small area, it doesn't exist at all'), were fully exposed by Jerusalem's churned-up soils. As a consequence, important questions, such as when the city started to expand over the western hill, remained unsettled.

After 1967, several large-scale excavations were conducted in Jerusalem by Israeli archaeologists. B. Mazar excavated large areas near the Haram esh-Shariff (1968–77), N. Avigad explored the Jewish Quarter of the Old City (1969–78), while Y. Shiloh tackled the southeastern hill again (1978–85), picking up where Kenyon and, before her, R.A.S. Macalister had left off. Some of these areas were real *terra incognita*, where no digging had previously taken place.

These excavations were characterized by excellent organization and intensive use of technical appliances, a preference for the exposure of large areas with much attention to architecture and little to stratigraphy, and the composition of a corpus of complete pots from floors instead of the detailed analysis of sherd material. Their foremost aim was the reconstruction of a visible and visitable national history, mainly from the so-called First and Second Temple periods, which encompass the Iron Age and the Herodian period. Although these excavations added enormously to our knowledge of ancient Jerusalem, the very quick way of digging with the help of inexperienced volunteers often resulted in hasty and controversial interpretations.

For most of its ancient history, Jerusalem was not located within the boundaries of the present-day 'Old City', but to the south of it, on the small southeastern hill, now (again) called the 'City of David'. King David himself would surely not recognize it, because in his days the landscape looked different. The Kidron Valley was about 15 m deeper, and the slope of the hill was much steeper and more difficult to climb. The road along the houses was not a road at all, but a valley, called the 'Valley of the Cheesemakers' in Josephus' time (that is, last quarter of the first century CE). The repeated destruction of Jerusalem has succeeded in filling up the valleys, and piling up a layer of debris more than 10 m high on the slopes of the hill.

The many large-scale excavations that have been conducted in Jerusalem since the end of the nineteenth century have demonstrated beyond doubt that the ancient city was built on the southeastern hill near the Gihon spring. Already in the Early Bronze Age, from 3000 BCE onwards, some people settled on this hill, built a small shrine there and left some tombs. In the Middle Bronze Age a fortified town sprang up near the spring. It is, however, the Jerusalem of the Iron Age that is the focus of attention in this article. In it I will survey the development of the ancient town of Jerusalem in the Iron Age (1200–587 BCE), based solely on the archaeological remains discovered during excavations.

Jerusalem in Iron Age I: A Stronghold

The traditional (biblical) picture of Jerusalem in Iron Age I (1200–1000 BCE), which is presented in most studies, is that it was a small, well fortified town, inhabited by Jebusites and the centre of a independent city state. Later, this town was taken by King David and transformed into his capital. Although historical sources for this period are almost non-existent, biblical references, most of which were only later written down, are used as historical evidence.

However, what was actually found tells a different story. In Jerusalem, a new 'settlement' was built on the southeastern hill, above the Gihon spring. Both Kenyon and Shiloh excavated a series of terraces on the eastern slope of the hill, built of narrow stone walls with a filling of earth and stones. The terraces were constructed over an earlier building that had a complete collared rim jar lying on its plastered floor. These jars are usually found in the villages in the highlands of Canaan, both west and east of the river Jordan, and date from Iron Age I. The discovery of this jar beneath the terraces means that the terraces cannot have been constructed before that date. The terrace system consisted of seven 'steps', descending the slope of the hill and bounded in the south side by a solid stone wall. The whole structure was at least 20 m high. Most steps were very small. Only the third terrace was large enough to build upon. One has to assume that the important buildings connected with this system were constructed on top of the hill. The pottery found in the fill of the terrace system puts it firmly in Iron Age I. Sherds from Kenyon's excavations have been analyzed and published.[4] Cahill and Tarler, who work on the material from area G of Shiloh's excavations, also date this structure to Iron Age I.[5]

The terrace system is an impressive architectural achievement, but *why* was it built? Why was such an enormous task undertaken at all? Careful analysis of bedrock from old maps and excavation reports suggest an answer. On top of the hill, a 3 m high rock ridge ran from east to west, forming a natural northern protection wall for any settlement south of it. It had actually functioned as such for the Middle Bronze Age town. However, immediately south of this rock ledge a large erosion gully had eaten away most of the rock surface. If the Iron I inhabitants wanted to use the rock ridge as a northern protection wall, they would have to fill in this gully to provide enough building space there. In the Middle Bronze Age this did not matter, as there was enough space south of the gully for building purposes. However, in Iron Age I, this clearly presented a problem. The question is: Why did people need the space right behind the rock ridge and so take all this trouble to fill in the gully? The only solution seems to be that they did not build a complete town, but only one structure: a building that needed the protection of the high rock ridge. Nothing of this structure has remained. It could have been anything from a farmstead to a sanctuary. However, because of the need to protect its northern side, a fortification of some sorts—a stronghold—seems more likely. Thus, we have a small stronghold that required a great deal of effort to build. It could not have housed many people, but it would have dominated its surroundings. If this interpretation is correct, then it would be the only fortified settlement in the hill country known from Iron Age I.

Any answer to the question of *who* built the terraces can (also) only be speculative. At a certain moment, the area near the Gihon spring was taken over by a group of people who intended to build not a village but a fortification. Several groups can be mentioned as candidates. First of all, it

---

4.   M. Steiner, 'Redating the Terraces of Jerusalem', *IEJ* 44 (1994), pp. 13-20; *idem, Excavations in Jerusalem by K.M. Kenyon 1961–67.* III. *The Settlement in the Bronze and Iron Ages* (Copenhagen International Seminar, 9; Sheffield: Sheffield Academic Press, 2001); H.J. Franken, *A History of Pottery and Potters in Ancient Jerusalem* (London/New York: T&T Clark International, forthcoming).

5.   J. Cahill and D. Tarler, 'Response', in *Biblical Archaeology Today 1990—Proceedings of the Second International Congress on Biblical Archaeology: Jerusalem, June 1990* (Jerusalem: Israel Exploration Society, 1993), pp. 625-26.

could have been the local farmers—the most unlikely solution. The only argument in favour of this hypothesis would be the material culture found in the terraces, mostly pottery, which is hardly distinguishable from that of the contemporary villages. Nevertheless, no village displayed the building techniques used in the terraces of Jerusalem, except perhaps Giloh.[6] Another possibility would be the Egyptian Empire. Indeed, at the end of the thirteenth century BCE, Egypt attempted to intensify its hold over Palestine and built fortresses (Beth-shean, Tel Mor) and residencies (Aphek, Tell es-Sa'idiyeh) along important routes. On the other hand, neither the pottery nor the building style of the terraces in Jerusalem show any Egyptian influence, in contrast to the other fortresses and residencies. The last possibility is that mutinous or lost mercenaries, from whatever place of origin, built the terraces on their own authority, on a location suitable for levying toll and raiding the area. In my opinion the most likely scenario is that Egypt erected the fortress to guard important military and trade routes to Beth-shean and Moab. Egyptian interest in this area is attested for earlier periods. The stronghold may have been garrisoned by mercenaries (Jebusites?), who continued to live there after the Egyptian domination ended. Where they learned their skill in terrace building remains an interesting question. Later in Iron Age I, a small village may have been connected with the fortress, because on the southern part of the slope some traces of occupation have been found from the eleventh century BCE.

Jerusalem in the Beginning of Iron Age II: A Regional Administrative Centre

In the beginning of Iron Age II (1000–587 BCE), historically the period of the monarchies for ancient Israel and its neighbours, the situation changed. The traditional picture of Jerusalem, based on the biblical stories of Kings David and Solomon, is that of a large beautiful town, with fortifications, palaces and storehouses, and crowned with a magnificent temple. Recent publications by Jamieson-Drake[7] and Thompson,[8] on the other hand,

---

6.   A. Mazar, 'Iron I and II Towers at Giloh and the Israelite Settlement', *IEJ* 40 (1990), pp. 77-101.

7.   D. Jamieson-Drake, *The Scribes and Schools in Monarchic Judah: A Socio-Archaeological Approach* (Social World of Biblical Antiquity, 9; JSOTSup, 109; Sheffield: Almond Press, 1991).

8.   T.L. Thompson, *Early History of the Israelite People: From the Written and Archaeological Sources* (Leiden: E.J. Brill, 1992).

describe the site as a small market town: the most important town of a small agriculturally based state, a situation that existed from the Middle Bronze Age onwards.

However, on the basis of an analysis of the archaeological material now available, we can revise and supplement this picture of Jerusalem. It seems that in the tenth and ninth centuries BCE, Jerusalem was neither a large royal city nor a small market town, but an administrative centre of at least regional importance. Unfortunately, no agreement has yet been reached on the dating of the pottery from this period. Pottery and buildings, commonly ascribed to the tenth century BCE (and thus to the period of the United Kingdom of biblical texts) might easily date from the early ninth century BCE or even later. The pottery found in Jerusalem is not very helpful in this respect, as it comes mainly from fills.

Several public structures from the tenth or ninth century BCE have been found. Most conspicuous is what is commonly called the 'stepped stone structure'. Elements of it were already discovered by Macalister and Garrow Duncan,[9] who called it the 'Jebusite Ramp'. Other parts have been found by Kenyon and Shiloh.[10] The structure consists of a mantel of stones and some adjoining terraces laid out over the pre-existing buildings and debris on the slope of the hill. Originally it must have been at least 27 m high and 40 m wide at the top, which makes it by far the largest and most impressive structure of this kind. It must have had a defensive function.

Linked with this structure is a casemate wall, of which a very small part has been discovered on top of the hill. This wall ran north. Building elements normally used for public buildings, such as a large number of fine ashlars and a very large proto-aeolic capital, were found in destruction debris near the stepped stone structure. The capital has been dated to the ninth century BCE.[11] A fragment of a wall made of fine ashlars was found in Kenyon's site SII and subsequently published by Mazar and Mazar.[12]

---

9. R.A.S. Macalister and J. Garrow Duncan, *Excavations on the Hill of Ophel, Jerusalem, 1923–1925: Being the Joint Expedition of the Palestine Exploration Fund and the Daily Telegraph* (PEFA, 4; London: The Committee of the Fund, 1926).

10. M. Steiner, 'The Jebusite Ramp of Jerusalem: The Evidence of the Macalister, Kenyon and Shiloh Excavations', in *Biblical Archaeology Today* (1990), pp. 585-88.

11. Y. Shiloh, *The Proto-Aeolic Capital and Israelite Ashlar Masonry* (Qedem, 11; Jerusalem: Institute of Archaeology, the Hebrew University, 1979), p. 21.

12. E. Mazar and B. Mazar, *Excavations in the South of the Temple Mount: The Ophel of Biblical Jerusalem* (Qedem, 29; Jerusalem: Institute of Archaeology, the Hebrew University, 1989), pp. 9-12, Pl. 13.

Some luxury items came from Shiloh's dig: a bronze fist that may have belonged to the statue of a god (Baal?), and part of a large pottery stand portraying a bearded man.[13]

These finds indicate the existence of defensive walls, fortifications and public buildings, maybe even a temple (for Baal?) in the settlement. What is missing in the archaeological record are houses. Compared to the finds from the earlier Middle Bronze Age and the later seventh century BCE, the difference is striking. In those periods, a city wall was built lower down the slope of the hill to protect a residential quarter. Since the top of the hill apparently did not offer enough space for the inhabitants of the town, they had to use the slope. Not so, however, in the tenth/ninth century. The slope was then partly covered by the stepped stone structure, but no town wall was discovered here, and no houses at all. It seems that the building area was restricted to the top of the hill. The town was apparently fortified (if at all) by walls along this top. The above-mentioned casemate wall may have functioned to connect this built-up area with another quarter more to the north. Excavations north of the 'City of David' by Benjamin and Eilat Mazar have uncovered a large tower-like structure there, possibly a gate, dating from the ninth century BCE.[14]

Based on the archaeological remains uncovered, the Jerusalem of the tenth/ninth century BCE can be described as a small town occupied primarily by public buildings. Its size would not have exceeded 12 hectares and it may have housed up to 2000 inhabitants. This means that in the tenth or the ninth century BCE, a new town was founded with impressive public buildings, but without a large residential quarter. The emphasis is on the word 'new', for no town had existed in the previous period. New towns were often founded in the context of new political entities, as capitals of new states. The new town of Jerusalem, with its impressive fortifications and public buildings, will have functioned as an administrative centre or as the capital of a small, newly established state. Surveys in the hill country of Judah have confirmed this picture of Jerusalem as the centre for the region in Iron IIA.[15] It seems unlikely, however, that this Jerusalem was

---

13. Y. Shiloh, *Excavations at the City of David*. I. *1978–1982: Interim Report of the First Five Seasons* (Qedem, 19; Jerusalem: Institute of Archaeology, the Hebrew University, 1984), p. 17, Pl. 29.

14. Mazar and Mazar, *Excavations*, pp. 13-17.

15. A. Ofer, '"All the Hill Country of Judah": From Settlement Fringe to a Prosperous Monarchy', in I. Finkelstein and N. Na'aman (eds.), *From Nomadism to*

the capital of a large state, such as the capital of the United Monarchy of the biblical texts. Jerusalem was very similar to other towns of the tenth and ninth centuries BCE. Megiddo, Hazor, Gezer and Lachish were all small towns showing the same characteristics: large fortifications, ashlar masonry, public buildings and hardly any ordinary houses. Based on the archaeological record alone, one could reasonably assume that these were the seats of the governments of several small regional states that only later fused into the historically attested states of Israel and Judah.

Jerusalem at the End of Iron Age II: A Primate City

In the seventh century BCE the situation had changed drastically, probably as a result of the Assyrian campaigns at the end of the eighth century BCE. The destruction of the city by the Babylonians in 587 BCE resulted in massive debris layers, yielding an enormous amount of architecture and objects. This makes it possible to reconstruct life in the city in the second half of the seventh century, just before its tragic end.

Jerusalem was then about 50 hectares in size (although its precise dimension and limits are still being debated) and it may have housed up to 10,000 people. It was fortified by city walls 5-7 m wide, which had been built at the end of the eighth century BCE. Water was supplied by several technically sophisticated underground systems. Surveys in the area around Jerusalem show a definite growth of population from the eighth century BCE onwards. The area inside the city walls was taken up, at least on the southeastern hill, entirely by residential units. None of the many excavations here or in other parts of Jerusalem has revealed the remains of public buildings, such as palaces or storerooms, constructed during the seventh century. On the contrary, the impressive stepped stone structure had gone out of use and houses were built on top of it. What have been excavated are houses, belonging to what may be called the 'elite' of Jerusalem: wealthy artisans and traders. A residential quarter was laid out on top of the stepped stone structure, whose defensive function had been overtaken by the new city wall. Streets 2 m wide and at right angles with each other gave access to houses, which were one or two stories high. These streets had underground water channels and some houses were equipped with toilets. In one house, excavated by Kenyon, a bronze workshop was discovered, with stone implements, pieces of bronze and iron and a collection

Monarchy: Archaeological and Historical Aspects of Early Israel (Jerusalem: Yad Izhak Ben-Zvi, 1994), pp. 92-121.

of stone weights.[16] The famous House of the Bullae yielded 51 bullae,[17] the remains of an archive. Shiloh interpreted this as a state archive,[18] but the bullae were found among broken household pottery (cooking pots) and other small objects, indicating family life: an iron knife, a bronze earring, a stone pestle. An interpretation as a private archive seems more plausible. In two locations, caches of more than 100 loom weights were excavated, attesting to commercial weaving activities. In the south part of the south-eastern hill, another suburb was discovered dominated by a large building called the 'Ashlar House' by its excavators.[19]

It cannot be stressed enough how profoundly Jerusalem had changed in the seventh century BCE. Not only had it grown from 12 to 50 hectares, but its political and economic position was completely different as well. In the year 701 BCE, at the very end of the eighth century, the Assyrian king Sennacherib marched against Judah, destroying most of its towns. Jerusalem itself was, as if by miracle, saved, but had to pay a heavy tax and became a vassal state of Assyria. Before that fatal year, a hierarchically structured settlement system existed, with Jerusalem as its most important town. There were administrative towns (Beersheba, Lachish), towns with specialized production (Tell Beit Mirsim, Gibeon) and residential towns (Tell en-Nasbeh), as well as fortresses, villages and isolated farms. This settlement pattern gives evidence of a complex economic structure. Most agricultural products were apparently processed and stored in the smaller towns, while some 'cash crops' such as olive oil and grain will have been exported through inter-regional trade contacts concentrated in Jerusalem.

In the beginning of the seventh century BCE, this system had disappeared because of the destruction the Assyrians wrought. In the Taylor Prism, discovered at Nineveh, the Assyrian king Sennacherib noted: 'As for Hezekiah the Judaean, who did not submit to my yoke, 46 of his strong, walled cities, as well as the small cities in their neighbourhood, which were without number, [...] I besieged and took...'[20] But the Assyrians

---

16. R.B.Y. Scott, 'Weights from the 1961–1967 Excavations', in A.D. Tushingham, *Excavations in Jerusalem 1961–1967* (Toronto: Royal Ontario Museum, 1985), I, pp. 197-212.

17. J. Shoham, 'A Group of Hebrew *Bullae* from Yigal Shiloh's Excavations in the City of David', in H. Geva (ed.), *Ancient Jerusalem Revealed* (Jerusalem: Israel Exploration Society, 1994), pp. 55-61.

18. Y. Shiloh, 'A Group of Hebrew Bullae from the City of David', *IEJ* 36 (1986), pp. 16-38.

19. Shiloh, *Excavations*, p. 14.

20. *ANET*, pp. 287-88.

destroyed not only Judah's towns, they destroyed its entire urban infrastructure. Many towns never recovered from these damages. Excavations
at Beersheba, Tell en-Nasbeh, Tell Beit Mirsim and Beth Shemesh show
that in most towns the destroyed fortification walls were not repaired,
while new habitation on those sites was either on a much smaller scale or
entirely absent. At Lachish, new fortifications were built, but occupation
within those walls was limited, and the administrative buildings were never
used again. Other important towns as Gezer and Timnah (Tell Batash) had
been given to the Philistines by the Assyrians.

Judah was certainly not left completely unpopulated. The surviving
inhabitants of the destroyed towns will have settled in the countryside,
while some certainly returned to their homes in the towns after the
Assyrians had left. However, we can safely assume that these towns, dismantled as they were, could not have fulfilled their former administrative
tasks—the collection of taxes, development of trade and industry, the
storage and distribution of goods and the protections of the villages in
their neighbourhood. This must have had great consequences for the economic and political structure of the country. Now there was only one city
left: Jerusalem. Instead of being the capital, the most important town of
the region, Jerusalem was now the *only* town of the country. It had become
the only centre of administration, the only centre of trade and commerce,
thus growing not only in size but also in economic and political importance.

The second half of the seventh century BCE was certainly not a period of
economic decline for Judah. Not only did Jerusalem expand, but everywhere new settlements were found. In the Judaean desert new farms were
built, while along the Dead Sea and in the Jericho oasis, settlements were
built that were connected with the large-scale cultivation of balsam and
dates, as well as the exploitation of salt and bitumen. In every region,
fortresses were erected, while at Ramat Rachel, near Jerusalem, a luxuri-
ous palace was built for the king.

According to Tatum,[21] this 'construction boom' was connected with a
campaign of the king to establish a strongly centralized state and reflected
a political struggle between the king and the old elite. Therefore, the new
settlements were built on new sites, and the old urban centres were not
revitalized. However, it seems to me questionable whether this old elite
still had much power after half a century of non-existence. Maybe the

---

21. L. Tatum, 'King Manasseh and the Royal Fortress at Horvat 'Usa', *BA* 54
(1991), pp. 136-45.

political and economical infrastructure of the country had simply been oriented towards Jerusalem to such a degree that the short-lived period of independence in the second half of the seventh century BCE and the connected economic prosperity only enhanced that bias.

Not only did the number of inhabitants of Jerusalem grow, so did the economic diversity of the settlement. Kenyon and Shiloh's excavations yielded information on a number of specialized professions. The metal smith must be mentioned here, as well as the trader of the House of the Bullae, and the weaving ateliers mentioned above. Three complete ostraca discovered by Kenyon under the floors of a street are of an administrative nature, mentioning jars of grain and olive oil, both important export products.[22]

Evidence on trade relations with other regions was also obtained. Imported products ranged from wine (jars) from Greece or Cyprus to wooden furniture from northern Syria, ivory from Syria or Mesopotamia and decorative shells from the Red Sea. Bronze must have come from either Cyprus or Transjordan. During Shiloh's excavations, three inscriptions in South Arabic have been found, inscribed on local pottery types. According to the excavator, this might be an indication of relationships between Judah and southern Arabia, connected with the incense trade. Fish bones have been found in some houses, showing that fish were brought to Jerusalem from the Mediterranean, the Nile and the Jordan. All this indicates trading and political relationships with a wide range of regions from Greece to Egypt and from Assyria and Babylonia to Transjordan.

To put Jerusalem's size in perspective, it is necessary to compare it with other towns in the region. In Judah itself during the seventh century BCE, there seem to have been no other towns, as mentioned already. In the rest of the region, many towns did not exceed 6 hectares, while only Ekron, with 20 hectares, was larger. However, even that settlement did not come anywhere near Jerusalem in size. Until the end of the Iron Age, Jerusalem remained what geographers call a 'primate city', a city that not only surpasses all other settlements in size, but where all economic, political and social power is concentrated as well.[23] The annals of King Nebuchadnezzar illustrate this beautifully. There are no references to 'strong-walled cities'. In the Babylonian Chronicle, it is stated simply: 'In the seventh

22. A. Lemaire, 'Les Ostraca Paleo-Hebreux des Fouilles de l'Ophel', *Levant* 10 (1978), pp. 156-60.

23. H. Carter, *An Introduction to Urban Historical Geography* (London: Edward Arnold, 1983), p. 99.

year, the month of Kislev, the king of Akkad mustered his troops, marched to the Hatti-land and encamped against the city of Judah, and on the second day of the month of Adar, he seized the city and captured the king'.[24]

Conclusions

In a period of 600 years, from the beginning Iron Age I to the end of Iron Age II, Jerusalem developed from a small stronghold, dominating only its immediate surroundings, to an administrative town, the capital of a small state, and then to a very large city, trading with the empires of Egypt and Mesopotamia. We have seen a development from the use of only local pottery to a wealth of imported material. Changes in political and economic relationships and power are evident here.

There seems also to be a development from a town with public buildings mainly (in the tenth and ninth centuries BCE) to a city where no new public buildings are to be found, and where public buildings were dismantled to make way for the rich houses of a wealthy elite of traders and artisans. This could be seen as evidence for an interesting development. Maybe the state and the king were losing some of their influence on the economic and political life of the city, which was transferred to the commercial elite. If this is true, then we see here a definite change in internal political relationships, concerning the division of power within the city and the state.

There is a third conclusion possible. If we think of Jerusalem as a holy city, a city special in the eyes of god and the people, then, in my opinion, the seventh century BCE would be the first period that this special status could be attached to the city—this is because it was only in the seventh century that Jerusalem was 'special', so to speak. It was the only town in the wide region that had not been taken by the mighty Assyrians. It had grown to huge dimensions, mainly because of the many refugees fleeing to this 'safe haven'. All economic and political power of the country was concentrated within its walls. This 'special status', in so many respects, could have given rise to a change in religious significance and importance as well. All three developments, in economic, political and religious significance, can only be mentioned here and deserve a more in-depth study. In this, the archaeological evidence can certainly be of great use.

24. A.D. Barnett, *Illustrations of Old Testament History* (London: British Museum, 2nd edn, 1977), p. 80.

ROME, SYRIA AND THE JERUSALEM HIGH PRIEST:
THE INTERNATIONAL BASES OF THE HIGH PRIEST'S RULE
OF THE JERUSALEM CITY-STATE (175–63 BCE)

Sara Mandell

Once a portion of Jerusalem was constituted a city-state (*polis*) in 175 BCE,[1] it would have been legal and proper to refer to Judah and Jerusalem simply as Jerusalem or the Jerusalem State.[2] During the Hellenistic Era, the *polis* was not necessarily defined by its physical formation, but by its Greek/Hellenized citizenship and by its way of life.[3] Even prior to the Hellenistic Era (before 325 BCE), a *polis* was a city or portion of a city that may have been, but need not be fortified. The term *polis* could even refer to a group of towns. However, the term *polis* was properly applied to the country or even to the citizenship. A *polis* usually included a citadel.[4]

---

1. The Jerusalem city-state, called Antioch, and the special group of young men designated Antiochenes (2 Macc. 4.7-10), are not to be confused with Antioch and its citizens in Syria. Likewise it is not to be confused with the 'City of David' (re)built and fortified by Epiphanes in 167 BCE (1 Macc. 1.33-36).

2. In the Greek Bible, 1 Macc. 6.48 refers to the *polis* as Judaea and Mt Zion. In contrast, 1 Macc. 7.24 refers to the perimeter of Judaea. Clearly, at the time of 1 Maccabees, there were different designations for the same entity, and they most likely were used synonymously without regard to political niceties. For 1 Maccabees' use of the term 'City of David' as applying to the entire area of Jerusalem, see Bezalel Bar-Kochva, *Judas Maccaabaeus: The Jewish Struggle against the Seleucids* (Cambridge: Cambridge University Press, 1989), pp. 446-51 with n. 5.

3. J.K. Davies, 'Cultural, Social, and Economic Features of the Hellenistic World', in *CAH* 7.1.304-20, for changes in the nature of the polis. Davies (p. 309), notes that the 'boundaries of the *polis* became more permeable' during the Hellenistic era. For the *polis* as organized on the basis of political institutions as well as physical attributes, see John H. Hayes and Sara R. Mandell, *The Jewish People in Classical Antiquity: From Alexander to Bar Kochba* (Louisville, KY: Westminster/John Knox Press, 1998), p. 28.

4. The term *akra* means 'high place', an abbreviation for *acropolis*, meaning 'high place of the *polis*'. In Archaic Greece, the *polis* was the citadel, and it was part of the

Where the surrounding lands, hamlets or towns were not actually incorporated into the *polis*, they were either the property or under the control
of the citizens of the *polis*. By the Hellenistic period, *poleis* (city-states)
were often subject to a king, priest or military leader. During the Hellenistic period, the Temple State and the subsequent Jerusalem State was a
theocracy, in which the high priest ruled.[5]

The reality of Jewish Hellenization, particularly in cities or *poleis*, including Jerusalem/Antioch, Alexandria, (Syrian) Antioch, and other cities
in the Hellenistic world, is discernible in the treatment of Jews who served
either Egypt or Syria. Egypt, for the most part, controlled Coele-Syria
from 301 until 201 BCE. It then lost it temporarily, regained it and lost it
permanently in 200 BCE at the battle of Paneion. However, it was not
totally under Syrian control until 198 BCE. Egypt's first Hellenistic monarch, Ptolemy I, had given citizenship to Jews in Alexandria in Egypt (*Ant.*
12.1.1 §§6-10). Seleucus Nicator, the founder of the Seleucid kingdom in
Syrian and Asia Minor, had granted Jews who had participated in a
military campaign with him citizenship in cities he had founded as well as
in the Syrian capital of Antioch. Additionally, Nicator gave them equal
status with Macedonian Greeks (12.3.1 §119), a policy that was continued
by some of his successors. Nicator also ordered the Gymnasiarchs and/or
the treasuries to give money for oil to those Jews who did not want to
use 'foreign oil', for use in the gymnasia (12.3.1 §120), which by definition would only be frequented by Hellenes or those who had become
recognizably Hellenized. The policy of giving money for oil for use in a
gymnasium was continued by other Seleucid monarchs, including Antiochus the Great.[6]

But, the reality of Jewish Hellenization can also be seen in the way
that both Egypt and Syria treated the Jews of the Temple State, which was
part of the geo-politically important land bridge of Coele-Syria. Given
the extent of Hellenization in Jerusalem, it is not surprising that under
Antiochus Epiphanes the Jewish Hellenizer Jason, the Tobiad, requested
and was granted permission to establish a gymnasium. Likewise, that

city (*astu*). By the Classical era, the term *polis* frequently denoted the city and, where
appropriate, the lands around it.

5.   Although this is often referred to the Temple State prior to the establishment of
Hasmonaean kingship, the term 'Jerusalem State' is a more accurate representation of
the Jerusalem *polis* after 175 BCE.

6.   SEG 2.663.

members of Judas Maccabaeus' own entourage were Hellenized more than simply their Greek names would suggest.[7]

The decree of the Roman Senate[8] of 196 BCE as well as Flamininus' 'Isthmian Proclamation',[9] in effect declared Rome the patron over all Greek speaking (= Hellenized) people. Jerusalem's constitution as a *polis* in 175 BCE, therefore, rendered any subsequent Greek speaking high priest the ruler capable of interacting with Rome, whether or not he already was subject to a Hellenistic ruler. When Judas and the *ethnos* (or 'nation') of the Jews sought some form of Roman alliance or diplomatic agreement in 161 BCE,[10] he arbitrarily activated a patron–client relationship that was already implicit in the protection of the freedom of the Greeks—*patro-cinium libertatis Graecorum*—according to the decree of the Roman Senate of 196 BCE. That is, Jerusalem, and by extension Judah, as part of the *polis* of Jerusalem and subject to the high priest who sought Rome's patronage,[11] became a Roman client kingdom (*Ant.* 12.5.1 §237; 2 Macc. 4.7).

Even after 175 BCE, the Jerusalem *polis* remained subject to the Seleucid king, who therefore had the right to appoint its ruler. In 175 BCE, Antiochus Epiphanes had given the high priesthood to the Tobiad Jason/Jesus, the brother of the High Priest Onias III (*Ant.* 12.5.1 §237; 2 Macc. 4.7). Josephus hints that the succession could have evolved upon Onias' son (Onias IV) had he not been an infant (*Ant.* 12.5.1 §§237-38), and that Onias then gave it to his younger brother. However, 2 Maccabees (4.7-9) attributes Jason's appointment to bribery. It was in this priestly crisis that the request was made for Epiphanes' permission that the Jews set aside traditional practice, adopt Greek customs and build a gymnasium in Jerusalem.[12] In any case, Epiphanes' removal and replacement of Jason/Jesus

7. See, e.g., Sara Mandell, 'The Beginnings of Roman Hegemony over Judah and Jerusalem', in J. Neusner (ed.), *Approaches to Ancient Judaism* (Atlanta: Scholars Press, 1993), pp. 3-83.

8. *Senatus Consultum* = *SC* (Polybius 18.44.2; Livy 33.30.1-2).

9. Polybius 18.46.5; Livy 33.32.5, 33.5-7; 34.41.3; 39.37.10.

10. It does not matter whether they sought the specific form of an alliance or an *amicitia* or a *societas et amicitia*. By the second century BCE, Rome treated all alliances as if they were simple *amicitiae*, that is, 'friendships' or diplomatic accords.

11. The irony of this is that the legitimate high priest, appointed by the Seleucid monarch, may well have invoked Rome's aid on the same basis. Possibly, however, he looked to the Greek garrison on the *Akra* for his protection.

12. *Ant.* 12.5.1 §§240-41; 2 Macc. 4.7-10; for its ramifications, see 2 Macc. 4.13-15.

as high priest in 172 BCE, with either his youngest brother[13] or Onias/ Menelaus, a brother of Simon,[14] shows that he did have the power to appoint the high priest. In fact, Epiphanes had this legal authority to appoint its new high priest and ruler because the Jerusalem State was his vassal.

Because Rome rarely altered the religious practices of its clients,[15] Rome continued Antiochus the Great and Seleucus IV's respective policies when the Jerusalem State became a Roman client. As the Seleucid monarch had permitted the *ethnos* of the Jews to live by its paternal laws and even supplied it with payment for temple sacrifices,[16] so did Rome who, however, did not remove Judas or the *ethnos* from Seleucid hegemony.[17] Antiochus the Great had obtained *de iure* control when he gained possession of Coele-Syria. He obtained such control *de facto* when the Jews willingly surrendered themselves to him and received him into Jerusalem (*Ant.* 12.3.3 §§133, 136). Becoming a client to Rome simply imposed Rome on the Jerusalem *polis* as an additional suzerain.[18]

13. Who like his older brother Onias III was also named Onias (*Ant.* 12.5.1 §238). There may be some confusion of names in the tradition, but that is not relevant.

14. A temple administrator according to 2 Macc. 4.23.

15. Rome usually preferred that its clients be self-governing. Some scholars confuse this with liberty as we understand it. They maintained their own religious practices, since this obviated the necessity and cost of a military presence. Those who presume that Rome granted any *amicitia* gratuitously, with 'no strings attached', ignore the nature of Roman foreign policy.

16. *Ant.* 12.3.3 §§140-142; see also 2 Macc. 3.3 for Seleucus' payment for temple sacrifices. In effect, the limited self-government Antiochus the Great and subsequently Seleucus IV had granted this particular sectarian group, constituted the *ethnos* as some type of recognizable legal entity, which may be why Rome included them in the diplomatic accord (*amicitia*) it granted Judas. It may be that the *ethnos* was in fact the militarily defined *laos*, which, as James C. VanderKam has noted, ultimately proclaimed Simon and Jonathan respectively to be high priest ('People and High Priesthood in Early Maccabean Times', in William Henry Propp, Baruch Halpern, and David Noel Freedman [eds.], *The Hebrew Bible and its Interpreters* [Winona Lake, IN: Eisenbrauns, 1990], pp. 205-25).

17. Likewise, when Jannaeus became subject to, or under the hegemony of Aretas (*Ant.* 13.152 §392), he may have been removed from Seleucid and Roman hegemony, but this was not done legally insofar as Rome was concerned.

18. This is easily accomplished since Rome's legal hegemony over Syria was established by virtue of the peace it had granted Antiochus III at Apamea in 188 BCE. The relationship between Rome and Syria is shown by the fact that in 163 BCE, after Epiphanes had died, Rome sent a triumvirate to administer the kingdom on behalf of Eupator. For the Syrian Lysias as regent, see, however, 1 Macc. 6.17.

Once Judas had been granted an *amicitia* ('friendship' = diplomatic arrangement) with Rome, the Maccabees and the *ethnos* of the Jews became subject to an occasionally and ultimately escapable Seleucid hegemony,[19] as well as to an inescapable Roman dominance.[20] Therefore by seeking and being granted diplomatic interaction with Rome, Judas and the *ethnos* acknowledged that they willingly agreed to subject the Jerusalem State and themselves to live under the tenets Rome superimposed on them.[21] By virtue of the *amicitia*, Rome acknowledged Judas' already established right to represent the people (*ethnos*) and his newly established right to represent the Jerusalem State (*polis*). Moreover, since rulership over the state devolved upon the high priest, the acquisition of the high priesthood implicitly acknowledged a person as the legitimate ruler of the

---

19. *Ant.* 13.9.3 §§267-69. The literary and numismatic data suggest that Judah and Jerusalem may never have been emancipated legally from Seleucid, or at least Syrian, hegemony, no matter what the temporary status was. For example, under Alexander Jannaeus or Alexandra or even Hyrcanus II, until Scaurus, Pompey's lieutenant took Damascus. Antiochus Sidetes' grant of the privilege of minting to Simon (1 Macc. 15.2-9) indicates a ruler–vassal relationship, since the right of coinage requires the explicit permission of the ruler. Even Hyrcanus' refusal to furnish the Seleucid king aid (*Ant.* 13.10.1 §§272-74) may not have released the state from Seleucid hegemony as is commonly assumed (but without supportive evidence). Josephus merely says, 'neither as subject nor friend did he furnish them anything' (*Ant.* 13.10.1 §274). That is, he reneged on his duties. It is possible that the Temple State was not liberated from Syrian dominance when it was changed into a kingdom by either Aristobulus I (*Ant.* 13.11.1 §301) or Alexander Jannaeus (Strabo 16.2.40), as is illustrated by the actions of Antiochus Dionysus (who became Syrian king c. 86/85 BCE), who either took it as his right to pass through (Josephus, *War* 1.4.7 §§99-102) or actually invaded Judaea (*Ant.* 13.15.1 §§387-93) as part of his campaign against the Arab king, Aretas.

20. After Pydna, everyone with whom Rome had a diplomatic relationship (of any sort and however defined) became part of Rome's *clientelae*. That is, all such states became Roman vassals.

21. We do not know exactly what defined the *ethnos* of the Jews prior to 161 BCE, but there is no evidence that it comprised the majority of the Jews in Jewish Palestine, much less in Judah and Jerusalem. The position of the *ethnos* as the true Israel may well have been a theological, and perhaps a theo-political reality, but it did not become a political reality until 161 BCE. It is the interaction with Rome that established it as the 'nation of the Jews', as opposed to other Jews. This gave legal status to its ideological claim, which re-established (or perhaps first established) Jerusalem as the center of the Jewish universe. Of more importance is the fact that Rome's recognition, which was accorded by virtue of the *amicitia*, in and of itself permitted the development of the Hasmonaean state, with its base in Jerusalem, as a Roman client.

state, whether or not he was given the title 'king'. So, it is important that Judas was already high priest, according to Josephus, when the diplomatic agreement with Rome was granted (*Ant.* 12.10.6 §§414, 419; see also 12.11.2 §434).

Prior to Jason/Jesus' obtaining of the high priesthood from Antiochus Epiphanes, that office had been hereditary.[22] There were certain limitations and infighting between eligible families, and the succession had to be recognized, or even granted, by the Temple State's ruler. Subsequently, neither Judas Maccabaeus' brothers nor their successors inherited the right to rule because of their relationship to Judas, and even less because of their military prowess. Nevertheless, these conditions may have put them in a position to gain the privilege of ruling.[23] Judas and subsequent Hasmonaean rulers obtained their position (with one or two significant exceptions)[24] in one of three ways: (1) they were appointed high priest by the military assembly,[25] as was Judas; (2) they arrogated the appointment to the high priesthood, as John Hyrcanus seems to have done (*Ant.* 13.8.1 §230); or (3) they were appointed or acknowledged as high priest by the Seleucid or Roman ruler (13.2.2 §45, 5.4 §146). For example, Simon was first made commander by Antiochus Sidetes (13.7.2 §223) and, subsequently, appointed as high priest by the Jewish masses (13.6.7 §213), and acknowledged as such by Sidetes (13.7.2 §§223-24). Hyrcanus II, whose appointment as high priest by Alexandra (13.16.2 §408) may well have been viewed as theologically invalid by certain sectarian Jews, was subsequently given the high priesthood by Pompey (14.5.4. §73).

No matter how appointed, many Hasmonaean rulers renewed the diplomatic accord (*amicitia*) with Rome,[26] to whom the temple—that is, the Jerusalem State—was now subject. Membership in Rome's network of clients was inalienable and the Jerusalem state was still subject to the

---

22. J.C. VanderKam (*An Introduction to Early Judaism* [Grand Rapids: Eerdmans, 2001], p. 18) notes that with this 'The highest ranking official in Judaism became a direct appointee of the foreign overlord'.

23. VanderKam's precepts regarding the *laos* and the proclamation of the high priest are particularly significant here ('People and High Priesthood in Early Maccabean Times', *passim*).

24. The most notable of which is Alexandra's appointment of Hyrcanus II as high priest so that she herself could rule (*Ant.* 13.16.2 §408).

25. The *laos* (*Ant.* 12.10.6 §414) is the military assembly.

26. E.g. Jonathan (*Ant.* 13.5.8 §§163-65), Simon (13.7.3 §227); and Hyrcanus I (13.9.2 §§259-66), with possibly a second time as well.

Seleucid king, who was himself a subject of Rome.[27] This renewal was the concluding part of the Jewish king's investiture as ruler, which began with the appointment as high priest and the granting of the 'purple' by the Seleucid monarch. Thus, even Hyrcanus I, whose arrogation of the high priesthood is covered up by Josephus,[28] made peace, submitted to Syria (*Ant.* 13.8.3 §§245-48) and made or renewed the diplomatic accord (*amicitia*) with Rome.[29] Since Rome never granted an eternal *amicitia*, but rather defined the *amicitia* as having to be renewed with each new monarch or ruler as he came to power, the renewal of the *amicitia* with Rome actually acknowledged the right of the new sovereign to rule the Jerusalem *polis*. This was not accidental. As a matter of policy, Rome held the 'keys to the kingdom' for each and every city, city-state and kingdom in its federation. This was based on a Hellenism enforced with either a 'velvet glove' or an 'iron fist', however needed.

It is significant that 1 and 2 Maccabees each have a different explanation for the building of the gymnasium in Jerusalem. They use it to account for a diminution of self-government to express different aspects of Hellenization,[30] which they wished to obfuscate. Antiochus Epiphanes, a Roman vassal who had actually been a hostage at Rome prior to his elevation to kingship in 175 BCE,[31] had to adhere to the decree of the (Roman) senate (*SC* of 196 BCE). Moreover, he needed to support the expanded policy set forth in the Isthmian Proclamation regarding Hellenized people. As vassal, he also had to accept Caius Popillius' mandate—however arrogantly presented—to retreat from Egypt and from the war with Ptolemy

27. The two monarchs who did not do so were making a political statement and perhaps asserting some type of independence. This was, however, never acknowledged by Rome. Significantly, only Aristobulus I, a self-made king who was never recognized by Rome and who ruled for only a year (104–103 BCE), and Alexander Jannaeus did not renew the *amicitia* (or *societas et amicitia*) with Rome. Jannaeus took advantage of the Seleucid civil war to increase his own power —thus explaining why he was not appointed high priest by the Seleucid monarch—and against whom his own people revolted (*Ant.* 13.13.5 §372).

28. Who suggests it is an inherited or paternal right (*Ant.* 13.8.1 §230).

29. *Ant.* 13.9.2 §§259-66, and renewed it if, as is likely, 14.10.22 §§247-55 refers to Hyrcanus I rather than II.

30. It does not matter that 2 Maccabees, which attributes the building of the *gymnasium* to bribery, differs from 1 Maccabees, which attributes it to renegade Jews. The two apologetic explanations are not mutually exclusive.

31. 1 Macc. 1.10. This status was established in 188 BCE by the peace Rome gave Antiochus the Great at Apamea.

(Polybius 29.27.1-10; Livy 45.12.3-8; *Ant.* 12.5.2 §244). Epiphanes did so grudgingly and unwillingly (Polybius 29.27.1-10; *Ant.* 12.5.3 §244). He then entered Jerusalem in 169 BCE (1 Macc. 1.20), having been helped (*Ant.* 12.5.3 §246) and even invited (1 Macc. 1.11-16) by his Jewish supporters to carry out what was his right as ruler. Many Jews willingly accepted his prohibitions of paternal customs (1 Macc. 1.41-50; 2.16, 18), though others were unwilling (*Ant.* 12.5.4 §255). What matters is not that 1 Maccabees and Josephus differ regarding Jewish willingness to comply, but rather that Epiphanes was taking away some of Jerusalem's self-government—an issue which the account in 2 Maccabees ignores.

This makes the actions of Judas, who had succeeded Mattathias (*Ant.* 12.6.5 §284; 1 Macc. 3.3-9), understandable. By 'purifying the land', Judas was acting as a political messiah whether or not he had yet been anointed to the office. He also assumed the functions, but not yet the title, of high priest, even though a legitimately appointed high priest was still alive.[32] The Jews in the citadel (*akra*) of Jerusalem went to Antiochus Eupator, who had succeeded his father on the Syrian throne in 164 BCE. They asked for help against Judas, whom they feared would take the citadel (*Ant.* 12.9.3 §§362-66). They were afraid that he would usurp the government of the state from the appointees to whom it had been entrusted, when Epiphanes had prohibited the so-called 'paternal customs'.[33] When 1 Maccabees (4.59) represents the entire congregation of Israel, with Judas and his brothers, as authoring the decree of the new holiday celebrating the purification of the temple, it suggests that Judas had acted falsely on theological grounds. 1 Maccabees may, however, have attributed the decree of the new eight-day holiday to Judas, Judas' brothers and the entire congregation of Israel in order to hide and possibly legitimize Judas' usurpation of the high priestly function of decreeing such a new holiday.

Such usurpation of the high priest's functions explains why the author of 1 Maccabees (6.18-27) understood the garrison in the *akra* of Jerusalem to be detrimental to the Maccabaean cause. For those Jews, as well as the non-Jewish Macedonians in the *akra*, it was Judas and his brothers who were the renegades. They themselves had followed the rule of the rightful patron. It was Judas and his brothers who were the persecutors, while they

---

32. However, Mattathias' deathbed designation of Symeon—whose name is more likely a patronymic for Judas than an alternate form of Simon—as 'a father' (1 Macc. 2.65), may well have been an appointment of Judas as high priest.

33. For which see 1 Macc. 1.41-51.

themselves were the persecuted and the protectors of the persecuted. It is no accident, therefore, that the Judaeans in the *akra* stress that they were suffering terribly at the hands of their countrymen, because they had acted in accordance with the precepts of Eupator's father, Epiphanes (*Ant.* 12.9.3 §§364-65; 1 Macc. 6.23). Although Eupator had considered granting Judas a treaty (*Ant.* 12.9.6 §381), he merely granted him a peace[34] (*sic*: *amicitia* = 'peace, friendship, diplomatic accord'). Perhaps he was emulating Roman policy. Nevertheless, Eupator may have been trying give some type of legitimacy to his acceptance of Judas, rather than the deposed High Priest Onias/Menelaus, as the ruler of the Jerusalem State. This is implied by Eupator's violation of his oaths regarding the peace when he ordered the razing of the citadel's wall (1 Macc. 6.22) and put Onias/Menelaus to death.[35] This recognized, or at least rationalized, Judas' actual assumption of the high priesthood, as his followers did not believe the later appointed high priest, Alcimus, to be legitimate.

In fact, Josephus again hides Judas' true standing when he states that 'Alcimus, the one also called Jakeimos, became High Priest after Menelaos' death' (*Ant.* 12.9.7 §385). Although it was most likely Soter who had chosen the Zadokite Alcimus,[36] 1 Maccabees hides the legitimacy of Alcimus' high priesthood by referring to him as an 'apostate'. Josephus also hides this by ignoring the Seleucid monarch's right to make the appointment. He further obscures Alcimus' legitimacy when he states that Alcimus was not a member of the high priestly family.[37]

Even while denying its legitimacy as *polis* and treating the state as Judah and Jerusalem, Judas had to secure his right of succession as high priest and ruler. It needed to be his by some inalienable means as before, and he was able to secure it by approaching the Seleucid ruler's suzerain—namely, Rome. This was expedient since Rome had the right to help Judas and the *ethnos* of the Jews by virtue of the decree of the Senate

34. *Ant.* 12.9.7 §382. According to 1 Macc. 6.58-61. The terms, however, included permission to follow the paternal laws and customs.

35. *Ant.* 12.9.7 §§383-86; see also, 2 Macc. 13.4 for the death of Menelaus.

36. 1 Macc. 7.9. There is some discrepancy between Josephus, 1 Maccabees and 2 Maccabees, which itself is self-contradictory in regard to which Seleucid had appointed Alcimus, and when the appointment was made. Josephus hedges (*Ant.* 12.9.7 §§385-86), but does so in such a way that it appears to have been Eupator who had appointed him.

37. *Ant.* 12.9.7 §387, 1 Macc. 7.14 had referred to him as the original High Priest, Aaron's seed, without any further specification.

resultant on Philip's defeat at Cynoscephalae in May 197 BCE, and of Flamininus' Isthmian Proclamation of June/July of 196 BCE, which altogether established the Senate's role as the protector of Greek freedom.[38] By concluding the diplomatic accord with Judas, if in fact they did so directly with Judas rather than with the *ethnos*, the Romans acknowledged him to be the legitimate ruler—that is, the high priest, with whom they could have diplomatic interactions.

Josephus depicted Alcimus and others as coming before Soter, the son of Seleucus Philopator, and accused 'the entire *ethnos* as well as Judas and his brothers' of treasonable acts against the king and of having driven the lawful high priest and others present out of the state.[39] From this perspective, Alcimus should have been the rightful ruler of the Temple State or of the Jerusalem *polis* by virtue of being the high priest. He thereby had the right to come before the Seleucid monarch. Because Judas seemed to have usurped power that was not his and appeared to have committed treason, Soter, who came to power in 162 BCE, put Alcimus under his own protection and condemned Judas. He did not at first succeed in putting Judas and his men to death (*Ant.* 12.10.2 §393). That happened in 160 BCE (1 Macc. 9.1-22).

Soter had not yet had his own investiture as Syria's hegemon acknowledged by Rome, who had held him hostage until his escape.[40] Polybius and Josephus differ here. In Polybius' account, the Romans ultimately acknowledged Soter as king in 160 BCE (Polybius 31.33.1-5) because of the support of Tiberius Sempronius Gracchus and his political party, when they received Soter's ambassadors at Rome (32.2.1–3.13). Josephus gives no indication of Roman recognition of Soter as king, but tells us that he was a self-crowned monarch to whom the people surrendered after he had returned to Syria with mercenaries (*Ant.* 12.10.1 §389-90). If Josephus is correct, the self-crowned Soter did not have a legal right either to

38. Sara R. Mandell, 'Was Rome's Early Diplomatic Interaction with the Maccabees Legal?', *Classical Bulletin* 64 (1988), pp. 87-89; 'The Isthmian Proclamation and the Early Stages of Roman Imperialism in the Near East', *Classical Bulletin* 65 (1989), pp. 89-94; 'Did the Maccabees Believe that they had a Valid Treaty with Rome?', *CBQ* 53 (1991), pp. 202-20.

39. *Ant.* 12.10.1 §§391-92. 1 Macc. 7.6 has him accuse them of treasonable acts, but not of driving out the lawful high priest. In this account, Alcimus is presented as wanting to be, not as being, high priest.

40. Polybius 31.11.1–15.12. Twice, the Roman Senate had refused to release him: Polybius 31.2.1-7, 11.4-12; Appian, *Historia Romana* (*Syriaca* = Syrian Wars) 46-47.

acknowledge or confirm Alcimus or any other high priest, though he could in fact do so. Similarly, the people did not have the right to invest Judas in office after Alcimus' death. However, in Polybius' account, Soter was the ruler acknowledged by Rome. If Polybius is correct, this recognition of Soter as Syria's patron legitimates Soter's sovereignty over Syria as well as his right to appoint or confirm the high priest in Jerusalem. When Soter later appointed Alcimus (1 Macc. 7.9) and sent him with his 'friend' Bacchides to exact justice in Israel, he was acting well within his rights.[41]

Judas' strength caused Alcimus to seek help from Soter (1 Macc. 7.25). In this way, Judas tried to safeguard himself by sending envoys to Rome to request an alliance and friendship (*societas et amicitia*). After Pydna (168 BCE), this status would be have been treated simply as one of *amicitia* ('peace') and would have made the Jerusalem State a client kingdom.[42] He also asked that the Romans rid them of 'foreign oppression' (1 Macc. 8.17-18) and that they inform Soter in writing that he is not to make war against the Jews.[43] Judas was taking advantage of Roman party politics by asking for protection from Soter, who, with the support of the Sempronii Grachi, had openly defied the Roman Senate by returning to Syria. The Roman Senate supported Judas and the Jerusalem *ethnos* and granted them a diplomatic accord of alliance and goodwill. They forbad Soter from making war against the Jews (*Ant.* 12.10.6 §§416-18). At the same time, the senate also acknowledged Soter as the lawful king in Syria. These self-contradictory acts probably reflect the interplay of party politics in the Roman Republic, which had little concern for the internal politics of the Jerusalem State.

After the death of Alcimus, who most likely was appointed legitimately,[44]

---

41. 1 Macc. 7.8-11. Significantly Alcimus' position was accepted by the Hassidim and other learned men (7.12-13) as well as others who had gained control over the state (7.22).

42. E.S. Gruen (*The Hellenistic World and the Coming of Rome* [2 vols.; Berkeley: University of California Press, 1984], p. 146, see also p. 147) indicates that *eleutheria/ libertas* was 'quite consistent with the suzerainty of larger powers over smaller'.

43. *Ant.* 12.10.6 §§415-16. The addition of 1 Macc. 8.31-32 suggests that Josephus' account is correct.

44. Alcimus was legally appointed by Eupator and confirmed by Soter, if Polybius' account of the acknowledgment is correct. He was unlawfully appointed by Soter, if 1 Maccabees' testimony of relative silence is accurate. The confirmation was unlawful, if Josephus' account is correct.

The people gave the High Priesthood to Judas, who, when he had heard about the Roman power and that they had subdued Galatia—before whom even the Macedonian monarchs cringed—as well as Iberia and Libyan Carthage—once the most powerful potentate in the Mediterranean—and he had heard that, in addition to these, they had conquered Greece and the kings Perseus, Philip, and Antiochus the Great, he took it to mean that this had (already) brought about a friendship with them.[45]

Josephus makes it abundantly clear that it was Judas' knowledge of Rome's status as conquerer of the Graeco-Macedonian monarchs and of the policy resulting from that series of conquests that had caused him to send envoys to Rome to seek alliance and friendship.[46] But he ignores the fact that it was Judas' assumption of the high priesthood, given him by the people, that gave him the illusion that he had the right to send envoys to Rome. Josephus rather presents his account in such a way that it seems as if the *ethnos* of the Jews were the lawful representatives of Judah and Jerusalem.[47] Josephus does not link the giving of the high priesthood to some Roman desire to embarrass Soter. He rather refers to Judas' knowledge of Rome's most significant conquests and specifically with those that afforded her suzerainty over the world. He also links that knowledge with Judas' understanding of Roman foreign policy from 198 BCE onward, under which both close ties with, and protection by, Rome had already been predicated for Judah and Jerusalem. Most importantly, he represents the people as giving Judas the high priesthood! However, as there is no indication of confirmation by the Seleucid king, we may assume that Josephus understood what Rome had intended.

After Judas' death, the people appointed Jonathan commander (*Ant.* 13.1.1 §§5-6; but see 1 Macc 9.31). Driven out of Jerusalem by Soter's

45. *Ant.* 12.10.6 §414. All translations are my own.

46. *Ant.* 12.10.6 §415. Mandell 'Did the Maccabees have a Valid Treaty with Rome?', *passim*.

47. If the *ethnos* is to be equated with the *laos*, then VanderKam's correct observation that the *laos* was a military entity makes the Jerusalem temple itself, as well as rulership over Judah and Jerusalem, a military prize ('People and High Priesthood in Early Maccabean Times'). So, it is important that, as I indicated above, the Roman acceptance of Judas' embassy did give confirmation to his appointment as high priest despite the possible irregularity of the initial appointment and despite the lack of formal recognition of that appointment. Whereas the decree signed by Eupolemus and Jason 'on behalf of Judas, the high priest of the *ethnos*, and (on behalf) of his brother Simon, its commander' (*Ant.* 12.10.6 §419), would seem to imply that the agreement was struck by Rome, with Judas as high priest and Simon as commander of the *ethnos* of the Jews.

general, Bacchides, Jonathan and Simon lived in semi-exile in the country (1 Macc. 9.43-49) and, after two years, their enemies in Jerusalem asked Soter to arrest Jonathan (*Ant.* 13.1.5 §23). Ultimately, Baccides made a 'friendship and alliance' with Jonathan, who accepted the amnesty, lived in Michmash, and administered his followers' business from there, purging the government of the 'impure' (*Ant.* 13.1.6 §§33-34; 1 Macc. 9.73). It is significant that it was Baccides, not Soter, who made the alliance, and that Jonathan did not go to Jerusalem, but to Michmash. In effect, he was not legally invested as general since this appointment would have to have come from the king himself, and to have been supported, or at least acknowledged, by Rome.

Soter only conceded Jonathan's position when he needed to do so, and then, only after Alexander Balas, Epiphanes' son, encouraged by the Romans, had become a threat to him in 153/152 BCE. That Soter then gave Jonathan permission to act as ruler in Jerusalem is indicated by Jonathan's move to Jerusalem and by the description of his actions. There, he read Soter's letter permitting him to raise an army (*Ant.* 13.2.1 §§37-40; 1 Macc. 10.1-6). He resided in Jerusalem and, in addition to rebuilding and repairing (1 Macc. 10.10-11), acted according to his own counsel (*Ant.* 13.2.1 §41)—that is, he acted as ruler.

Like Soter, Balas attempted to court Jonathan (1 Macc. 10.15-20). He offered him a diplomatic agreement. He exercised his prerogative as Seleucid overlord to appoint Jonathan high priest and to endorse him as his 'friend'. Technically, this means that he installed him in some form of public office. Accordingly, Balas invested Jonathan in the purple robe and gold crown, symbols of office. He asked Jonathan further to treat him reciprocally and with equal respect (*Ant.* 13.2.2 §§43-45; 1 Macc. 10.15-20). Josephus highlights the importance of Balas' appointment of Jonathan by noting retrospectively that there had not been a high priest during the four years after Judas' death (*Ant.* 13.2.3 §46). Soter had not yet been recognized by Rome, which still saw Balas as the rightful monarch. Significantly, Balas had invested Jonathan already prior to Soter's attempt to win Jonathan over to his side.

In Ptolemais (151 BCE), Balas treated Jonathan magnificently. Not only did he grant him protection, he named him 'first of the king's friends'— that is, he gave him a pre-eminent political position, perhaps governor of Judaea.[48] Despite Soter's attempt to win him over (1 Macc. 10.22-46),

---

48. Josephus, *Ant.* 13.4.2 §§83-85; 1 Macc. 10.62-66. For Balas' appointing Jonathan high priest and Provincial Governor, see 1 Macc. 10.18-21.

Jonathan favored Balas. Josephus suggests that Jonathan did not behave as a subject to the Syrian monarch (*Ant.* 13.4.3 §§88-90). Yet, the information Josephus himself presents suggests otherwise and 1 Maccabees shows that Josephus is incorrect.

When Demetrius Nicator, Soter's son, became king (148–147 BCE), Jonathan went to war, defeating Nicator's officer. Later, he took the citadel in Jerusalem (*Ant.* 13.4.9 §§121, 5.4 §§145-46; 1 Macc. 10.68-69; 11.20). Ultimately, Nicator acknowledged Jonathan's status (*Ant.* 13.4.9 §§124-30; 1 Macc. 11.33-37) and confirmed him as high priest, addressing him as 'brother'.[49]

Once Jonathan was established, he sent envoys to Rome to renew the former *amicitia* (*Ant.* 13.5.8 §§163-64; 1 Macc. 12.3) and thereby have his present status acknowledged. The Romans ratified the former decrees and gave them letters of safe conduct. These were addressed to all the kings of Asia and Europe as well as to the magistrates in various cities (*Ant.* 13.5.8 §165). This implies that those kings and magistrates were themselves subordinate to Rome. Once his position has been diplomatically secured, Jonathan had his brother secure the fortresses throughout Judaea and Palestine (13.5.10 §180). With his brother, Simon, Jonathan was then able to return to Jerusalem and fortify both the city and countryside—that is, the *polis* (13.5.11 §183).

With the death or what appears to be the death of Jonathan—Josephus' *Antiquities* is confused regarding this matter—the *ethnos* of the Jews seemed to be without a leader. Simon wanted the position and actively sought it (*Ant.* 13.6.3 §§196-200). The people specifically chose Simon to be their ruler (*Ant.* 13.6.4 §201; 1 Macc. 13.1-9), and then further selected him as high priest (*Ant.* 13.6.7 §213). Simon was the first to be chosen as both hegemon and high priest by the people. He is also the first to be described as the benefactor and leader of the Jews.[50] Perhaps it is this that has led scholars to the erroneous conclusion[51] that the Hasmonaean state became independent under Simon and remained so until 63 BCE. Josephus

---

49. *Ant.* 13.3.9 §§125-26. The subordinate status of Judaea, nevertheless, is recognized, yet not understood by Josephus, who condemns Nicator for demanding the tribute that the *ethnos* of the Jews had paid from the time of the first kings (*Ant.* 13.3.9 §§142-43). Josephus does not seem to understand that Jonathan is a Seleucid vassal, and Judah and Jerusalem a vassal kingdom, in spite of evidence that he himself brings out, supporting this vassalage (*Ant.* 13.5.8 §165).

50. Either *ethnarch* or *eparch* of the Jews (*Ant.* 13.6.7 §214).

51. Based on the misinterpretation either by or of 1 Macc. 13.41.

does not indicate that Simon had removed the *ethnos* or the state from Macedonian hegemony, but rather that he brought them immunity from tribute and what was called 'freedom'.[52] As noted above, this does not mean emancipation from rule by a greater power. During the Hellenistic Era, *eleutheria/libertas* is a restricted form of freedom in which the city-state, people or nation is still subject to one and possibly more than one ruler.[53]

Consequently, Antiochus Sidetes acknowledged Simon when he proposed the friendship and alliance that Simon accepted, although he had not himself appointed him high priest (*Ant.* 13.7.2 §§223-24). By virtue of accepting this, Simon confirmed his subordinate relationship to the Seleucid ruler, as is also suggested by his large gifts of money and provisions. This relationship was, moreover, acknowledged by Sidetes' appointment of Simon as a 'closest friend', which was a purely political appointment. Later, Sidetes forgot Simon's benefits to him and Simon not only defeated him in battle, but renewed the diplomatic accord with Rome (*Ant.* 13.7.3 §225).

Perhaps the account in 1 Macc. 15.26-31 is more realistic. According to that report, Sidetes refused the proffered aid and broke off the alleged 'alliance' with Simon and the *ethnos*. We must remember that he had not appointed Simon, but simply acknowledged him as high priest. He may well have viewed Simon's actual assumption of power as illegal, or even threatening. In this case, Sidetes' actions imply the Seleucid right to make the appointment, and so imply Seleucid hegemony. Simon's 'alliance' with the Romans, with whom he renewed the *amicitia*, is important as, according to Josephus, he made this alliance after he had defeated the Seleucid king (*Ant.* 13.7.3 §227).

John Hyrcanus succeeded Simon (135 BCE) and was or became subject to Syria. When Hyrcanus broke away, Syria attempted to resume its suzerainty. Sidetes invaded and was on the point of conquering Judaea, when Hyrcanus offered terms, which, with some changes, were accepted (*Ant.* 13.8.2-3 §§236-48). Although Hyrcanus extended his territory when Sidetes was killed in battle by the Parthians, there is no evidence to suggest that he freed himself from Syria. Rather, that the Syrian king

52. *Ant.* 13.6.7 §213. Meaningfully, the immunity affected by Simon is from a tax that had been imposed by Antiochus Epiphanes in 167 BCE (1 Macc. 1.29) that had been one of the causes of the Maccabaean revolt.

53. And, by this time, its nature is predicated on the doctrine enunciated in Livy 45.18.

Antiochus Grypus made an *amicitia* with Hyrcanus suggests just the oppo-site (13.10.1 §270). Most importantly, Hyrcanus renewed the *amicitia* with Rome (13.9.2 §§259-66). The official status of being an independent entity continued to exist within the framework of the pyramidal structure so common in the Graeco-Roman world. This acknowledged the nationhood of the Hasmonaean state. The *ethnos* of the Jews did represent the Jewish State, which by that time may well have extended beyond the Jerusalem *polis*; yet the Hasmonaean ruler was also both a Seleucid and a Roman client prince.

If the lack of data for the renewal of the treaty by Aristobulus I (104–103 BCE), Alexander Jannaeus (103–76 BCE), and Queen Alexandra (76–67 BCE), indicates that the treaty was not renewed, this would have been meaningful to the Jewish state, but not to Rome. Only Rome could permit a state to opt out of her alliance. If these three rulers did believe that they were independent of Rome—and there is no data, only silence, regarding the topic[54]—their successor Hyrcanus II did not. His assumption of either royal power or the high priesthood is dated to the consulship of Quintus Hortensius and Quintus Metellus.[55] His use of the Roman method of dating by consular years here is perhaps very important and the dating by consular year (70/69 BCE) for the first time in the *Antiquities* may signal that Hyrcanus II was clearly under Roman suzerainty.

Hyrcanus II, however, soon gave up the kingship to his brother Aristo-bulus II. It is not clear whether he also abdicated from the high priesthood, though it is likely that he did so. In a simplistic account, Josephus attributes what happened to malice against Aristobulus by Antipater, an Idumaean friend of Hyrcanus. Hyrcanus fled to the Arab Aretas, who made and won a war against Aristobulus (*Ant.* 14.1.3–2.1 §§8-19). This, however, would make the state subordinate to Aretas, which would be intolerable to Rome. It is not surprising, then, that Scaurus went to Judaea in the spring of 65 BCE since their client kingdom was in danger of defection to Rome's enemy (14.2.3 §§29). His support of Aristobulus is not surprising either since, in the process, he forced Aretas to withdraw, and thereby re-estab-lished Roman hegemony. What does not make sense is that Hyrcanus also sought Scaurus' support (14.2.3 §§29-31).

---

54. That Aristobulus I changed the nature of the state, making it a kingdom (*Ant.* 13.11.1 §301), does not mean that he also altered its status as client.

55. Together with the Greek year dated by Olympiads, by Josephus (*Ant.* 14.1.2 §4).

We may view this in yet another way. When the Romans captured Damascus (*Ant.* 14.2.3 §29) and took over the role of the Seleucid monarch, they went on to Judaea, where both Aristobulus and Hyrcanus were seeking Scaurus' aid (14.2.3 §§29-31). In so doing, they acknowledged the Roman right to judge between them and to appoint the ruler of the Jewish state.[56] This is confirmed by the fact that Jewish envoys were sent to Pompey, who had arrived in Damascus (14.3.1-3 §§34-37). In Damascus, Pompey heard the arguments of both the Jews and their leaders who were vying for the high priesthood.[57] It is therefore clear that they sought to legitimate the appointment as ruler by the only suzerain to whom they were now subject, Rome. Pompey, understanding this, appointed Hyrcanus II high priest, but not king, over the truncated nation. This nation was once again the Jerusalem State (14.4.4 §73), which he made tributary to Rome (14.4.4 §74).

56. Pompey was acting lawfully in giving audience in Damascus to the Jews and to their leaders who were vying for the high priesthood (*Ant.* 14.3.2-3 §§41-46) since, under the Manilian Law of 64 BCE, Pompey had the legally granted power (*imperium infinitum*) to exercise Rome's right to appoint a legitimate ruler.

57. Not ostensibly the kingship (*Ant.* 14.3.2 §41; see also *Life* 153).

HEROD AND JERUSALEM: THE HELLENIZATION OF AN ORIENTAL CITY

John Strange

One of the most delicate and difficult tasks in archaeological and historical (re)construction is to assess the degree of foreign influence on a culture or country or city. This is because when we try to assess the origin of an institution, or component of an institution, whether cultural, political or economical, we face a choice. It could be an indigenous development or diffusion from outside, or it could be implementation by foreign rulers or even the result of immigration, or it could be a conscious effort from a ruler or ruling class to change society. The important thing to assess is not so much the individual artefact or class of artefacts. Greek pottery does not make Greek culture in the Persian period in the history of the Holy Land, it is often a sign of trade. The important thing to assess is the influence on the institutions, for example, as it might be reflected in the buildings. Here, a fortress made after a modern, foreign fashion is not significant, but a theatre is, because the theatre, being an at least quasi-religious institution in the Classical world, reflects a new religious attitude in a society. Even pottery styles can be important when they reflect a change in diet.

The aim of this study is to show that Jerusalem was changed from an oriental provincial capital into a Hellenistic metropolis by King Herod and, in passing, to take a look on the policies and character of King Herod.

The Hellenistic Period and Culture

Hellenism was one of the most profound and enduring cultural movements in history. It was inaugurated by Alexander's conquest of the Persian Empire close to 300 BCE and it ended only in the Levant when the Abbasid period began with Baghdad's ascendancy c. 750 CE. In this period the Near East was Hellenized, that is, was influenced by Greek culture, both material, literary and religious, and later, from the period of the Principate, it was also under heavy influence from Roman culture, which, in my opinion, must be regarded as an extension and intensification of the Hellenistic culture developed in the East.[1] The degree of Hellenization varied considerably from place to place. In the Levant it was strongest in North Syria where already Alexander's successor began building Greek cities followed by Seleucus who built a number of large cities: Antiokia, Laodikaea, Seleukia and Apamea, together called Tetrapolis. This was to be the centre of gravity of the Seleucid kingdom until its fall and of Syria even up to the Arab conquest in 638 CE. Further to the east and to the south, the Greek-Hellenisitc culture was much more a veneer upon a largely unchanged society. This is obvious alone in the rapid 're-semitization' in the wake of the Arab conquests in the seventh–eighth centuries CE.

Palestine

When Alexander died in 323 BCE, the regions of Palestine both east and west of the Jordan river came under Egyptian rule under the Ptolemaic kings, after some vacillations. Unfortunately, we do not know very much about the country in the following century. The country was ruled by a *strategos*, but the Ptolemaic kings seem to have had an interest only in the coastal region. However, the so-called Zenon papyri—reports from an official travelling in the country—give some information. Archaeology does also, but most of the material has been lost because later Roman and Byzantine builders used very deep foundation for their monumental buildings. As for the change in pottery styles that can be observed—from predominantly Palestinian to a rather high proportion of Hellenistic styles—these considerations should be remembered. The important thing to assess is normally not so much the individual artifacts, or classes of artifacts, which have come into the country, as the influence on the economic, political and cultural institutions. It is very hard to assess the degree of Hellenization in the Ptolemaic period.

When Antiochus III won the battle at Paneion (Banyas) in 198 BCE against Ptolemy V Epiphanes, Palestine became part of the Seleucid Empire. The Seleucid kings, especially Antiochus IV Epiphanes who ascended the throne in 175 BCE, tried, together with the leading families, to Hellenize Palestine.[2] That triggered the Maccabaean revolt, which, in my opinion,

1.   For this concept of the Hellenistic period see further J. Strange, 'Hellenism in Archaeology', in K. Jeppesen, K. Nielsen and B. Rosendal, *In the Last Days* (Aarhus: Aarhus University Press, 1994), pp. 175-80.

2.   See Sara Mandell's article 'Rome, Syria and the Jerusalemite High Priest' in the present volume, as well as M. Hengel, *Juden, Griechen und Barbaren* (Stuttgarter Bibelstudien, 76; Stuttgart: KBW Verlag, 1976), pp. 152-75.

largely stopped the process, even though the ruling class felt themselves to be a Hellenistic dynasty and great segments of the population were more or less under the influence of Hellenistic ideas.[3]

The degree of Hellenization is again hard to assess, and it is probable that the degree varied from place to place, the 'resistance' against acculturation being greatest in the parts of Palestine governed by the Maccabees and the Hasmonaeans. It is instructive to take a look at the Decapolis,[4] a league of a varying number of 'Greek' cities created by Pompey when he conquered Palestine in 63 BCE. The names of most of them were Semitic until late: Beth-shean, later Scythopolis (derived from *skyth*, 'a village'); Amman, in Zenon-papyri called Ammanitis, later Philadelphia; Gerasa (probably Semitic *garash*); Fahl, later Pella; Capitolias—later Arabic Beth Ras; Abila (from Semitic *abel*, 'stream'); Hippos (Greek for *Susita*, derived from 'horse'); Kanatha (from *qanat*, 'reed'); Dion, Rafana and Damascus.

Even if cities like Scythopolis, Pella, Abila and Gerasa were fortified with soldiers and colonists, there is no evidence of them having had a Greek *polis* status[5] in the Ptolemaic period and no coins were minted except perhaps for Damascus. In the following Seleucid period, it seems that most of the towns were governed by tyrants, or they were under Hasmonaean rule. There is no sign of minting of coins and no trace of Greek institutions like *bouleuterion* or *theatre*. On the other hand, we see the first Zeus temples (at Gerasa and Scythopolis). The Hasmonaeans and the Nabateans fought over the territory east of the Jordan in the former part of the first century BCE, and the Nabateans were 'masters' as far north as Damascus, where Paul lived under Nabatean jurisdiction in the Nabatean quarter. It is not certain that the Nabatean suzerainty encompassed the whole city. Although there were many Nabatean monuments in the Decapolis, it is not certain that there were many Nabateans living there.

After Pompey's conquest in 63 BCE, he took the conquered cities and placed them under his own governor. He rebuilt Gadara and gave the cities Hippus, Scythopolis, Pella and Dium back to their inhabitants. Following his early departure, the area came under Roman governors. Later, when

3. See E.S. Gruen, *Heritage and Hellenism* (Berkeley: University of California Press, 1998), pp. 1-40.

4. The following paragraph draws heavily on D. Graf, 'Hellenisation and the Decapolis', *Aram* 4 (1992), pp. 1-48.

5. For this, see M.H. Hansen 'The Hellenic Polis', in *idem* (ed.), *A Comparative Study of Thirty City-State Cultures* (Historisk-Filisofiske Skrifter, 21; Copenhagen: Det Kongelige Danske Videnskabernes Selskab, 2000), pp. 141-87.

Herod became king of Judaea, he was made *strategos* over Coele-Syria, including most of the cities in the Decapolis. Gadara and Hippos were added to his kingdom and, although several delegations were sent to Rome to ask for transfer to Syria's authority, this was done only after Herod's death.

It was under Augustus and Herod that Hellenization became apparent. Temples were built and true urbanization was introduced under Trajan and Hadrian in the second century CE. Now, at last we find the typical Greek institutions: *boule* or *gerousias*, *ekklesia* or *demos*. We find buildings like *bouleuterion*, *odeon* and *teatron*.[6] The onomasticon is Greek, even if the persons behind the names were probably not Greek, but predominantly Semitic.[7] People were recruited into the Roman army and the Hellenisitc cities of Philadelphia, Gerasa and Gadara are mentioned on tombstones. Finally, it must be mentioned that Roman town planning is found in the Roman period. In the Hellenistic period, Jerash, for example, was a fortified village with a temple for Zeus. A new temple was founded in 22/23 CE and later, after Hadrian's visit to the Levant 129–131 CE, a real Roman city plan is found with a *cardo*- and *decumanus*-system from 170 CE. The town had its Seleucid name reinstated and it was given status as a *polis* with the name *Antiochenes Chrysorhoas, earlier the Gerasenes*. From a little later, we find coins with the honourable titles: *autonomia* and *hiera asylos*. It is thus surprising how late it was that the area of the Decapolis was truly Hellenized.

The Coastal Cities and Idumaea

The cities on the coast—Ptolemais, Dora, Joppa, Azotus, Ashcalon and Gaza—were in much closer contact with the Hellenistic world and more open to Hellenistic influence. It must be remembered that these cities were populated by the Peoples of the Sea at the beginning of the Iron Age, with the Philistines in the south and others in the north. These peoples had contact with the west over a long period and, even if they were subject to acculturation, they had not been assimilated. To a certain degree, they had

---

6.   All theatres in the Decapolis are from the Roman period, the oldest being in Gerasa from between 38 and 96 CE. Earlier theatres in the southern Levant are in Jerusalem (28 BCE), Sebaste (26 BCE) and Caesarea (10 BCE): all Herodian. And in Petra from the reign of Aretas IV (9 BCE–40 CE).

7.   Avi-Yonah reckons the ratio between Greek and Semitic was between 1:15 and 1:20.

kept their own culture through the Iron Age.[8] I am convinced that this cultural distinctiveness persevered into the Hellenistic period and that the peoples along the coast had close connections with the Hellenic world, whether from Crete, Asia Minor or Greece itself, as may be seen from stories in later texts and from archaeological finds.[9] The cities were independent from the Maccabaean and Hasmonaean dominance for a long time, and they were free cities under Greek and Hellenistic influence until very late in the period. Accordingly, at Ptolemais, Dora, Azotus and Ashkelon, traces of Hellenistic town planning have been found[10]—a sign of real influence.

The cities of Idumaea, Marissa and Adora were also in close contact with the Hellenistic world and open to its influence. They formed a corridor from the Nabataean kingdom to the coast and were populated by new settlers, partly nomads coming from the east to settle, and partly town dwellers, as in Marissa, where a Hippodamian town plan[11] has been found preserved, perhaps because the town was destroyed by the Persians in 40 BCE (Josepus, *Ant.* 14.13.9) and never rebuilt.

Jerusalem before Herod

In Antiquity, Jerusalem had been built on two hills:
1. The Eastern Hill, a spur of Palestine's Central Range, comprises Bezetha, Haram al-Sharif, Ophel, the area between the Haram and the so-called Nehemiah's Tower. The southeastern slope, the original 'City of David', ends where the Kedron and Hinnom Valleys meet at Siloam.
2. The northern part of the Western Hill begins at the Christian Quarter and continues south of David Street in the Armenian and Jewish quarters. The Southwestern Hill—the present Mount Zion—lies south of the present wall and north of the Hinnom Valley.

---

8. B.J. Stone, 'The Philistines and Acculturation: Culture Change and Ethnic Continuity in the Iron Age', *BASOR* 298 (1995), pp. 7-35; J. Strange, 'The Philistine City States', in Hansen (ed.), *A Comparative Study*, pp. 129-39.

9. See, e.g., J. Strange, *Caphtor/Keftiu* (Leiden: E.J. Brill, 1980), pp. 122-23.

10. See *NEAEHL*, I, pp. 22-25, 101-102, 110, 362-63.

11. For Hellenistic–Roman town-planning, see A.N. Barghouti, 'Urbanization of Palestine and Jordan in Hellenistic and Roman Times', *Studies in the History and Archaeology of Jordan* 1 (1982), pp. 209-29.

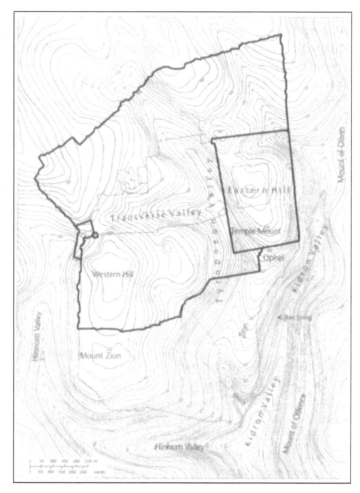

Figure 1. *Contour Map of Jerusalem*
(reproduced from John Strange [ed.], Bible Atlas *[New York: American Bible Society, 1999 [Danish original 1998], p. 53 [Map 67])*

There are some valleys of importance for the topography:

1. Between the two hills, lies the Tyropoeon Valley, partly filled in, from the Damascus Gate and along el-Wad Street. It continues under the southwest corner of the Haram and continues all the way to Siloam, where it empties into the Kidron valley.
2. A transversal valley from the Tyropoeon runs to the west along David Street, and empties into the Hinnom Valley north of the citadel.

3. A transversal valley from the Kedron Valley runs toward the west under the northeastern corner of the Haram and divides into two branches, one going to the northwest and the other slightly to the southeast under the Haram, where it meets an artificial moat cut from the Tyropoeon Valley. This is undoubtedly the northern limit of the Temple Mount before Herod expanded the platform to the north. Just north of this trench, at the northwestern corner of the Haram, there is a hill, 750 m high, on which the boys' school is situated today.

Hasmonaean Jerusalem was situated mainly on the Eastern Hill, but it extended on the Western Hill south of David Street where the Upper City was situated. The extent and date of this part of the city is, however, disputed. Even if there had been a considerable urban area in the later periods of the kings, especially after Hezekiah c. 700, as may be seen from Johns' and later excavations at the citadel, and from Avigad's excavations in the Jewish Quarter, no buildings have been found from the Iron II C period (the post-exilic, Persian period) on the Western Hill, not even in the citadel. This is due to the fact that Jerusalem was very poor at the beginning of the post-exilic period and was confined to the Eastern Hill. How far north the urban area stretched is uncertain, but the northern limit of the Temple area and city was probably the valley and moat under the northern part of the Haram, just north of the Dome of the Rock. There is no evidence that either Zerubbabel or the Hasmonaeans enlarged the Temple area to the north. The area north of the Haram, Bezetha, was not built up, apart from the Antonia and Probaticon, before Herod Agrippa built the 'third wall' in 40–44 CE.

The Western Hill is a subject of some controversy. The maximalists, led by Avigad,[12] claim that the whole Western Hill south of David Street, including Mount Zion, was surrounded by a wall, and that this quarter was built up at least from the Hasmonaean period. They base their assumption partly on the presence of Hellenistic pottery all over the Western Hill. On the other hand, the minimalists, led by Tushingham,[13] claim that there is no reliable material showing any buildings before Herod, except perhaps

12. See N. Avigad, *Discovering Jerusalem* (Jerusalem: 'Shiqmona' Publishing Company, 1983), pp. 64-79, and 'The Upper City', *Biblical Archaeology Today* (1985), pp. 469-75.

13. See D. Tushingham, *Excavations in Jerusalem 1961–67* (Toronto: Royal Ontario Museum, 1985), pp. 9-44, and 'The 1961–67 Excavations in the Armenian Garden, Jerusalem', *PEQ* 120 (1988), pp. 142-45.

in the Citadel, where finds point to a settlement after 100 BCE (or rather after 40 BCE). I believe that until the archaeologists, Broshi, Geva and others who have worked on the Western Hill, publish reliable material, one should side with the minimalists to be on the safe side.

Be this as it may, we at least have written evidence of new buildings in Jerusalem in the Hellenistic period. There were apparently attempts by the citizens—and supported by the Syrian rulers—to turn Jerusalem into a Greek *polis*. The High Priest Jason obtained permission from Antiochus IV Epiphanes to build a *gymnasium* in 175 BCE (2 Macc. 4.9) and Josephus mentions a *boule* (city counsel building). Also the *Akra* must be mentioned. It was a fortress built by Antiochus IV Epiphanes in 168 BCE to control Jerusalem and was captured by Simon Maccabee in 141 BCE. It was probably situated where later the Baris, built by John Hyrcanus in c. 134 BCE, and the Antonia, built by Herod in 37 BCE, stood.[14] Another building is known from literature. The Hasmonaean palace was probably built in the Upper City on the Western Hill and connected with the Temple Mount by a bridge (Josephus, *War* 1.7.2; 2.17.3). Neither of these buildings survived and their ruins have disappeared. Archaeological excavations have uncovered only a few remains from the Hellenistic period, and no coherent area shows town-planning of a Hippodamian plan. Although the excavations of the Hellenistic remains in Samaria from the third and second century BCE, where a Macedonian colony had been established by Alexander's general, have a great proportion of Hellenistic pottery forms with the black glaze imitated by a black wash and also cooking pots, casseroles and lamps, based on Hellenistic forms (alongside of imports from Greece and the Aegean), it is remarkable that, in Jerusalem, only very few black-glazed Hellenistic vessels or black-washed copies are found. Cooking pots and casseroles, based on Hellenistic forms, are virtually absent.[15] The Temple was surrounded by two courtyards before 200 BCE (Josephus, *Ant.* 11.3.3). Otherwise, the design of the Temple was not altered.[16] A degree of Hellenization may, however,[17] be seen in the many Hellenistic tombs which have survived.

---

14. J. Strange, 'Jerusalems topografi i hasmonæisk tid—Akra-problemet', *DTT* 54 (1991), pp. 81-94.

15. Kathleen Kenyon, *Jerusalem* (London: Thames & Hudson, 1967), p. 136; see also her *Digging up Jerusalem* (London: Ernest Benn, 1974), pp. 188-204, for an assessment of the Hellenistic material from Jerusalem.

16. J. Strange, 'Theology and Politics in Architecture and Iconography', *SJOT* 5 (1991), pp. 23-44 (32-34).

17. See, most conveniently, *NEAEHL*, III, pp. 747-56.

The attempts to Hellenize Jerusalem culminated in 165 BCE, when an altar dedicated to the Olympian Zeus was set up on the alter of burnt offerings in the Temple and the Jewish religion was suppressed (1 Macc. 1.41-64). This triggered the Maccabaean revolt, which effectively put an end to further Hellenization. It seems to me that whatever the degree of Hellenization of Palestinian society had been, Jerusalem was not really touched by it.

Herod

King Herod, a Judaized Idumaean, tried all his life to Hellenize Judaism. He 'laboured to raise Judaea to the rank of one of the greatest client-kingdoms of Rome, by secularizing it as far as possible and giving it a definitely Hellenistic structure, on another side his policy bore a strong Jewish imprint'.[18]

Herod was the most important of all the client-kings in Augustus' Empire and the linchpin for Roman rule in the East.[19] To understand his importance in the Roman Empire, one should remember that he rose to power when the whole empire was in the turmoil of civil war. First were the wars between Caesar and Pompey, and after Caesar was murdered in 44 BCE, the conflict continued between the conspirators Cassius and Brutus and the triumvirs Octavian, Antony and Lepidus and, finally, between Octavian and Antony. All this time, Herod managed to be on the winning side. At the same time, Rome was at war with the Parthians, who had invaded Palestine in 40 BCE. Key events were his meetings with Antony in Bithynia in 41 and later with Octavian in Rhodes in 30 BCE. Herod was the grandson of Antipater, the Idumaean strategos of the Hasmonaean king Alexander Jannaeus. His father, also called Antipater and made a Roman citizen by Caesar in 47 BCE, had even greater power during the reign of Hyrcanus II and appointed Herod as governor of Galilee. In the year 40 BCE, Herod was appointed king of Judaea in Rome by Anthony, with Octavian's approval, while Hyrcanus was still alive and his nephew Antigonus ruled the land, having been named king by the Parthians. With the help of a Roman army, Herod conquered 'his' kingdom in the following

18. A. Momigliani, 'Herod and Judaea', in *CAH*, X, pp. 316-39 (322).

19. For client-kings, see D.N. Jacobson, 'Three Roman Client Kings: Herod of Jerusalem, Archelaus of Cappadocia and Juba of Mauretania', *PEQ* 133 (2001), pp. 22-38.

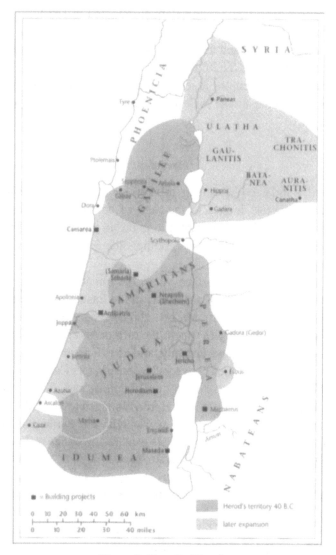

Figure 2. *Herod's Kingdom*
(reproduced from John Strange [ed.], Bible Atlas *[New York: American Bible Society, 1999 [Danish original 1998], p. 46 [Map 54])*

years (40–37 BCE) and entered Jerusalem in 37 BCE. His first building was the fortress Antonia (named in honour of his benefactor Anthony), which dominated the Temple and Jerusalem as a whole. It was built where the Syrian fortress *Akra* had been constructed by Antiochus IV Epiphanes in 168 BCE and later substituted by the Baris, which was built by John

Hyrcanus in 134 BCE. Herod became the undisputed ruler of a kingdom larger than either Solomon or Alexander Jannaeus. The keys to success were his Roman citizenship, inherited from his father and his friendship and unstinting support to Augustus. Augustus, on the other hand, gave him a free rein in pursuit of power in Syria-Palestine (Josephus, *Ant.* 15.10.3).

Herod was originally an Idumaean and, because his father had proselytized to Judaism, he was also a Jew. To my mind, his true religious conviction, if he had any, was that of a syncretistic agnostic. This may be seen from his attitudes: where necessary and possible, he built temples for Rome and Augustus, an abomination to the Jews. He also gave large donations to temples elsewhere. On the other hand, he gave the Jews a more beautiful temple in Jerusalem by restoring and embellishing the temple of Zerubbabel. In so doing, he altered the entire concept: from a temple dedicated to Adonai Elohim to a syncretistic monument.

Herod's Building Activities

From texts, we know quite a lot about Herod's building activities, both outside (in Phoenicia and Syria as well as in Asia Minor or Greece) and inside Palestine and, of course, in Jerusalem. In all three areas, he provided for or built a staggering amount of buildings and other projects.

Outside Palestine we find evidence of Herod's building activity in 25 places. In Phoenicia and Syria, he is engaged, for example, in Damascus, Tyre, Byblus, Berytus, Tripoli, Laodicea and Antioch. In Asia Minor and Greece, there are activities in Lycia, Ionia, Pergamum, Rhodes, Cos, Chios, Samos, Delos and even Athens, where he gave donations to the Acropolis and other places.

In Palestine, he built in 40 places. He built whole cities, such as Caesarea, Sebaste, Antipatris and Phasaelis, harbours in Caesarea and the fortress-palaces of Masada, Machaerus, Herodium and Jericho, as well as other palaces in, for example, Alexandreion, Ascalon, Hyrcania, Betharamphtha, Sepphoris and Banyas. In Caesarea, Sebaste and Banyas, he built temples to Rome and Augustus, in Si'a near Canatha to Ba'al Shamem, and other religious memorials in Hebron and Mamre. He built theatres, amphitheatres, hippodromes, aqueducts, baths, pools and gardens, fortresses and fortifications, gates, streets and colonnades.[20]

---

20. For a full list, see P. Richardson, *Herod* (Edinburgh: T. & T. Clark, 1999), pp. 198-202.

Figure 3. *Jerusalem in the Time of Jesus*
(reproduced from John Strange [ed.], Bible Atlas *[New York: American Bible*
Society, 1999 [Danish original 1998], p. 56 [Map 75])

Most of these building activities were meant to enhance his reputation
as the most important of Augustus' client-kings and indeed the greatest
ruler in the East. This is perhaps one of the reasons that he confined his
building activities to the East. It is interesting that he furnished the hippodrome in Caesarea with an obelisk on the *spina*. As this was a symbol of
royal power and divinity in Egypt and was later taken over by the Roman
emperors when they were deified while still living, a more megalomaniac
and cunning piece of propaganda is hard to find. Symbolically, it made
him equal to Augustus himself.

Jerusalem in Herod's Time

In Jerusalem, Herod carried out a huge building program throughout his reign. Already in 37 BCE, when he took control of Jerusalem after a siege, he built the fortress Antonia[21] on the site of the Hasmonaean fortress Baris, at the northeastern corner of the Temple Mount. Its function was probably to secure control of events should the city become a centre for resistance against his policy (Josephus, *Ant.* 13.11.2; 15.8.5, 11.7; 18.4.3; *War* 5.238-46). Over the next 30 years he changed Jerusalem into a Hellenistic city. He rebuilt the Hasmonaean palace (*War* 2.344), and later a great palace in the Upper City near the present Western Wall (*Ant.* 15.9.3; *War* 5.156-83), the podium of which has been found in the Armenian Garden.[22] Of its towers: Phasaelis, Mariamme and Hippicus, Phasaelis is still to be seen near the Jaffa Gate.[23] He built a tomb for his family north of the Damascus gate (*War* 5.108, 507). For himself, he built the Herodeum as mausoleum[24] and tomb. Finally, he built purely Hellenistic Roman buildings: a theatre (*Ant.* 15.8.1), an amphitheatre (15.8.1) and a Hippodrome (17.10.2).

He rebuilt the city according to a Hippodamian town plan, with streets running east–west and north–south. The main thoroughfare ran from Wilson's Arch to the Citadel where he built his palace. Another notable street ran from the northwestern corner of the Temple Mount below the Antonia along the Temple platform and continued all the way to Siloam.[25] Part of this grid is still discernible in Jerusalem, even as today's grid was part of Aelia Capitolina and built after the destruction of Jerusalem in 70 CE and is to be associated with Hadrian's reconstruction of Jerusalem as a Roman city, much as we see it on the Madaba map in a Byzantine version.

Herod rebuilt the walls of Jerusalem and he probably incorporated the quarter that lies north of David Street, west of the Haram al-Sharif and east of the present Khan el-Zeit and Suq el-Attarin. This pushed the city westwards to the quarries where Golgotha was situated. He may have built a wall across the Tyropoeon valley from Mount Zion to Birket Hamre, but

---

21. For a description, see A. Schalit, *Koenig Herodes* (Berlin: W. de Gruyter, 1969), pp. 366-68.

22. Tushingham, *Excavations*, pp. 25-32.

23. See I. Nielsen, *Hellenistic Palaces: Tradition and Renewal, Studies in Hellenistic Civilization* (Aarhus: Aarhus University Press, 1994), p. 182; Schalit, *Koenig Herodes*, pp. 368-70.

24. Richardson, *Herod*, p. 183.

25. J. Wilkinson, 'The Streets of Jerusalem', *Levant* 7 (1975), pp. 118-36.

this is uncertain, as it has not been possible to show any occupation on the eastern slope of the southwestern hill.

Perhaps most enduring and important, Herod gave Jerusalem water-works large enough to support a large population. Before his time, Jerusalem had been dependent mostly on the water from the Gihon spring in the valley of Kedron under David's city. Herod furnished Jerusalem with many pools with large catchment areas and aqueducts. To the north of the city was Sheep Pool (Probaticon), Pool of Israel and Strouthion Pool; to the east, Birkat Sitte Miryam and to the west, Pool of Mamillah and Heze-kiah's Pool. He repaired the Gihon Spring and Hezekiah's tunnel, and he built the Siloam and Hamra Pools. Beyond this, he built huge water reser-voirs south of Bethlehem, now called Solomon's Pools, which led the water in an aqueduct to Jerusalem.[26] This increase in the water supply of Jerusalem allowed the possible number of inhabitants to grow to c. 75,000.

The Temple

The crowning effort in Herod's Hellenization-program was the rebuilding and embellishing of the old Jewish Temple.[27] According to the Bible, it had originally been built by Solomon, the legendary king who, nearly a millennium before, had ruled a vast empire with Jerusalem as its centre, much as Herod did in his new world. Jerusalem had earlier been destroyed by Nebuchadnezar and rebuilt by Zerubbabel. Much as this Zerubabel had reinstated in his person the tradition of David and Solomon's Empire when Jerusalem became a provincial capital of the Persian Empire, now Jeru-salem, as the capital of a client kingdom in the Roman Empire, had Herod as spiritual son of both David and Solomon.

Herod first enlarged the platform on which the Temple stood to the north, where he cut part of the hill north of the Temple courtyard away. This may be seen in the artificial scarp formed at the northern edge of the Haram. He also extended the platform to the south and to the west by ter-racing on pillars across the Tyropoeon Valley. This created the greatest open space of any Classical city. It measured 280 by 485 m, with a height of 170 m, the present Haram in the Old City of Jerusalem. On this plat-form, Herod built one of the most remarkable building complexes ever

26. The list is taken from Richardson, *Herod*, p. 198, for an overview of the water supply, see J. Wilkinson, 'Ancient Jerusalem its Water Supply and Population', *PEQ* 106 (1974), pp. 33-51.

27. For a description see also Strange, 'Theology and Politics', pp. 34-36.

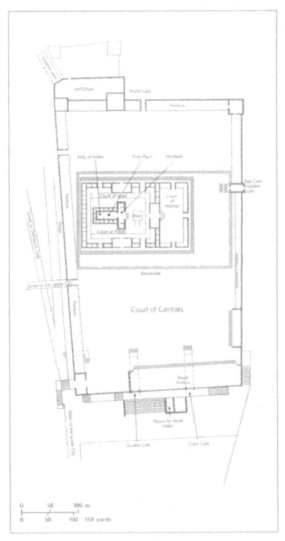

Figure 4. *Herod's Temple*
*(reproduced from John Strange [ed.], Bible Atlas [New York: American Bible
Society, 1999 [Danish original 1998], p. 55 [Map 74])*

constructed in Palestine. The old temple was not torn down, but probably
restored and embellished on the old foundations, foundations which may
even have belonged to a pre-exilic Temple.[28] In its tripart construction of

28. See Josephus, *Ant.* 15.11.1; cf. also Strange, 'Theology and Politics', p. 32.

Vestibule, Holy Place and Holy of Holies, it continued the Jewish Temple tradition. This can also be seen in the surrounding Court of Priests and the Court of Israel, separated from the outside by a balustrade with warnings to foreigners against trespassing on penalty of death.[29] Outside these structures, and separated from them by a balustrade, he added two areas: the Court of Women and the Court of Gentiles. These he surrounded by porticoes, thereby making the whole building into a Hellenistic monument. The Jewish Temple took up about one third of the platform. The rest may be described as a northern and a southern Agora. Already the old temple had probably been surrounded by porticoes or roofed colonnades with an aisle. Herod may have simply taken over the portico known as Solomon's Portico, toward the east, from the earlier temple court. On the other sides, where the platform had been enlarged, he built new porticoes. These were double colonnades, that is, colonnades with two aisles. The most magnificent was the one towards the south, called the Royal Portico (*stoa basileia*). It was a three-aisled building with a central aisle 31 m high, 185 m long and 33 m deep.[30] Only the Temple itself, which was about 46 m (100 cubits) high, and the towers of Antonia stood higher. It must be remembered that still at the time of Herod the higher grounds to the west and northwest of the Haram had not been built upon. The Temple, standing on its platform in the then northeast corner of Jerusalem, dominated the city completely.

The whole plan had seven 'spheres'. Entering from the outside, one proceeded through the Court of Gentiles, Court of Women, Court of Israel, Court of Priests, the Vestibule, the Holy Place and finally the Holy of Holies. It was like a journey through the seven planet spheres, a Hellenistic concept linked to astrology.[31] In my opinion, it was calculated to send a signal to the Graeco-Roman world. Here, in Jerusalem, the true *kosmos* was to be found. It made Jerusalem a counterpart to Rome, a capital of Empire.

The Temple area must have looked like the Acropolis of Athens or at least the Pergamon, towering above all Jerusalem.[32] It was undoubtedly

---

29. See *NEAEHL*, II, p. 744.

30. For a description see A. Businsk, *Der Tempel von Jerusalem* (2 vols.; Leiden: E.J. Brill, 1980), II, pp. 1187-232.

31. See, e.g., C. Singer, *A Short History of Scientific Ideas to 1900* (Oxford: Oxford University Press, 1959), pp. 81-91; O. Neugebauer, *The Exact Sciences in Antiquity* (New York: Dover, 2nd edn, 1969), pp. 152-207.

32. An artist's view is found in J.B. Pritchard, *The Times Atlas of the Bible* (London: Times Books, 1987), pp. 166-67.

meant to serve both as a Jewish place of worship—anything else was unthinkable—and also as a market place and a centre for Greek thinking, like the Agora in Athens with its Stoa. It was a grandiose attempt to make Judaism respectable and to harmonize it with other Hellenistic religions. This was the place where the oldest religion in the world, the religion of Abraham, had culminated in the sacrifice of Isaac on Mt Moriah (Gen. 22). It was the very spot where Solomon had built the First Temple (2 Chron. 3.1). Herod intended that this religion was now to be united with other Hellenistic religions.

Herod began his restoration of the Temple in 20/19 BCE, but died long before the project had been realized. Only in 64 CE was the project finished. By then, other forces in Jerusalem had prevailed and Jerusalem had become the provincial capital of Judaea, ruled by the Romans as part of the province of Syria. Moreover, within Jerusalem, the elements who would keep Judaism clean from foreign influence at any price were gaining power. It ended in the Jewish War, in which the Hellenistic Temple and all Jerusalem was destroyed and replaced by the Roman city Aelia Capitolinus.

JERUSALEM IN THE AGE OF THE KINGDOM OF JUDAH

Firas Sawah

From the birth of archaeology as an independent discipline in the nine-teenth century, no part of the world has witnessed archaeological excavation on the scale of that carried out in Palestine. Over the span of a century and a half, excavations have been undertaken on almost every hillock: from the Mediterranean in the west to the Jordan valley and Red Sea in the east; from Galilee in the north to the borders of Sinai in the south. The motives underlying this hectic activity were made explicit from the start by the Palestine Exploration Fund, which was established in Britain in 1865 and was the first organization of its kind in Europe. The primary objectives, as laid down by the organization's program, were to be 'the accurate and systematic investigation of the archaeology, the topography, the geology, the physical geography, the traditions and customs of the Holy Land for Biblical illustration'.[1] Thus, archaeology in Palestine was born as biblical archaeology, to be placed at the service of theology. The search for the origins of Israel in the Holy Land, and verification of the historicity of the biblical narratives, became the sole objective of the programs of exploration in question, beginning, immediately after the Fund's establishment, with that of Captain R.E. Warren. Archaeology in Palestine was at the mercy of sponsors concerned primarily with theological issues; and this remained the case even after responsibility for finding sponsorship had been passed to major universities in Europe and the United States. The pursuit of archaeological activity was still subject to the need to satisfy these sponsors.

The end result of this flurry of activity, undertaken by explorers grasping a Bible in one hand and a pickaxe in the other, was, ironically, the opposite of what had been foreseen. The cycles of biblical narrative began, one after the other, to move from the sphere of history to that of religious

---

1. K. Kenyon, *Digging Up Jerusalem* (London: Ernest Benn, 1974), p. 3.

literature. None of the biblical accounts showed themselves to be historically and archaeologically viable, apart from a small number related to the final decades of the kingdoms of Samaria and Judah. Archaeology can show that most famous stories of the Bible did not happen as the Bible records them, especially those of the Pentateuch. As for the Deuteronomistic history, only few events and characters are verified by archaeology or extra-biblical sources. And even here such scanty details as were supplied remained obscure, confused and overloaded with theological elements that set them apart from history in the sense of accurate documented information.

Up to the mid-twentieth century, it was easy for archaeologists and historians to formulate arbitrary interpretations, in terms of the events of biblical narrative, of the results of archaeological exploration in Palestine. This was due to the paucity of sites where archaeological strata had been comprehensively explored, to concentration on separate and isolated sites and to primitive methods of excavation and of dating archaeological finds. However, following the excavations carried out in Palestine by the British archaeologist Kathleen Kenyon—notably her excavation program in Jerusalem from 1960 to 1967—and the results (revolutionary by the standards of the time) emerging from these and due to the improvements she introduced into the nascent field of stratigraphy,[2] excavation programs intensified. This was especially true in the Palestinian highlands, the traditional regions of Samaria and Judah that came under Israeli control in the wake of the June 1967 war. Between the early 1970s and late 1980s, a young generation of Israeli archaeologists initiated and developed a different style of excavation, involving comprehensive regional survey of specified geographical areas, as opposed to digging in remote and geographically separate areas. The University of Tel Aviv organized various archaeological teams, supported by experts in a number of related fields. Over the past two decades, the members of these teams, working on foot, have surveyed every square meter of the Palestinian highlands, gathering, in the process, a body of valuable information that has revolutionized the archaeology of Palestine.

As ever more archaeological data were gleaned, set down and analyzed, it became ever more difficult for historians and archaeologists to correlate the information with biblical narrative about the origins of Israel in the

---

2. Stratigraphy is a method of dating buried archaeological finds and buildings, through the inspection and dating of fragments of pottery contained in the covering soil.

land of Canaan and about the rise of the so-called United Kingdom which was followed by the twin kingdoms of Samaria and Judah. This state of affairs eventually led the eminent Israeli archaeologist, Israel Finkelstein, to call for the liberation of archaeology from its domination by the biblical narratives. In a symposium on the origins of Israel, held at Ben Gurion University in 1998, Finkelstein maintained that biblical sources formerly dominant vis-à-vis research on the origins of Israel have lost most of their importance and should, as such, no longer be numbered among the main and direct sources. The biblical narratives, he went on, as they were written long after the events they described, reflected a theological bias that rendered exceedingly difficult, if not impossible, the search for the historical seeds of the biblical narratives themselves. It was, Finkelstein felt, essential to examine archaeological data in a free and objective manner, independently of the biblical text.[3]

In the light of the most important findings of the regional archaeological survey undertaken over the past two decades, it is now clear that the groups settling in the Palestinian highlands in Iron Age I, between 1200 and 1000 BCE (the alleged period of the arrival and settlement of the Hebrew tribes in the land of Canaan, the so-called Age of Judges) did not leave Egypt in a mass wave of emigration. They did not enter Palestine after a period of wandering in the desert, did not bring with them a religion revealed in Sinai, and did not wipe out or displace the local inhabitants. The culture of these early settlers, as reflected in their material remains, points to, and shows continuity with, the late Bronze Age culture (1550–1200 BCE) dominant throughout the Palestinian region, albeit with tendencies linked to these settlers' characteristic modes of economic life. It may be beside the point now to talk of the settlers' common genealogy, or of their descent from the twelve children of Jacob. It is not possible to deduce on the existing evidence any spread of conquest or infiltration of new settlers coming from outside Palestine, carrying with them different cultural traditions which mark a break between the late Bronze Age and the Iron Age. Such a break, which the biblical archaeologists tended to emphasize, seems now entirely unwarranted.[4]

3.   I. Finkelstein, 'The Rise of Ancient Israel', in S. Ahituv and E.D. Oren (eds.), *The Origin of Early Israel: Biblical, Historical and Archaeological Perspectives; Irene Levi-Sala Seminar, 1997* (Beer-Sheba: Ben-Gurion University of the Negev Press, 1998).

4.   For further elaboration on the historicity of the Patriarchal Age, Exodus, Judges and Joshua, see J. Van Seters, *Abraham in History and Tradition* (New Haven: Yale

What happened in the Palestinian highlands during Iron Age I is that several groups of Palestinian inhabitants, originally uprooted during the long period of aridity affecting the east Mediterranean area from the middle of the Late Bronze Age onwards, were returning to a life of agriculture and stability following a long period of pastoral migration. This phenomenon was not confined to the Palestinian highlands. Archaeological surveys carried out in other major regions in Palestine, including the territories east of the Jordan, have revealed that the settlement history of these territories in the Late Bronze and Early Iron Age I, was broadly similar to those of the highlands, and people here lived in the same kind of villages, in similar houses, used similar pottery, and led an almost identical way of life. Yet, we know that they were not descendants of the twelve sons of Jacob as the highlanders were surely not. The inhabitants of the Palestinian highland established a number of small scattered villages and cleared the evergreen woodland to provide agricultural land, and lived on subsistence agriculture over an extended period. In time, such villages came to be closer together, and family ties grew stronger, with a consequent need for co-operation and a sense of ethnic identity. Three centuries on, the highland inhabitants had come to form the basis first of the Kingdom of Samaria and then of the Kingdom of Judah.[5]

University Press, 1975); G. Garbini, *History and Ideology in Ancient Israel* (London: SCM Press, 1988); T.L. Thompson, *The Historicity of the Patriarchal Narratives: The Quest for the Historical Abraham* (Berlin: W. de Gruyter, 1974); idem, *Early History of the Israelite People* (Leiden: E.J. Brill, 1992); N.M. Sarna, 'Israel in Egypt', in H. Shanks (ed.), *Ancient Israel: A Short History from Abraham to the Roman Destruction of the Temple* (Englewood Cliffs, NJ: Prentice–Hall, 1988), pp. 31-52, as well as J. Callaway, 'The Settlement in Canaan', pp. 53-84 in the same volume; Firas Sawah, *Aram, Damascus and Israel: History and Biblical Narratives* (Damascus: Aladeen Publishers, 1994).

5. The 1980s and 1990s witnessed a series of new publications contributing to a significant shift in perception vis-à-vis the nature or existence of early Israel in the Bronze–Iron Age transition. Dissatisfied with the standard histories of ancient Israel, the authors of these works were attempting to respond to significant changes taking place in the discipline, especially following the publication of Israel Finkelstein's book, *The Archaeology of the Israelite Settlement* (Jerusalem: Israel Exploration Society, 1988), which provided vital survey data from a distinguished and professional archaeologist. The following list of publications is not intended to be comprehensive: N.P. Lemche, *Early Israel: Anthropological and Historical Studies* (Leiden: E.J. Brill, 1985); G.W. Ahlström, *Who Were the Israelites?* (Winona Lake, IN: Eisenbrauns, 1986); R.B. Coote and K.W. Whitelam, *The Emergence of Early Israel in Historical Perspective* (JSOTSup, 12; Sheffield: JSOT Press, 1987); N.P. Lemche, *Ancient Israel:*

So wide is the gulf between archaeology and biblical sources, with respect to the origins of Israel, that we find ourselves faced with two quite different communities (even if these do share the same geographical location). Biblical Israel is a literary construct, which cannot be called 'realistic' merely on the grounds of its being presented on a real geographical stage, any more than the *Arabian Nights* can be so because events are portrayed as taking place in Baghdad, Kufa, Basra or Cairo. By the same token, the highland inhabitants of Iron Age I, as defined by archaeology, would have failed to recognize themselves as they are portrayed in the five Books of Moses, Joshua, and Judges. They certainly did not see themselves as Israelites in the biblical sense, nor did they worship the biblical God. On the contrary, material remains from highland sites in Iron Age I show conclusively that the inhabitants followed a traditional Canaanite religion, that their modest temples were consecrated to the old Palestinian gods and that no evidence exists, direct or indirect, for the seeds of biblical religion. Some of these temples have been discovered by Adam Zertal on Mt Ebal, Amihai Mazar in Manasseh and Israel Finkelstein in Shiloh.

What, then, can be said of the history set down in the books of Samuel and 1 Kings? Does the biblical text record events of a broadly authentic nature? Did the tribes that inhabited the highlands for two centuries in the Age of the Judges (corresponding to Iron Age I) call, for the first time, for unification under the banner of a king? Was a United Kingdom formed in the Palestinian highlands between the late eleventh and late tenth centuries BCE, ruled successively by Saul, David and Solomon, which annexed most of Palestine and a large part of southern Syria in the wake of King David's storming military campaigns?

Up to the late 1970s, many scholars believed the age of the United Kingdom, beginning with the reign of Saul in 1025 BCE and ending with the death of Solomon in 931 BCE, to be the first historically credible period of biblical narrative. Now, however, archaeological fieldwork has—just as with the earlier cycles of biblical narrative—removed the events of the United Kingdom from the sphere of history to that of religious literary construct. We know now that, up until the end of the eleventh century BCE (the alleged period for the beginning of the United Kingdom), the northern

A New History of Israelite Society (The Biblical Seminar, 5; Sheffield: JSOT Press, 1988); R.B. Coote, *Early Israel: A New Horizon* (Minneapolis: Fortress Press, 1990); T.L. Thompson, *The Early History of the Israelite People* (Leiden: E.J. Brill, 1992). P.R. Davies, *In Search of 'Ancient Israel'* (JSOTSup, 148; Sheffield: JSOT Press, 1992).

highlands (Samaria) had a mere 200 small agricultural villages, inhabited by no more than a few thousand people.[6] As for Shechem, the only city in the northern highlands before Samaria was built, it was in ruins and abandoned. Other, smaller townships, such as Bethel, Geba, Shiloh and Tirzah, were in a slightly better state. They were still unimpressive sites, with no more than a few hundred inhabitants each.[7]

In the southern region (the highlands of Judah), the situation was apparently still more depressing. Up to the end of the tenth century BCE—the alleged period for the end of the United Kingdom—the population was scanty, not exceeding 2000 people scattered over several dozen small hamlets. Hebron was almost void of inhabitants. Jerusalem, the alleged capital of the United Kingdom, was neither functioning nor inhabited throughout the tenth century BCE.[8] By the evidence of archaeology, the United Kingdom did not exist. There was insufficient population; there was no capital or significant urban centers; and the Palestinian highlands were incapable of developing any real state infrastructure before the ninth century BCE, when the state appeared in the north first, following the building of Samaria in 880 BCE.

After the death of King Solomon, so we read in 1 Kings, his kingdom was divided between his son Rehoboam, who governed the Kingdom of Judah from Jerusalem, and Jeroboam, son of Naboth, the former governor of the northern regions, who ruled over the ten northern tribes called Israel. As such, the biblical editors depict twin, fully developed states, each controlling a part of the former United Kingdom. Yet archaeological excavations and the field survey of the Palestinian highlands point to origins for both Israel and Judah that are totally at odds with the biblical narrative. We know now that the state in the north rose at least a century and a half before the southern state came into existence. Towards the end of the tenth century BCE, and early in the ninth century BCE, the population in the northern highlands numbered close on 45,000. Shechem developed into an important regional center, while small townships such as Bethel, Shiloh and Tirzah also flourished. When Samaria was built around 880

---

6.   T.L. Thompson, *The Bible in History* (London: Jonathan Cape, 1999), p. 159. For further elaboration on the settlement of the Palestinian highlands, see Thompson's *Early History*, Chapters 4, 6 and 7.

7.   K. Kenyon, *Archaeology in the Holy Land* (London: Methuen, 4th edn, 1985), pp. 230-342

8.   For further elaboration on the pattern of settlement in the highland regions of Benjamin and Judah, see Thompson, *Early History*, pp. 288-92.

BCE, the northern highlands (so archaeological evidence indicates) had already been placed under general central administration, as evidenced by the rise of major centralized industries, such as oil and pottery, which were operated and controlled by the state. A few decades later, the whole region had been united into a single powerful state that became the most important in Palestine and one of the major states south of Syria.[9] In the Assyrian texts, the state was called the 'Humri country', or 'Humri land', referring to King Omar (biblical Omri),[10] who built Samaria and established the state. The name 'Israel' is documented only in two local texts: one the Mesha Stele (the inscription of Mesha, king of Moab), which was discovered in a region east of the River Jordan; the other a stele of King Hazael of Damascus, discovered in a hillock (Tell Dan) in northern Palestine.

Samaria was born as a Palestinian Canaanite state, and flourished as an independent kingdom for about a century and a half (880–721 BCE), in Iron Age II. Its inhabitants came from other Palestinian lowlands and they had no connection with the legendary ten tribes of Israel. This kingdom extended over the northern highlands from Bethel in the south to the Jezreel valley in the north, but invaded further lands to the north and the east whenever its kings felt powerful. Samaria's expansion put her face to face with Damascus, the major power in Syria at the time. The two kingdoms contended over the control of Jezreel valley, with its strategically important passage, and regions east of the river Jordan, through which ran a trade route of major importance. The two states would come together by virtue of military pacts concluded by Damascus to face Assyrian military pressure; and they would become disunited due to a clash of interests. This explains the successive states of war and peace between the two. This state of affairs ended when Assyria destroyed the independence of Damascus in 732 BCE, after devastating wars between the two kingdoms for more than a century. Samaria itself was destroyed in 721 BCE and annexed to the Assyrian crown, so permanently losing its status as an independent political entity.

While Samaria was developing into a powerful state in the early ninth century BCE, the southern highland region remained as isolated and backward as it had been in the tenth century BCE and earlier. There were no

9. For further field data on the rise of the Kingdom of Israel see Thompson, *Early History*, pp. 221-29, 316-39; see also Chapter 7 of his *The Bible in History*.

10. In a text of the Assyrian king Shalmanesser III, one king of Samaria, Ahab son of Omri (biblical Ahab), is called 'the Israelite'.

more than 20 agricultural villages, along with some rural groups living as pastoral nomads. The pottery and other material remains of these people show strong links with Late Bronze Age culture, which is evidence of their coming from other Palestinian regions rather than from a different country. As for the two main urban centers, Jerusalem and Hebron, there is no indication of these becoming significant regional centers during the ninth century BCE.[11]

Although settlement activity accelerated during the eighth century BCE, leading to a significant increase in population, there is hardly any evidence for the rise of a central authority in the region. The oil and pottery industries retained a primitive family identity, developing into major centralized industries only in the early seventh century BCE The same holds true for large-scale use of writing, along with other indications of bureaucratic activity such as monumental inscriptions, ostraca, inscribed stone weights, and so on. Ashlar masonry appears in the early seventh century BCE, two centuries after its appearance in Samaria, but falls short, in terms of size and architectural beauty, of similar buildings in the north.[12] In sum, the region of Judah, according to archaeological evidence, did not achieve mature statehood before the transitional period between the eighth and seventh centuries BCE

The history and archaeology of Jerusalem reflect this general picture of the southern highlands. The excavations carried out by Kathleen Kenyon show Jerusalem to have risen as a walled town, for the first time, early in the Middle Bronze Age (c. 1800 BCE),[13] covering, at that time, an area of no more than four and a half hectares on the crest of the Ophel Hill, down the present southern wall of the Haram esh-Sharif between Kidron Valley east and Tyropoeon Valley west.[14] This built-up area is not much greater than the areas of large Neolithic villages, such as Jericho in the Jordan Valley, while major Syrian towns of the Middle Bronze Age covered areas of between 50 and 100 hectares. The area covered by Hazor, in Upper Galilee, was 75 hectares. The early inhabitants had apparently been attracted by the spring of Gihon in the Kidron Valley. Rainfall in Palestine is completely seasonal. From about April to November there is virtually non. Early settlements had to be within reach of a perennial water supply.

11. I. Finkelstein, *The Bible Unearthed* (New York: Free Press, 2001), pp. 158-59.
12. Finkelstein, *The Bible Unearthed*, pp. 229-50.
13. Kenyon, *Digging Up Jerusalem*, p. 83.
14. Kenyon, *Archaeology in the Holy Land*, p. 347.

The favourable climate predominant in the eastern Mediterranean region during the Middle Bronze Age meant that Jerusalem enjoyed an active economic life. The period was characterized by high levels of rainfall, and this enabled a large number of Palestinian sites to develop into walled townships, each controlling a certain area of land around it. Early in the second millennium BCE, the long period of drought, which had characterized the Early–Middle Bronze transitional period, was in retreat, and the wet, rainy weather encouraged inhabitants uprooted from their agricultural land to return to a settled way of life. Villages appeared in all the fertile plains, old urban centers flourished and new ones came into existence. None of these centers was, however, sufficiently large or strong enough to control an extensive, centrally governed province, let alone a major kingdom bringing the whole Palestinian region together in a political, integrated unity. The political system remained a tribal one based on local chieftains and influential ruling families, who were incapable, as yet, of establishing royal dynasties with stable power.[15] Then, from the early decades of the Late Bronze Age, a new and prolonged wave of drought gradually took effect, and put an end to the flourishing Bronze Age civilization. This is particularly noticeable in the Palestine region, where population decline mirrored the retreat of cultural aspects of all kinds, as indicated by pottery, plastic arts, architecture and fortifications. Agriculture was first hit in those highlands most susceptible to drought. Farmers began to abandon their lands early in the fourteenth century BCE, and the main provincial centers, including Jerusalem, also were to be abandoned.[16]

A comprehensive archaeological survey in the Judean highlands, conducted by the Israeli archaeologist Ari Ofer, shows that human settlement ceased in the regions around Jerusalem early in the Late Bronze Age, and that it was resumed only in the transitional period between the tenth and ninth centuries BCE. Commissioned by the British Institute of Archaeology in Jerusalem to re-date the archaeological findings of the Jerusalem site, Professor H. Franken and his colleague Margreet Steiner, both of Leiden University, produced results showing Jerusalem to have been deserted, without inhabitants, during the second half of the Late Bronze Age. There were no traces of fortifications, gates or any other archaeological findings

15. Thompson, *The Bible in History*, pp. 105-24.
16. For fresh information on climatic factors underlying the collapse of Late Bronze culture, see H. William and J.R. Stiebing, 'Climate and Collapse', *BR* (August 1994), pp. 19-27.

indicative of life in the site. Such findings were plentiful for the archaeological strata of the Middle Bronze Age, and any claim that the findings of the Late Bronze Age were swept away for some reason remains baseless.[17]

There is no reason to think that the situation in Jerusalem changed in Iron Age I or early in Iron Age II, in the tenth century BCE. During the 1970s and 1980s, there was a search for remains from the tenth century BCE and the United Kingdom, led by Yigal Shilohm which focused on the so-called city of David (which is identical with the Middle Bronze Age city called the Jebusite City, after its Canaanite Jebusite inhabitants). The results were disappointing, no traces being found to indicate that life returned to the town during the supposed period of David's and Solomon's rule. According to the archaeologist David Ussishkin, of Tel Aviv University, this absence of evidence applies not only to large buildings but to small pottery and similar findings, which might indicate the presence of active life. Since the site of the City of David has provided us with numerous such findings, from various strata of the Middle Bronze Age and from the eighth and seventh centuries BCE, Ussishkin concluded that the most optimistic assessment of this negative evidence is that tenth-century Jerusalem was a typical small hill country village within the backward highland region.[18] There is some evidence of human activity on the Ophel Hill early in the ninth century BCE, but no houses or any indication that a large number of people lived there. The probability is, therefore, that the site was the administrative center of a modest political authority, and that we are dealing with the beginnings of a nascent town not in existence a few centuries earlier.[19]

In the course of the ninth century (that witnessed the rise of the Samarian kingdom, the formation of the Shephelah, Philistia and Transjordanian city-states, and the transformation of Damascus into a dominant power in

17. For the results of Avi Ofer's survey, see A. Ofer, 'All the Hill Country of Judah—From Settlement Fringe to a Prosperous Monarchy', in I. Finkelstein and N. Na'aman (eds.), *From Nomadism to Monarchy* (Jerusalem: Yad Izhak Ben-Zvi/ Israel Exploration Society, 1988), pp. 92-121. For the results of Franken and Steiner's dating of the excavation material from Jerusalem, see M.L. Steiner's recent book, *Excavations by Kathleen M. Kenyon in Jerusalem 1961–1967.* III. *The Settlement in the Bronze and Iron Ages* (Copenhagen International Seminar Series, 9; Sheffield: Sheffield Academic Press, 2001).

18. Finkelstein, *The Bible Unearthed*, p. 133.

19. M. Steiner, 'David's Jerusalem, Fiction or Reality: Archaeology Proves a Negative', *BARev* (July–August 1998), pp. 26-33, 62.

Syria) Jerusalem developed into an inhabited town as the settlement process accelerated in the Judean highlands. Scrublands were cleared and
turned into arable use. Farm products were sent to Jerusalem and Hebron,
which became central markets for the southern highlands, along with
Lachish, the main town in Shephelah plain. These three towns competed
for the control of the arable lands in the southern highlands, where the
villages were not as yet under any central authority. Towards the end of
the eighth century, this competition led Jerusalem to put an end to the
independence of Hebron, and to extend its authority over the entire Judean
highland. As for Lachish, Jerusalem had to wait for the Assyrians to
destroy it around 701 BCE in order to gain full control of its trade and have
free hand in Shephelah.[20]

The destruction of Samaria, the end of independence in the Northern
Kingdom and the annexation of the latter to the Assyrian crown in 721
BCE affected the nascent Southern Kingdom favorably. In the wake of the
Assyrian campaigns against Samaria between 734 and 721 BCE, the region
took in large numbers of farmers emigrating from the north, providing the
south with skilled agricultural labor. Archaeological field surveys indicate
that, in the second half of the eighth century BCE, the number of agricultural villages between Jerusalem and Beer-sheba reached about 300 and
that many existing villages had developed into well-organized towns.
Some scholars estimate the population of Judah in the late eighth century
BCE at about 120,000—indicating that the region experienced a population
explosion following a long period of demographic vacuum.[21] Archaeological excavations in Jerusalem reveal the swift and sudden development
taking place in the city. Early in the eighth century BCE, the Jebusite town
on the Ophel Hill was fortified and extended northward, annexing the area
between the southern wall of the Haram esh-Sahrif and the northern wall
of the Jebusite town (the area mistakenly called the 'Solomonic Extension'
by Kathleen Kenyon).[22] By the late eighth or early seventh century BCE,

20. See Thompson, *Early History*, pp. 288-92, 332-33, and *The Bible in History*,
pp. 161-64.

21. For the number of settlements in Judah toward the end of the eighth century
and its population, see Finkelstein, *The Bible Unearthed*, p. 245.

22. According to Kenyon, the date of the eastern walls of the northern expansions,
on the basis of the deposit found against them, is—on the field estimate of the pottery—
eighth century or earlier. Having noted, however, that these walls were constructed of
re-used stones of a character identified as Phoenician at Samaria, she concluded these
walls were originally Solomonic. Solomon's use of Phoenician masons is undoubted,

the residential area had been extended westward across the central valley, dividing the eastern from the western ridges of the Jerusalem mountains, and the new residential area was surrounded by a huge wall. Some scholars have estimated the town's population at 15,000 by the late eighth century BCE, in an area exceeding 50 hectares.[23]

This archaeological picture of Jerusalem is supported by the historical one. Throughout the millennium between the eighteenth and eighth centuries BCE, the town was on the margin of events. It is mentioned only twice in Egyptian texts, and is completely ignored by Assyrian and local Syrian texts. The Galilee town of Hazor is mentioned in the texts of Ebla as early as the middle of the third millennium BCE, and is also mentioned around 20 times in the archives of Mari in the eighteenth century BCE as being an important commercial town in northern Palestine. By contrast, Jerusalem, which rose contemporaneously with the Mari archives, was completely unknown to the commercial and diplomatic missions exchanged by the courts of Mari and Hazor.

Jerusalem is first mentioned in the Egyptian Execration Texts, which date back to the eighteenth century BCE. These were magical texts inscribed on pottery vessels, which were then smashed in a rite supposed to cause harm to those named in the inscriptions. The names of Jerusalem, and of its ruler, were included in a list of Palestinian and Phoenician towns regarded as enemies of Egypt in the region.[24] Since the kings of Egypt did not control Palestinian regions and had no permanent military presence there at such an early date, Egyptian hostility toward the towns mentioned in the Execration Texts must have been provoked by the rulers of these towns through their interception of Egyptian trade caravans and the heavy taxes they imposed on them. As for the few documented campaigns against Syria in the period of the Middle Kingdom, their aim was simply to chastise local governors and secure the trade routes connecting Egypt to Syria, Babylon and Asia Minor. One such campaign, carried out by Sen-Usert III, took him to Shechem in the northern highlands.[25]

More than four centuries after the Execration Texts, Jerusalem is mentioned in the Tel el-Amarna archive, which was discovered in the royal

and it is a reasonable inference that, close at hand, there was a wall at the time of Solomon, from which the builders of the eighth century BCE derived their stones. See Kenyon, *Digging Up Jerusalem*, pp. 115-16.

23. Finkelstein, *The Bible Unearthed*, p. 243.

24. J.A. Wilson, 'Egyptian Rituals and Incantations', in *ANET*, p. 328.

25 J.A. Wilson, 'Egyptian Historical Texts', in *ANET*, p. 230.

palace of King Akhenaton, in the middle of the fourteenth century. The larger part of the archive's contents comprises letters exchanged between the princes of Egypt's vassal states in southern Syria and the Egyptian court: letters describing the chaos prevalent in the region as a result of the weakening of the Egyptian military hold, hostilities among local kingdoms and the rise of the armed Apiru: mercenaries fighting in the service of the highest bidder. Among these were found five letters sent to Akhenaton by the governor of the Jerusalem area, named as Abdi Heba. The governor complains of attacks by neighbors, brought about because of his allegiance to the Pharaoh, and of Apiru attacks on his area; he asks Egypt for support and protection. The Tel el-Amarna letters have long been regarded as evidence that Jerusalem was an important and strong city-state in the fourteenth century BCE. We now know, however, that the core of Judah, that is, the area between Jerusalem in the north and Hebron in the south, had no more than eight small villages at this time and a population not exceeding 1500 people, Jerusalem included. In view of this, Margreet Steiner believes that Abdi Heba was not a king over a city but a governor over a limited area of land, with the responsibility for protecting Egyptian interests there and that he lived in a small fortress near the Gihon spring, in the valley below the Ophel Hill. In the view of the Israeli historian Nadav Na'aman, Abdi Heba's Jerusalem was no more than an administrative quarter, where a small group of elites managed the affairs of a small number of agricultural villages and pastoral groups.[26] Careful perusal of Abdi Heba's letters shows that they do not in fact refer to Jerusalem as a city, nor do they have anything to say about fortifications or gates. The letters refer consistently to 'the lands of Jerusalem'. Certain minor details in the letters indicate the slight importance of this Jerusalem region. In one letter (EA 289), Abdi Heba details his critical position and the dangers facing him from the towns in revolt against the Pharaoh, and from the Apiru—he then asks the court for a military force of a mere 50 Egyptian soldiers to protect him.[27]

After the Tel el-Amarna letters, history remains completely silent about Jerusalem until the late eighth century BCE, when its King Ahaz is mentioned in a list of kings west of the Euphrates who paid tribute to the

26. For Nadav Na'aman's rejoinder ('It's There: Ancient Texts Prove It') to M. Steiner's interpretation (It's Not There: Archaeology Proves a Negative), see their two articles in *BARev* (July–August 1998), pp. 42-44.

27. Wilson, 'Egyptian Rituals and Incantations', p. 489.

Assyrian king Tiglath-pileser III, in around 735 BCE.[28] This historical silence is no coincidence, nor does it spring from any gap in our historical information. The first half of the first millennium BCE is a historically well-documented period. No kingdom in the Syro-Palestinian area went unnoticed by the Assyrian chronicles. Hence, the only possible explanation for the Assyrian kings' lack of interest in Jerusalem is that the town was poor and insignificant, and that the Judean highlands had nothing to attract the Assyrian conqueror.

The reference to Jerusalem in the Assyrian archives is contemporaneous with the development of the town into a strong regional capital, extending its control over the whole of the Judean highlands. Only by the late eighth century BCE do archaeological finds begin to indicate the establishment of an integrated central state in the southern highlands: population growth, ashlar masonry, seals and seal impressions indicating the spread of writing, inscribed weights, the central production of pottery, oil and wine in large workshops, the appearance of middle-sized towns serving as provincial centers.[29]

The first real town on the Jerusalem site is that dating from the reign of King Ahaz, and it is the only one on which we have sufficient archaeological and historical documentation. Hence, the historian can only study the political, cultural and religious history of Jerusalem, and of Judah in general, from the reign of this king onwards. Anything before this period is 'pre-history'. As for the eleven kings, descendants of the mythical King David, who (as we are told by the editors of 1–2 Kings), succeeded him on the throne of Jerusalem, these could, by the best estimate—and assuming they existed—belong only to some time in the early eighth century BCE.

Ahaz found himself embroiled in complex Syrian politics, with the Assyrians pressing hard on the regions west of the Euphrates following the battle of Qarqar, in 854 BCE, between the Syrian alliance led by Hadadezer, king of Damascus, and Shalmaneser III, king of Assyria. During the time of Tiglath-pileser III, the Assyrians adopted the policy of annexing conquered lands to the Assyrian crown. The Kingdom of Damascus was still confronting Assyria, powerfully and obdurately, defending itself and other kingdoms west of the Euphrates through military coalitions that proved effective over more than a century of fierce wars between the Syrians and

28. See A.L. Oppenheim, 'Babylonian and Assyrian Historical Texts', in *ANET*, pp. 267-317 (282).

29. For archaeological indications of mature state formation in the southern highlands, see Finkelstein, *The Bible Unearthed*, pp. 229-50.

Assyrians. Damascus made no attempt to carve out an extensive empire west of the Euphrates, being instead content to establish a regional system enabling the kingdom to protect the area militarily and lead it politically. Damascus felt bound, in consequence, to intervene militarily against any Syrian state that made peace with Assyria or that agreed to pay tribute to it. The Kingdom of Israel was the first to receive a fatal military blow by Damascus when Ahab's successors broke the agreement held between the two countries before the battle of Qarqar (in which King Ahab had fought under Damascus leadership and brought substantial military strength to the battle). King Hazael, who succeeded Hadadezer, invaded the Kingdom of Israel and destroyed its military power, so that King Jehoahaz, as we read in 2 Kings 30, was left with no more than 50 cavalry and ten chariots. Ben Hadad, the son of Hazael, led a military campaign against the Kingdom of Hamat for the same reason, besieging King Zakir in his royal quarters in the town of Hatrica with the help of an alliance of six north Syrian kingdoms. This campaign is documented in a text written in Aramaic by Zakir himself.[30]

When Ahaz ascended the throne of Jerusalem around 735 BCE, Damascus was striving to maintain its hold over the Syrian kingdoms, but was politically, militarily and economically exhausted, having paid a great price in the Syrian–Assyrian wars. It appears that Rahiano, the last king of Damascus, was preparing a new coalition to face the bitter assault expected on the middle and south of Syria, and he tried to convince Pekah, king of Samaria, and Ahaz, king of Jerusalem, to join him in the expected battle. Pekah agreed, but Ahaz had decided to submit to Assyria and so avoid exposing his young kingdom to new dangers in the face of Assyrian military might. He opted to pay tribute to Tiglath-pileser and refused to join the new Damascus pact. Thus he initiated a policy, which was maintained after him in Judah and the kingdom flourished as a result, moving on to a golden age. Damascus, for its part, was not prepared to accept an Assyrian vassal state in its southern region—one not only paying tribute to Assyria but also (as subsequent events were to show) providing it with military assistance. Rahiano, king of Damascus (called Rezin in the biblical text), and Pekah, king of Samaria, joined forces to fight Ahaz, marching on Jerusalem and laying siege to the town, with the aim of conquering it and setting on its throne another king who would withdraw the allegiance to Assyria. Our sources for this war are 2 Kings 16 and Isaiah 7.

---

30. F. Rosenthal, 'Canaanite and Aramaic Inscriptions', in *ANET*, pp. 655-56.

The editor of 2 Kings gives no convincing reason as to why Damascus and Samaria should have attacked Jerusalem. We read only:

> Then Rezin king of Syria and Pekah son of Ramaliah king of Israel came up to Jerusalem to war and they besieged Ahaz but could not overcome him... So Ahaz sent messengers to Tiglath-pileser king of Assyria saying, 'I am thy servant and thy son: come up and save me out of the hand of the king of Syria, and out of the hand of the king of Israel, which rise up against me'. And Ahaz took the silver and the gold that was found in the home of the Lord, and in the treasure of the king's house, and sent it for a present to the king of Assyria. And the king of Assyria hearkened unto him: for the king of Assyria went up against Damascus and took it, and carried the people of it captive to Kir and slew Rezin. And King Ahaz went to Damascus to meet Tiglath-pileser king of Assyria... (2 Kgs 16.5-10)

This account might lead us to suppose that Tiglath-pileser had accepted Ahaz's bribe and had crossed the Euphrates with his army solely to save Jerusalem. Assyrian records, however, give an indication of what really happened at this time. Around 733 BCE, Tiglath-pileser led a campaign against the regions west of the Euphrates and southern Syria, especially Damascus and Samaria, who were preparing a new alliance. He first besieged Samaria and deposed the rebel king, replacing him by one of his generals, Hoshea. Then, he annexed to the Assyrian crown all the Samarian possessions outside the northern highlands. Next, he marched on Damascus and laid siege to the city, but, unable to take it, avenged himself on Rahiano by burning the Ghota orchards around the city before finally withdrawing. A year later (732 BCE) he attacked Damascus once more and ended its independence. It appears King Rahiano was killed during the attack on the city. Samaria was soon to follow Jerusalem. Rebelling once more in 722 BCE, it was conquered and destroyed in 721 BCE, and a large number of its inhabitants were taken captive to Assyria by the Assyrian King Sargon II.[31] From this date on, Samaria never again rose as an independent state: it remained first an Assyrian, then Persian, then Hellenistic, and finally Roman province.

Ahaz, when he assumed power, placed himself in the service of Assyria, but did not reap the fruit of his vassalage until after Damascus had lost its independence in the campaign, for which Jerusalem supplied token forces, and until after the destruction of Samaria, the main rival to Jerusalem in the region. After 721 BCE, Judah experienced a sudden demographic growth and real social and economic evolution. Jerusalem underwent an

---

31. Oppenheim, 'Babylonian and Assyrian Historical Texts', p. 248.

unprecedented population explosion, with its residential areas expanding from its previously populated narrow eastern ridge to cover the entire
western ridge. A similar picture of population growth emerges from
archaeological surveys in the southern highlands. By the late eighth century, there were about 300 settlements of all sizes in Judah, from the
metropolis of Jerusalem to small farmsteads, where once there were only a
few villages and modest towns. The sudden growth of settlement far to the
south of Beer-sheba Valley may hint that Judah took part in the intensification of the Arabian trade in the late eighth century under the Assyrian
domination. On the other hand, the sudden flourish of oil, pottery and wine
production indicate that Jerusalem became a center for cash-crop exchange
on a large scale. Wealth began accumulating, especially in Jerusalem,
where the economic, social, religious and political affairs of the country
were centrally controlled by a trained bureaucratic elite. The reason behind
this series of rapid development is that Judah not only became a vassal
state to Assyria, but also cooperated with and even incorporated itself into
the economy of the Assyrian Empire.[32]

Ahaz appointed his son Hezekiah crown prince and co-ruler while still a
young man, and Hezekiah ruled with his father for 14 years before finally
assuming full power on the latter's death. His reign extended, therefore, from 729 to 696 BCE. The editor of 2 Kings celebrates the reign of
Hezekiah in a manner unmatched by that for any other king. He is the
good king who restored the worship of Yahweh in the temple of Jerusalem, after his father had fallen away from the orthodox faith and turned
to the worship of others' gods. He it was who enlarged the lands of the
kingdom by annexing new areas to it, who fortified Jerusalem and the
other towns of Judah, who increased agricultural production and heads of
livestock and made the trade routes safe and who drew the waters of the
Gihon spring into an underground tunnel, running from the Kidron Valley
to the Siloam pool in the central valley. Hezekiah made the first and last
attempt to rebel against Assyria, spurred on by promises of Egyptian
support. There is, in fact, no reason to disbelieve the portrayal of Hezekiah
supplied by the editor of 2 Kings. Recent excavations on the Jerusalem site
indicate significant improvements, additions and reparations to the city
wall that may be assigned to the time of Hezekiah, while earlier excavations had already discovered the tunnel dug by Hezekiah beneath the site
of Jebusite Jerusalem to draw the waters of the Gihon spring from the
eastern side of the Ophel Hill to the western side, pouring into the pool of

---

32. Finkelstein, *The Bible Unearthed*, pp. 243-46.

Siloam, which lay in a hidden site easily defensible should the area be besieged. On the other hand, the decision to rebel against Assyria, taken by a state that was economically and politically stable (albeit a partner in the Assyrian economic system and an upholder of its interests), indicates the power and self-confidence now enjoyed by Jerusalem and the ability of its ruling class to provide the necessary resources for a confrontation with Assyria.

Sargon II left Jerusalem to its own devices and chose not to go near its lands, despite the destruction he had brought down on Samaria and a number of towns on the Philistine plain, such as Ashdod, Gaza and Ekron. Scenes of the invasion of these towns are represented on a bas-relief found at Sargon's palace. Ahaz contrived to gain favor with Sargon, just as he had done with his two predecessors, Shalmaneser V and Tiglath-pileser III. However, Hezekiah's ambition, and his feeling that Jerusalem was capable of playing a significant regional role in Palestine and the rest of southern Syria, led him on to a decision he thought sound at the time. After the death of Sargon II, the Assyrian armies disappeared from the region west of the Euphrates for about four years. Their power and their ability to wage new raids had become less certain and this encouraged a number of the southern Syrian states to revolt and refuse payment of tribute. To Hezekiah, it seemed preferable to seize the present opportunity rather than remain the satellite of an imperial power he saw to be in decline. Moreover, Egypt, which in the past had promised help but failed to keep its promise, was now moving fast. Before Assyrian forces arrived to crush the new rebellion, Egyptian forces were already intensifying their presence in Palestine, ready to intervene in support of Hezekiah and other kings to whom they promised help.

In 701 BCE, King Sennacherib led a campaign against the region west of the Euphrates, targeting the rebellious kingdoms of Phoenicia and Palestine. Having made Phoenicia subject to him, Sennacherib moved down the Philistine plain and subdued Ashkelon, the head of the rebellious cities in Philistia. He then moved up the plain of Shephelah and besieged Lachish, its main town, before overrunning it and utterly destroying it. Hezekiah had already gone out to confront Sennacherib, camping in a place called Al-ta-qu in the Assyrian text, most probably the biblical site of Eltekeh, some kilometers south of Ekron. The battle ended, however, with the defeat of Hezekiah and the supporting Egyptian forces. Hezekiah then withdrew to Jerusalem, where he was besieged by an Assyrian army that had already destroyed 46 villages and towns in Judah. After a long siege,

Hezekiah agreed to pay tribute and made himself subject to Assyria once more. Sennacherib then withdrew, without invading the town.[33]

2 Kings 18–19 provide the biblical version of Sennacherib's campaign against Jerusalem. As usual, the biblical editor is here either unconcerned with events on the local and international levels or totally ignorant of what was going on. He leads us to believe that Sennacherib's campaign was basically aimed at Jerusalem, whose king had renounced allegiance to Assyria, and that, when Sennacherib's army reached the Shephelah plain and besieged Lachish, Hezekiah took fright and sent his messengers to Sennacherib, renewing his allegiance and promising to pay tribute. Then, after Sennacherib had accepted the tribute, he sent three of his generals, who subjected Jerusalem to a long siege. They incited the people of Jerusalem to mutiny against their king, promising to take them to a land better than theirs if they would open the gates of their town, rather than perish inside with their families. When the town was about to fall, however, the God of Israel intervened and struck Sennacherib's army. When the people of Jerusalem woke, they found the Assyrian soldiers dead and Sennacherib nowhere to be seen.

The findings of the archaeological excavation confirm the account of this campaign by Sennacherib. Lachish was completely destroyed, never to regain its former state. From Sennacherib's palace in Nineveh, we have a bas-relief from the throne hall portraying, in minute detail, the Lachish siege, the Assyrian weapons and tools of siege, the people defending it, the fall of the town and the captivity of its people. In the Judean region, signs of destruction appear everywhere, showing that Sennacherib did not simply mean to teach Hezekiah a stern lesson, but also intended to destroy the kingdom's economic infrastructure and resources.[34] After Sennacherib's campaign, Assyrian texts are completely silent on Jerusalem. Apart from two casual references to King Manasseh, who succeeded Hezekiah, the Assyrian records do not recount what was happening in Judah or mention any of its kings. This remained the case up to the end of the Assyrian Empire a century later, even though Assyria had occupied Egypt and the forces of Esarhaddon and his son, Ashurbanipal, were passing through Palestine on their way to the Nile Valley, chastising, in the meantime, towns that opposed Assyria. This indicates that Jerusalem kept allegiance to Assyria, playing its part in the Assyrian regional system.

33. Oppenheim, 'Babylonian and Assyrian Historical Texts', pp. 287-88.

34. Kenyon, *Archaeology in the Holy Land*, pp. 287-88; Finkelstein, *The Bible Unearthed*, pp. 260-63.

Five years after Sennacherib's campaign, Hezekiah died and, in 696 BCE, was succeeded by his son, Manasseh. 2 Kings gives an unfavorable account of this king, who abandoned the worship of Yahweh and followed other gods. He was, nevertheless, the strong ruler who restored the kingdom to its former state in the wake of the general destruction caused by Sennacherib's campaign. Manasseh realized, with sound pragmatic sense, that the only way to rebuild Judah was to submit to Assyria once more and seek its protection, joining the state economy to that of Assyria. Within two decades of Manasseh's accession, in a reign lasting around 50 years, the country had been restored to health and had embarked, indeed, on a period of unprecedented prosperity. Exploiting the destruction of its western neighbor, Lachish, Jerusalem now held complete control over trade in the Shephelah and the Philistine plain. Moreover, Jerusalem expanded its boundaries westward, to cover a large part of the Shephelah and eastward, to cover the whole area on the Dead Sea shore, beginning with Jericho. As Jerusalem absorbed large numbers of immigrants from the Shephelah, following Sennacherib's campaign, its population increased notably. The population of Judean agricultural areas increased likewise, leading to a rise in production as agricultural villages spread over the arid eastern and southern areas, which, in the eighth century BCE, had had no permanent agricultural settlements. The Assyrian regional economic system was largely founded on the oil production and trade, and on control of trade with the Arabian Peninsula. In both of these fields, Jerusalem played an important role, both to its own advantage and that of Assyria. It appears that the caravan stations on the route through Sinai up to Judah were placed under the direct supervision of the Jerusalem court. A large proportion of Arabian goods flowed into Jerusalem, to be re-exported to other regions. The conspicuous presence of Arab merchants is indicated by south Arabian inscriptions found in several sites throughout Judah. In Jerusalem, three ostraca with south Arabian script, and a typical seventh-century seal that seems to carry a south Arabian name were uncovered.[35]

The reign of Manasseh marks the climax of Judah's monarchic history. It seems that the Deuteronomistic History of King Solomon's reign was drawn up with Manasseh's reign in mind. The visit of the queen of Sheba to Solomon and the grandeur she saw of his court and palaces, can only be related to the situation of the capital during the later decades of king Manasseh's reign. The cultural and economic contacts with Arabia were as

35. Finkelstein, *The Bible Unearthed*, pp. 267-70.

never before. It is possible that a cordial visit from one of the queens of north Arabia to the court of Manasseh is behind the fictive story of queen of Sheba. Female rulers of Arabian tribes were documented in Assyrian texts from Tiglath-pileser III to Ashurbanipal. So we learn from Esarhaddon's chronicles (680–669 BCE) about an Arabian queen called Ishkalatu who was taken hostage to Nineveh after her defeat, and about an Arab princess called Turbua who grew up in the king's palace and was cultivated there before sending her back to rule over her people. From Ashurbanipal's chronicles (668–633 BCE) we learn, as well, about queen Adia and her husband Uate who were seized in the battle and brought to the king. From the older records of Tiglath-pileser III (744–727 BCE) we learn about queen Zebibi who paid tribute to Assyrian, and about queen Samsi who fled like a wild donkey-mare after her defeat.[36]

Manasseh was succeeded after his death by his son Amon, who died two years later. He was succeeded by his son, Josiah, who, just eight years old at his accession, enjoyed a long reign (639–608 BCE). His reign was contemporaneous with the stormy period that saw the end of Assyria and the succession of the Chaldean ruling dynasty in Babylon, which inherited the Assyrian possessions west of the Euphrates. There followed a Babylonian–Egyptian tussle over the Assyrian legacy. The part played in this by Jerusalem led to its end and to the destruction of the Kingdom of Judah.

After the death of King Ashurbanipal in 633 BCE, the Chaldean Nabopolassar proclaimed himself king over Babylon, independent of Assyria. He concluded a pact with the Persian kingdom of Media, and their two armies, marching from the south and east, attacking the towns of the Assyrian triangle—Nineveh, Nimrod and Ashur—which fell one after the other between 614 and 612 BCE. The last Assyrian king, Ashur-uballit, withdrew beyond the river Tigris and set up temporary headquarters in Haran, in northern Syria, from where he sent to Pharaoh Neco of Egypt asking for help. Egypt had become independent from Assyria towards the end of Ashurbanipal's reign, and now began to dream of regaining control over southern Syria. Neco gave the Assyrians an immediately favorable response, for he preferred to keep the ailing Assyrian state alive rather than see a young empire entertain designs on regaining Assyrian possessions in Egypt.

In 609 BCE, Neco marched up to the Euphrates region to ease Babylonian pressure on the Assyrian king in Haran. At that time, Josiah, failing to

36. For these texts, see Oppenheim, 'Babylonian and Assyrian Historical Texts', pp. 267-301.

realize the full extent of Babylon's power, thought he would be able to fill up any vacuum created by the absence of Assyria from the region. Therefore, as noted in 2 Kgs 23.30 (though without any explanation as to why Josiah should have taken such a step), he decided to intercept Neco and waited for him in the Jezreel Valley near Megiddo. Neco strove vainly to convince Josiah that he had no intention of attacking Jerusalem, and that the interception was therefore unnecessary. Disguised in a soldier's uniform (as was the habit of some kings at this time), Josiah joined battle, and his army was swiftly defeated. Moreover, Josiah himself, seriously wounded, was taken to Jerusalem, where he died.

Josiah reaped the fruits of the seventh-century BCE boom. He inherited from his father a rich, stable kingdom and a vast wealth accumulated by the ruling classes from managing Assyrian interests in the region, along with other forms of wealth accumulated by the priests in the Jerusalem Temple. Unlike his father Amon and his grandfather Manasseh, Josiah did what was right in the sight of the Lord, and followed in the steps of David. As the editor of 2 Kgs 23.25, put it: 'Before him there was no king like him, who turned to the Lord with all his heart, with all his soul, and with all his might, according to all the law of Moses; nor did any like him arise after him'. The editor of 1 Kings had described King Solomon in a similar fashion, as we read in 1 Kgs 3.12: 'so that there shall not be any among the kings like unto thee all the days'. Josiah led the most extensive religious reform after that of Hezekiah. He removed all symbols of foreign worship from the Temple of the Lord, cleared it of the priests who worshipped idols, pulled down the high places facing Jerusalem, built by Solomon for Asherah and other Canaanite deities, drove the priests from the high places and killed them in all the lands of Judah.

The narrative in 2 Kings says little about the outcome of Neco's campaign. On the basis of fragmentary information from Babylonian annals, we learn that Nebuchadnezzar, who inherited the Babylonian throne, had defeated Neco, near Carchemish on the Euphrates, around 605 BCE. Neco then withdrew, setting up temporary headquarters for himself at Riblah (west of present-day Homs, toward Harmel). From there he began to act as ruler over central and southern Syria, and reorganized the political situation there. Hence the editor of 2 Kgs 23.31-35, tells us that Neco sent his forces to Jerusalem, arrested King Jehoahaz, son of Josiah, took him captive to Riblah, and, in his place, set up his brother Jehoiakim, who promised allegiance and payment of tribute to Egypt.

However, after winning control over the Euphrates region, Nebuchad-nezzar decided to put an end to Egyptian ambitions in southern Syria. He led a campaign against Neco, forced him to retreat, and pursued him to the Egyptian frontiers. On his way back, he made a stop in Jerusalem, Egypt's ally, arrested its King Jehoiakim and took him captive to Babylon. Then he appointed the king's son, Jehoiachin, in his place, the latter having promised allegiance to Babylon. But the new king, who had inherited the allegiance to Egypt from his father, was himself soon to rebel against Babylon. In consequence, Nebuchadnezzar led a new campaign against southern Syria and the king he himself had appointed. In this connection, we read, in 2 Kgs 24.10-17, how Nebuchadnezzar besieged Jerusalem and conquered it (around 597 BCE). He arrested its king and took him captive to Babylon, along with 10,000 captives from among the people of Jeru-salem. He looted the treasures of the temple and the king's house. He then appointed Zedekiah, the uncle of the deposed king, in the latter's place. The Babylonian annals contain a brief text, without details, to the follow-ing effect: 'Year 7, month Kislino: The king of Akkad moved his army into Hatti land, laid siege to the city of Judah and the king took the city on the second day of the month Addaru. He appointed it a new king of his liking, took heavy booty from it and brought it into Babylon.'[37]

Zedekiah failed to learn his lesson from Nebuchadnezzar's campaign against Jerusalem and its consequences. As soon as the Assyrian armies had left the region, he began sending envoys to the kings of Phoenicia and Transjordan in an attempt to form a new coalition. It appears, so we gather from Isa. 27.3, that the kings of Adom, Moab, Ammon, Sidon and Tyre, or their representatives, had met in Jerusalem, at the invitation of King Zedekiah. Such meetings were encouraged by Egypt. After Nebuchad-nezzar's final campaign against Jerusalem, Pharaoh Psametichus, so we learn from an Egyptian papyrus, made a peaceful military tour, visiting a number of Palestinian and Phoenician kingdoms with a view to gaining their support.[38]

The Babylonian reaction was prompt and decisive. Egyptian promises quickly evaporated as a new Babylonian campaign was initiated against a number of Palestinian kingdoms, including Jerusalem. Nebuchadnezzar laid siege to the city, then returned to his headquarters in Riblah to manage

37. A.L. Oppenheim, 'Babylonian and Assyrian Historical Texts', in *ANET*, pp. 555-67 (504).

38. S.H. Horn, 'The Divided Monarchy', in Shanks (ed.), *Ancient Israel*, pp. 109-49 (147).

his other punitive campaigns. After a siege of two years, as we are told by the editor of 2 Kings 25, the Chaldean army took the city, burnt it down completely, and took its people captive to Babylon, leaving only the poor of the land. Zedekiah was taken to Nebuchadnezzar in Riblah and there, after his family had been put to death in front of him, his eyes were gouged out before he was finally sent captive to Babylon. By 587 BCE, therefore, the Kingdom of Judah had disappeared forever from the political map of the ancient Near East, being now reduced to a poor Babylonian province and a backward rural region. For the next three centuries, no source other than the Bible mentions the city or what was happening in the Palestinian highlands in general. We have no Babylonian text dealing with the last campaign against Jerusalem and its destruction. Excavations have, however, found traces of destruction and conflagration almost everywhere within the city walls of Jerusalem, that go back to the beginnings of the sixth century BCE. There are also signs of destruction in a number of major sites in Judah and no signs of habitation are found in those parts for about a century.[39]

Following this detailed survey of political life in Jerusalem, we may note that the biblical editor, despite his ignorance of events in the local and international spheres during the lifetime of the Kingdom of Judah, has given us a number of chronicles which, in general and sometimes in detail, agree with outside sources, starting with the age of King Ahaz, in the late eighth century BCE, and continuing up to the end of the seventh and the early sixth century BCE. The reason for this, as I see it, is the spread of writing for the first time in the southern highlands and the rise of a bureaucratic sector in Jerusalem that took to recording regular annals of kings, following the example of the earlier Samarian annals, as well as the Phoenician and the Assyrian annals. The biblical editors, so often, refer to such records of Samaria and Judah and call them the book of Chronicles of the Kings of Judah and the book of Chronicles of the Kings of Israel. Some modern scholars doubt the existence of these two sources used by the biblical editors. I see no reason, however, for any such doubt, nor do I see why the kings of Samaria and Jerusalem should not have ordered such a record of events in their reign, following, in the first place, the example of their Phoenician neighbours, who had such records available to them. I do doubt, though, whether these two sources ever actually reached the biblical editors in their original versions. It is, I think, more likely that

39. Kenyon, *Digging Up Jerusalem*, pp. 166-72; Finkelstein, *The Bible Unearthed*, pp. 294-95.

what reached them were fragments, copied at several removes from the original text. Even so, the biblical editor was eclectic in his choice of events taken from those fragments, to say nothing of the distortions he introduced to suit the ideological perspective of Jerusalem priests in the Persian age, who were formulating an account of the origins of the Jerusalem community, and of the biblical religious belief now forming, for the first time, in the small region the Persians called 'Yehud', after the ancient name of Judah. This distortion is seen primarily in theological matters.

Until recently, scholars have taken as authentic the biblical editor's description of religious life in Jerusalem and the Kingdom of Judah. We are told how the people of Judah followed the orthodox creed set out in the Torah, and how they had no sooner deviated from this creed than they returned to it, asking the God of Israel for pardon and forgiveness. However, excavation carried out in the Palestinian highlands over the past two decades has provided us with a wealth of archaeological information demonstrating that the people of Jerusalem and the rest of Judah—like the people of Samaria—knew nothing of the Pentateuch, had not heard of the revelation to Moses on Mt Sinai, and did not hold to a biblical creed that was in fact formulated long after the destruction of Jerusalem. We do not indeed have a single piece of archaeological evidence or one inscription to indicate that the people of Judah had any knowledge of such a creed. The idolatry of the people was not a departure from their earlier monotheism. It was, instead, the way the people had worshipped for hundreds of years.

Historians of religion, cannot explore the religious belief of a particular culture, separated from us in time, if the people of that culture have left no indication of their beliefs and rites, such as places of worship, images of gods, cult objects, religious artifacts, and so on. Where relevant material remains are supported by written evidence from the same period, then the historian of religion will have all the direct evidence enabling him to form a general picture of that religious belief. In fact, all the direct evidence left us by the people of Judah shows the religion of the kingdom, on both the official and popular levels, to have been a natural continuation of the religion of Canaan in Iron Age I and earlier, exactly as was the case with religion in Samaria: in both regions the gods worshipped were the traditional Canaanite gods. All the excavated religious centers, small or large, were consecrated to the fertility worship that had deep roots in the region from the earliest times. The god Yahweh, who was chosen by the priests of Jerusalem to be worshipped alone in the Second Temple period, was just one of the ancient gods of Palestine, and an eminent member of the

Judahite pantheon, worshiped together with other deities, such as Baal, Asherah, and the Host of Heaven. He was also the husband of the goddess Asherah, who is very well known to us from Canaanite texts, especially the Ugaritic texts.

The first thing confronting us, in connection with the Palestinian religious scene, is the thousands of female figurines, called by archaeologists pillar figurines, where the artist shows the head, torso, and naked breasts only. Such statuettes have been found in almost all excavation sites, whether religious centers or normal places of residence. In Jerusalem and the rest of Judah, the pieces found number more than 3000 to date, all of them belonging to the age of the Kingdom of Judah between the eighth and seventh centuries BCE. There is no doubt that these pillar figurines represent the goddess Asherah and that they were used in special rites to activate the powers of fertility governed by the goddess. The discovery of ever more of these archaeological finds has led conservative archaeologists (who were, until recently, fostering the viewpoint of the biblical editors on the question of the religion of the people of Judah) to reconsider the matter and take the worship of the goddess Asherah more seriously than before. The conservative archaeologist William Dever, says:

> We do not know for sure what the belief in the god Yahweh meant for the average Israelite. Although the biblical text tells us that most Israelites worshipped Yahweh alone, we know that this is not true... The discoveries of the last fifteen years have given us a great deal of information about the worship of the ancient Israelites. It seems that we have to take the worship of the goddess Asherah more seriously than ever before.[40]

The biblical editors tell us nothing about these statuettes, nor do they give them any special name. They do, though, describe the worship of the goddess Asherah among the people of Samaria and Judah, in three manifestations, whether in the family shrines or in major religious centers. In the first form, the goddess Asherah was present through her images and statues displayed in temples and homes. The mother of King Asa of Jerusalem had a statue of Asherah displayed in her home shrine (1 Kgs 15.13). King Manasseh had a statue of Asherah displayed in the temple of Jerusalem (2 Kgs 21.7). In the second form, asherah was a green tree planted near the altar, especially in the high places where rituals were conducted in

---

40. An extract from '*BARev* Interviews, William Dever', *BARev* (September–October 1996), pp. 36-37. Raphael Patai was the first to identify the pillar figurines with Asherah. See R. Patai, *The Hebrew Goddess* (New York: Ktav, 1967 [2nd edn = Detroit: Wayne State University Press, 1990]).

the open air (Deut. 16.21; Judg. 6.25). In the third form, asherah was a cut tree trunk, displayed in the temple near the altar. Asherah (the plural form being asherim) is mentioned as a cut tree trunk in 18 different places in the Old Testament.

We have substantial evidence now to believe that Yahweh, the principal god of monarchic Judah and Israel, had a consort. Our main evidence comes from two archaeological sites where several inscriptions suggest quite explicitly that Yahweh had a female consort. In Khirbet el-Qom, a short distance east of Hebron, a tomb cut in the rock has recently been discovered, where the inscription on the wall reads: 'May you be blessed by the god Yahweh and his Asherah'. At the site of Kuntillet 'Ajrud, north of Sinai, a trade caravan station has been discovered where a small shrine contains storage jars with inscriptions mentioning the gods El, Baal and Yahweh. Other inscriptions mention Yahweh and his wife Asherah, as we read: 'May you be blessed by Yahweh the god of Samaria and his Asherah'. Also: 'May you be blessed by Yahweh, the god of Temen and may you be blessed by Yahweh and his Asherah. May Yahweh bless and protect you and stand by you.' These inscriptions have been dated back to the eighth century BCE.[41]

Under the inscription mentioning the god of Samaria, there are three figures. The two in front are men, with huge male organs, and one of these is certainly Yahweh, for the second line of the inscription merges with the tip of his head cover, which is in the shape of a lotus flower. The third, at the back, is that of a woman sitting on a chair, playing a lyre. Undoubtedly this is Asherah, since the back of the jar portrays a tree borne by a lion, with two pairs of goats on the two sides of the tree, attempting to nibble its leaves. This stylized sacred tree was a standard motif in most cultures of the ancient Near East, and symbolizes the fertility goddess by her different names: Ishtar, Anat or Asherah.

A good deal of information concerning the religious life and beliefs of Judah in the late monarchic period and early post-exilic Period, comes

41. For these inscriptions and the current debate concerning them, see the follow-ing articles: Z. Meshel, 'Did Yahweh have a Consort?', *BARev* (March–April 1979), pp. 53-61; A. Lemaire, 'Who or What was Yahweh's Asherah?', *BARev* (November–December 1984), pp. 42-51; R. Hestrin, 'Understanding Asherah', *BARev* (September–October 1991), pp. 50-59; J.G. Taylor, 'Was Yahweh Worshipped as the Sun?', *BARev* (May–June 1994), pp. 53-61; E. Stern, 'Pagan Yahwism', *BARev* (May–June 2001), pp. 21-37; U. Anver, 'Sacred Stones in the Dessert', *BARev* (May–June 2001), pp. 31-41.

from the papyri-archival documents found in the Elephantine Island in upper Egypt. These documents belong to a Judean community who lived there from early fifth century to early fourth century BCE, and they show clearly that the cult of Yahweh (who is called here Yaho) is a syncretistic mixture of Yahwism and other Canaanite cults of Anat-Yaho, Eshem, Eshem-Bethel, Herem-Bethel and Anat-Bethel. This is because the names of these deities appear in Juridical oaths and salutations used in the Elephantine documents.

From these documents we know as well, that there were two main temples in the Island, one for the god Yahweh and another for the Egyptian god Khnub. The names of these deities appear in texts invoking blessing, as we read in a letter: 'To my lord Micaiah, from your servant Geddel, I send you welfare and life, I bless you by Yaho and Khnub'. But the temple of Yaho was destroyed, as we know from a correspondence exchanged around 410 BCE between Yedonia, the head of the Elephantine community on the one hand, and the two governors of Jerusalem and Samaria on the other. Yedonia was asking for their help to rebuild Yaho's temple, and their response was positive. They did not hesitate to offer him whatever they could.[42]

All this indicates that a century after the returned exiles rebuilt their second temple in Jerusalem, the worship of Yahweh alone was not yet deeply rooted in Judah. The Elephantines did not take offence at finding their syncretistic faith parallel to that of their Judean brothers, nor the Judeans refrained from giving help to rebuild the temple of Yaho being one of the several gods in the Elephantine Pantheon.

The religious centers discovered so far in monarchic Judah, confirm what the textual evidence conveys about the syncretistic faith of the Judeans. All of these centers are consecrated to the traditional Palestinian gods and show an unbroken continuity of Canaanite religious traditions. Some of these centers were discovered in southern Judah between Arad and Beer-sheba. But the most interesting Canaanite religious center was discovered in monarchic Jerusalem itself, during Kathleen Kenyon's excavations of 1961–67, and the excavator ascribed it to some time between the mid-eighth century and the early seventh century BCE. This center lies about 300 m of the boundary of the supposed Jerusalem temple outside the contemporary walls. Two main features led the excavator to interpret the building as a fertility shrine: the two standing stones of Mazzeboth,

42. For the Elephantine texts, see H.L. Ginsberg, 'Aramaic Letters', in *ANET*, pp. 490-94.

symbol of Canaanite fertility deity, and a large cave served the function of *favissa*, containing a large deposit of objects offered in the sanctuary which would not thereafter be returned to profane use. Among these objects there are around 400 human and animal figurines. Most of the human figurines were female of the fertility goddess type. Large number of the animal figurines represent horses with a disk on the forehead, suggesting possible association with the horses of the sun mentioned in 2 Kgs 23.11.[43] Some scholars, however, believe that in both Israel and Judah Yahweh was symbolically represented by the sun.[44]

Away from these main religious centers, sacrifices were offered at shrines within domestic compounds, at family tombs, and at open altars throughout the countryside. The archaeological finds of clay figurines, incense altars, libation vessels, and offering stands throughout monarchic Judah suggest that the practice of religion was highly varied, geographically decentralized and certainly not restricted to the worship of Yahweh in the temple of Jerusalem, about which there is no archaeological evidence. The existence of high places and other forms of ancestral- and household-god worship was not apostasy from an earlier, purer faith, but was part of the timeless tradition of the hill country.[45]

The question now arising is: Did Jerusalem have a large temple like the one described in 1 Kings and ascribed to King Solomon, and was it situated in the area called the Temple Mount where the Haram es-Sharif now stands? We have no archaeological evidence whatsoever that such a temple was erected during the time of monarchic Judah or prior to it. The non-Islamic remains on the Temple Mount (such as the Hamam platform and the Wailing Wall of the Jews) are relics from King Herod's temple which was built in the late first century BCE. Nothing earlier have survived. It has become certain now that King Solomon's temple belongs to the fictive imagination of the biblical editors, since from the tenth century BCE there is no archaeological evidence of a town in Jerusalem, let alone a big regional capital. It is almost certain, too, that such a temple could not have been built in the ninth century BCE; for at that time Jerusalem was a small administrative center with public buildings but only a small residential quarter, and its chieftains had not attained sufficient wealth of sufficient power to enable them to undertake such a costly architectural project.

---

43. Kenyon, *Archaeology in the Holy Land*, pp. 133-43.
44. Taylor, 'Was Yahweh Worshipped as the Sun?'.
45. Finkelstein, *The Bible Unearthed*, pp. 241-42.

Was the temple, then, built at some time during the transitional period, between the eighth and seventh centuries BCE, the period in which Jerusalem was turned into a significant capital? Although there are no archaeological indications at all of the existence of a Jerusalem temple in the age of the Kingdom of Judah, we cannot simply deny its existence on negative evidence alone. A large regional capital such as Jerusalem in the seventh century BCE would certainly have needed a temple like the one described in 1 Kings and ascribed to King Solomon. The kings of Jerusalem were certainly then capable of financing a project of this scale. Accordingly, I tend to believe that the Jerusalem temple was built in stages, over a period extending from the reign of King Ahaz, in the latter years of the eighth century BCE, until the reign of King Manasseh, which continued up to the middle of the seventh century BCE. Ahaz would have initiated the building of a modest temple, which was subsequently enlarged in two stages: one in the time of Hezekiah, and the other in the time of Manasseh, who would have provided the building with all the grandeur described in 1 Kings. The enlargement process went hand in hand with the economic revolution in Judah and the growing role of Jerusalem as a political, economic and religious center for the whole county.

What is certain, nevertheless, on the basis of the above archaeological evidence about the religious beliefs and practices of the people of monarchic Judah is that the temple of Jerusalem was not consecrated to the worship of the biblical Deity, but rather to the worship of the ancient Palestinian Yahweh and his Asherah, and that other gods were undoubtedly worshiped there alongside them. Moreover, archaeological excavations carried out in Syria during the last 50 years have shown that the builders of Jerusalem temple were following an earlier Syrian temple plan known to the archaeologists now as the Syrian symmetrical temple type, of which more than 20 temples have been discovered so far. Among these are the temples of Alalakh, Ain Dara, Tell Ta'ynat and Hazor.

Conclusion

Jerusalem remained an isolated small country town throughout most of its history. It made no contribution to the beginnings of agricultural settled life, as did Jericho. It was of no importance in the Early Bronze Age, compared with the important towns of Megiddo, Hazor, Beth-shean and Lachish. As far as the archaeological and historical evidence goes, Jerusalem appeared for the first time as a small walled town in the Middle

Bronze Age (1950–1600 BCE), probably around 1800 BCE; but after less then three centuries the site was deserted. In the Late Bronze Age (1600–1200 BCE), judging by the fact that no remains from that period have been found—not even a single sherd of pottery or other small finds indicating human activity—Jerusalem seems to have been a dead city. This archaeological situation persists in Iron Age I (1200–1000 BCE), and the paucity of archaeological evidence continues into the tenth century. Some time between the end of the tenth century and the beginning of the ninth century BCE we have evidence of a small town again on the site, occupied mainly by public buildings but with a small number of inhabitants.

Only towards the end of the eighth century BCE do we have evidence of a real city on the site. Jerusalem became an important regional center and capital of the newly established Kingdom of Judah: At that time only, the name of Jerusalem appeared in the Assyrian records among many states in southern Syria who paid tribute to the Assyrian king.

Judah flourished as an independent state for about a century and half, and gained much power and wealth under the Assyrian protection. The new situation created by the collapse of Assyria and the rise of the new Babylonian Empire encouraged the kings of Jerusalem to get involved in the international politics. But their failed attempt to participate in the game of great powers led the kingdom to its gloomy end. The Babylonians destroyed Jerusalem around 587 BCE, and the Kingdom of Judah vanished from the political scene forever.

Judah was born, flourished, and ended as a Palestinian Canaanite state. Its inhabitants came from other Palestinian lowlands, with a large number coming from the adjacent steppe lands after the gap in occupation caused by the great drought. As far as the archaeological evidence go, this settlement process was slow and took over two centuries. The material culture of those early inhabitants, their language and their religion were Canaanite and they have no connection whatsoever with the biblical tribe of Judah. The history of their kingdom, as well as that of Israel, belongs to the Palestinian history that we have recently become able to write. That history was confiscated by the biblical editors, who, during the Persian period, were creating a story of origins about the community of the Yehud province, and another story of origins about the biblical ideology that was in the making during the same period. But archaeology has begun recently to disengage the real history of Israel and Judah from the biblical narrative—narrative that is moving faster then ever from the realm of histography to the realm of theological literature.

ETHNIC GROUPS IN JERUSALEM

Lester L. Grabbe

'Thus spoke the Lord God to Jerusalem, "Your origins and birth are from the land of the Canaanite; your father was an Amorite and your mother a Hittite".' This statement in Ezek. 16.3 is symbolic of Jerusalem's story. In its long history, Jerusalem—like 'Galilee of the nations' (Isa. 8.23)—was inhabited by many different peoples and ethnic groups. There are enormous gaps in Jerusalem's history, and my discussion here can only be partial: I can talk about only what we know and not about what we do not. Nevertheless, what we do know is interesting and relevant for the issue of ethnicity and the city of Jerusalem.

The aim of this article is the simple one of doing what the title suggests: to investigate the various ethnic groups that have inhabited Jerusalem. The period covered is from the earliest records to the Roman period. A major problem is how to define 'ethnic group'. For purposes of this article, it is not necessary to become entangled in a lengthy discussion of definition. One of the reasons is that we do not have the data to determine ethnicity according to the criteria of any modern definition.[1] All we can go on is the names of peoples found in ancient written sources. It is these that we shall consider here.

The Earliest References to Jerusalem

According to current (incomplete) knowledge, our earliest information on Jerusalem is archaeological, with remains from as early as the Calcolithic Period (fourth millennium BCE) in the form of debris-filled pits. It has been accepted that Jerusalem first appeared in historical records from about the Middle Bronze I period (early twentieth century BCE) in the 'Execration Texts' from Egypt. These texts come from the custom of writing on a

---

1. M.G. Brett (ed.), *Ethnicity and the Bible* (BIS, 19; Leiden: E.J. Brill, 1996), esp. pp. 3-15.

pottery object the names of places and their leaders that one wished to curse and then breaking it in a cursing ceremony. Since Egypt attempted to dominate Palestine all through the second millennium BCE, any opposition would be dealt with by magical as well as military means. This is why various cities of Palestine and their kings occur in the extant Execration Texts. Some of these, from the nineteenth and eighteenth centuries BCE, have the place name *Rwšȝmm*. This has been thought to be the Egyptian way of trying to reproduce the name of Jerusalem which was to the Egyptians a foreign name in a foreign language, being read something like *(U)rushalimum*, which is quite close to the name in the Amarna tablets (see below). However, Na'aman[2] has argued that the first part of the name should be read as *rôš* ('head'), to give a reading something like Rosh-ramem. If so, although Jerusalem was already a walled city in the Middle Bronze II (eighteenth century BCE), as the archaeological remains demonstrate,[3] it was not sufficiently important to be mentioned in the Egyptian texts at this time.

Our first extensive information on Jerusalem comes from the fourteenth century BCE, in the Amarna letters. At this time, Palestine was a part of the Egyptian New Kingdom. Much of the territory was under the control of various Canaanite city-states who were vassals of Egypt. The capital of Egypt under Pharaoh Amenophis IV (Akhenaton) was at Amarna, a city that was abandoned after his death. When the city was excavated in the nineteenth century, among the recovered archives were copies of correspondence between the Egyptian administration and many of these Canaanite kings. These so-called 'Amarna Letters' give us a unique insight into events in Palestine during this period. Among those who wrote letters to the Pharaoh was the king of Jerusalem (*Urusalim*). We have six letters from him,[4] plus a couple of other letters that refer to him (EA 284, 366). In the passages that follow, the term used for the head of the various city-states is usually *hazannu* which normally means 'mayor' or chief administrator of a city; however, it is used here of the petty kings of the city-states. The 'commissioner of the king' was, of course, an Egyptian official who represented the Pharaoh to the local rulers. The king of

---

2. N. Na'aman, 'Canaanite Jerusalem and its Central Hill Country Neighbours in the Second Millennium B.C.E.', *UF* 24 (1992), pp. 275-91 (278-79).

3. M. Steiner, 'The Earliest City Wall of Jerusalem', *IEJ* 38 (1988), pp. 203-204.

4. EA 285-90. The translation used here is from William Moran (*The Amarna Letters* [Baltimore: The Johns Hopkins University Press, 1992]), though his italicized passages are not indicated so as to increase ease of reading.

Jerusalem is called 'Abdi-Ḫeba. Other kings include Suwardata of Gath and Lab'aya of Shechem. One term that appears several times is "Apiru' or 'Ḫapiru'.[5] The word seems originally to mean someone outside the social system or an outcast or a refugee. However, in the Amarna Letters, it always seems to have a pejorative connotation along the lines of 'outlaw' or 'bandit', perhaps because banditry was one of the few ways that those outside the system could survive.

EA 285:

> [And n]ow as for me, may the king [give heed to 'Abdi]-Ḫeba, his servant. [If th]ere are no archers available, may the king, my lord, [sen]d [a commissione]r that he may fetch [the ma]yors to himself… And as for [the garrison] that belongs [to Adday]a, the commissioner of the king, [I] want their house. So may the ki[ng] provide [f]or them, and may he send a mess[enger qu]ickly.

EA 286:

> Say [t]o the king, my lord: Message of 'Abdi-Ḫeba, your servant. I fall at the feet of my lord, the king, 7 times and 7 times. What have I done to the king, my lord? They denounce me: …(I am slandered) before the king, my lord, "Abdi-Ḫeba has rebelled against the king, his lord'. Seeing that, as far as I am concerned, neither my father nor my mother put me in this place, but the strong arm of the king brought me into my father's house, why should I of all people commit a crime against the king, my lord? As truly as the king, my lord, lives, I say to the commissioner of the king, [my] lord, 'Why do you love the 'Apiru but hate the mayors?' Accordingly, I am slandered before the king, my lord. Because I say, 'Lost are the lands of the king, my lord', accordingly I am slandered before the king, my lord, May the king, my lord, know that (though) the king, my lord, stationed a garrison (here), Enḫamu has taken i[t al]l away… [Now], O king, my lord, [there is n]o garrison, [and so] may the king provide for his land. May the king [pro]vide for his land! All the [la]nds of the king, my lord, have deserted. Ili-Milku has caused the loss of all the land of the king, and so may the king, my lord, provide for his land. For my part, I say, 'I would go in to the king, my lord, and visit the king, my lord'. But the war against me is severe, and so I am not able to go to the king, my lord. And may it seem good in the sight of the king, [and] may he send a garrison so I may go in and visit the king, my lord. In truth, the king, my lord, lives: whenever the commissioners have come out, I would say (to them), 'Lost are the lands of the king', but they did not listen to me. Lost are all the mayors; there is not a mayor remaining to the king, my lord. May the king turn his attention to the

---

5. N.P. Lemche, 'Habiru, Hapiru', in *ABD*, III, pp. 6-10.

archers so that archers of the king, my lord, come forth. The king has no lands. (That) 'Apiru has plundered all the lands of the king. If there are archers this year, the lands of the king, my lord, will remain. But if there are no archers, lost are the lands of the king, my lord. [T]o the scribe of the king, my lord: Message of 'Abdi-Ḥeba, your [ser]vant. Present eloquent words to the king, my lord. Lost are all the lands of the king, my lord.

EA 287:

May the [kin]g know (that) all the lands are [at] peace (with one another), but I am at war. May the king provide for his land. Consider the lands of Gazru, Ašqaluna, and L[akis]i. They have given them food, oil, and any other requirement. So may the king provide for archers and the mayors will belong to the king, my lord. But if there are no archers, then the ki[ng] will have neither lands nor mayors. Consider Jerusalem! This neither my father nor m[y] mother gave to me. The [str]ong hand:…(arm) [of the king] gave it to me. Consider the deed! This is the deed of Milkilu and the deed of the sons of Lab'ayu, who have given the land of the king <to> the 'Apiru. Consider, O king, my lord! I am in the right! With regard to the Kašites, may the king make inquiry of the commissioners. Though the house is well fortified, they attempted a very serious crime. They [t]ook their tools, and I had to seek shelter by a support for the roof: …A[nd so i]f he is going to send [troop]s into [Jerusalem], let them come with [a garrison for] (regular) service. May the king provide for them; [all] of the land might be in dire straits on their account. May the king inquire about the[m. Let there be] much food, much oil, much clothing, until Pauru, the commissioner of the king, comes up to Jerusalem. Gone is Addaya together with the garrison of soldiers [that] the king [pro]vided. May the king know (that) Addaya [sa]id to me, '[Beh]old, he has dismissed me'. Do not abandon it, [and] send this [year] a garrison, and send right here the commissioner of the king.

EA 288:

It is, therefore, impious what they have done to me. Behold, I am not a mayor; I am a soldier of the king, my lord. Behold, I am a friend of the king and a tribute-bearer of the king. It was neither my father nor my mother, but the strong arm of the king that [p]laced me in the house of [my] fath[er]… I gave over [to his char]ge 10 slaves. Šuta, the commissioner of the king, ca[me t]o me; I gave over to Šuta's charge 21 girls, [8]0 prisoners, as a gift for the king, my lord. May the king give thought to his land; the land of the king is lost. All of it has attacked me. I am at war as far as the land of Šeru and as far as Ginti-kirmil. All the majors are at peace, but I am at war. I am treated like an 'Apiru, and I do not visit the king, my lord, since I am at war. I am situated like a ship in the midst of the sea. The strong hand (arm) of the king took the land of Naḥrima and the land of Kasi, but now the

'Apiru have taken the very cities of the king. Not a single major remains to the king, my lord; all are lost. Behold, Turbazu was slain in the city gate of Silu. The king did nothing. Behold, servants who were joined to the 'Api[r]u smote Zimredda of Lakisu, and Yaptiḫ-Hadda was slain in the city gate of Silu. The king did nothing. [Wh]y has he not called them to account? May the king [pro]vide for [his land] and may he [se]e to it tha[t] archers [come ou]t to h[is] land. If there are no archers this year, all the lands of the king, my lord, are lost. They have not reported to the king that the lands of the king, my lord, are lost and all the mayors lost. If there are no archers this year, may the king send a commissioner to fetch me, me along with my brothers, and then we will die near the king, our lord.

EA 289:

Milkilu does not break away from the sons of Lab'ayu and from the sons of Arsawa, as they desire the land of the king for themselves. As for a mayor who does such a deed, why does the king not <c>all him to account? Such was the deed that Milkilu and Tagi did: they took Rubutu. And now as for Jerusalem, if this land belongs to the king, why is it <not> of concern to the king like Ḫazzatu? Ginti-kirmil belongs to Tagi, and men of Gintu are the garrison in Bitsanu. Are we to act like Lab'ayu when he was giving the land of Šakmu to the Ḫapiru? Milkilu has written to Tagi and the sons <of Lab'ayu>, 'Be the both of you a protection. Grant all their demands to the men of Qiltu, and let us isolate Jerusalem'. Addaya has taken the garrison that you sent in the charge of Haya, the son of Miyare; he has stationed it in his own house in Ḫazzatu and has sent 20 men to Egypt. May the king, my lord, know (that) no garrison of the king is with me. Accordingly, as truly as the king lives, his *irpi*-official, Pu'uru, has left me and is in Ḫazzatu. (May the king call (this) to mind when he arrives.) And so may the king send 50 men as a garrison to protect the land. The entire land of the king has deser[ted]. Send Ye'eh'enḫamu that he may know about the land of the king, [my lord].

EA 290:

Here is the deed against the land that Milkilu and Šuardatu did: against the land of the king, my lord, they ordered troops from Gazru, troops from Gimtu, and troops from Qiltu. They seized Rubutu. The land of the king deserted to the Ḫapiru. And now, besides this, a town belonging to Jerusalem, Bit-^{d}NIN.URTA by name, a city of the king, has gone over to the side of the men of Qiltu. May the king give heed to 'Abdi-Ḫeba, your servant, and send archers to restore the land of the king to the king. If there are no archers, the land of the king will desert to the Ḫapiru. This deed against the land was [a]t the order of Milki[lu and a]t the order of [Šuard]atu, [together w]ith Gint[i]. So may the king provide for [his] land.

Much could be said about these letters in another context, but this is outside the present concern. 'Abdi-Ḥeba was one of the many kings of the Canaanite city-states. We need to keep in mind that only 'Abdi-Ḥeba's side of the story is given in his letters. His claims to loyalty and being a victim of treacherous neighbors need to be considered alongside other letters, letters from those very same neighbors who accuse him of treachery, aggression, and disloyalty toward the Pharaoh!

EA 280:

> Mes[sage] of Šuwardata, [yo]ur servant, the dirt at your feet… The king, my lord, permitted me to wage war against Qeltu… Why did 'Abdi-Ḥe[b]a write to the men of Qeltu, '[Ac]cept silver and follow me'? Moreover, may the king, my lord, conduct an inquiry. If I took a man, or a single ox, or an ass, from him, then he is in the right! Moreover, Lab'ayu, who used to take our towns, is dead, but now [an]other Lab'ayu is 'Abdi-Ḥeba, and he seizes our town.

Shechem was one of the more powerful kingdoms in Canaan at this time, whereas Jerusalem was a rather smaller, minor state.[6] When Shechem's ruler Lab'ayu died, 'Abdi-Ḥeba evidently took the opportunity to try to expand his territory to the west. This was at the expense of the kingdom of Gath whose ruler was Šuwardata. This is why the latter complains to the Egyptian king that 'Abdi-Ḥeba had become another Lab'ayu throwing his weight around. However, in the political maneuverings and shifting alliances that one expects of the region at this time, Šuwardata and 'Abdi-Ḥeba were able to make common cause when they were both threatened by ''Apiru':

EA 366 (letter from Šuwardata):

> May the king, my lord, be informed that the 'Apiru that rose up…against the lands, the god of the king, my lord, gave to me, and I smote him. And may the king, my lord, be informed that all my brothers have abandoned me. Only 'Abdi-Ḥeba and I have been at war with (that) 'Apiru. Surata, the ruler of Akka, and Endaruta, the ruler of Akšapa, (these) two also have come to my aid…with 50 chariots, and now they are on my side in the war.

In the end, we do not know what happened to 'Abdi-Ḥeba, but it is in his letters that Jerusalem first appears in history. The name 'Abdi-Ḥeba means 'servant of (the Hurrian) goddess Ḥeba'; however, as far as we can tell he was a native Canaanite. As will be noted in the next section, later

---

6. Na'aman, 'Canaanite Jerusalem', pp. 288-89.

traditions speak of a number of different Canaanite tribes. To what extent these traditions reflect reality will be discussed, but it is to be expected that there were various local groups in an area the size of Canaan. But we have no further information about 'Abdi-Ḥeba.

Traditions in the Hebrew Bible

The Hebrew Bible (or Old Testament) contains many traditions whose origins and value have been much debated by scholars over the past two hundred years and more. It was widely believed that the Pentateuch was made up of four sources, dating from about the eighth to fifth centuries BCE, which were edited together about the fifth century BCE. Alongside this was the 'Deuteronomistic History', the biblical books of Joshua to 2 Kings. The Deuteronomistic History was believed to be made up of a variety of traditions, some early and some late. But large sections of the history were written by the final compilers, the Deuteronomistic school. Despite some debate and even dissenting opinion,[7] this basic understanding is still widely held in scholarship.

If this analysis is correct, the contents of the biblical books of Genesis to 2 Kings contain a mixture of traditions ranging from perhaps the ninth century BCE to the exile (sixth century BCE) and even to the fifth or even fourth century BCE. The earliest traditions provide an insight into the situation of their time, but significant sections of the text were probably written in the Persian period, long after the events allegedly being described. It is not always easy to know how to sort out or evaluate the various sorts of material in the text. We can catalogue the different textual statements without always knowing what to make of them, as we shall see. With regard to the subject of the present paper, the different traditions in the text suggest that a number of different peoples (tribes, ethnic groups, or whatever one wishes to call them) have inhabited Jerusalem in the three millennia for which we have information on the city.

The first mention of Jerusalem in the Bible seems to be in Genesis 14. According to the story here, a coalition of five kings had raided the area and taken Abraham's nephew Lot captive. Abraham assembled a small army of his servants and attacked the drunken camp of the invaders, freeing his own relatives and taking much booty. Afterward, Abraham

---

7. E.g. N. Whybray, *The Making of the Pentateuch: A Methodological Study* (JSOTSup, 53; Sheffield: JSOT Press, 1987).

paid tithes to 'the king of Salem', a figure named Melchizedek, who appears in the narrative without an introduction except for the statement that he was 'priest of El Elyon' (Gen. 14.18). Genesis 14 has been variously dated, with some giving it a quite early dating, including the argument that El Elyon represents an early form of a Canaanite divine name;[8] others, however, argue that it is late.[9] Assuming there are any historical data in the story, it might suggest memory of a time when Jerusalem was a Canaanite city-state and was ruled by a priest-king, a figure perhaps like 'Abdi-Ḫeba of the Amarna letters.

The Bible gives a story of how the sons of Jacob married, had children, and their descendents multiplied in Egypt until they left in the exodus as a great multitude and eventually conquered the land of Canaan in a period of only five years, divided up the land and settled down as a nation with God as its king. It is an appealing and fascinating story, but recent scholarship has called the whole scenario into question. Some sources have pointed to another, rather different reconstruction of how Israel became a nation: the two sources of archaeology and some other biblical traditions, especially those in the book of Judges, give another story.

First, rather than coming about by the immigration of an outside group into the country, the group called Israel most likely coalesced from the indigenous peoples in Palestine. Exactly how this came about is much debated, but the fact that the Israelites were Canaanites who formed a new grouping in the central hill country is now widely accepted. If there was an exodus from Egypt, it was of a small group. But there was no 'conquest' as in the book of Joshua, and Israelite control of the entire country took many centuries, if it ever occurred at all. This makes evaluation of the statements in the text a complicated matter. Therefore, we must first look at what the text says and only then discuss the implications in light of recent study.

In the tradition of the Israelite conquest in the book of Joshua, the king of Jerusalem named, Adoni-zedek, organized a coalition of five 'Amorite' kings that fought against the Israelites and was defeated (Josh. 10). Nevertheless, Josh. 15.63 states that the sons of Judah were not able to drive out the Jebusites from Jerusalem but that the Judahites and Jebusites

---

8. H.J. Zobel, '*'elyôn*', in *TDOT*, XI, pp. 121-39.

9. For the history of interpretation, see C. Westermann, *Genesis 12–36: A Commentary* (trans. J.J. Scullion; Continental Commentaries; Minneapolis: Fortress Press, 1985), pp. 189-90.

lived side by side in the city. In a parallel account, Judg. 1.4-8 speaks of the defeat of the 'Canaanites and Perizzites' and the capture of their leader Adoni-bezek. The text does not state Adoni-bezek's city, but he is brought to Jerusalem where he dies, and Jerusalem is captured. A few verses later, however, it is stated that the Benjaminites were not able to drive out the Jebusites who lived in Jerusalem but they continued to live in the city in the territory of Benjamin (Judg. 1.21). The city was also called Jebus (Judg. 19.10; cf. Josh. 18.28).

After David was anointed king in Hebron, he went up against Jerusalem (2 Sam. 5.6-9). The Jebusites were said to be the inhabitants of the territory. David took the city and renamed it the 'City of David'. However, a later story suggests that some of the Jebusites continued to live in the city. 2 Samuel 24.16-25 is part of an incident in which a plague was devastating Israel because of David's sin. In order to stay the plague, David was told to set up an altar on the threshing floor of 'Araunah (*hā'ᵃrawnâ*) the Jebusite', which he purchased. The suggestion is that it was this threshing floor which later became the site of the temple built by Solomon. The word 'Araunah' is curious. It does not look like a typical Hebrew name, and in part of the episode the word occurs with the article which is not normal with names. It has been explained as a Hittite word meaning 'aristocrat' or a Hurrian word meaning 'lord'. Either explanation suggests that the owner of the threshing floor was the (former?) king or lord of the city, which is also one way of reading the Hebrew text of 2 Sam. 24.23: 'Araunah the king gives all to the king (David)'.

A further possible indication of Jerusalem's pre-Israelite history is the high priest Zadok. He suddenly appears without introduction, but his name may be connected with the deity Ṣedeq who seems to have been a deity associated with Jerusalem. It was once widely accepted that Zadok was a priest of the pre-Israelite cult of Jerusalem.[10] Arguments have been advanced against this interpretation, along with an attempt to demonstrate that Zadok was an Aaronic priest;[11] however, this draws on the picture of Zadok in 1 Chronicles which itself is likely an effort to make Zadok 'orthodox'. Although one cannot be certain, there are a number of factors pointing to the thesis that one of the measures taken by David to consolidate

10. H.H. Rowley, 'Zadok and Nehushtan', *JBL* 58 (1939), pp. 113-41; C.E. Hauer, 'Who Was Zadok?', *JBL* 82 (1963), pp. 89-94.

11. F.M. Cross, Jr, *Canaanite Myth and Hebrew Epic* (Cambridge, MA: Harvard University Press, 1973), pp. 195-215.

his position over the Jerusalem was to make an existing Jebusite priest (Zadok) one of his priests.[12]

One other story indicates the presence of other ethnic groups in Jerusalem. This is the well-known story of David and Bathsheba (2 Sam. 1.11). Bathsheba was married to Uriah the Hittite (11.3). Uriah's name looks Hebrew, but the label 'the Hittite' may come about because of ancestry rather than his being an actual foreigner in Jerusalem. His place in David's army suggests someone with a good reputation, and a house close enough to the palace to be observed from there implies someone who was a native to Jerusalem. But, in any case, it seems likely that the story wants us to understand Uriah as at least of Hittite descent. Another of David's officers Ahimelech is also said to be Hittite (26.6), though his name is also pure Hebrew.

It is difficult to know what to make of the various traditions just outlined. They represent diverse traditions, and some of them seem even mutually contradictory. For example, the straightforward story of Joshua tells us that the land of Canaan was conquered in five years and then divided up among the tribes, with most of the Canaanites killed or made slaves. Yet the book of Judges suggests that the Israelite displacement of the Canaanites was a slow, complicated process that lasted for several generations, even centuries. The picture is further complicated in that most recent studies have argued that the Israelites were not a people who invaded from outside, but rather a group that developed among the indigenous inhabitants of the country. That is, the Israelites were not an ethnic group that came into the country, but were simply a selection of Canaanites who coalesced together into a particular political structure because of particular historical circumstances. This conclusion is based on a variety of data: archaeological, biblical and inscriptional.[13] Later on, when Israel

---

12. L.L. Grabbe, *Priests, Prophets, Diviners, Sages: A Socio-Historical Study of Religious Specialists in Ancient Israel* (Valley Forge, PA: Trinity Press International, 1995), pp. 60-62.

13. N.K. Gottwald, *The Tribes of Yahweh: A Sociology of the Religion of Liberated Israel, 1250–1050 B.C.E.* (Maryknoll, NY: Orbis Books, 1979); N.P. Lemche, *Early Israel: Anthropological and Historical Studies on the Israelite Society before the Monarchy* (VTSup, 37; Leiden: E.J. Brill, 1985); I. Finkelstein, *The Archaeology of the Israelite Settlement* (Jerusalem: Israel Exploration Society, 1988); L.L. Grabbe, '"Canaanite": Some Methodological Observations in Relation to Biblical Study', in G.J. Brooke, A.H.W. Curtis and J.F. Healey (eds.), *Ugarit and the Bible: Proceedings of the International Symposium on Ugarit and the Bible, Manchester, September 1992* (Ugaritisch-Biblische Literatur, 11; Münster: Ugarit-Verlag, 1994), pp. 113-22.

had established its own identity, the biblical writers invented a 'Canaan' and 'Canaanites' that they could demonize from a religious perspective, but this was not the historical Canaan or Canaanites.[14]

But if this is the case, where do these traditions come from? It was noted above that, despite some criticisms and revisions, scholars by and large accept the thesis of the 'Deuteronomistic History'—the narrative of the biblical books of Joshua to 2 Kings—made up of inherited traditions that have been put together by editors, shaped according to their purposes, and filled out with much material that they wrote themselves. This literary creation clearly has certain theological aims that dominate and structure the material. Overall, there are patterns of divine deliverance and return, sin and falling away, punishment by captivity and exile, deliverance and return and so on. This leads to the image of Israel as the people of God who were allowed to go into captivity in Egypt but who were then delivered by God's own intervention and given the land promised to Abraham. But this interpretation, which arises from considering the Deuteronomist's aim, automatically requires that the land be conquered from the native (but illegitimate) inhabitants.

The book of Judges, however, probably represents more closely the chaotic origins of Israel, with a diversity of 'tribes' fighting one another but sometimes forming alliances that extended over several groups, out of which eventually came the nation of Israel (or at least the nations of Israel and Judah, since whether they were ever a united nation under David and Solomon is currently a point of debate).[15] The stories in Judges seem to remember a Jerusalem that came into Israelite hands only relatively late and continued to have the earlier people as a part of the population for some time afterward.

In a number of passages are listed the various 'tribes' or peoples who lived in the land and opposed the Israelites.[16] The lists differ among themselves but tend to list the Canaanites, Hittites, Perizzites, Amorites, Jebusites, Hivites and sometimes the Girgashites; other names are also

14. N.P. Lemche, *The Canaanites and their Land: The Tradition of the Canaanites* (JSOTSup, 110; Sheffield: Sheffield Academic Press, 1991); cf. Grabbe, '"Canaanite": Some Methodological Observations'.

15. See the essays in L.K. Handy (ed.), *The Age of Solomon: Scholarship at the Turn of the Millennium* (Studies in the History and Culture of the Ancient Near East, 11; Leiden: E.J. Brill, 1997).

16. E.g. Gen. 15.19-21; Exod. 3.8; 23.23; 33.2; Josh. 3.10; 1 Kgs 9.20; Ezra 9.1; Neh. 9.8.

occasionally found.[17] The question is to what extent these names reflect actual peoples in Iron Age Palestine. We know that 'Canaanite' was a generic term for the inhabitants of the whole region. In the biblical text, the term 'Canaanite' seems also at times to be a generic term for the whole people in the region (cf. Gen. 12.6), but in these lists the name appears to be a single tribe alongside the other tribes of the land. This suggests that the writer was either unfamiliar with who the Canaanites were or was really only interested in creating an artificial list to use for his theological purposes.

Hittites and Amorites were also major peoples of the ancient Near East. In the second millennium BCE the Hittites had an empire in the area of Asia Minor.[18] The Hittite Old Kingdom straddled the line between the Middle and Late Bronze Ages (c. 1650–1500 BCE). The Hittite empire, also known as the 'Hittite New Kingdom', flourished later in the second millennium (1450–1200). After the end of the Hittite empire, a series of 'Neo-Hittite' states arose in Syria. As for the Amorites, a 'kingdom of Amurru' in Syria is known from references in the Amarna letters, Ugaritic texts and the texts from the Hittite capital known from its modern place name of Boghazköy in Turkey.[19] Other texts are less definite, referring to smaller groups or perhaps even individuals at various places, mainly in the Euphrates region. In the first millennium BCE Neo-Assyrian and Babylonian texts used the term 'Hittite' (*Hatti*) as a generic term for the West. It is possible that in the first millennium BCE individual Hittites or Amorites or even small groups of them lived in various places in Palestine (e.g. Uriah the Hittite). However, the picture of a 'Canaanite tribe', 'Hittite tribe' or an 'Amorite tribe' alongside other local tribes looks distinctly like an artificial creation of the author.

In order to understand what has happened, we can consider the case of the Rephaim. The Rephaim were supposedly one of the original inhabi-

---

17. T. Ishida, 'The Structure and Historical Implications of the Lists of Pre-Israelite Nations', *Bib* 60 (1979), pp. 461-90.

18. O.R. Gurney, *The Hittites* (Harmondsworth: Penguin, 1990); F. Cornelius, *Geschichte der Hethiter, Mit besonderer Berücksichtigung der geographischen Verhältnisse und der Rechtsgeschichte* (Darmstadt: Wissenschaftliche Buchgesellschaft, 1976 [repr. 1992]).

19. G. Buccellati, 'Amorites', in E.M. Meyers (ed.), *The Oxford Encyclopedia of Archaeology in the Near East* (5 vols.; Oxford: Oxford University Press, 1997), I, pp. 107-11; T.L. Thompson, The Historicity *of the Patriarchal Narratives: The Quest for the Historical Abraham* (BZAW, 133; Berlin: W. de Gruyter, 1974), pp. 67-171.

tants of the Transjordanian region,[20] yet, in the Ugaritic texts, they are the deceased ancestors.[21] Also, Og of Bashan, labelled as a remnant of the Rephaim, dwells in Ashtarot and Edrei,[22] the same area in which the god Rapha'u of a Ugaritic incantation seems to dwell (*KTU* 1.108). Other passages[23] associate the Rephaim with the dead. It appears that myth has been historicized, and the shades of the dead have been turned into ethnographical entities. Thus, the writer seems to have taken traditional or mythical names and used them to create a narrative about ethnic groups.

The ultimate extreme is found in Ezra 9.1 and Neh. 9.8, which give the traditional list of tribes opposed to Israel. It is unlikely that these identifiable ethnic groups still existed in Palestine at this late date in the Persian period, even if they ever had. In sum, a case can be made that the nations alleged to be in Canaan and driven out or conquered by Israel were a least partially a literary fiction, in which the authors have taken traditional names and used them to create fictional lists of the pre-Israelite inhabitants of Jerusalem. Some of these names may indeed have been the names of actual peoples or tribes of ancient Canaan, but we know for certain that others were not. *Prima facie*, the unknown names were more likely to be a genuine memory of early tribes or groups than those more widely known. Interestingly, the Jebusites seem to exist independently of these lists of names and to be consistently labeled as constituting the pre-Israelite inhabitants of Jerusalem.

What the various traditions suggest, therefore, is that there was a collective folk memory of a time when Jerusalem was not Israelite, and even that it came into Israelite hands much later than some of the surrounding territory. This is a remarkable memory, especially if we keep in mind that it would have been more convenient to believe (as the book of Joshua has it) that Jerusalem was conquered with the rest of the territory and divided up by the Israelites without any complications.

Jerusalem to the Coming of the Romans

Jerusalem was taken by the Babylonians in around 587 BCE, with much of the city destroyed. Exactly who lived in the city for the next decades, if anyone, is not indicated. The books of Ezra and Nehemiah claim to tell us

20. E.g. Gen. 14.5; 15.20; Deut. 2.11, 20; 3.11, 13.
21. Cf. *KTU* 1.21 (= Aqhat IVa); *KTU* 1.161 (a ritual text?).
22. Deut. 1.4; 3.10-11; Josh. 9.10; 12.4; 13.12.
23. Such as Job 26.5; Ps. 88.11-13; Isa. 26.14, 19; Prov. 9.18.

about events in the early part of the Persian period.[24] According to the book of Ezra, the city of Jerusalem was settled by Jews early in the Persian period (539–333 BCE). However, we have some curious statements about 'foreigners' in the country that need to be looked at more closely. Ezra 4 speaks of 'the people of the land', who hindered the rebuilding of the temple, as being deportees from Mesopotamia who were living in Samaria. The matter is complicated because events of the time of Cyrus (539–530 BCE) are confused with references to correspondence which is dated to the time of Artaxerxes I (465–404 BCE). According to one letter quoted, the people had been brought from Erech (Uruk), Babylon and Elam to settle in Samaria (Ezra 4.9-10, 17).

That deportees from Mesopotamia were brought in to replace those deported from Samaria when it was conquered seems to be established. The problem with the book of Ezra is that it fails to acknowledge what we also know: that many of the people living in the land of Judah in the Persian period were Jews themselves, descendents of those who were not deported by the Babylonians at the conquest of Jerusalem in 587–586 BCE. Only a minority of the Jews were deported after Judah fell but the majority were left living in the land.[25] When some Jews returned from exile in the early Persian period, they must have found many Jews already in the land, yet the book of Ezra fails to say anything about this. Thus, when it speaks of the 'people(s) of the land(s)',[26] we must realize that these were likely to have been Jews or at least to have included Jews. They were not all foreigners, as the writer of Ezra would have us believe, but many were fellow Jews.

Thus, in Ezra 9–10, where Ezra is alleged to have led a move to make those who had married 'foreign' wives separate from them and their children, were these wives really non-Jews? Those who had married them, including priests in some cases, had seen no problem with the marriages. This suggests that their wives were probably Jews in many cases, but Jews from the native population rather than from the *golah* (returnee) community. Thus, if we ask whether ethnic groups other than Jews lived in Jerusalem in this period, it is difficult to say whether they existed or not. The desire of the book of Ezra and also Nehemiah (cf. Neh. 13.23-27) to

24. For a discussion of these books and their historicity, see L.L. Grabbe, *Ezra and Nehemiah* (Readings; London: Routledge, 1998).

25. H. Barstad, *The Myth of the Empty Land: A Study in the History and Archaeology of Judah during the 'Exilic' Period* (Oslo: Scandinavian University Press, 1996).

26. Ezra 4.4; 9.1, 11; 10.2, 11; cf. Neh. 10.29, 31.

brand certain peoples of Palestine as foreign may mask a conflict within the Jewish community itself, with one group of Jews (the *golah* community) discriminating against another portion of the Jewish community (the natives of Judah who had never been taken captive).

One other episode is described in Neh. 13.23-27. Here Nehemiah is said to have been appalled because 'Jews had married Ashdodites, Ammonites, and Moabites' (13.23). There are a number of questions about this passage. The 'foreign women' seem a strange combination, including women from one of the old Philistine cities and from the peoples of the Transjordanian area. Why were only these areas—from the western and eastern extremes of the region—involved? Some scholars feel that this section of Nehemiah is not part of Nehemiah's own writing.[27] Is the account based on an actual incident, or has a later writer created an action for Nehemiah to be parallel to Ezra's experience with regard to 'mixed marriages'? In any case, it is not suggested that these women were living in Jerusalem.

One of the most interesting aspects of ethnicity and the books of Ezra and Nehemiah concerns an often-overlooked possibility that some of the temple servants were of non-Israelite origin. These were the Netinim. Ezra 2 ostensibly lists those who returned with Zerubbabel and Joshua to Judah in the early Persian period. A section of the list is made up of temple personnel of various sorts: priests, Levites, singers, gatekeepers, Netinim servants and Solomon's servants (Ezra 2.36-58). Another list (Neh. 11) includes priests and Levites but also 'sons of Solomon's servants'. However, these 'sons of Solomon's servants' are not found as such in the detailed list later on in the chapter; instead we have 'gatekeepers', 'Netinim' and 'singers'. The singers are evidently seen as a part of the Levites.

When Ezra is about to lead a group of Jews from Babylon back to Jerusalem, he makes a detour in order to include some Levites in his caravan (Ezra 8.15-20). The community of Levites is said to include a group of Netinim. They are described as a group whom David and his officials had appointed to help with the work of the Levites, but here they seem to be considered as a part of the Levite community. The names of the Netinim in these passages do not look typically Hebrew, but foreign.[28] According to Josh. 9.23, 27, one of the native Canaanite peoples, the Gibeonites, were made temple slaves. The place of the Gibeonites is not further discussed in the text, nor is any specific connection made between the

---

27. Known as 'Nehemiah's Memorial', which is usually believed to include much of Neh. 1–6.

28. J. Blenkinsopp, *Ezra–Nehemiah* (OTL; London: SCM Press, 1989), pp. 90-91.

Gibeonites and the Netinim. But several of the textual data point to the Netinim as being non-Israelites who, under unknown circumstances, became temple servants. Apparently, they eventually became a part of the Levites serving in the temple itself.

Throughout the entire period of Persian, Greek and finally Roman rule, Jerusalem was seen by both Jews and non-Jews as primarily a Jewish city, the capital of the Jewish nation. Writing not long after Alexander's conquests, in about 300 BCE, the Greek author Hecataeus of Abdera believed that Moses had founded the city of Jerusalem.[29]

> But the greater number were driven into what is now called Judaea, which is not far distant from Egypt and was at that time utterly uninhabited... The colony was headed by a man called Moses, outstanding both for his wisdom and for his courage. On taking possession of the land he founded, besides other cities, one that is now the most renowned of all, called Jerusalem.

Nevertheless, there are indications that other groups lived in Jerusalem alongside the Jews during the period of Greek rule. Jerusalem became a Greek city (*polis*) for a short period of time after 175 BCE.[30] Nothing is said about inhabitants of Jerusalem other than Jews, but as a Hellenistic city Jerusalem would have seen itself as cosmopolitan, and some non-Jews may have lived there as a minority population. A few years later, the Syrians placed a garrison in Jerusalem which was one of the events associated with the Maccabean revolt.[31] This garrison was there for almost 30 years before the citadel was finally taken by the Jews under the leadership of Simon Maccabee about in 142 BCE (1 Macc. 11.20-53; 12.35-36; 13.49-52). The members of this garrison may not have left a permanent presence in Jerusalem, but we cannot be sure.

The independent Jewish state that arose under Hasmonean rule brought a new situation, leading to a new group with strong associations to Jerusalem: the Idumeans. These were evidently the descendants of the ancient Edomites. According to Josephus, the Edomites were forcibly converted to Judaism by the Hasmonean ruler John Hyrcanus (*Ant.* 13.9.1 §§257-58).

---

29. As quoted in Diodorus Siculus 40.3.1-7; B. Bar-Kochva, *Pseudo-Hecataeus, On the Jews: Legitimizing the Jewish Diaspora* (Hellenistic Culture and Society, 21; Berkeley: University of California Press, 1996), pp. 7-43.

30. 2 Macc. 4; see further L.L. Grabbe, *Judaism from Cyrus to Hadrian*. I. *Persian and Greek Periods*; II. *Roman Period* (Minneapolis: Fortress Press, 1992 [British one-volume edn = London: SCM Press, 1994]), pp. 277-81.

31. 1 Macc. 2.31; cf. Grabbe, *Judaism*, pp. 283-84, 298-99.

This is a difficult episode to interpret since the Idumeans seem to have remained faithful to their new religion. One would have expected them to revert to their old religion at the first opportunity, but most Idumeans appear to have continued as converts to Judaism. This suggests something more complicated than a simple forced conversion; indeed, it appears that the conversion was voluntary for the most part.[32] In any case, we read several times of Idumeans who clearly have a connection with Jerusalem.

The most important figure who may have been Idumean was Herod the Great. The question of his ancestry is not a straightforward one since there were traditions that he claimed descent from Babylonian Jews, and he clearly lived as a Jew.[33] But if Josephus is right that he was of Idumean descent, he could still have been seen as a Jew and lived by the precepts of Judaism for the reasons noted above. Various members of his court were also Idumean, judging by their names which contain the theophoric element –*co*–, which seems to be a reflex of the old Edomite deity Qaus (*Ant.* 2.5.2-3 §§72-79).

The Idumeans showed their continuing loyalty to Judaism by also being supportive of the Jews in their resistance against the Romans at various times. In the 'war of Varus' that broke out after Herod's death (4 BCE), when a number of revolts started and had to be suppressed by the Roman commander Varus, Idumea apparently joined the revolt, or at least a large group of Idumeans participated, including some of Herod's own relatives (Josephus, *War* 2.5.3 §§76-79). Seven decades later, during the siege of Jerusalem by the Romans, a large body of Idumeans came to Jerusalem to aid their brethen in their fighting (4.4.1–6.1 §§224-353). However, when they got caught up in internecine warfare between different Jewish factions, most of them eventually left (2.5.2-3 §§71-79; 4.9.11 §§566-70).

After the fall of Jerusalem in 70 CE the Jews apparently continued to live there, but there was a strong Roman presence. The Tenth Legion was stationed in Jerusalem on a permanent basis. This state of affairs continued for another 60 years until the Bar Kokhba revolt in 132–35 CE. After this second war with Rome, there was widespread destruction in the country. In addition, the Romans founded a new city, called Aelia Capitolina, with

32. Strabo 15.2.34; see S.J.D. Cohen, *The Beginnings of Jewishness: Boundaries, Varieties, Uncertainties* (Hellenistic Culture and Society, 31; Berkeley: University of California Press, 1999), pp. 110-19; Grabbe, *Judaism*, pp. 329-31.

33. P. Richardson, *Herod: King of the Jews and Friend of the Romans* (Studies on Personalities of the New Testament; Columbia: University of South Carolina Press, 1996); Grabbe, *Judaism*, p. 364.

a pagan temple on the original site of Solomon's temple. Jews were forbidden to enter this city on pain of death, a regulation that continued in effect for several centuries.

Summary

Archaeology indicates that Jerusalem was a fortified town by the eighteenth century BCE, one of many Canaanite cities in existence at the time. Jerusalem enters history with the Amarna Letters of the fourteenth century BCE, which were written at a time when Palestine was part of the Egyptian empire. These letters include correspondence from the Canaanite city-states to the Egyptian king. Among them are several relating to the city-state of Jerusalem and its leader. This is our first detailed information on Jerusalem.

The biblical text contains a variety of traditions, some of them written down long after the events they purport to describe. Thus, it is not always possible to take a biblical tradition at face value since the account may be the author's own creation based on certain ideological or theological aims. Despite this evaluation, which is accepted by most biblical scholars, some traditions go against the expected interpretation and indicate that Jerusalem was not under Israelite control at an early time. Thus, according to Joshua 10 the king of Jerusalem led a coalition of Canaanite kings that was defeated by Joshua, after which the king of Jerusalem was put to death. Yet a number of biblical passages suggest that Jerusalem did not come into Israelite hands until much later.

Even the book of Joshua recognizes that the Benjaminites could not drive out the Jebusites who inhabited Jerusalem (Josh. 15.63), and a number of passages in Judges suggest the same thing (Judg. 1.21; 19.10). The most important passage is in 2 Sam. 5.6-9, where the city of Jebus remains outside Israelite control until the time of David, who is the one who takes the city and makes it the 'City of David'. Nevertheless, the Jebusites continued to live there, and Araunah, who sold his threshing floor to David on which to build an altar, and on which Solomon later is said to have constructed the temple, seems to have been the last Jebusite king of the city (2 Sam. 24.16-25). There are good arguments to suggest that one of David's two high priests, Zadok, was originally a Jebusite priest. Also during David's reign, the husband of Bathsheba was Uriah the Hittite. Perhaps he was a man of Hittite descent rather than an immigrant, but he provides further evidence that other ethnic groups continued to live in Jerusalem even after it came into Israelite hands.

Jerusalem was destroyed by the Babylonians in 587/586 BCE and the Kingdom of Judah came to an end. In the Persian period the temple was rebuilt, and Jerusalem returned to Judean control until well in the Roman period. However, Jerusalem became a cosmopolitan city in which individuals of diverse ethnic background lived. One group that had a lot to do with Jerusalem was the Idumeans (Edomites). Although the Idumeans were converted to Judaism, they retained their own ethnic identity. According to some sources (though not all) Herod the Great was of Idumean descent.

Jerusalem was captured by the Romans after a disastrous Judean revolt in 66–70 CE, and the temple destroyed. The temple itself was never rebuilt, though Jews continued to inhabit the city for the next 60 years. After another revolt against Rome in 132–35 CE, however, the city was turned into a Roman city called Aelia Capitolina. A pagan temple was established on the former temple site, and Jews were forbidden to enter the city for a long time afterward.

From Zion to Zion:
Jerusalem in the Dead Sea Scrolls

Philip R. Davies

Since the destruction of the last Jewish temple in Jerusalem 2000 years ago, Judaism has become a religion of dispersion, built around domestic and social structures, expressing the virtues of strong communal solidarity and personal obedience to the divine law. It has also developed, like Islam and Christianity, its own mystical traditions, many of which clearly originated already in biblical times.[1] Judaism as it has been since the end of the first century CE has had no functioning priesthood, no sacrificies, and of course no sanctuary. The synagogue is no sanctuary, but essentially a place of prayer and reading of the scriptures. Paradoxically, it is Christianity that has adopted the language of priesthood, of altar, of sacrifice. The loss of first the temple and then residence in Jerusalem by order of Hadrian led to a radical re-creation of the religion of the Jews into a system where the sanctuary-centred structures of holiness and of communion with the deity through sacrifice were transformed. The temple and the land are nostalgically portrayed in the Mishnah (written c. 200 CE), but in effect the life of Jews proceeds without them, through obedience to the law of Moses as continually developed and applied to the everyday life of Jews individually and corporately.

Before these disasters, before the creation of rabbinic Judaism, when Palestine (including the province of Judea and many surrounding territories where Jews were in the majority), was still the homeland of the *ethnos* of the Jews, the city and temple dominated to a tremendous extent not only religion but politics and economics. Jerusalem's eminence was entirely dependent on its status as a major sanctuary city, on the many visitors the temple attracted to its festivals and on the enormous appetite for sacrifical meat that its cult enjoyed. In the Jewish scriptures and in

---

1.   See, e.g., Christopher Rowland, *The Open Heaven: A Study of Apocalytpic in Judaism and Early Christianity* (London: SPCK, 1982).

other Jewish literature of the Second Temple period (500 BCE–70 CE), 'Jerusalem' meant the temple. It was a holy city because the temple was holy. It was important not primarily because it was the capital of a Jewish land, but because it was the place where the Jewish god whom the Jews believed had chosen them had also chosen to live himself. For much of the Second Temple period the high priest was the political representative of the Jews.

By the first century BCE, of course, there were more Jews living outside Palestine than inside and to these Jerusalem was also the focus of their religious life. It was not merely the capital city of Judea (never mind that the Romans regarded Caesarea as the political capital of the territory), and not merely the centre of the land of Israel, but the centre of the Jewish people in the world and indeed, the centre of the world that their god himself had created.

Outside Palestine, this focus was represented by the annual temple tax, and by the institution of prayers and Torah readings in local Jewish assemblies as a kind of reflection on the real cult in Jerusalem. Where possible, it was also the destination of many pilgrims. But outside Jerusalem no religious cult was permitted. Beyond the reach of the city of Jerusalem, Judaism had to be something different, an ever-present idea but not a reality. It was the temple hill that was called 'Mt Zion': the place nowadays called 'Mt Zion' at the southwest corner of the Old City is incorrectly named. And the place of the Jerusalem temple in the mind of Diaspora Jews is indeed the earliest expression of 'Zionism'. Rabbinic Judaism built upon a Judaism that existed as a true world religion, a religion equally valid anywhere and everywhere, regardless of the temple, even of the land of Israel. But the physical absence of the Jerusalem temple had much less effect on Diaspora Jews. It remained an idea, but its physical absence lent a powerful nostalgia to a people now called 'Jews' ('Judeans'), but without the land or the temple to represent that name in material, geographical form.

The followers of Jesus also at first respected the sanctity and importance of the cult of the Jerusalem temple, and only gradually, as the religion essentially defined by Saul/Paul of Tarsus spread among non-Jews, and emphatically after the fall of the temple, did Christianity develop in a way that ignored altogether the centrality of Jerusalem. The end of the temple was interpreted in the New Testament Gospels as a vindication of Jesus' message and mission, so that Jesus was recorded as having predicted its downfall (Mt. 26.61; Lk. 21.5-6, etc.) and possibly predicting his own body as a replacement (Jn 2.20-22).

We have few Jewish sources directly from Palestine in the century when the temple was lost, and certainly hardly any literary sources preserved in Hebrew. The manuscripts found at Qumran by the Dead Sea in 1947 are by far the most important evidence for Palestinian Judaism in the last 150 years or so of the temple's existence. These scrolls show that for a number of Jews living in Palestine at this time, the place of the temple in their religion was rather complex. We cannot attribute all the writings in this archive to a single community, though it is probable that they represent the attitudes and doctrines of certain Jewish groups and sects that were related to each other and came into existence in the last two centuries BCE. All of these groups and sects probably came into existence, or at least formed sects, as a result of their opposition to the priestly families that were at the time in charge of the Jerusalem temple. Their opposition forced them to reconsider the place of the temple itself in their religious system. But they addressed this problem in different ways, ranging at one end from accepting that Jerusalem and its holy place remained the absolute centre of the universe, to, at the other end, believing that there was no place for an earthly temple in bringing together the god of Israel and the people he had chosen.

I suspect that this range of views about the temple reflects a chrono-logical sequence by which this movement, opposed to the priests of Jeru-salem, gradually loosened its allegiance to the temple, first by rejecting just its personnel, then by rejecting the temple itself, and finally by abandoning even the idea of an earthly temple. But the chronology is not as important as the typology, and many Qumran scholars do not agree with this opinion. However, as already mentioned, we might also see a parallel in early Christianity of this detachment from allegiance to the temple: the community led by James the brother of Jesus remained close to the sanctu-ary; even Paul respected the priority of Jerusalem within his network of churches. Only later was Jerusalem supplanted by Rome as the capital of Christianity.

Within the Jewish Diaspora, too, we can find clues suggesting that Judaism should be, or indeed already was, universalized, that its principles were essentially those of Plato, or even of universal human reason.[2] So even if the specific grievances and theology of the writers of the Dead Sea Scrolls were unique, these writers were not the only Jews to approach the notion of Judaism without a temple, which meant a Judaism without

---

2.   I am thinking especially of the writing of Philo of Alexandria (first century CE), or books such as *3 Maccabees* (from about the same time or a little earlier).

Jerusalem. But since these writers were Palestinian Jews, and in their time the temple still existed and exerted a strong influence on their society, the abandonment of the temple involved a theological struggle, and we can doubt whether they ever managed to free themselves of the dominance of the temple in their religious life.

And so I shall now look briefly at examples of the range of attitudes to Jerusalem and its temple among the Dead Sea Scrolls. The view most favourable to the temple emerges in the Temple Scroll,[3] which describes in detail an ideal temple and its cult, a temple almost as large as the city of Jerusalem itself at that time. This temple was the centre of a set of concentric circles that represented areas of holiness. Thus, the Most Holy Place at the centre of the temple was also the centre of the created universe, and here God could visit, be invisibly present; beyond this empty room were the temple courts: the court of priests, then the court of Israelites and finally of women. Beyond the temple was the holy city, beyond the holy city the holy land of Israel and finally, beyond the land of Israel the rest of the world, in which there was little or no holiness. The rabbis in fact reflected this view in their writings, and although the temple was gone, the land of Israel remained subject (at least in theory) to certain laws that did not apply elsewhere, such as tithing and the dedication of the first-fruits and firstborn.

The temple and city of the Temple Scroll are here idealized. Scholars are divided on whether the vision in the scrolls represents an expectation for the future or a plan of how things should have been in the first place. The contents certainly reflect a number of contemporary views about the status of the temple and city of Jerusalem. Criticism of the existing priestly regime is implied in the laws that regulate the temple cult, but there are no explicit accusations. The Damascus Document, however, very clearly does express strong criticisms.[4] This document was found in several copies at Qumran, but in fact it was first discovered a century ago in a synagogue

---

3.   This was recovered by Yigael Yadin in 1967 and subsequently published by him in 1977 (in Hebrew). The English translation is Y. Yadin, *The Temple Scroll* (Jerusalem: Israel Exploration Society, 1983). See also *idem, The Temple Scroll: The Hidden Law of the Dead Sea Sect* (London: Weidenfeld & Nicholson, 1985); J. Maier, *The Temple Scroll: An Introduction, Translation and Commentary* (JSOTSup, 34; Sheffield: JSOT Press, 1985).

4.   For a comprehensive analysis of the first part of the Damascus Document, see P.R. Davies, *The Damascus Covenant: An Interpretation of the 'Damascus Document'* (JSOTSup, 25; Sheffield: JSOT Press, 1983).

in Cairo, where two copies from about the tenth century were recovered.[5] In the *Damascus Document*, which probably has no connection with the real city of Damascus, but is so called because of the use of the 'land of Damascus' in the document as a symbol, we encounter a Jewish sect that almost certainly had its headquarters in Jerusalem. But, critical of the ritual code practised by the temple priesthood, this text separates the true law from the temple and relocates it among its own settlements, effectively decentralizing the sanctuary in one aspect. Because of these differences, and in particular because this sect held to a different calendar from the Jerusalem priests, the members of the sect could participate in only a small number of temple activities, such as private offerings. This document, and others that emanate from the same sect, thus express a full approval of the centrality of the Jerusalem temple, provided it is properly run, but have to cope with the fact of a real temple whose priests are regarded as disobeying the will of God.

A further distancing from the temple is implied in the text known as *Songs of the Sabbath Sacrifice*, or *Angelic Liturgy*.[6] Here we find written down the praises of the heavenly angels in the presence of God in heaven. It seems as if the members of the group that produced this text were directing their devotion not to the actual Jerusalem temple, not even to an ideal Jerusalem temple that might one day exist, but away from Jerusalem to the temple of heaven, where God was worshipped in person every sabbath (and perhaps even continually) by his heavenly ministers, led, it seems, by Melchizedek, the heavenly high priest. This text suggests to many scholars hat the writers had turned their back on the Jerusalem temple and had moved towards a form of worship that was to be spiritual. It can be argued whether this abandonment of Jerusalem was expected to be temporary or permanent. I don't think it matters, because the writers believed things would only change at the end of time. In the *Rule of the Community* from Qumran,[7] we find a clarification of the position of these

5.   Published by Solomon Schechter in his *Documents of Jewish Sectaries* (Cambridge: Cambridge University Press, 1910 [repr. with a Prolegomenon by J.A. Fitzmyer = New York: KTAV, 1970]), pp. ix-69, 1-10.

6.   First published by Carol A. Newsom, *Songs of the Sabbath Sacrifice: A Critical Edition* (Atlanta: Scholars Press, 1985); see now J.H. Charlesworth and Carol A. Newsom, *The Dead Sea Scrolls: Hebrew, Aramaic, and Greek Texts with English Translations*. IVB. *Angelic Liturgy: Songs of the Sabbath Sacrifice* (Tübingen: J.C.B. Mohr [Paul Siebeck]; Louisville, KY: Westminster/John Knox Press, 1999).

7.   See J.H. Charlesworth, *The Dead Sea Scrolls: Hebrew, Aramaic, and Greek Texts with English Translations*. I. *Rule of the Community and Related Documents*

writers. Here is written down an explicit rejection of the value of sacrifices, and a claim that the central shrine of the temple where God dwelt was now reconstituted by a community of men dedicated to lives of the utmost holiness. They would be a 'human sanctuary' and their sufferings and their personal holiness would take the place of sacrifices.

These texts from Qumran, which I think emanate from a group that was different from the sect of the *Damascus Document*, show us the development of a theology in which Jerusalem and its temple were replaced even before Jerusalem itself was actually destroyed. Despite living in Palestine, which meant effectively within the shadow of the Jerusalem temple, these people felt obliged to create a Judaism based on ritual activities that symbolically functioned in place of that cult. We may contrast this with the attitude in the book of Daniel to the destruction of the cult in Jerusalem. According to Daniel (in its present Hebrew/Aramaic form dated to c. 165 BCE), neither God nor the Jewish people could long survive the absence of the daily sacrifices, and so the end of history had to come soon. The writers of the *Community Rule*, written probably within a century, have taken a different path, even if they too believed that the end of time was almost upon them because of the wickedness of Israel.

Conclusion and Summary

The destruction of the temple in Jerusalem was, and is still regarded as, a very great tragedy in the history of Judaism. However, to many Jews at the time it was something that they could adapt to, while for others, as we have seen in the Dead Sea Scrolls, it could be interpreted as a vindication of their opposition to the wicked priests who controlled the temple. To Christians it came also to be seen as divine judgment.

Rabbinic Judaism also adapted to this loss, and this adaptation ensured the survival of Judaism. As it has been known for 2000 years, Judaism needs no temple. Zionism has focussed rather on the city and the land. The city of Jerusalem itself has taken the place of the temple: it is now the 'eternal holy city', not so much the home of God but of Israel. What, then, is the importance of Mt Zion to modern Jews? There are many answers. A few Jews, of course, would like to reinstitute the temple and its cult, which would certainly boost the livestock economy and contribute to local air pollution. For other Jews, the Temple Mount, the real Mt Zion, is now in

(Tübingen: J.C.B. Mohr [Paul Siebeck]; Louisville, KY: Westminster/John Knox Press, 1994).

some symbolic or perhaps even real way inhabited by their god, who has again blessed them. For secular Jews, it is perhaps not important at all except as an important archaeological relic of one of the architectural wonders of the ancient world and of course another monumental witness to Jewish ownership of the city many centuries earlier.

The situation, then, is today, as it was 2000 years ago, highly varied with regard to the temple hill of Zion. Basically, it seems to me, the *city itself* has assumed the symbolic role of the temple as a holy relic to challenge the scroll of the law that held sway for two millennia (and in terms of daily life outside Israel, still largely does). To a lesser extent, this is also true of the 'land of Israel' itself (I mean as defined by the rabbinic texts and not by international law). But the symbols of city and law pull in opposite directions, one universal and one particular. This opposition between a universal spiritual Judaism and a nationalistic and Jerusalem-centred Judaism is not a new one. It is as old as Judaism itself, and it has generated not only the many forms of Zionism, but some forms of anti-Zionism as well.

THE MAKING OF THE HOLY CITY:
ON THE FOUNDATIONS OF JERUSALEM IN THE HEBREW BIBLE[*]

Thomas M. Bolin

The rise of urban culture 5000 years ago in lower Mesopotamia can be attributed to the development of sustainable agriculture in the alluvial plain, the division of labor and resources, and consequent social stratification.[1] Cities have always functioned as a means to pool resources and to defend against outsiders. They are distinctively human, among the most visible of markers that separate us from the other animals. They are the tangible aspect of the intellectual and social worlds necessary for sustainable and enduring human life.[2] When Aristotle observes in his well-known remark that human beings are by nature 'political' animals (*Politics* 1253a), it merits mention that the root of the word 'political' is the Greek πόλις ('city'). Similarly, in that most famous of ancient Near Eastern texts, the *Epic of Gilgamesh*, the wild man Enkidu is tamed by a woman in a step-by-step process culminating in his being brought to a city, 'Uruk-the-Sheepfold'.[3] In a standard process that seeks to validate cultural constructs, a city is almost always understood as the result of much more than the pragmatic matters of safety, economic efficiency, or social cohesion, being attributed instead to the work of divine or human heroes. In the Hebrew Bible, the authors' important city is, of course, Jerusalem, and for them their metropolis is not simply founded by one great hero from the Israelite past, but by a series of major biblical figures. This essay will look

*   An earlier version of this essay was read on 12 November 2001 to the Senior Seminar at the Institut for bibelsk Eksegeses of the Københavns Universitet. I am grateful to the members of the Seminar for their comments and criticism.
    1.   Detailed discussion of this process is in N. Yoffee, 'The Economy of Ancient Western Asia', in *CANE*, III, pp. 1387-99.
    2.   Cf. P. Berger and T. Luckmann, *The Social Construction of Reality: A Treatise on the Sociology of Knowledge* (New York: Doubleday, 1966).
    3.   See the new edition of A. George, *The Epic of Gilgamesh: A New Translation* (Harmondsworth: Penguin, 1999).

at the different ways urban foundations were portrayed in antiquity. These data will then be brought to bear on the biblical texts that speak of the founding of Jerusalem. Doing so reveals a wide array of textual strategies that the biblical authors employed in the service of an ideology that sought to exalt Jerusalem's role among the educated Diaspora of the Hellenistic era.[4]

Beliefs Concerning the Foundation of Cities

The different traditions concerning the founding of cities in the ancient world may be grouped into two broad categories comprising those stories in which the city is founded by a deity and those that tell of a foundation by a hero.

The City Founded by a Deity

One of the main cultural purposes of ancient cities was to house temples, understood as domiciles of the protecting deities. Thus it is no surprise that many cities developed aetiologies attributing their foundations to divine action.[5] There are Mesopotamian traditions that claim that all distinctive aspects of human life, for example, culture, art, technology, were gifts from the gods brought by the *apkallu*, the sages, semi-divine or divine figures, usually seven in number. In the opening and closing verses of the *Epic of Gilgamesh*, Gilgamesh the king of Uruk boasts of his city's walls: 'Were its bricks not fired in an oven? Did the Seven Sages not lay its foundations?'[6] Such an exalted pedigree also serves as powerful propaganda in the city's policies toward either its own citizens or outsiders. A brief look at two of the better-known examples will illustrate the logic at work in this kind of mythopoesis.

---

4.   A different approach from that of L. Hoppe, who looks at the theology of Jerusalem in the Psalms, the Prophets and the Deuteronomistic writings (*The Holy City: Jerusalem in the Theology of the Old Testament* [Collegeville, MN: Liturgical Press, 2000]).

5.   Stories of deities choosing to dwell in cities already in existence or commanding cities to be built by their followers are not included here. Strictly speaking, these kinds of stories belong under the category of cities founded by heroes because they carry out the divine will in these traditions. Divine approbation in the story thus serves to validate the role of the hero.

6.   George, *Epic of Gilgamesh*, pp. 2, 99. For a discussion of the *apkallu*, see J. Van Seters, *Prologue to History: The Yahwist as Historian in Genesis* (Louisville, KY: Westminster/John Knox Press, 1992), pp. 68-77.

First is the Babylonian creation story known as the *Enuma Elish*.[7] Although written in the mid-second millennium BCE, the text achieved prominence in the first millennium BCE, especially because of the rise to prominence of the Neo-Babylonian power in the sixth century. The myth's new lease on life was doubtless due to its ability to furnish a divine sanction for the dominance of Babylon in the seventh and sixth centuries BCE. The text deals with creation in several different arenas. First, the primeval couple, Apsu and Tiamat, begets the first generation of gods. After a cosmic battle between Marduk and Tiamat, the victorious Marduk, now acknowledged as king of all the gods, embarks on a series of creations, beginning with the heavens, which he makes from the bisected corpse of the defeated Tiamat. Next comes the creation of the constellations, the moon, time and the seasons. Then the land of Mesopotamia is made, including the Tigris and Euphrates. Finally, as the culmination of the cosmogony, Marduk decides to create a city in the middle of the new world, and to call it *bab-ilu*, ' the gate of god'. Here, Marduk and the other gods will dwell and be served by humankind, newly created expressly for this purpose. In gratitude for his wisdom and beneficence, the other gods proceed to make Marduk's 'house' in the new city: his great temple Esagila and ziggurat Etemenanki, fashioned 'as counterpart to Esharra [heaven]'.[8] The order of creation in the epic runs, then: heavens and earth, the city of Babylon, people, and Marduk's temple Esagila.

When one surveys the arrangement of the newly made world at the end of the *Enuma Elish* the prominence given to Babylon is difficult to

---

7. Translation and commentary in B. Foster, *Before the Muses: An Anthology of Akkadian Literature* (2 vols; Bethesda: CDL Press, 2nd edn, 1996), I, pp. 350-401.

8. Foster, *Before the Muses*, I, p. 381. The Sumerian terms *e-sagil* and *e-temen-an-ki* mean, respectively, 'house whose top is high' and 'house whose foundation is heaven and the underworld' (A. George, *House Most High: The Temples of Ancient Mesopotamia* [Winona Lake, IN: Eisenbrauns, 1993], pp. 139-40, 149). T. Jacobsen notes that in the text, Babylon is the last act of *divine* creation on earth (*The Treasures of Darkness: A History of Mesopotamian Religion* [New Haven: Yale University Press, 1976], p. 181). In Christian tradition, Jerusalem is understood as a counterpart to heaven, but in an antithetical way. Thus Rev. 21.9-27, recycling and reinterpreting passages from Ezek. 40–48, contrasts the heavenly Jerusalem with the earthly city. For more discussion on Jerusalem in the Christian tradition, see Hoppe, *The Holy City*, pp. 6-14, and, more fully, H. Busse and G. Kretschmar, *Jerusalemer Heiligtumstraditionen in altkirchlicher und frühislamischer Zeit* (Wiesbaden: Otto Harrassowitz, 1987), and R. Wilken, *The Land called Holy: Palestine in Christian History and Thought* (New Haven: Yale University Press, 1993).

overlook. The city occupies the exact center of the cosmos, between the realm of the gods who dwell below and those who are above. The text's purpose is obviously to extol the city of Babylon and its patron deity, Marduk. Just as he is the *bel*, or lord, of all the gods, so too is Babylon the master of all other cities in the world. Babylon is portrayed as the culmination of *every* divine act of creation in the cosmos, the place chosen by Marduk for his abode and the dwelling place of all the gods as well. Further evidence of the myth's use in support of this ideology is available in the Assyrian versions of the *Enuma Elish* in which the Assyrian national god Assur takes the place of Marduk, and the Assyrian capital of the same name occupies the cosmic center instead of Babylon.[9] It is only natural that in an infinite cosmos there can be infinite 'centers'.[10]

The second example is the Egyptian text known as the *Memphite Theology*, an Old Kingdom composition (c. 2700–2200 BCE) preserved in an inscription dating from the 25th Dynasty (eighth–seventh centuries BCE).[11] The text seems to combine two separate traditions: one about the supremacy of the god Horus (symbol of Lower Egypt) over his uncle Seth[12] (symbol of Upper Egypt), with another that asserts the primacy of the god Ptah and his city of Memphis. As with Marduk and Babylon in the *Enuma Elish*, in the Egyptian text Ptah is extolled as creator of cosmos, gods, and proper worship, and then his city Memphis is praised:

> He [Ptah] gave birth to the gods, he made the towns...he settled their offerings, he established their shrines, he made their bodies according to their wishes... The Great Throne [Memphis] that gives joy to the heart of the gods in the house of Ptah is the granary of Ta-teten the mistress of all life, through which the sustenance of the Two Lands is provided... Thus Osiris

---

9.   Foster, *Before the Muses*, I, p. 350. Concerning Assur, J.N. Postgate remarks that 'Assur the god is hardly more than the deified city, and plays no role in any other pantheon known to us' ('Royal Ideology and State Administration in Sumer and Akkad', in *CANE*, I, p. 406).

10.   See J. Borges, 'The Library of Babylon', in *idem, Ficciones* (trans. A. Bonner; New York: Grove, 1989), pp. 79-88.

11.   Translation and discussion are in M. Lichtheim, *Ancient Egyptian Literature*. I. *The Old and Middle Kingdoms* (Berkeley: University of California Press, 1975), pp. 51-57.

12.   Lichtheim, *Ancient Egyptian Literature*, I, p. 56. In Egyptian mythology, Horus is the son of Osiris. Osiris was murdered by his brother Seth and his body found at Memphis. Thus, the two stories, while distinct, are related. See J. Van Dijk, 'Myth and Mythmaking in Ancient Egypt', in *CANE*, III, pp. 1702-706, for an overview of the Osiris myths.

came into the earth at the Royal Fortress [Memphis]... His son Horus arose
as king of Upper Egypt, arose as king of Lower Egypt.[13]

It should be emphasized again that in both the Babylonian and Egyptian
texts theology is at the service of social and political needs. The claims to
supremacy of Babylon and Memphis are 'underwritten', as it were, by
their respective divine patrons. The dominant role of these cities is understood to be part of the primal cosmic arrangement. Just as the natural
world has been so since the beginning, so too, the texts maintain, has the
political realm been fashioned. The prestige and power of these cities is a
fact of existence; it is simply the way things are. The city, and its corresponding political, social and cultic roles, is portrayed as a cosmic datum
like the stars, the mountains or the sea. To stand against the power of the
city is, consequently, madness, as if one to were to attempt to defy nature
and the elements.[14]

The City Founded by a Hero
Many cities in antiquity connected themselves to heroes. These figures
could be legendary or historical, and have come from the remote or recent
past. Traditions of heroic city-founders take several distinct forms. Some
cities fashion tales of their founding by a hero who in turn functions as an
eponym for the city. To give an obvious example, Rome traced its origins
and name to its founder, Romulus.[15] Eponymous founders need not be
solely legendary. The Assyrian king, Sargon II (reigned 721–705 BCE),
built a new capital on the Tigris and named it *Dur-Sharrukin*, 'the Fortress
of Sargon'.[16] Alexander the Great founded numerous cities that he named
Alexandria. After destroying Jerusalem in 135 CE, the Roman emperor
Hadrian rebuilt the city and named it Aelia Capitolina after his own family
(Aelius) and the Capitoline gods, Jupiter, Juno and Minerva. Constantine
built a magnificent capital on the Bosporus in 330 CE and named it Con-
stantinople.[17] In the Bible, David's general Joab takes the city of Rabbah

13. Lichtheim, *Ancient Egyptian Literature*, I, pp. 55-56.
14. Cf. P. Berger, *The Sacred Canopy* (Garden City, NY: Doubleday, 1967 [repr. =
New York: Anchor Books, 1990]), pp. 29-52.
15. Livy, *Roman History* 1.3-6. The traditions surrounding the founding of Rome
involve more than the Romulus legend; see the discussion below concerning the
competing narratives of Romulus and Aeneas.
16. See the discussion below concerning David's renaming of Jerusalem 'the City
of David' in 2 Sam. 5.
17. A city may also be founded and then named after someone important to the
founder. Among several such examples provided by Herod the Great is the instance in

and, in a gesture of insolence, threatens to rename it after himself (2 Sam. 12.28).

Closely related to the foundation of a city by a hero is the practice of colonization. In the period spanning the ninth–fifth centuries BCE many cities sent out groups of citizens to found other cities. This is the case of the famous Greek settlements in Sicily and Magna Graecia on the Italian peninsula. The head of such an expedition merited the title of οἰκιστής ('founder'). As head of the new colony, the founder was responsible for seeking divine sanction for the new colony from the Delphic oracle. He would then oversee the colony's foundation and governance, including the proper transfer and institution of the cults from the mother-city. After his death, the founder was often granted heroic honors, among these being the right to have offerings made at his grave. Many new cities were founded in this manner throughout the Mediterranean world during the Hellenistic period as well. Among these foundations were cities that had already existed for centuries, and whose subsequent 'foundation' consisted of assuming Greek names and social structures.[18] The ideology used to support such expansionism involved the exaltation of the mother-city and the emphasis on the colony's connection with both the mother-city and their own legendary founder. The historical reality of city foundations thus easily coalesced with legendary tales about city-founders. This resulted in a continuum in which historical founders would take on heroic qualities, and cities that did not know their origins would create founder traditions. In some instances, cities would change their founders as political expediency demanded.

Existing cities subject to conquest were often portrayed as being founded anew. In Antiquity the conquest of a city was understood as a transfer of ownership. The victor, in a show of his hegemony over the city, was free to destroy the city and rebuild it, to slaughter or exile its inhabitants and repopulate the city, or to replace the local elites with people subservient to him. Whatever course he chose to take, the official explanation given for a conqueror's action often involves the ideology of improvement. The city

c. 10 BCE when he built a sumptuous city on the site of an earlier Palestinian coastal site and named it Caesarea in honor of the Roman emperor Augustus, who had given the city to him.

18. 'City-Founders', in *OCD* (2nd edn), p. 244; 'Colonization, Greek', in *OCD* (2nd edn), pp. 264-65, and A. Graham, *Colony and Mother City in Ancient Greece* (repr., New York: Barnes & Noble, 1971). For urban foundations in the Hellenistic period, see H. Koester, *Introduction to the New Testament. I. History, Culture, and Religion of the Hellenistic Age* (Berlin: W. de Gruyter, 2nd edn, 1995), pp. 71-75.

was now better, as good as new, or a new thing altogether, possibly with a new name. In an inscription describing his destruction of the city of Samaria in 722 BCE, Sargon II of Assyria claims to have led Samaria's inhabitants into exile and then to have 'rebuilt the city, better than it was before and settled therein peoples from countries which I myself had conquered'.[19] Conquest is thus understood as foundation in the fact that it is represented as a new beginning that conclusively breaks with the past. Ancient texts regularly use the dichotomy of order and chaos to illustrate this shift. Before a city is conquered it is ruled by the forces of darkness, evil and chaos, in other words the antithesis of civilization. After conquest, things are put into order, understood as a state of affairs where the right person has power and his subjects are obedient and industrious. Things are then as they should be, according to the nature of reality.[20] The Cyrus Cylinder is a parade example of this type of rhetoric. Babylon has fallen into disarray because of the apostasy of an evil king. At the command of the gods Cyrus comes to restore the proper order and is greeted as the conquering hero. The Assyrian text of Sargon quoted above is also explicit on this point. According to the inscription, prior to Sargon's intervention the city of Samaria was populated with ungrateful clients who did not know how to show proper respect to the Assyrian king. Afterward, the new city is ruled over by a faithful vassal and peopled by inhabitants who know what is expected of them as Assyrian clients: 'I placed an officer of mine as governor over them and imposed upon them tribute as is customary for Assyrian citizens'.[21] As with those explanations that attribute the city's foundation to the gods, so too here the attempt is to claim that a certain political state of affairs, that is, the rule of a city by a particular person or a city's rule over others, is in fact part of the natural order which stands in opposition to the threatening, disordered realm of rule by a false king or city. Consequently, to be against the city or a particular ruler is to be an enemy of the civilized human world and an accomplice of the forces

19. *ANET* (2nd edn), p. 284.

20. K. Younger, *Ancient Conquest Accounts: A Study in Ancient Near Eastern and Biblical History Writing* (JSOTSup, 98; Sheffield: JSOT Press, 1990), pp. 65-69; M. Liverani, *Prestige and Interest: International Relations in the Near East ca. 1600–1100 B.C.* (Pauda: Sargon SRL, 1990); G. Bellia, 'Note sulla spazialità dell'Oriente antico', in S. Manfredi and A. Passaro (eds.), *Abscondita in lucem: Scritti in onore di mons. Benedetto Rocco* (Palermo: Salvatore Sciascia, 1998), pp. 23-53. These remarks also draw upon T. Bolin, 'Warfare', in J. Barton (ed.), *The Biblical World* (2 vols.; London: Routledge, 2002), II, pp. 33-53.

21. *ANET* (2nd edn), p. 284.

of destruction. Anyone with but a passing familiarity with modern political rhetoric realizes the persistence of this ideology.

Conversely, founder traditions can be used to protect a vulnerable city from destruction by recourse to an implied or explicit threat of divine punishment on any who would dare violate an ancient and revered settlement. This was the rationale behind declaring German occupied Rome an open city during the Second World War as the Allied armies advanced on it. It worked for Rome, but not for the 1500 year-old Benedictine abbey of Monte Cassino south of Rome, which was completely destroyed by American bombs in 1944. Divine protection over a city can also be used to calm an anxious populace facing the possibilities of destruction or siege.[22]

One may also speak of a symbolic conquest. This is at work in a city's boast of having been paid a visit by a great hero. These tales lend prestige to the city in question through connection with a famous personage and in turn also enhance the 'conqueror's' heroic stature. Josephus claims that Alexander the Great paid a visit to Jerusalem on his way to Egypt and offered his respects to the high priest and the Jewish god (*Ant.* 11.325-39, discussed below in relationship with Gen. 14). The Cyrus inscription concerning Babylon mentioned above hints at this in its claim that Cyrus captured the great city without a battle. In the New Testament Gospels, Jesus' entry into Jerusalem is described as a figurative capture. He rides into the city acclaimed as a king by the people, and then symbolically destroys the city by expelling temple personnel from the sacred precincts and predicting the fall of Jerusalem at the hands of the Romans.[23] Setting this 'conquest' immediately prior to Jesus' crucifixion, the Gospel writers portray in story the Christian belief that the ignominious death of Jesus is, in fact, a victory.[24]

As in the case of foundation stories involving the gods, explanations for the founding of cities that have recourse to heroes also exist to serve the

22. Cf. also the remark of Poseidon in *Iliad* 21.446-47 about his having made the walls of Troy impregnable after being tricked by the Trojan king.

23. These elements are present in all four of the canonical Gospels, but are most easily seen in Lk. 19.28-47, where they occur in sequence without any intervening material.

24. The victory of Jesus over Jerusalem, represented in the persons of the chief priests and scribes, is also stressed by the Gospel writers in the many confrontation stories placed in between Jesus' entry into Jerusalem and his death. In all of these, Jesus comes away the winner. In John, the cleansing of the Temple is placed at the beginning of Jesus' career (2.13-25). That Gospel stresses the victory of Jesus in his death with different literary elements.

political ends of specific groups, helping to justify local or regional pre-eminence and resultant dominance over neighboring cities. Conquest stories in particular explain the change in political control in terms of the institution or restoration of order and the inauguration of a new city, either on the site of the previous one or quite simply identical with its predecessor in everything but name. That other cities might also have similar origin stories is not a complication here. These differences can be ignored as long as possible and, should this tack fail, they may always be sorted out on the battlefield, with subsequent revision to stories an option if necessary.

Biblical Texts about the Founding of Jerusalem

There is no single narrative tradition in the Hebrew Bible about the founding of Jerusalem. This is a curious fact, given the city's centrality in the overwhelming majority of the biblical texts. Equally remarkable is that none of the biblical traditions explicitly claims primeval divine foundation for the city, as does the *Enuma Elish* for Babylon and the *Memphite Theology* for Memphis. The creation story of Genesis 1 bears many resemblances to that of the *Enuma Elish*: in both myths the primeval waters are defeated by the chief deity of the pantheon and a world is created in the midst of the waters below and above. Yet in the Genesis account there is no city or temple in the center of the newly created world. Instead of being made as a place for the gods to live, the world exists as an exclusively human habitat. One wonders whether the author wrote during the exilic period when the city of Jerusalem and its temple did not exist, or whether the text is a Diaspora polemic against Jerusalem and its temple, or is an extended philosophical critique of all cosmogonies that envision a world that could possibly contain a radically transcendent divinity. In contrast, Isa. 60.3-13 places Jerusalem in the center of the cosmos, but this vision is eschatological rather than primeval. Jerusalem's centrality leads to the understanding that it is the place where the wealth and honor of the entire world come to be housed. In this manner it is more like the Persian imperial ideology of center and periphery visually expressed in the palace reliefs at Persepolis.[25] At best, one could point to Ps. 78.69, which says of Yawheh that 'he built his temple like the heights, like the earth which he established for eternity' (ויבן כמו רמים מקדשו כארץ יסדה לעולם), or Ezek. 38.12, which refers in passing to Jerusalem as 'the navel of the

---

25. A. Kuhrt, *The Ancient Near East c. 3000–330 B.C.* (2 vols.; London: Routledge, 1995), II, pp. 676-82.

earth' (טבור הארץ).[26] More common is the recurrence in Deuteronomy 12 of the enigmatic phrase 'the place that Yahweh your god chooses' (המקום אשר יבחר יהוה אלהיכם), which most, if not all, scholars assume refers to Jerusalem.[27] There is also the divine endorsement of Solomon's temple in 1 Kgs 9.3, where Yahweh promises Solomon that he will forever dwell in the temple built for him by the wise king.[28] However, for the most part there are few occurrences of the divine-founder theme for Jerusalem in the Hebrew Bible. This fact is all the more significant given that some biblical texts are hostile to the idea that Yahweh dwells in a city. In addition to Genesis 1's cosmology, devoid of a city and temple, Yahweh tells David in 2 Sam. 7.5, when the latter proposes to build a temple for him, 'Are you the one to build me a house to live in?' (האתה תבנה־לי בית לשבתי).[29] Yahweh's resistance to the idea of a temple also allows the author to juxtapose two different meanings of the Hebrew בית ('house'). It is not David who will build a house (i.e. temple) for Yahweh, but Yahweh who will build a house (i.e. dynasty) for David.[30] Similarly in

26. These texts are discussed in J. Levenson, *Sinai and Zion: An Entry into the Jewish Bible* (Minneapolis: Winston, 1985), pp. 102-37. Levenson uses these texts to substantiate the claim that the Hebrew Bible does contain mythology similar to that found in the *Enuma Elish* about the temple and city being established by god on the primeval cosmic mountain. However the meager evidence in the biblical text leads Levenson to maintain that the biblical authors were trying to downplay religious similarities with their non-Israelite neighbors. His reading of the biblical text is also influenced by later rabbinic exegesis, which did have a developed tradition of Jerusalem as the primeval center of the created world.

27. More specifically in Yahweh's words of 1 Kgs 11.36: 'the city where I have chosen to put my name'. Numerous places in the Psalms speak of Yahweh's choice of Jerusalem (referred to as Zion) as a dwelling place. See also the essays by P.R. Davies and I. Hjelm in the present volume.

28. There are other signs of divine favor. In 1 Kgs 8.10-11 a cloud designated as 'the glory of Yahweh' fills the temple at its dedication. Prior to this, the temple's site is chosen after David beholds a vision of an angel and is commanded by Yahweh to erect an altar on a threshing floor belonging to a non-Israelite inhabitant of Jerusalem (2 Sam. 24.15-25; cf. the different account in 1 Chron. 21.18–22.1).

29. The parallel text of 1 Chron. 17.4 is more explicit: 'You shall not build me a house to live in' (לא אתה תבנה לי הבית לשבת).

30. So 2 Sam. 7.11: 'Yahweh declares to you that he will make you a house' (והגיד לך יהוה כי בית יעשה לך יהוה). On the different nuances of the Hebrew term בית, see the extensive discussion surrounding the *bytdwd* inscription discovered in 1993 at Tel Dan in P.R. Davies, '*Bytdwd* and *Swkt Dwyd*: A Comparison', *JSOT* 64 (1994), pp. 23-24; E. Ben Zvi, 'On the Reading "Bytdwd" in the Aramaic Stele from Tel Dan',

1 Kgs 8.16 Yahweh declares that he did not choose a *city* (i.e. Jerusalem) but a *man* (i.e. David). Strictly speaking, the presence of Yahweh in his temple and the exalted status of Jerusalem, while related in the Hebrew Bible, are not equivocal.[31] This ambiguity in the divine attitude toward Jerusalem is one of the ongoing interpretive cruxes for biblical scholars.

The absence of a clear divine-founder tradition allows for the possibility that the biblical texts substantiate the importance of Jerusalem through the use of hero tales, and that is exactly what one finds in the texts. None of the heroes involved in these stories functions as an eponymic referent for the city of Jerusalem *as such*,[32] although the alternate name of Jerusalem, the 'City of David', takes its name from the famous Israelite king. As mentioned above, cities may be tied to heroes through visitation, conquest or foundation. All three of these explanations are present in biblical texts about Jerusalem. Examination of the relevant passages reveals that the biblical authors' aim was to validate the importance of Jerusalem not by reference to a single event in the past that could be interpreted as the city's origin, but rather by constructing a series of such foundation events spanning the entirety of Israelite history as it is assembled in the Hebrew Bible.[33] Each of these stories is examined here.

Visit by a Hero: Abram

The tale of Abram's defeat of five kings in Genesis 14 is one of the more enigmatic passages in the Patriarchal Cycle.[34] The text may be divided into

---

JSOT 64 (1994), pp. 25-32; E.A. Knauf, A. de Pury and T. Römer, '**BaytDawid* ou **BaytDod*? Une relecture de la nouvelle inscription de Tel Dan', *BN* 72 (1994), pp. 60-69. See also N.P. Lemche's essay in the present volume.

31. Discussed already by M. Noth, 'Jerusalem and the Israelite Tradition', in *idem*, *The Laws in the Pentateuch and Other Studies* (trans. D. Ap-Thomas; London: Oliver & Boyd, 1966), pp. 132-44).

32. The etymology of Jerusalem is uncertain; see the overview in P. King, 'Jerusalem', in *ABD*, III, pp. 747-66 (751).

33. By 'history' I mean the intellectual process and resultant literary construct that seeks to create a coherent narrative about a past that can be real or imagined (or, more often, a mixture of both). My use of the term does not mean to imply the historical accuracy of some of the biblical stories under discussion. Indeed, as my remarks below indicate, the biblical stories have more to do with the 'present' of their authors than with any real past. For more on this see T. Bolin, 'History, Historiography, and the Use of the Past in the Hebrew Bible', in C. Kraus (ed.), *The Limits of Historiography: Genre and Narrative in Ancient Historical Texts* (Leiden: E.J. Brill, 1999), pp. 113-40.

34. A thorough discussion and bibliography concerning the lack of supporting extra-biblical and archaeological evidence for Gen. 14 is in T.L. Thompson, *The*

three sections:[35] (1) a legendary passage written in annalistic style of the defeat of a coalition of five rebellious vassal kings by another coalition of four patron kings (vv. 1-11); (2) a story in which Abram assembles a small group of warriors from his household, routs the four patron kings who have taken his nephew Lot captive, and returns both with Lot and a great deal of plunder, the latter which he gives to the grateful king of Sodom (vv. 12-16, 21-24); (3) an episode in which Abram is met and blessed by Melchizedek, king of Salem (i.e. Jerusalem[36]) who in return is given by Abram one tenth of the spoil (vv. 18-20).

The legendary character of the passage is clear.[37] Abram appears uncharacteristically as a military hero, whereas in the remainder of the material about him in Genesis he is a semi-nomadic foreigner wandering to and fro

Historicity of the Patriarchal Narratives: The Quest for the Historical Abraham (BZAW, 133; Berlin: W. de Gruyter, 1974), pp. 187-95. For discussion and bibliography dealing with source-, form- and tradition-critical issues, see C. Westermann, *Genesis 12–36* (Philadelphia: Fortress Press, 1985), pp. 182-208; F. Anderson, 'Genesis 14: An Enigma', in D. Wright, D.N. Freedman and A. Hurvitz (eds.), *Pomegranates and Golden Bells: Studies in Biblical, Jewish, and Near Eastern Ritual, Law, and Literature in Honor of Jacob Milgrom* (Winona Lake, IN: Eisenbrauns, 1995), pp. 497-508. I was unable to consult K. Baltzer, 'Jerusalem in den Erzvätergeschichten der Genesis? Traditionsgeschichtliche Erwägungen zu Gen 14 und 22', in E. Blum, C. Macholz and E.W. Stegemann (eds.), *Die hebräische Bibel und ihre zweifache Nachgeschichte. Festschrift für Rolf Rendtorff zum 65. Geburtstag* (Neukirchen–Vluyn: Neukirchener Verlag, 1990), pp. 3-12.

35. Following Westermann (*Genesis 12–36*, pp. 190-92) but without subscribing to his dating of the constituent parts. Cf. S. Bigger, 'Genesis: History or Story?', in *idem* (ed.), *Creating the Old Testament: The Emergence of the Hebrew Bible* (Oxford: Basil Blackwell, 1989), pp. 98-102.

36. The equation is accepted by nearly all biblical scholars and appears early in the Jewish tradition in both the Hebrew Bible (Ps. 76.3) and the Qumran literature (1Qap Gen[ar] 22.13). For a full discussion, see J. Emerton, 'The Site of Salem, The City of Melchizedek (Genesis XIV 18)', in *idem* (ed.), *Studies in the Pentateuch* (VTSup, 41; Leiden: E.J. Brill, 1990), pp. 45-71. Melchizedek is only mentioned in one other biblical text (Ps. 110.4), but played a significant role in later Jewish and Christian tradition. See the surveys in J. Fitzmyer, 'Melchizedek in the MT, LXX, and the New Testament', *Bib* 81 (2000), pp. 63-69, and M. McNamara, 'Melchizedek: Gen 14,17-20 in the Targums, in Rabbinic, and Early Christian Literature', *Bib* 81 (2000), pp. 1-31.

37. Westermann (*Genesis 12–36*, pp. 196-97) concludes that the story puts forward 'the impossible notion that Abraham conquered four kings of powerful empires with 318 men and chased them through the whole of Palestine' (pp. 201-202).

across the ancient Near East.[38] Important to notice is the intrusiveness of the Salem/Jerusalem episode in the story. In vv. 18-20, Abram is met by Melchizedek, the priest-king of Jerusalem who brings Abram an offering of bread and wine and blesses him by the West Semitic deity El Elyon. In response, Abram gives Melchizedek one tenth of the spoil and equates El Elyon with the Israelite god, Yahweh (v. 22).[39] However, Salem is not one of the cities threatened by the four invading kings; nor is it even mentioned in the text prior to v. 18. Abram's giving of a portion of the booty to Melchizedek contradicts and detracts from Abram's boast to the king of Sodom in vv. 22-24 that Abram will return to him all but those provisions necessary for his men.

At work in Genesis 14 is a founder tradition that portrays the great hero visiting a city. Abram's credentials as a hero are established in the first part of the chapter with the account of his stunning defeat over a coalition of mighty foreign kings (arguably the only act of his in the Bible that can be termed 'heroic' in the classic sense). Immediately afterwards, Melchizedek, the king and priest of Jerusalem, meets Abram outside of his city and acknowledges Abram's exalted status. In turn, Abram honors the city by presenting an offering to its god, represented by the god's broker, Melchizedek. Abram goes further by equating Jerusalem's god with his own. The intrusiveness of the Melchizedek episode into the battle account of Genesis 14 lends credence to the contention that it is an insertion into

38. So too Bigger, for whom 'it was evidently within the author's intention to create a story in which Abram figured as a victorious military man' ('Genesis: History or Story?', p. 100). The passage has affinities with the military conquests recounted in the book of Judges, most specifically the Gideon story in Judg. 6–7 (Westermann, *Genesis 12–36*, pp. 191, 201). The image of Abram/Abraham as the perpetual foreigner (Hebrew: גר) is explored further in T. Bolin, '"A Stranger and an Alien among You" (Gen 23,4): The Old Testament in Early Jewish and Christian Self-Identity', in J. Hills (ed.), *Common Life in the Early Church: Essays Honoring Graydon F. Snyder* (Nashville: Trinity Press International, 1998), pp. 57-76.

39. Discussion and bibliography in E. Elnes and P. Miller, 'Elyon', in *DDD* (2nd edn), pp. 293-99. The equation of Yahweh and El Elyon does not occur in the LXX of Gen. 14.22. The process whereby the names of other deities are transformed into epithets for Yahweh is common in the Hebrew Bible (cf. Exod. 6.2-3, which equates Yahweh with El Shaddai). The same phenomenon is present in the final two tablets of the *Enuma Elish* which enumerate 50 glorious names of Marduk, many of which are the names of other gods (Foster, *Before the Muses*, I, pp. 388-400). The epic ends extolling Marduk as 'the Enlil of all the gods' (I, p. 400). Enlil is also the proper name of the chief deity of the Sumerian pantheon; as such, Enlil appears in many texts.

the story. Abram's role as a victorious military commander is the most fitting place to have him 'found' Jerusalem. That is to say, that his presence as a hero in the city and the honor he extends to the place validates it. The tale's format closely resembles the legend of Alexander the Great's visit to Jerusalem and his acknowledgment of the Jewish high priest and his god that is narrated in the *Jewish Antiquities* of Josephus, a text that also seeks to claim an exalted status for Jerusalem. Josephus recounts that after the siege and destruction of Tyre, Alexander was eager to go to Jerusalem (*Ant.* 11.325). While on the way to the city, he was met by Jaddua the high priest in full sacerdotal regalia. Alexander approached Jaddua and, prostrating himself before the high priest, extolled the Jewish god as the one who had commanded him to embark on his conquests and had ensured his victory (*Ant.* 11.329-35). Alexander then went into the Jerusalem temple to make offerings to the Jewish god (*Ant.* 11.336). The parallels with Genesis 14 are striking. In both accounts a victor fresh from battle is met outside the city by the priest/leader of Jerusalem. The hero returns the honor given him by the priest by acknowledging the city's god, and by so doing shows great honor to Jerusalem. It is unclear whether the story about Alexander is purely the work of Josephus, or whether he is drawing upon earlier legends.[40] That Genesis 14 may be influenced by an earlier legend about Alexander visiting Jerusalem that was also reworked by Josephus has not been explored.[41]

Conquest: Joshua and David

The Hebrew Bible has two narrative traditions of the conquest of Jerusalem by the Israelites, each tradition existing in two variants. The first tradition is set during the period of the Israelite appropriation of Palestine under Joshua (Josh. 10; Judg. 1). Apparent in the text of Joshua 10 are the many plot similarities with the story of Abram and Jerusalem in Genesis 14. The Israelite hero battles against a coalition of kings, four in the case

40. For discussion, see E. Bickerman, *The Jews in the Greek Age* (Cambridge, MA: Harvard University Press, 1988), pp. 1-7.

41. J. Soggin ('Abraham and the Eastern Kings: On Genesis 14', in Z. Zevit [ed.], *Solving Riddles and Untying Knots: Biblical, Epigraphic, and Semitic Studies in Honor of Jonas C. Greenfield* [Winona Lake, IN: Eisenbrauns, 1995], pp. 283-89) dates Gen. 14 to the Hellenistic period. In a different vein, G. Rendsburg dates the story to the time of David and reads the text as an *apologia* for David's choice of the (putatively) non-Israelite Zadok to be high priest ('Biblical Literature as Politics: The Case of Genesis', in A. Berlin [ed.], *Religion and Politics in the Ancient Near East* [Bethesda: University of Maryland Press, 1996], pp. 58-59).

of Abram, five for Joshua (Josh. 10.3-5, but note the coalition of five kings in Gen. 14.8).[42] The hero engages in nocturnal military maneuvers and routs the enemy (Gen. 14.15; Josh. 10.9). The enemies take flight, but are entrapped by some natural impediment, either tar pits (Gen. 14.10) or caves (Josh. 10.16-18).[43] A prominent role is played in the two accounts by the king of Jerusalem, whose names are very similar: Melchizedek in Genesis 14 and Adonizedek in Joshua 10.[44] Joshua 10 does not explicitly state that Jerusalem was taken by the Israelites, however it is assumed in the fact that Joshua kills Adonizedek. Additionally, the list of defeated kings in Joshua 12 includes Jerusalem (v. 10) and the variant account of Judges 1 clearly states that the Israelites took Jerusalem (this time under Judah rather than Joshua): 'The sons of Judah fought against Jerusalem and took it. They put its inhabitants to the sword and fired the city' (וילחמו בני יהודה בירושלם וילכדו אותה ויכוה לפי חרב ואת העיר שלחו באש, Judg. 1.8).

This seemingly straightforward account of the taking of Jerusalem by the newly arrived Israelites is muddied by the persistent biblical tradition that the city's pre-Israelite inhabitants, known in the biblical text as the Jebusites, continued to live there. So Josh. 15.63 states that 'The sons of Judah were not able to drive out the Jebusites, the inhabitants of Jerusalem. So the Jebusites dwell with the sons of Judah in Jerusalem to this day' (ואת היבוסי יושבי ירושלם לא יוכלו בני יהודה להורישם וישב היבוסי את בני יהודה בירושלם עד היום הזה).[45] Similarly, Judg. 19.10— a text that occurs ostensibly after the Israelite capture of Jerusalem—notes that a traveling Levite chose not to stay in Jebus (identified parenthetically with Jerusalem) because it was a non-Israelite city. The toponym 'Jebus' (and the corresponding term 'Jebusite') does not occur outside the Hebrew

42. Ps. 48, which extols the grandeur of Jerusalem, also speaks of the defeat of a coalition of foreign kings See the discussion in J. Levenson, 'Zion Traditions', in *ABD*, VI, pp. 1099-101.

43. Ancient Near Eastern literary parallels discussed in Younger, *Ancient Conquest Accounts*, pp. 220-25.

44. The two Hebrew names, Melchizedek and Adonizedek, have practically the same meaning: 'my king is righteous' and 'my lord is righteous', respectively. The variant account of the taking of Jerusalem in Judg. 1 gives the name Adonibezek for the king. This is also the reading of the LXX in both Josh. 10 and Judg. 1 and is followed by Josephus, *Ant.* 5.121-24.

45. The parallel passage in Judg. 1.21 speaks of the tribe of Benjamin rather than Judah. This contradicts the statement of Judg. 1.8, quoted above, that the Israelites completely destroyed Jerusalem and its inhabitants.

Bible and its provenance and meaning are unknown.[46] From a literary standpoint, however, the enduring presence of the Jebusites in Jerusalem creates the necessity for taking the city from them again, which David does in 2 Samuel 5. However, the David traditions about Jerusalem are not without their own ambiguity in this respect. 1 Samuel 17.54 states that after killing Goliath, David removed his head and brought it to Jerusalem, implying that the city was under Israelite control even though David does not take the city from the Jebusites until 2 Samuel 5. After capturing Jerusalem, David renames the city after himself: 'David settled in the fortress and called it the City of David' (2 Sam. 5.9),[47] the first occurrence of this place name in the Hebrew Bible. Used most often in the burial notices of the kings of Judah found in 2 Kings and 2 Chronicles, it can refer either to portions of Jerusalem or to the entire city.

The accounts of David's capture of the city in 2 Samuel 5 and 1 Chronicles 11 in many ways comprise a standard tale of a siege. As in other such tales, there is the taunting of the besieging army by the city's inhabitants in 2 Sam. 5.6 where the Jebusites boast that their city is so impregnable that even the physically disabled could withstand David's forces. In 2 Sam. 5.8, David refers to the now famous *tzinnor* (Hebrew צנור),[48] as the way for the Israelites to take the city from the Jebusites. The parallel account in 1 Chronicles 11 does not mention the *tzinnor*, but does say that David's lieutenant Joab led the assault on the city, thus earning the right to command David's army. The parallel accounts of 2 Samuel 5 and 1 Chronicles 11 contain the fragments of the literary motif of the single valiant soldier, in this case Joab, gaining entry into a city due to some structural weakness on its part, this being the water channel. This motif occurs elsewhere in ancient literature, for example in the account of Herodotus

---

46. A summary of the historical problems surrounding this term is supplied by S. Reed, 'Jebus', in *ABD*, III, pp. 652-53.

47. The explanation is different in 1 Chron. 11.7, where Jerusalem is called the City of David because he lived there and not because he renamed it.

48. The translation of the Hebrew of 2 Sam. 5.6-8 has puzzled commentators. P. McCarter (*II Samuel* [AB, 9; New York: Doubleday, 1984], pp. 136-40) reads vv. 6-8 so as to understand that the blind and the lame incite the Jebusites to taunt David in v 6. This explains his hatred of them and their cultic exclusion in v. 8. McCarter's reading is subject to some difficulties. It requires the two occurrences of the phrase 'the blind and the lame' to refer to two different groups of people: those already so disabled who urge the Jebusites to resist David and those defenders who may be disabled in the Israelite assault on the city.

(*Histories* 1.84), which tells of the capture of Sardis by Cyrus the Great of Persia. In this story, Cyrus offers a reward to any of his soldiers who can penetrate the city, which by then had been under siege for 14 days. One of Cyrus' men observes one of the city defenders clamber down a seemingly impassible sheer rock face to retrieve his helmet that had fallen. Cyrus' soldier is thus able to climb up the rock himself and finds a way for the Persians to take the city. As in the two accounts of David's capture of Jerusalem, the story in Herodotus tells of a general rewarding an act of individual bravery on the part of one of his men which involves some feat of physical daring that exploits a weakness in a city's defenses.[49] Much historical speculation on 2 Samuel 5 centers on the possibility of whether *tzinnor* refers to the water shaft discovered by Charles Warren in 1867 and dated by archaeologists to the tenth century BCE. However, it is practically impossible for someone to come through this passageway and into the city. On the other hand, another water channel, known as Hezekiah's Tunnel, allows for relatively easy passage into the city. To this day, tourists in Jerusalem walk through it, beginning outside the ancient city walls at the Gihon spring and ending up inside the city at the Siloam Pool. The possibility that the *tzinnor* of 2 Samuel 5 refers to this water channel has not been seriously explored by scholars, since most agree that Hezekiah's Tunnel was built roughly three centuries after the putative time of David, and the assumption of 2 Samuel's historicity makes it imperative either to identify the *tzinnor* with a known pre-ninth century archaeological feature in Jerusalem or to translate the term so that its meaning has nothing to do with the topography of Jerusalem.[50] It seems more likely that the

49. 1 Chron. 11.15-19 continues with another such heroic story in which three of David's men enter the Philistine stronghold of Bethlehem in order to fulfill David's wish to drink water from its well. Upon being presented with the water, David is so humbled by his men's devotion and bravery that he offers the water to God (cf. a similar story told about Alexander in Plutarch, *Alex.* 42). S. Holm-Nielsen maintains that Joab did not climb up a water shaft during the siege, but rather captured the source of the water shaft that supplied Jerusalem, thus forcing the city's capitulation ('Did Joab Climb "Warren's Shaft"?', in A. Lemaire and B. Otzen [eds.], *History and Tradition of Early Israel: Studies Presented to Eduard Nielsen* [VTSup, 50; Leiden: E.J. Brill, 1993], pp. 38-49). On water systems in Jerusalem, see Y. Shiloh, 'Underground Water Systems in Eretz-Israel in the Iron Age', in L. Perdue, L.E. Toombs and G.L. Johnson (eds.), *Archaeology and Biblical Interpretation: Essays in Memory of D. Glenn Rose* (Atlanta: John Knox Press, 1987), pp. 215-22.

50. According to McCarter, David tells his men in v. 7 to strike enemy soldiers in the windpipe (McCarter's translation of צנור), presumably so that their wounds

author of 2 Samuel is referring to Hezekiah's Tunnel anachronistically because he is recounting a legend about a heroic king set many centuries in the past.

The two biblical traditions of the Israelite conquest of Jerusalem have distinct literary forms. The tale of Joshua 10 (with a similar account in Judg. 1) draws upon a theme present also in Genesis 14 of a pitched battle with a coalition of enemy kings that results in a rout and the complete destruction of the city. The parallel stories of David's capture of the city take the form of a siege tale known in many variants in the ancient world in which the siege is successful on account of an act of individual heroism. Both traditions speak of the continuing presence of the pre-Israelite inhabitants in the city. The evidence for this in Joshua and Judges is discussed above, and in these texts it functions partially as a plot device that provides the motive for the taking and renaming of Jerusalem by David. The further mention of Jebusites in Jerusalem after David's conquest is more puzzling. As is the case with Josh. 15.63 and Judg. 1.21, 1 Kgs 19.10 refers to the non-Israelite residents of Palestine, among them the Jebusites, whom the Israelites were unable to drive out and who consequently still dwelled in the land. Moreover, 2 Samuel 24 and the parallel text in 1 Chronicles 21 recount how the land for the Jerusalem temple was purchased from a Jebusite inhabitant of the city (called Araunah in 2 Samuel and Ornan in 1 Chron. 21).[51]

---

will be fatal and there will be no enemy wounded to tend. McCarter assumes that 'in tenth-century B.C. Hebrew the range of meaning…must be included "(wind)-pipe, gullet," and thus "throat"' (*II Samuel*, p. 140). This translation, however, is founded upon an unattested extension of the meaning of *tzinnor* from a water pipe or channel to the windpipe. Apart from speculations about what must have been the case in ancient Hebrew, whether ancient writers would have known about the anatomical structure of the trachea cannot be assumed. For arguments on the basis of comparison with Ugaritic in favor of reading צנור as 'water shaft', see T. Kleven, 'The Use of *ṣnr* in Ugaritic and 2 Samuel 5 v. 8: Hebrew Usage and Comparative Philology', *VT* 44 (1994), pp. 95-204.

51. Rendsburg claims that the non-Israelite population was 'assimilated' by David's force after the taking of the city and that the previous king-priest was Zadok, whom David subsequently retained as high priest. Rendsburg reads the proper name 'Araunah' as a title, related to the Hurrian word for 'lord'. He thus equates Zadok with the man who sold David the land for the temple. Thus Rendsburg's reconstruction is as follows: David takes the city of Jerusalem from its king-priest Zadok. David retains Zadok as high priest and buys the land upon which Zadok performed cultic functions in order to build a temple to Yahweh ('Biblical Literature as Politics', pp. 55-57).

Colonization: Ezra and Nehemiah

The narratives of Ezra–Nehemiah are fraught with numerous unresolved historical questions concerning their date, authorship and sources.[52] Two things, however, are clear from reading the text. First is that, from the vantage point of the author, this story of Jerusalem's re-founding is something from the distant past. Second is that the figures of Ezra and Nehemiah were once independent of each other and have been brought together secondarily in the narrative. The two men deal with different Persian kings and are only together in the great rededication ceremony of Nehemiah 8–9, appearing not to know of each other in the remainder of the story. This is an odd state of affairs, given their prominence in both Jerusalem and the Persian court. The distinct Ezra and Nehemiah traditions that exist in early Judaism also speak to the artificial nature of their combination in the biblical text.[53]

The composite work of Ezra–Nehemiah is an extended foundation story for Jerusalem and contains all the essential elements to describe the colonization of a new settlement in Antiquity as is discussed above.[54] The two main characters share the duties of the founder. Both men lead a group of settlers to found the colony with the blessing of their local leadership. To Ezra is given the task of ritual purification, which involves offering prayers on behalf of the people and giving instruction in the Law of Yahweh. To Nehemiah fall the activities of building fortifications, populating the city with worthy inhabitants, and establishing commercial, cultic and social regulations. The picture in Ezra–Nehemiah is thus one in which a city is built from the ground up, complete with a temple, walls, population and necessary social structures. The twist here is that the

52. See the summary of the issues and bibliographies in L.L. Grabbe, *Judaism from Cyrus to Hadrian*. I. *The Persian and Greek Periods* (2 vols.; Minneapolis: Fortress Press, 1992), pp. 30-38. Cf. also the contributions of Lester Grabbe and Thomas Thompson in the present volume.

53. Concerning Ezra, there are the variant Greek versions of Ezra, which make only passing reference to Nehemiah. For Nehemiah there is the legend recounted in 2 Macc. 1, along with the famous encomium of Jewish heroes in Sir. 49.13, neither of which mentions Ezra. For a skeptical appraisal of the Ezra traditions, see G. Garbini, *Hsitory and Ideology in Ancient Israel* (New York: Crossroad, 1988), pp. 151-69.

54. Although the martial imagery of Neh. 4 along with the repeated expulsion of foreigners bears resemblance to the conquest narratives discussed above. For another use of Greek colonization stories and their relationship to the Bible, see W. Wilson, 'Urban Legends: Acts 10,1–11,18 and the Strategies of Greco-Roman Foundation Narratives', *JBL* 120 (2001), pp. 77-99.

mother-city whose cult must be honored in the colony is not the city from which the colonists have come (i.e. Babylon and its environs or, in the case of Nehemiah, Susa), but is rather the destroyed Jerusalem of the past. Put another way, the mother-city is not remote in distance, but in time. This is all part of the emphasis that Ezra–Nehemiah places on the dynamic interplay between continuity and rupture. The temple to Yahweh is rebuilt in Jerusalem, but it is nothing like the splendid building erected by Solomon (Ezra 3.12). The ancient law of Moses is once again being followed in Jerusalem, yet it has to be re-taught to the people as if it were a new thing because it has been forgotten (Neh. 8).[55] Jerusalem is a city that is empty and deserted after the Babylonian destruction; yet repeated mention is made of indigenous peoples who live there. For instance, according to Ezra 9.1, the Jebusites still dwell in the city. Consequently, both Ezra and Nehemiah are required to purify the population of such foreign influence (Ezra 9–10; Neh. 13), thus creating another literary paradox of a purified people in the midst of the enduring presence of outsiders, parallel to that found in the other biblical stories' mention of the persistence of the Jebusites in Jerusalem after it becomes an Israelite city.

Outside of the Bible is another tradition that describes the founding of Jerusalem in terms of colonization. The writings of the Greek historian Hecataeus of Abdera (c. 300 BCE) survive only in fragments quoted in the writings of Diodorus of Sicily (c. 50 BCE) and Josephus. In one of these, from a work dealing with the history of Egypt, Hecataeus narrates a story in which, after a plague has struck, foreigners are expelled from Egypt in an attempt to stave off divine wrath.

> The greater part of them were sent into what is now called Judea, a land not far from Egypt and entirely uninhabited at that time. The leader of the colony (ἀποικία) was called Moses, who was famous for his wisdom and courage. After taking possession of the land he founded, in addition to other cities, the one most renowned now, Jerusalem.[56]

After founding Jerusalem, Moses builds the temple and promulgates both cultic and civil norms. Hecataeus is clearly influenced by the colonization process at work in the Greek world, and indeed the Greek word he uses to

---

55. For further discussion of this see T. Bolin, 'When the End is the Beginning: The Persian Period and the Origins of the Biblical Tradition', *SJOT* 10 (1996), pp. 3-15.

56. Greek text, translation and commentary in M. Stern, *Greek and Latin Authors on Jews and Judaism* (3 vols.; Jerusalem: Israel Academy of Sciences and Humanities, 1974), I, pp. 20-44.

describe the nascent Jewish settlement (ἀποικία) is the same term used by Greek writers to talk about colonization.[57] There are also significant points of contact with Ezra–Nehemiah.[58] Like Ezra and Nehemiah, Moses founds Jerusalem, builds the temple, and establishes laws. Each account also tells of the founder enacting land reform. In Neh. 5.13, Nehemiah in his capacity as governor must upbraid the Jewish nobility in Jerusalem for charging exorbitant interest rates on loans to farmers and then appropriating the debtors' land when they default on the loans. Similarly, Hecataeus writes that Moses forbade the selling of land in order to prevent it from falling into the hands of a few wealthy owners.[59] This story about Moses from Hecataeus is tantalizing in that his source is unknown. Both Menahem Stern and Doron Mendels argue that Hecataeus used elements in his narrative that originated among Jewish circles.[60] This raises an interesting question, because in the Hebrew Bible arguably the single most important hero (i.e. Moses) has nothing to do with Jerusalem. Could an extra-biblical tradition about Moses that connected him with the founding of the city have originated among Egyptian Jews in the Hellenistic age? If so it would provide an interesting analogue to the kind of literary creation at work in the founder stories of the Hebrew Bible.

Conclusion

The multiplicity of founder stories in the Hebrew Bible raises the question of why the biblical authors collected and arranged numerous variants of the same tradition. Simply to say that the stories recount historical events in the order and manner in which they happened, or even to say that the stories preserve historical kernels, does not sufficiently explain the literary similarities and highly stylized nature of the texts, nor does it adequately address the considerable amount of contradictory historical evidence in the archaeological and textual sources. The solution lies instead in the

57. Citations can be found in Stern, *Greek and Latin Authors*, I, p. 30; see also I. Gafni, '"Pre-Histories" of Jerusalem in Hellenistic, Jewish and Christian Literature', *JSP* 1 (1987), pp. 5-22.

58. Cf. D. Mendels, 'Hecataeus of Abdera and a Jewish "patrios politeia" of the Persian Period (Diodorus Siculus XL, 3)', *ZAW* 95 (1983), pp. 96-110.

59. So too Mendels, 'Hecataeus of Abdera', pp. 107-108.

60. Stern, *Greek and Latin Authors*, I, pp. 21-24; Mendels, 'Hecataeus of Abdera'. Conversely, Gafni maintains that this account 'does *not* derive from an otherwise lost historical account' but rather exhibits aspects that are 'fixtures of the Greek ethnography of the period' ('"Pre-Histories" of Jerusalem', p. 7).

fundamental purpose of city-founder stories to justify a city's claim to prestige and dominance. This need, and the means devised to meet it, is the concern of urban elites, the creators of the 'Great Tradition', to use the term of sociologist Robert Redfield.[61] In the case of the biblical accounts, the repeated foundation of Jerusalem by a series of heroic figures from the authors' 'mythic past' serves to emphasize through repetition Jerusalem's claim for pre-eminence among ancient Jews. The fact that all but one of these stories is closely related to or contains cultic elements underscores the authors' desire to enhance the sacred status of Jerusalem as the place where Yahweh's one true temple stands. Thus Abram is blessed by the priest of Jerusalem and, following the law of Deut. 14.22-23, offers a tithe to Yahweh there. After taking Jerusalem, David transfers the ark into the city and purchases the land upon which his son Solomon will build the temple. The returning exiles in the book of Ezra build the temple and, as soon as it is completed, the priest Ezra arrives to furnish it and make offerings. Both Ezra and Nehemiah preside over re-dedication ceremonies in which the people of Israel swear allegiance to Yahweh and his Torah, an act designed to ensure that a holy people inhabits the holy city.[62] Related to this emphasis on cult is the Bible's concern with non-Jewish inhabitants in Jerusalem explicit in all of the tales. The Jewish heroes in the biblical narrative continuously live side by side in Jerusalem with 'outsiders', be they Jebusites, Samaritans, faithless Jews, or the עם הארץ ('the people of the land'). The stories thus represent the reality of the authors' world as one in which they were required to exist with 'outsiders'. In this way too, the stories portray the heroes as examples insofar as they persist in their fidelity to Yahweh and his Torah despite the presence of foreigners in their midst or, conversely, despite their being in the midst of foreigners.[63]

The urgency at work in these literary attempts to sustain Jerusalem's sacred status among Jews by stressing the exclusivity of its temple to Yahweh in the light of significant, extended contact with non-Jews seems

61. Cf. Bolin, '"A Stranger and an Alien among You"', pp. 57-59.

62. One could here cite the example of Judah Maccabee who, after taking Jerusalem from the foreign general Lysias, cleanses and re-dedicates the temple. On the idea that Jerusalem's holiness is derived in Israelite tradition secondarily due to the presence of the temple, see Noth, 'Jerusalem and the Israelite Tradition'.

63. Of course, the presence of other stories in the Hebrew Bible that fantasize about the expulsion of all foreigners from Jerusalem and Palestine, for instance, Ezek. 40–49 and the conquest traditions of Joshua, are evidence of another way of dealing with the presence of outsiders. This viewpoint is intensified in the Qumran literature.

to fit best with the cultural and historical contexts of the Hellenistic era, when the Jewish Diaspora was settled in renowned and prestigious cities such as Alexandria, Babylon and Sardis. The biblical stories are the temple elites' attempt to assert to their fellow Jews the sovereignty of Jerusalem over the other cities of the Hellenistic οἰκουμένη.[64] Rival temples to Yahweh were built in Egypt and elsewhere in Palestine, thus creating the need for the Jerusalem temple personnel to claim religious priority. Also, the extended contact of Jewish intellectuals with the culture and tradition of the Hellenistic world was seen by some Jewish elites as a threat to their cultural and religious identity. Consequently, the stories portray the ongoing presence of non-Jews in Jerusalem, yet also make clear how this fact does not in any way compromise the heroes' religious and cultural purity. The stories of heroic foundations of a city in general and of colonization in particular, that is, just the kind of tales about Jerusalem in the Hebrew Bible, are more typical of Hellenistic rather than ancient Near Eastern literature, which prefers to offer divine origins for cities.[65] As Isaiah Gafni has shown, the same narrative phenomenon as that under discussion in the Hebrew Bible is also present in rabbinic Jewish writings as well, which exhibit 'a tendency...to attach central issues, events and persons of the early biblical narrative to the city of Jerusalem'.[66] In particular, traditions which claimed that Adam had been created from the earth of Jerusalem,

64. D. Schwartz argues that during the Hellenistic period, Diaspora Jews had favorable views of Jerusalem as a Jewish city and that these views had nothing to do with the presence of the temple. Indeed, the temple was viewed negatively by these same Diaspora Jews ('Temple or City: What Did Hellenistic Jews See in Jerusalem?', in M. Poorthuis and Ch. Safrai [eds.], *The Centrality of Jerusalem: Historical Perspectives* [Kampen: Kok, 1996], pp. 114-27). In support of Schwartz' distinction, one could point to the strong emphasis on cult in the majority of the founder traditions in the Hebrew Bible. *Contra* Schwartz, Gafni's discussion shows how the rabbinic tradition (albeit textually later than the Hellenistic period) stressed the importance of Jerusalem precisely because it was the site of the Temple ('"Pre-Histories" of Jerusalem', pp. 10-11).

65. For discussion of the Hellenistic dating of the biblical traditions using different yet supporting criteria, see Bolin, '"A Stranger and an Alien Among You"'; T.L. Thompson, *The Bible in History: How Writers Create a Past* (London: Jonathan Cape, 1999); and the collection of essays both for and against such a dating in L.L. Grabbe (ed.), *Did Moses Speak Attic? Jewish Historiography and Scripture in the Hellenistic Period* (JSOTSup, 317; Sheffield: Sheffield Academic Press, 1999).

66. Gafni, '"Pre-Histories" of Jerusalem', p. 6. Gafni also shows how the idea that Yahweh founded Jerusalem at the creation of the world becomes widespread first in the rabbinic period.

and subsequently buried there were prevalent in later Jewish texts, until they were replaced by alternate traditions in light of the growing Christian interest in the city.[67] However, rabbinic traditions did not limit themselves to tales about Adam's contact with Jerusalem but created 'a certain conscious continuity in the successive relationship of each biblical figure to the place'.[68]

The preservation of multiple founder traditions is not limited to ancient Jewish literary circles, but occurs also in the traditions surrounding the origins of Rome, and these function as a supporting example to the kind of phenomenon being argued for the Hebrew Bible. Several competing narratives about Rome's foundation were preserved in Antiquity; these may be divided into two categories. The first comprises those stories that attribute Rome's foundation to the Trojan hero Aeneas who figures in the *Iliad*. The earliest known occurrence of this tradition is in the writings of the fifth century BCE historian Hellanicus of Lesbos.[69] The second category comprises those traditions that attribute the city's founding to Romulus. These stories appear in numerous written and pictorial representations beginning in the third century BCE. One of the longer discussions of these multiple foundation traditions occurs in Book 1 of the *Roman History* of Dionysius of Halicarnassus. Writing the in first century BCE, Dionysius notes seven different foundation stories for Rome among Greek authors and three from Roman writers. Most of the Greek authors speak of an eponymous founder, either male or female, named 'Rhome' or 'Rhomus'. In these different aetiologies, the founder of Rome is understood alternatively as the wife, son or grandson of Aeneas.[70] The Latin authors all

67. Gafni, '"Pre-Histories" of Jerusalem', pp. 10-16.

68. Gafni, '"Pre-Histories" of Jerusalem', p. 6.

69. A fragment preserved in Dionysius of Halicarnassus, *Roman History* 1.72. Emilio Gabba (*Dionysius and the History of Archaic Rome* [Berkeley: University of California Press, 1987], pp. 12-13) describes the literary context of the reference to Rome in Hellanicus as 'an ethnographic framework that is typically Greek and whose aim was to gather centripetally into the Hellenic world whatever new peoples the Greeks encountered'.

70. Dionysius of Halicarnassus, *Roman History* 1.72-73. W. Donlan ('The Foundation Legends of Rome: An Example of Dynamic Forces', *CW* 64 [1970], pp. 109-14), traces the tradition history of the Greek and Roman founder tales. Donlan demonstrates that the Greeks took up the Romulus traditions, yet set him alongside a brother, Rhomus, who functioned as the eponymous founder of the city. The Romans, wanting to maintain Romulus as the founder, altered the eponymous Rhomus into the ill-fated twin Remus.

attribute the city's founding to Romulus. Dionysius reconciles these competing Greek and Latin founder traditions by means of chronological
arrangement, although he was not the first to do so.[71] Thus, Aeneas founds
the city of Lavinium after defeating the indigenous population in battle.
His son, Ascanius, founds the colony of Alba Longa. Numitor, the thirteenth king of Alba Longa, sends out his grandsons, Romulus and Remus,
to found a colony that will be known as Rome[72] (this last element incor-
porating another tradition that claimed that Rome was founded by colonists from Alba Longa). Note the similarity of this composite narrative to
the city-foundation tradition in the biblical texts, which also include
conquest and colonization tales. The complex tale of Rome's foundation
became the canonical version, and figures also in the first century CE
writers, Virgil and Livy.[73] The specific purpose of the Roman tradition is
twofold. First, it provides for Rome the requisite Greek pedigree by
linking the city with the Homeric hero, Aeneas.[74] Indeed, Dionysius states
explicitly that his aim is to make the reader acknowledge that 'Rome is a
Greek city' (Ἑλλάδα πόλιν αὐτήν), and that 'no one can find a nation
that is more ancient or Greek' (οὐδὲν εὕροι τῶν ἐθνῶν οὔτε αρχαιό-
τερῶν οὔτε Ἑλληνικώτερῶν) than the Romans.[75] Second, it creates
divine approval and patronage for the city. Aeneas is the son of Aphrodite.
Rome's other founder, Romulus, is the son of Mars and he himself
becomes divine, eventually being worshiped in Rome under the name of
Quirinus.

The biblical authors had different aims from their classical counterparts,
yet they employed similar compositional and rhetorical strategies in their
repeated use of foundation stories to stress the ongoing sanctity and consequent importance of Jerusalem throughout Israelite history. This series of

71. Already in the third century BCE, the Roman poet Ennius had done so. Concerning the high level of fidelity with which Dionysius utilized his sources, see Gabba,
Dionysius, pp. 10-12.

72. Dionysius of Halicarnassus, *Roman History* 1.53-71; 2.2.

73. Virgil, *Aeneid* 1.272; 6.756; Livy, *Roman History* 1.1-2.

74. Greek logographers had already attributed to Aeneas the foundation of the city.
The Romans subsequently incorporated this into the canonical version; see Donlan,
'Foundation Legends', pp. 110-11; Gabba, *Dionysius*, p. 12. Similarly, by providing
Abraham origins in 'Ur of the Chaldees', the biblical authors establish for their
Israelite ancestor a connection with the ancient and venerable culture of Mesopotamia.

75. Dionysius of Halicarnassus, *Roman History* 1.89. See also the remarks of
Gabba, which state that the 'principal aim' of Dionysius was 'to establish the Greek-
ness of the Romans' (*Dionysius*, p. 134; cf. also pp. 10, 35).

stories involves the pre-eminent figures in the Hebrew Bible, and its intended cumulative effect serves didactic and ideological aims. As did Abram, Joshua, David, Ezra, and Nehemiah, so every good Jew is should acknowledge the primacy of Jerusalem, make offerings to Yahweh there and nowhere else, and maintain strict fidelity to the Torah despite, or because of the presence foreign influence. Moreover, this is so because, of all the cities in the world, only Jerusalem should take pride of place among Jews, no matter what city they themselves would claim for their own.[76] Historical investigation has revealed that in the last three centuries BCE there were ongoing and at times fierce debates among Jewish intellectuals and elites concerning their cultural and religious identity—witness the so-called 'Samaritan schism' or the bellicose language of the Qumran sectarians. Each group involved in this discussion realized that appropriation of the past entailed an effective endorsement of its respective position, a process repeated in the struggle between Judaism and early Christianity concerning both interpretive control of the Hebrew Bible and of Jerusalem as a symbol. The biblical authors portrayed virtually every major figure of the tradition as a proponent of their particular vision of Judaism, and of Jerusalem's role in it. Such rhetorical 'overkill' was do doubt justified by the extraordinarily high stakes of the questions at issue. Struggles such as these are what give rise to religious literature.

76. A similar use of repetition as a literary device in the Hebrew Bible is the recurrence of the motif that tells of the recovery and reading of lost and forgotten law codes. This appears in the stories of Josiah (2 Kgs 22), Ezra (Neh. 8–9) and Judah Maccabee (2 Macc. 2). In each of the stories, the recovery of the laws leads to a renewed fidelity to Yahweh on the part of the people. Again, the didactic aim of the motif is clear in that the reader is to be like the characters in this story, each of whom is a faithful student of Torah.

Ingrid Hjelm

With the traditions of the Pentateuch, Jews and Samaritans place their
origins in the ancient world's cultural and political clashes between the
kingdoms and peoples of the Euphrates and the Nile. Coming out of
Mesopotamia and Egypt, Abraham and Jacob's descendants are given the
task of making fruitful and plenty the homeland given to them, the fertile
soil of Palestine, inhabited with various indigenous people, with whom
they can choose either to live in harmony or in conflict. While the fathers
seek peaceful solutions, their sons and their children are minded to drive
out these people, whom they call 'foreigners of the land'. Based on the
Pentateuchal laws about ethnic and religious purity, biblical narratives in
the so-called Deuteronomistic History (Joshua–2 Kings)[1] about the life
within the land are characterized by seemingly never ending internal and
external conflicts over sovereignty. The internal conflicts result in civil
wars between the tribes and develop a north–south opposition between
Israel/Ephraim and Judah, which in biblical tradition finds its solution in
Yahweh's removal of Israel/Ephraim in the eighth-century BCE Assyrian
conquest of Samaria. While this sad solution has given impetus to later
Jewish interpretations (especially that of the first-century CE Jewish-
Roman writer Flavius Josephus), which explain why the Samaritans
should be regarded as foreigners, the biblical Prophets and the so-called
Chronistic History (the books of Ezra, Nehemiah and Chronicles) expose

---

1.   This tradition is not shared by the Samaritans, who have their own, non-canoni-
cal, historical tradition, which in its oldest known manuscripts varies with much of the
Masoretic material in Judges–2 Kings, having no traditions about the dual monarchy
from the reign of Israel's king Jeroboam to Judah's king Jehoiachin and the Babylonian exile. Samaritan traditions dealing with the Persian, Hellenistic and Roman
periods are both independent of, and related to, traditions known from the biblical
books of Ezra and Nehemiah, Jewish-Christian Apocryphal and Pseudepigraphic
literature and Josephus. For bibliographical references, see the footnotes to section 3.

an ambivalence and argue for the status of Judah (and Benjamin) as right-ful heir to Yahweh's promise to Abraham. At the same time, it acknowl-edges Israel/Ephraim's role as firstborn.[2] It is on the basis of this role that the Samaritans claim, already in Josephus' time, to be the true descendants from the Pentateuchal traditions about Jacob's son Joseph and his sons Ephraim and Manasseh. At that time, the Samaritans—whose home had long been the central highlands of Palestine with its holy institutions: the mountain of Gerizim, the ancient traditions about Shechem, Bethel and Gilgal, the burial places of the Patriarchs, as well as Shechem's position as the capital city and the home of the Samaritans at least since the fourth century BCE—had numbered as many as the Jews with whom they shared many ancient traditions and belief. They did not share, however, the opin-ion that Jerusalem was the proper place for Yahweh's dwelling or that any other books than the Mosaic Torah should be given canonical status.

In the first section, I will deal with the biblical presentation of the origins of these two groups and consider some of the tensions between the biblical narratives and extra-biblical sources. In the second section I will deal with Josephus' argumentation of how the Samaritans came to be like Jews without actually being Jews. Finally, in the third section, a short presentation of Samaritan traditions will reveal that historical roots and claims are embedded in competing stories, each opting for its own tradi-tion. These stories, although shared by many peoples for centuries after-wards as part of their origin narratives, once merely belonged to those who wrote them. It is such ancient discussions that modern scholars must pre-sent and evaluate: not against our own values and realities, but against the realities of the ancient worlds that created the traditions.

1. *Abraham's Heir*

According to Jewish and Samaritan traditions, Palestine's earliest history began with Abraham's settlement in Canaan. Previous to this settlement, Abraham had separated himself from his family in Chaldea to go to a new homeland promised him by God (Gen. 11.27-32). In *Jubilees* (a non-biblical Jewish book from around the second century BCE), this departure

---

2.   Most explicitly argued in 1 Chron. 5.1-3's statement that although the birthright belongs to Joseph, Judah is given the role of being the chief ruler, which places this book in close connection with similar argumentation in second–first century BCE extra-biblical literature's struggle for Judaean hegemony based on the biblical concept of the twelve tribes of Israel.

also included a separation from his ancestral religion. Abraham's connection to Haran was well established in tradition and could not be denied, but any doubts that this relationship should imply a connection to the 'reform of King Nabonidus' in Haran, and that Abraham might have brought his god(s) from there, needed clear rejection. This was done in the story about Abram's burning of the house of idols in Ur, in which Abram's brother Haran died while trying to save the gods (*Jub.* 12.12). When Abram thereafter goes to the town of Haran (12.15), it is not Haran's gods but Yahweh who reveals himself and teaches Abram not to make signs from the sun and the moon. Only after the cutting of the covenant and the institution of Hebrew as the language of creation (12.22-27) does Abram travel to Canaan with his wife and his fatherless nephew Lot, who was the son of Abram's deceased brother Haran.

In the biblical narrative, it is implied that Lot is brought up as Abram's foster son, since Sarai had no children (Gen. 11.30-31; 12.5). On Abram's second arrival into Canaan, now from Egypt (the first arrival had been from Mesopotamia), the country is portrayed as too poor to feed the whole family (of three!),[3] so Lot departs to settle with his cattle and herdsmen in the Jordan rift valley, in the region around Sodom and Gomorrah. Having separated himself from what was left of his family—and we notice that Abram took the initiative in the separation rather than solving the problem through direct sharing (13.8-9)—Abram receives a third blessing,[4] promising that he shall become a great people (15.3-5). We also notice that Abram does not count Lot as his heir, but considers his servant Eliezer to have that honour (15.2). Because of Sarai's barrenness the blessing sounds hollow, as Sarai herself clearly recognized, when she suggested that Abram beget a son by his Egyptian slave woman Hagar (16.2). The arrangement turns out disastrously, and Sarai chases Hagar away after she has become pregnant (16.6). In the desert, Yahweh gives Hagar her own identity as a mother of a great people, the Ishmaelites (16.7-14). With Hagar's return to Abram's house, the author plays with his audience's knowledge of what will become of Hagar's child growing up in Abram's house, while Sarai has no children in spite of the blessing given to Abram. The question lingers in the background: Will Ishmael become Abram's heir?

---

3.   For the theme of scarcity as a paradigm for biblical discussion of violent monotheism, see R.M. Schwartz, *The Curse of Cain: The Violent Legacy of Monotheism* (Chicago: University of Chicago Press, 1997).

4.   The first blessing had been given before Abram's departure from Haran (Gen. 12.1-3) and the second right after Lot had separated from Abram (13.14-17).

However—in folk-tale fashion—not only Abram, but also his wife, are given new identities in preparation for the fulfilment of the blessings. Their names change to accord with what they are to become: the father and mother of nations and kings. This act takes place on the very day that Ishmael, ancestor of twelve princes (Gen. 17.20), is considered to have become a grown-up—he is in his thirteenth year. After the birth of Abraham and Sarah's son Isaac, Hagar and Ishmael once again are sent away. In the desert, Ishmael's life is threatened and then miraculously saved by God, who will make of him 'a great people' (21.18). Abraham and Sarah are left alone with their son Isaac, the heir of Yahweh's promise. Playing once again on the frailty of beginnings, Isaac's life is in turn threatened by Yahweh's request for a burnt offering (ch. 22). The narrative takes the audience's breath away. Will Ishmael after all become Abraham's heir? By divine intervention, Isaac is spared from Abraham's knife lifted for the ritual slaughter. Abraham had passed the test. Putting his faith in Yahweh, he had demonstrated his worthiness to become the ancestor of a great people. From then on no hindrances stand in the way of the blessings that had been given in the opening of Abraham's story (ch. 12). For Ishmael, the identity given him before his birth (ch. 16) and at his circumcision (ch. 17) is upheld as his family forms a barrier between the ever-threatening empires of Egypt and Assur (25.12-18).

With these synchronized narratives about the origins of the Ishmaelites and the Israelites, combined also with narratives about the peoples of the land (14.18-19), about Abraham's Egyptian connections (chs. 12 and 20), about his children with his second wife Keturah (25.1-6), about his Mesopotamian connections and Isaac's marriage with Abraham's relative Rebekah (ch. 24), the Bible offers a grand discourse on the question: Who is Abraham's rightful heir? The discourse is not progressive, though its surface makes it appear as if it were. It is schematic and philosophical. How can a single ancestor and a line of firstborn be established from Palestine and its vicinity's many peoples? How can a single people be established as a people of God with whom Yahweh establishes his covenant, as promised in Gen. 17.18-21, while explicitly excluding Ishmael from that covenant (vv. 18 and 20), but not from Yahweh's blessing.[5] Within this discourse, we must notice that although the author's intention is to establish this line of firstborns as a way of identifying Yahweh's people to be given the biblical land of Canaan, he also creates the 'nations'—

5.   T.L. Thompson, *The Origin Tradition of Ancient Israel: The Literary Formation of Genesis and Exodus 1–23* (JSOTSup, 55; Sheffield: JSOT Press, 1987), p. 96.

the Ishmaelites, Moabites, Ammonites, Midianites, Ashurites, Letushites, and so on[6]—in a segmented lineage belonging to Abraham's but not to his wife Sarah's lineage.[7] *Jubilees* 15.28-32 deals more explicitly with this problem, stating that Yahweh caused 'spirits' to rule over the many nations and peoples, while over Israel 'he did not cause any angel or spirit to rule because he alone is their ruler' (15.32).

The beginning is singular and its result is plural, as expressed in the wider narrative about Yahweh's people *within* the land; namely, the tradition about the sons of Jacob and the tribes of Israel. Reiterating the Ishmael and Isaac competition, we find a struggle over inheritance between Isaac's sons: Esau and Jacob, first- and second-born. Once again, the author plays the knowledge of the audience off against the knowledge of his characters.[8] With Esau almost dying from hunger after a (fruitless?) hunting trip, Jacob buys from him the right of firstborn with food produced from the land: lentils and bread. Easily done, as Esau, 'dying from hunger', has no need for his right of firstborn (Gen. 25.32). Ironic as the narrative is, he has need for it as soon as he has sold it. Done is done. Isaac has only a single blessing, which Jacob 'steals' (ch. 27). In that narrative, given as yet another example of the farmer and hunter's capabilities of bringing food in proper time, Rebekah helps Jacob prepare a mock-game meal prepared of two prime kids from the flock. Pretending to be Esau, wearing Esau's clothes and covered with skins from the kids, Jacob brings the meal to his aging father, who loves game (25.28), but cannot tell the difference. Neither can he tell the difference between a hunter and a farmer's smell. And so, he blesses Jacob with the fertile land abundant with grain and wine (27.28), while Esau, for whom Isaac, in fact, has no blessing, is cursed from that land to live a hunter's life in submission to his brother; until he casts off his yoke (27.39-40). The predicted fate of both, fighting from their mother's womb (25.22-23), becomes their unavoidable destiny. Once

6.   Many more are mentioned in the genealogies of Abraham's children with his second wife Keturah (Gen. 25.1-6) and the children of Ishmael (25.12-18).

7.   For references to this well-known literary topic in ancient Near Eastern as well as Graeco-Roman literature, see T.L. Thompson, *The Historicity of the Patriarchal Narratives: The Quest for the Historical Abraham* (Berlin: W. de Gruyter, 1974), pp. 311-14; K.L. Sparks, *Ethnicity and Identity in Ancient Israel: Prolegomena to the Study of Ethnic Sentiments and their Expression in the Hebrew Bible* (Winona Lake, IN: Eisenbrauns, 1998).

8.   Cf. the oracle given to Rebekah in the opening of the Esau–Jacob narrative: 'Two nations are in your womb, and two peoples born of you shall be divided; the one shall be stronger than the other, the elder shall serve the younger' (Gen. 25.23).

again irony forms part of the narrative as Jacob flees to Haran (27.43) and Esau becomes rich on the products of Canaan (36.6). The author's struggle with destiny's power suggests a pragmatic solution: 'stay there until your brother's anger is over', Rebekah advises her youngest son (27.44). At Jacob's return, Esau's anger is over. While scarcity governs Jacob's acts, abundance governs Esau's.[9] He has no need for anything that is Jacob's (33.9), not even the scarcity of a land that cannot support both families because of their wealth (36.7-8), as it similarly could not support Abraham *and* Lot's families (13.6).

These narratives of the patriarchs belong to the great cycles of stories, dominated by the motif of rejecting the firstborn in order to give place to the youngest. In an increasing plot-line, we find that in the Lot tradition the eldest 'brother' is a subordinate member of the segmented lineage, son of Abram's brother Haran, who has the role in the book of *Jubilees* of opposing Abram's burning of the idols. In the Ishmael tradition, he is reckoned as Abraham's illegitimate son; and finally in the Esau–Jacob tradition, he is the twin-brother, whose status of firstborn is to be challenged. It is this equal but rejected brother who makes the connection to the Edomite Yahweh (Gen. 32.4; 33.16; 36; Deut. 33.2; Judg. 5.4) and to the Ishmaelites (Gen. 28.8-9; 36.3), while Jacob, in the Pentateuch tradition, becomes connected exclusively to the Shechem, Bethel and Hebron stories (33.18–35.29), as did also Abraham his grandfather.[10]

We are dealing here with a type of literature that is found only in the Old Testament tradition and is unparalleled in Near Eastern literature.[11] This literature reworks the past in typological narrative, which, taking up the past, is able to reject it. 'From this comes the dissonance in various compositions, which are seen paralleled in entire books and collection, i.e. the dissonance between the Pentateuch and the historical books.'[12] That

9. The biblical discussion about scarcity as 'the origin of hatred and violence among brothers' (cf. Schwartz, *The Curse of Cain*, p. 83) is thus more sophisticated than Schwartz allows. Its voice is as critical to its characters' egoism as must be any modern reader.

10. I. Hjelm, *The Samaritans and Early Judaism: A Literary Analysis* (JSOTSup, 303; CIS, 7; Sheffield: Sheffield Academic Press, 2000), pp. 146-49.

11. D. Irvin, *Mytharion: The Comparison of Tales from the Old Testament and Ancient Near East* (AOAT, 32; Neukirchen–Vluyn: Neukirchener Verlag, 1978).

12. Hjelm, *Samaritans and Early Judaism*, p. 278 n. 8. Thompson, *The Origin Tradition*, p. 158: 'The narratives of this genre all begin with a series of three episodes which together perform specific functions of the chain narrative. They state the theme and frequently give the context of the later narrative. They set the mode of resolution

this rejection of past traditions is in fact to be identified with the implied progressive plot-line, has been strongly challenged by J. Van Seters' works on the Tetrateuch traditions.[13] In these works, he argues that the patriarchal traditions are younger and dependent on the chronologically much later 'Deuteronomistic History' of the monarchies of Israel and Judah. In Van Seters' argument, the narrative of history from creation to the death of Moses was not intended to supersede the Deuteronomistic History, but to provide it with a prologue that would give to it a new perspective and direction.[14] This was the work of an author who worked progressively from this past tradition to a new understanding, without rejecting that past entirely.[15] My own arguments have been much more based on assumptions of supersessionism's rejection of past traditions, related as they might be to Jewish–Samaritan controversies about traditions.[16] Whether one accepts Van Seters' argument as an explanation of a theological development of inner religio-political discussions over cult and belief, or one accepts my assumption of two separate groups (Samaritans and Jews) arguing each for their own perspective, the Pentateuch's solution that brothers should not fight brothers and that Yahweh will care for all the descendants of Abraham prevails; it is not Jacob and Esau who go into open conflict, it is their sons.[17]

for the plot-line and they take the first step in the plot-line of a greater story. It is usually the third of these episodes which sets the plot of the chain narrative moving and is found to echo through succeeding episodes of the larger narrative.'

13. J. Van Seters, *Prologue to History: The Yahwist as Historian in Genesis* (Louisville, KY: Westminster/John Knox Press, 1992), and *The Life of Moses: The Yahwist as Historian in Exodus–Numbers* (Kampen: Kok, 1994).

14. J. Van Seters, 'Joshua 24 and the Problem of Tradition in the Old Testament', in W.B. Barrick and J.R. Spencer (eds.), *In the Shelter of Elyon: Essays on Ancient Literature in Honor of G.W. Ahlström* (JSOTSup, 31; Sheffield: JSOT Press, 1984), pp. 139-58 (154); so also M. Rose, *Deuteronomist und Jahwist: Untersuchungen. zu den Berührungspunkten beider Literaturwerke* (ATANT, 67; Zürich: Theologischer Verlag, 1981), p. 327.

15. Van Seters, *Prologue to History*, p. 332: 'In ancient historiography, the "prologue" or *archaiologia* set forth the ancient background for the historical work, and in doing so often laid the principles by which the history was to be understood. By his presentation of the origins of humanity and that of the people's ancestry, the Yahwist has given a radical revision and reinterpretation of the national tradition.'

16. Hjelm, *Samaritans and Early Judaism, passim.*

17. Hjelm, *Samaritans and Early Judaism*, pp. 138-52 (151); Schwartz, *The Curse of Cain*, pp. 109-16.

Having settled Esau and his descendants *outside* the land (Gen. 36), the narrator is ready to continue his narrative about Israel's twelve tribes, who settle *within* the land. Short-lived as this settlement is, Jacob and his sons are forced to go to Egypt to survive from hunger, as Abraham also had been in his day. Reiterating the implied discussion of who can provide Jacob's second-youngest son Joseph, firstborn of Jacob's true wife Rachel in spite of her barrenness (30.22), provides food for his brothers and father at a time when hunger threatens their lives (45.11; 47.12). It is no coincidence that the verb used is reiterated in Joseph's last words, that he will provide for his brothers and their families (50.21). Given the obligation of securing a remnant for the land (45.7),[18] Joseph plays Yahweh's role of comforting and reassuring his brothers, who had done evil against him (50.15-21). Although his brothers sought to kill him and ended up selling him, because of their envy, his fate of becoming their leader, which was 'predicted' in his youth (37.5-11), could not be changed. Having stayed in Egypt for 400 years as predicted in the Abraham narrative (15.13), their return to the land, now inhabited with people mightier than the Israelites (Num. 13.25-29), reiterates, on a new level, the question of who the Israelites are and what has become of Israel's sons' right of firstborn. We cannot help thinking of Esau selling his birthright in order to survive. Ironically, the Israelites survived, but lost their inheritance, that land that had been inhabited with the ever-recurrent Canaanites, Hittites, Hivites, Perizzites, Girgashites, Amorites and Jebusites.[19] The regaining of the land is not easily done and certainly not pleasant, as Jacob's sons, not seeking peaceful solutions, kill or drive the people of the land out. Having thus removed these peoples (Josh. 24.11)[20] and the ancestral gods from Mesopotamia

18. The vocabulary reflects the remnant ideology of the Prophets (see, e.g., Isa. 37.31-32; 46.3; Ezek. 14.22; Mic. 4.7) and the book of Ezra (esp. ch. 9) and anticipates thematically the Exodus' saving function, albeit the specific vocabulary is connected with the survival from Babylonian rather than from Egyptian exile.

19. Deut. 7.1; Josh. 3.10; 9.1; 24.11; cf. Exod. 3.17; 23.23; 33.2; 34.11; Num. 13.25-29; the names occur as a stock motif in several texts. They might vary a bit, both in number and names; mostly they occur as either six (without the Girgashites), seven or ten peoples. In the spy and conquest narratives we find other regional names, not used as stock motifs.

20. Other passages in Joshua, Numbers, 1 Samuel and Chronicles claim that the Israelites did not conquer the land entirely, that these and other peoples had not been removed. In these narratives other ideologies direct their roles: for example, they are left for somebody else to conquer (Judah, David and Hezekiah). They lead the Israel-

and Egypt (24.14), covenant making and settlement give way to a new chapter in the never-ending story of the Israelites (24.25-28).[21]

In the book of Judges, divisiveness rather than unity sets the stage for Israel's people. The twelve tribes' attempt to cooperate and commit themselves to one central leadership is almost disastrous. Because there was no king, 'everyone did what he saw fit in his own eyes'. So, kingship is instituted as the story moves once again from diversity to unity, from the twelve judges to the one king (the books of Samuel). Kingship, however, does not solve the basic problem: Who shall rule, when there is more than one candidate and more than one region?[22] The position given in succession to King Saul from the tribe of Benjamin, youngest son of Jacob (Gen. 35.16–19.24), and to David and Solomon, both from the tribe of Judah, the fourth son of Jacob (29.35; 35.23; 46.12; 49.8), increase antagonisms. Although the narrative seeks to give the impression that the Davidic kingship finally united the tribes, this 'unity' was not created by resolving

ites to unfaithfulness and idolatry. In Josh. 24, it is Joshua who is granted the honour of having 'cleansed' the land, an act David, Josiah and Ezra reiterate.

21. As is clear from this paraphrase, no attention has been paid to the various questions of text composition related to uncertain sources, redactions and the like. The object of examination has been the medieval Masoretic text, without implying pre-Masoretic discussions about text traditions, variants, and so on. In its present canonical form, Josh. 24 functions as a transition chapter, which, in light of the preceding narrative (Genesis–Joshua), introduces the future fate of the Israelites within the land. At the same time, it also has the potential of commenting on this fate (presented in the Deuteronomistic History) in an admonition of a return to the 'innocent' period of the Patriarchs. The latter has been advocated especially by Van Seters, 'Joshua 24 and the Problem of Tradition', and *Prologue to History*, pp. 336-37. For further discussion, see, I. Hjelm, *Jerusalem's Rise to Sovereignty in Ancient Tradition and History: Zion and Gerizim in Competition* (London: T&T Clark International, forthcoming [2004]).

22. This conflict is anticipated in Gideon/Jerubbaal's Ephraimite son Abimelech's deceitful institution of the kingship at Shechem at the expense of his 70 brothers in the time of the Judges (Judg. 9). The narrative opens up a Pandora's Box of interrelated biblical texts that struggle with that theme. While the Benjaminite Gideon refused the offer to become king, because 'Yahweh shall reign' (Judg. 8.22-23), his Ephraimite son achieved a kingdom in the North (Shechem) 'supported' by money from Baalberith's temple (Judg. 9.4). It is not possible to go into detailed studies of the book of Judges' narratives about Ephraim, Dan and Benjamin's deceitful acts and struggles with the remaining tribes. It should, however, be noticed that in the Deuteronomistic History, Saul is a Benjaminite and Jeroboam is an Ephraimite, and that the tribe of Judah is never involved in any dishonourable acts of fratricidal war before the division of the kingdom and Rehoboam's civil war with Jeroboam's kingdom. In this narrative (1 Kgs 12), Yahweh orders Rehoboam not to wage war on his brother (v. 24).

former disagreements. Solomon's peaceful reign from Dan to Beer-sheba was one of exception rather than normality (1 Kgs 5.4-5), as everyday life did not long secure Israel and Judah's peoples a place under shading branches of fig and wine. Dispersion lies in wait.

Having moved from twelve to one, the story reverses paradigmatically. Two 'brothers' fighting over the divided territory *within* the land in a struggle for the role of the true Israel (1 Kgs 12). From Judah, Rehoboam, the son of Solomon, fights against Israel's Jeroboam, the son of Nebat, an Ephraimite from the tribe of Joseph and second-youngest son of Jacob (Gen. 30.24; 46.19; 49.22), but he is assigned the role of the firstborn (47.27–48.4) and receives a variation on the blessing given to Jacob (27.27-29; cf. 49.22-26).[23] The competition between these two tribes (Judah and Joseph/ Ephraim), geographically placed in Judaea[24] and Samaria,[25] forms the theme of the biblical books of Kings and Chronicles, and lies at the core of the prophetic literature's judgment of each group's political and religious behaviour.

The implicit question about sovereignty is not so much 'Who belongs to the lineage of firstborn?',[26] but 'Who will show himself to be the true Israel?' In a synchronic narrative setting, Ephraim/Israel, its kingship and its people, become rejected by Yahweh because of their conduct—their unfaithfulness towards Yahweh—while Judah is temporarily spared because of its faithfulness. This judgment of 'the faithless Israel' is dramatically spelled out and made paradigmatic for the narrative as a whole. At the centre of the narrative cycle, thematically designed as '*he walked in all the ways of Jeroboam the son of Nebat and in the sins which he [the king] made Israel to sin, provoking the Lord the God of Israel to anger by their idols*' (1 Kgs 11.1–2 Kgs 23.15), is the narrative about the Israelite

23. Extending this line of firstborn, the blessing also comes to include Joseph's sons Ephraim and Manasseh, respectively, the second-born and firstborn (Deut. 33.13-17), who for their part have their status exchanged in yet another variant of the Esau–Jacob narrative.

24. Biblical: Judah (and Benjamin); Assyrian: *ya-á-du, ya-a-ḫu-du* and *ya-ku-du*; Persian: *yehûd* or *yahûd*.

25. Biblical: Samaria/Israel; although never explicitly mentioned by tribes, the ideal Northern Kingdom includes the remaining ten (eleven) tribes on both sides of the Jordan. Geographically, the borders change according to political circumstances both before and after the Assyrian occupation; Moabite (Mesha Stele): *Israel*; Assyrian: *Sir-i-la-a, Bît Humri, Samerina*; Persian: *Abr-Nahara, Shomron*.

26. It should be remembered that Joseph and his son Ephraim are given that role (also in psalmodic and prophetic literature), while Judah never had it.

king Ahab son of Omri (Humri),[27] who sinned even more by marrying the daughter of the Sidonian king Ethbaal and by raising an altar for Baal in Samaria (1 Kgs 16.30-32). The reiteration of this theme throughout the books of Kings[28] relates the narratives to each other and forwards the fate of Israel; namely, its disappearance as a kingdom and a people after the Assyrian king Shalmanezer's conquest of Samaria and the deportation of its population around 722 BCE. In this narrative, Israel is not rejected by Yahweh because of its lineage, but because it was not the true Israel; that is, it is rejected because of its conduct, its unfaithfulness (2 Kgs 17.7-23; 18.12). Replacing Israel's population, Assyria introduced five other peoples from Babylon, Cuthah, Avva, Hamath and Sepharvaim.[29] In the first century CE Jewish-Roman writer Josephus' writings they are called Cuthaeans (Josephus, *Ant.* 1–20; *War* 1–7). I will return to this below.

In biblical literature, the 'event' is contrasted first to the religious and political reforms of the Judaean king Hezekiah, who is implicitly claimed to have saved his kingdom from the Assyrian attack (probably in 701 BCE), because of his faithfulness (2 Kgs 18.13; 18.17–20.19; parallel Isa. 36–39). Half a century later, the Judaean king Josiah, recalling both Solomon and Jeroboam's sins (that they did not serve Yahweh properly), destroys or defiles all the former cult places and marks every place outside of the walls of Jerusalem as unclean (2 Kgs 23.4-20). Reiterating the Passover celebration from the time of the Judges (23.22),[30] Israel and Judaea's royal pasts are made parenthetical as Judah regains its sovereignty as the chosen tribe and Jerusalem as the chosen place, albeit in a much-diminished form compared to David's reign. The intention of the reform is not unification

27. Missing in the LXX, which in other instances (e.g. 3 Kgdms 16.29) agree with the Masoretic tradition on Ahab's relationship with Omri.

28. 1 Kgs 15.34; 16.19, 26, 31; 22.53; 2 Kgs 3.3; 10.29, 31; 13.2, 11; 14.24; 15.9, 18, 24, 28; 17.22; 23.15.

29. 2 Kgs 17.24. The event is well testified in Assyrian sources. According to Assyrian Inscriptions it was Sargon II who took the city in the first year of his reign (721 BCE), removed its population (27,290 people), rebuilt the city 'more splendid than before', repopulated it with people of his conquered lands and placed one of his officials as governor there. Samaria had thus become the provincial capital of the Assyrian province Samarina. See D.D. Luckenbill, *Ancient Records of Assyria and Babylonia* (2 vols.; Chicago: University of Chicago Press, 1927 [repr. = New York: Greenwood Press, 1968]), II, §§4, 92, 99. See, however, the discussion of the chronological problems in B. Becking, *The Fall of Samaria: An Historical and Archaeological Study* (Leiden: E.J. Brill, 1992).

30. Possibly, even excluding that period, since no Passover is mentioned in the book of Judges.

but selection, in supersessionism's reiteration of the pre-monarchic past as wishful departure. In the Josiah story's transfer of the Law of Moses to Jerusalem (22.3-20), the reforms of Josiah not only signify that Israel's past as centred in the north is over, but also that Jerusalem's remnant has been chosen to bring it forward to a new beginning.[31]

Now we are back to the single tribe again: to Judah and Jerusalem's Davidic house. In the version in the books of Kings, this kingdom comprises the regions where Abram and Jacob began: from Shechem to Beer-sheba,[32] while in the versions in the books of Chronicles, it accords with the twelve tribes settled in their return from Egypt: from Dan to Beer-sheba.[33] The competition should be over and so there is no one to compete with. Or is there? In fact, there are many, as past relatives become present ghosts. In the biblical tradition, such ghosts make their entry on the scene, not in Josiah's cleansed Jerusalem, but in the ruins of an exilic, deserted Jerusalem. As in the Abraham and Jacob narratives, the first settlement in the land is short-lived, as is the Davidic–Solomonic kingdom, as is also Josiah's 'new-born' Jerusalem. Within less than two generations, the people are banned from the city (and the land), forced into Babylonian captivity and into flight to Egypt (2 Kgs 25). The judgment of Judah's religious conduct that led to this disaster is as harsh as had been the judgment of Israel's. Both are rejected, but only Judah (and Benjamin) returns.

In their return (40 or 70 years later; cf. the book of Ezra), the city (and the land), which had been claimed to be empty (2 Chron 36.21; Jer. 25.11) is, in fact, filled, not with giants growing great on the fruits of the land as in the Jacob–Moses tradition, but with 'ghosts', in a single term called 'the people of the land', the עַם הָאָרֶץ, who are claimed to be of foreign origin or of a mixed population. It is post-exilic Judaea's 'encounter' with these peoples that poses the greatest problems for the biblical writers' struggle with questions about secular and religious ethnicity. While the books of Ezra and Nehemiah give explicit voice to these struggles—rejecting any relationship with such past 'relatives'—most of the remaining books of the Bible implicitly seek to establish a common past for which hierarchy and heritage is accounted. This accounting, however, favours one group against

31. It hardly is coincidental that the term 'Lord, God of Israel' disappears in the Judaean parts of Kings' narrative after Solomon's reign, not to be taken up again before the Northern Kingdom has been removed from the scene (2 Kgs 18.5; 19.15, 20; 21.12; 22.15, 18).

32. Gen. 12.6-9; 13.18; 21.22-33; 27–35; cf. 2 Kgs 23.4-20.

33. Deuteronomy, Joshua and Judges; cf. 2 Chron. 34.3-7.

the other, Judaeans against Ephraimites. While the Pentateuch favours Ephraim, the Bible as a canon favours Judah, from which line came the Davidic kingship. Such favoritism has survived in literature and in scholarship.

As must now be clear from this survey, there is much more at stake for the biblical writers than what can be called a 'History of Palestine'. Considering that the author of 1 and 2 Kings shows no interest in Judaean history as such, but only in its comparison with Israelite history, we must realize that his historiographic perspective does not belong to history but to ideology. Knowing that for the centuries under consideration Israel and Judaea did not form a coherent state,[34] we cannot but wonder why the work's Jewish author put such great effort into convincing his reader that the Northern Kingdom had more to do with the petty state of Jerusalem, than had, for example, Gezer, Ashkelon, Lachish, Tyre, Sidon, and so on.[35] It is not the two-state structure or, in fact, the many-state structure that creates the problem for biblical exegesis. This situation is already a testified historical fact from as early as the Late Bronze–Early Iron period, and at least from the ninth century BCE onwards.[36] It is the 'utopian'

34. I. Finkelstein and N.A. Silberman, *The Bible Unearthed: Archaeology's New Vision of Ancient Israel and the Origin of its Sacred Texts* (New York: Free Press, 2001), pp. 149-50: 'As we have seen, there is no compelling archaeological evidence for the historical existence of a vast united monarchy, centred in Jerusalem, that encompassed the entire land of Israel. On the contrary, the evidence reveals a complex demographic transformation in the highlands, in which a unified ethnic consciousness began only slowly to coalesce.' T.L. Thompson, *Early History of the Israelite People: From the Written and Archaeological Sources* (Leiden: E.J. Brill, 1992), pp. 407-12.

35. Finkelstein and Silberman, *The Bible Unearthed*, p. 159: 'There is no doubt that the two Iron Age states—Israel and Judah—had much in common. Both worshipped YHWH (among other deities). Their peoples shared many legends, heroes, and tales about a common [*sic*], ancient past. They also spoke similar languages, or dialects of Hebrew ["West Semitic" is a better term for the language spoken also by Ugarites, Edomites, Moabites, Ammonites and Aramaeans], and by the eighth century BCE, both wrote in the same script. But they were also very different from each other in the demographic composition, economic potential, material culture, and relationship with their neighbours. Put simply, Israel and Judah experienced quite different histories and developed distinctive cultures. In a sense, Judah was little more than Israel's rural hinterland [sparsely populated and with a significant pastoral segment until the seventh century BCE (cf. *The Bible Unearthed*, pp. 154 and 159)]'.

36. Finkelstein and Silberman, *The Bible Unearthed*, pp. 153-59. Thompson, *Early History*, pp. 412-15.

unified state, with its single people structure, that creates the problem. As stated by Gary Knoppers: 'Historically, factionalism among the tribes may have been the norm, but the Deuteronomist upholds Israel as an 'organism', whose unity is quite apparent during the first period of Solomon's rule'.[37] Contrary to Knoppers' more historicizing reading of the biblical material, I do not think that we can use biblical 'evidence' for '(dis)unity' as 'a vital issue in the pre-exilic era', or as a witness to any historical reality at a time of 'factionalism among the tribes', since these 'tribes' are elements of the paradigmatic biblical narrative. The unity of Iron Age Palestine in extra-biblical sources is not a given and occurs only fragmentarily in references to various sorts of coalitions during the Assyrian period. Without the paradigmatic use of this idealized past of the first period of Solomon's rule,[38] we would not have had a biblical monarchic (or perhaps also pre-monarchic) history.[39] We might instead have had more objective stories about Palestine's petty kingdoms,[40] and about the ways they interrelated in their various dealings with internal and external enemies. We might have had stories about the highly developed Philistine culture, as well as about the impact of the Aramaean culture far beyond its own borders.[41] We might have had stories about life in the Assyrian province Samerina for the four-fifths of the indigenous population, which remained there.[42] Contrary to what the Bible purports and to what scholars

37. G.N. Knoppers, *Two Nations Under God: The Deuteronomistic History of Solomon and the Dual Monarchies* (HSM, 52; 2 vols.; Atlanta: Scholars Press, 1993), I, p. 6; note also: 'Indeed, there is evidence in a variety of biblical sources and within the Deuteronomistic History itself that (dis)unity was a vital issue in the preexilic era' (p. 4).

38. Knoppers, *Two Nations Under God*, I, pp. 54-56.

39. J. Van Seters, *In Search of History: Historiography in the Ancient World and the Origins of Biblical History* (New Haven: Yale University Press, 1983), pp. 316-17. On p. 320 Van Seters states: 'While the record of the monarchy in Kings focuses on evaluating the progress of people and their kings from the time of Solomon until the end, this appraisal does not make sense without the story of the rise of the monarchy, the enunciation of the divine promise to David, and the establishment of the true cult centre in Jerusalem under Solomon. The author must first set out these constitutional elements of the Israelite state by which all the "reforms" must be judged.'

40. Or larger ones, such as the Omride Dynasty; cf. Finkelstein and Silberman, *The Bible Unearthed*, pp. 169-95.

41. This lack of biblical as well as scholarly interest in Syria-Palestine's history, which do not serve biblical interests, was the concern of K.W. Whitelam, *The Invention of Ancient Israel: The Silencing of Palestinian History* (London: Routledge, 1996).

42. Finkelstein and Silberman, *The Bible Unearthed*, p. 221.

deceptively have concluded,[43] Samaria's population did not cease to exist after the Assyrian conquest.[44] It might not be wrong to understand this paradigm as mirroring the 'cessation' of Judah and Jerusalem after the Assyrian[45] and Babylonian conquests, which in literature did not lead to a repopulation of Jerusalem, but to the myth of the empty land.[46] How did these remaining people—citizens of Assyria—with their priesthood, royal houses, and so on function and interact with the rest of Palestine, most of which came under Assyrian dominion in less than one generation after the fall of Aram, Samaria and the Transjordan? How did they interact with the new settlers under Assyrian and Babylonian dominion with Samaria (and later Megiddo)[47] as provincial capitals and Bethel as an important cult site from the seventh century until well into the Persian period?[48]

43. Such a conclusion has even been made by some of those scholars who are most critical of the biblical presentation; for example, Thompson, *Early History*, p. 415: 'By the end of the sixth-century, the *Jerusalem* and *Judah* of the Assyrian period had ceased to exist as thoroughly as had the *Samaria* and *Israel* of the eight-century'; see, however, *idem*, 'A History of Palestine: The Debate', *The Journal of Palestinian Archaeology* 2.1 (2001), pp. 18-24, as well as his Introduction to the present volume ('An Introduction: Can a History of Ancient Palestine and Jerusalem be Written?'); N.P. Lemche, *Ancient Israel: A New History of Israelite Society* (The Biblical Seminar, 5; Sheffield: JSOT Press, 1988), p. 128; *idem*, *The Israelites in History and Tradition* (Louisville, KY: Westminster/John Knox Press, 1998), p. 85, arguing, however, also for a continuation of the material culture: 'The local population might have received a massive contribution of foreigners in the Assyrian period, something that should be reflected in the material remains, but most of it remained stable, tilling their farmland, breeding children, and living a peasant's uneventful life'.

44. Cf. B. Oded, *Mass Deportations and Deportees in the Neo-Assyrian Empire* (Wiesbaden: Reichert, 1979), pp. 26-32, 116-35, which clearly shows that while Phoenicia, lower Galilee, Judaea and the southern coastal areas were highly affected by several deportations, especially, from the time of Sennacherib onwards, only the town of Samaria itself had its population removed. In central Palestine most of its population remained unchanged.

45. According to Sennacherib's report of his conquest of Judaea in 701 BCE, 46 walled cities were conquered, 200,150 persons carried away as spoil and Hezekiah's kingdom remarkably diminished; cf. Luckenbill, *Ancient Records of Assyria and Babylonia*, II, §240.

46. H. Barstad, *The Myth of the Empty Land: A Study of the History and Archaeology of Judah during the 'Exilic' Period* (Oslo: Scandinavian University Press, 1996); Hjelm, *Samaritans and Early Judaism*, pp. 16, 149-51.

47. Finkelstein and Silberman, *The Bible Unearthed*, pp. 216-17.

48. Finkelstein and Silberman, *The Bible Unearthed*, pp. 221-22: 'In the hill country around the city of Samaria, which was destined to serve as the hub of the new

What opposition was created by the status given to Samaria as an administrative and political centre for Assyrian interests in Palestine? 2 Kings 17.24-41 offers an ironic play on tendencies of Assyrian dominion and cultural assimilation, when Samaria's replaced population worships Yahweh rather than Ashur.[49] We might have had documents to support these stories, rendering information, inscriptions memorializing the grandeur of, say, Philistine, Aramaean, Israelite and Judaean kings.[50] Did it all vanish after the writing of the biblical narratives? Did the Josianic scribes' attempt 'to authorise massive royal reforms', in order to 'reverse the outstanding transgressions committed by both his [Josiah's] southern and his northern predecessors',[51] eliminate competing stories?[52] Or does this authorization

Assyrian province, the deportation was apparently minimal… In the northern valleys, the Assyrians destroyed the Israelite administrative centers but left the rural population (which was basically Canaanite, Phoenician, and Aramean in tradition) unhurt… Indeed, surveys and excavations in the Jezreel valley confirm the surprising demographic continuity. And about half of the rural sites near Samaria continued to be occupied in subsequent centuries…a significant number of Israelites were still living in the hill country of Samaria, including the southern area of Bethel, alongside the new populations brought by the Assyrians.'

49. See further, Hjelm, *Jerusalem's Rise to Sovereignty* (forthcoming), Chapter 3.

50. G. Garbini, *History and Ideology in Ancient Israel* (London: SCM Press, 1988), pp. 17-20, rightly asks '"where are the Hebrew inscriptions of the Iron Age?", not one of the forty kings from Saul to Zedekiah has left a direct trace of his name' (p. 17); and, further, '[where are] "the documents of the Persian period?"': the epigraphic and archaeological remains are reduced to a tiny quantity until well into the Hellenistic period' (p. 19).

51. Knoppers, *Two Nations Under God*, I, p. 56.

52. Finkelstein and Silberman, *The Bible Unearthed*, p. 167: 'It was Josiah's ambition to expand to the north and take over the territories in the highlands that once belonged to the northern kingdom. Thus the Bible supports that ambition by explaining that the northern kingdom was established in the territories of the mythical united monarchy, which was ruled from Jerusalem; that it was a sister Israelite state; that its people were Israelites who would have worshipped in Jerusalem; that the Israelites still living in these territories must turn their eyes to Jerusalem; and that Josiah, the heir to the Davidic throne and to YHWH's eternal promise to David, is the only legitimate heir to the territories of vanquished Israel. On the other hand the authors of the Bible needed to delegitimize the northern cult—especially the Bethel shrine—and to show that the distinctive religious traditions of the northern kingdom were all evil, that they should be wiped out and replaced by the centralized worship at the Temple of Jerusalem. The Deuteronomistic History accomplishes all this'. Further: 'Had Israel survived, we might have received a parallel, competing, and very different history. But with the Assyrian destruction of Samaria and the dismantling of its institutions of royal

also belong to the mythic past, which in literature came to life again only in the second century BCE's extra-biblical documentation of the Maccabaean state.[53]

The argument in the Deuteronomistic History is not descriptive, but prescriptive. Moving backwards, we learn that when Israel was finally united under one ruler with its centre in Jerusalem, everyone lived in peace from the Euphrates to Gaza, from Dan to Beer-sheba (1 Kgs 5.4-5). This is exactly what the Assyrian cupbearer, the Rabshaqeh, offers (2 Kgs 18.31-32) and what Isaiah prophesies (2 Kgs 19.29-31) to Jerusalem's remnant. This, however, is a literary and not a historical departure. History is used and created. Both Van Seters and Knoppers fail to recognize that the creation of the idealized David–Solomonic past cannot have been modelled upon the biblical Josianic period of 2 Kings. In this book, the northerners are not invited to participate in the cult reforms or in the Passover celebration (2 Kgs 23). Unification is not within the scope of the narrative, and Josiah's reign does not signify the re-creation of Great Israel, but rather an election of Judah and Jerusalem after the disappearance of the Northern Kingdom. It is the books of Chronicles that offers us allusions to the warranted scenario (2 Chron. 34.9, 21; 35.4, 18). If for any reason Josiah's court dreamt of extending Judah's borders or perhaps succeeded in doing so, as has so often been maintained in biblical scholarship,[54] its 'royal archives', supposedly reflected in 2 Kings' narrative, are rather negligent of such idealistic political efforts.[55] Biblical scholars have deceptively filled in the gaps and read into the biblical narrative hopes and longings deducted from the 'false similarity' between Josiah's reign and

power, any such competing histories were silenced' (p. 223). Needless to say, it is the biblical narrative that informs us that such a competition ever existed!

53. Garbini, *History and Ideology in Ancient Israel*, pp. 174-75.

54. See the critique of such interpretations in N. Na'aman, 'The Kingdom of Judah under Josiah', *Tel Aviv* 18 (1991), pp. 3-71; G.W. Ahlström (with a contribution by Gary O. Rollefson), *The History of Ancient Palestine from the Palaeolithic Period to Alexander's Conquest* (ed. D.V. Edelman; JSOTSup, 146; Sheffield: JSOT Press, 1993), pp. 764-81; W.B. Barrick, 'On the Meaning of בֵּית־הַה/הַבָּמוֹת and בָּתֵּי־הַבָּמוֹת and the Composition of the Kings History', *JBL* 115.4 (1996), pp. 621-42; Finkelstein and Silberman, *The Bible Unearthed*, pp. 347-53 (Appendix F).

55. Ahlström, *The History of Ancient Palestine*, p. 766: 'It is inconceivable that the biblical writer would not mention anything about Josiah's extension of his kingdom, had it occurred, for such military-political success would have been a very important factor in the glorification of Josiah as the most important king after David. There was simply no space for Josiah to play a grand political role.'

the days of the United Monarchy.[56] Similarly, the often-argued expansion of Jerusalem (partly based on archaeological findings) and its increased importance in seventh-century BCE Palestine as the sole kingdom of the southern Levant, lacks consideration of the political dynamics of the entire region, in which especially the Philistine and later also the Phoenician areas shared Jerusalem's status as Assyrian vassals. While in its didactic setting the closure of the Josiah narrative—which predicts that also Jerusalem should become rejected—belongs to the narrative discourse of the Deuteronomistic History, the Hezekiah narrative (2 Kgs 18.17–20.19; Isa. 36–39) breaks into that discourse and claims a future for Jerusalem's faithful remnant in spite of that rejection. This perspective, however, does not belong to the authorial voice of the books of Kings. It belongs to the voice of the book of Isaiah, with which it shares significant linguistic and thematic traits.[57]

2. *From Past Relatives to Present Ghosts*

Now we have to return to past relatives, who for the post-exilic writers have become present 'ghosts'—'ghosts', because they represent a rejected past, a cursed past and a relationship which is now denied. Tragic as the narrative is, ambivalence drives the narrators (biblical and non-biblical) to reject that past, yet retain it for the sake of the heritage, the claim on the land.[58] In non-biblical literature, the first-century CE Jewish writer Flavius Josephus, in his identification of such 'ghosts' as 'Samaritans/Cuthaeans', offers elaborate narratives of how the Samaritans came to be like Jews, without in fact being Jews.

Josephus' portrait of the Samaritans[59] takes its point of departure from the book of Kings' story of the deportation of Samaria's population and its replacement by peoples from Babylon, Cuthah, Ava, Hamath and Sepharvaim (2 Kgs 17.24-41). In Kings' narrative, it is said that they did not know how to worship the god of the land. Having no intention of giving up their own gods, they introduced a syncretistic religion, using the temples made by the Samaritans (2 Kgs 17.29). Even when attacked by lions

56. Na'aman, 'The Kingdom of Judah under Josiah', pp. 55-60.

57. See further Hjelm, *Jerusalem's Rise to Sovereignty* (forthcoming).

58. Lemche, *The Israelites in History and Tradition*, pp. 86-88.

59. Given in five separate narratives, which are set in the eighth, sixth, fourth, third and second centuries BCE and are connected through theme and terminology. For an examination of these narratives, see Hjelm, *Samaritans and Early Judaism*, Chapter 5.

and requested to decide which god they would worship, they did not choose to worship Yahweh alone (as the Israelites did in Josh. 24.21-24), but decided to fear Yahweh and serve their own gods. It is central in the biblical text that they did not know how to worship the god of the land (2 Kgs 17.26-28) and that to worship Yahweh is to keep his ordinances (17.36-38). It is not said that they betrayed Yahweh in a manner similar to the Israelites, which had caused *their* removal from the country (17.7-24). The situation is the opposite. The Israelites, on the contrary, *knew how* to fear Yahweh, as is clearly stated in the opening paragraph (17.7-23) and reiterated in the midrash on the first commandment in the closing paragraph (17.34-41), but they failed to do so. In contrast, the foreigners did not know how and obviously were slow to learn, so these foreigners continued to 'fear Yahweh' in their own manner, breaking the first commandment of not serving other gods (vv. 35, 37 and 38). Indirectly, a critique is given of the Israelite priest 'carried away from Shomron', who is brought back to teach the newcomers how to fear the god of the land (17.28). He must be understood as belonging to the same stock as those who are claimed responsible for the idol worship that had led to a rejection of Israel. The author implicitly states that they did not change at all, since the foreigners continue to do so 'unto this very day', leaving the land as polluted as it was before (17.41).

Josephus' account of this story in 2 Kings is interpolated in his Hezekiah narrative, using the pious acts of the Judaean king Hezekiah as contrasting motifs to the impious acts of the Israelites, who did not accept Hezekiah's invitation to join the celebration of the Feast of Unleavened Bread in Jerusalem. They not only laughed at the king's message, as also in the biblical account (2 Chron. 30), but, in an elaboration of this narrative, they 'poured scorn upon them [the prophets] and finally seized them and killed them' (Josephus, *Ant.* 9.265). This stock motif, which frames Josephus' views on the Samaritans, is reiterated several times in his presentation of what he claims are historical events. It should not escape our notice that he also made use of this motif in his judgment of Hezekiah's son Manasseh's crime, that he 'imitated the lawless deeds of the Israelites' and 'killed all the righteous men among the Hebrews. Nor did he spare even the prophets, some of whom he slaughtered daily' (*Ant.* 10.37-38). In Josephus' account, we are at first surprised to notice that he has given a special status to one group of people who had been transported to Samaria (*Ant.* 9.279). Revealing the language of his own day, he calls them 'Cuthaeans'. The term conflicts with the biblical account, which speaks about Cuthaeans as but one among other peoples in 2 Kings 17, but which never uses the term elsewhere.[60] The name perhaps has 'survived', because of its implicit reference to a major Assyrian cult site for the underworld god Nergal in Cuthah from as early as the third millenium BCE. The worship of Nergal was an important part of the official Assyrian cult, and invocation of this deity occurs frequently in neo-Assyrian texts.[61] The location of Cuthah is uncertain; it might be modern Tell Ibrahim, 20 miles northeast of Babylon.[62] Josephus further mentions that the Cuthaeans originally had been five tribes, each of whom worshipped their own god and came from the Persian region and river valley called Cuthah (Josephus, *Ant.* 9.288; cf. 2 Kgs 17.30). In Josephus' treatment, the biblical 'lions' have become 'a pestilence' and an oracle advises that worship of the Most High God will bring deliverance. Although minor, these changes reflect a discussion, which we also meet in rabbinic literature from the second–fifth centuries CE. In this literature, the Samaritans are accused of having been forced to

---

60. In fact, the narratives about the deportation of *all* Israel and the importation of foreign peoples have no impact on the Bible's further 'history', which continues to speak of Samaria/Ephraim's population as if it were the biblical, pre-722 BCE Israel. It is only in the book of Ezra's narrative about the re-building of Jerusalem's temple, set in the Persian period, that some people are mentioned as brought in by Esarhaddon and Osnappar (that is, Asshurbanipal [Ezra 4.2, 10]), similarly not mentioned anywhere else. This have led commentators to suggest that 2 Kings' narrative was a late insertion, which could therefore not have influenced the narratives about the decline of the Judaean kingdom in the seventh–sixth centuries BCE.

61. R. Labat, *Le caractère religieux de la royauté assyro-babylonienne* (Paris: Librairie d'amérique et d'orient adrien-maisonneuve, 1929), pp. 251-74; H. Spieckermann, *Juda unter Assur in der Sargonidenzeit* (FRLANT, 129; Göttingen: Vandenhoeck & Ruprecht, 1982), pp. 255-56.

62. B. Meissner, *Babylonien und Assyrien I* (2 vols.; Heidelberg: C. Winters Universitätsbuchhandlung, 1920), pp. 12, 38; D.O. Edzard and M. Gallery, 'Kutha', in G. Ebeling *et al.* (eds.), *Reallexikon der Assyriologie* (6 vols.; Berlin: W. de Gruyter, 1932–83), VI, pp. 384-87. In Samaritan tradition, it is argued that because the Samaritans had been deported to that area during the reign of Darius, 'the Jews call them Kuthians, so that the name Samaritan and the name Israelite would fall into disuse'; see Abu'l Fath, *Kitab al Tarikh*, ch. 24, p. 88 (published in English with notes by P. Stenhouse, *The Kitab al Tarikh of Abu'l-Fath* [Sydney: The Mandelbaum Trust, University of Sydney, 1985] on the basis of the Arabic version, published by E. Vilmar, *Abulfathi Annales Samaritani* [Gothae: n.p., 1865]). (Hereafter Stenhouse's edition will be referred to as *AF*, with underlined page numbers referring to the pagination of the manuscript used by Stenhouse.) Cf. Hjelm, *Samaritans and Early Judaism*, p. 261.

convert because of attacks of lions, and one conclusion is drawn that their conversion cannot be regarded as valid.[63] While the biblical account claims that it was Yahweh who sent the lions, Josephus states that it had been the bringing of 'their own gods' that had brought the pestilence. The implicit critique fits the role of Nergal as a deity associated with plague, pestilence, war and sudden death.[64] The consequences of the oracle is thus changed, for surprisingly in *Ant.* 9.290 we read:

> ...after being instructed in the ordinances and religion of this God, [namely, Yahweh] they worshipped him with great zeal, and were at once freed of the pestilence. These same rites have continued in use even to this day among those who are called Cuthaioi, Cuthim, in the Hebrew tongue, Samaritans by the Greeks.

With a single artifice—the omission of any reference to religious syncretism—Josephus succeeded in combining the narrative of the biblical books of Kings with his further elaboration on the Samaritan question and avoided attacking their cult and religion (an attack, which it would have been difficult to defend[65]). Questions of ethnicity and relation to the Israelite tribes are the central themes of Josephus' narrative. This is further emphasized in *Ant.* 9.280, in his introductory remark to that story:

> ...the ten tribes of Israel emigrated from Judaea nine hundred and forty seven years after their forefathers went out of Egypt...

which is to be understood on the assumption that the ten tribes had never returned, again contrasting Samaria with the fate of the Judaean tribe(s), who had returned (*Ant.* 10.184-85).[66] His closing remark about the Samaritans in *Ant.* 9.291 serves the same purpose:

---

63. Cf. *b. Qid.* 75a-76a; *Masseket Kutim* (a *tosefta* to the Babylonian Talmud) 27; Hjelm, *Samaritans and Early Judaism*, pp. 105-106. The tractate is presented *in extenso* (and in English translation) in J.A. Montgomery, *The Samaritans: The Earliest Jewish Sect—Their History, Theology and Literature* (The Bohlen Lectures of 1906; Philadelphia: John C. Winston, 1907 [repr. = New York: Ktav, 1968]).

64. Cf. A. Livingstone, 'Nergal', in *DDD*, pp. 621-22.

65. L. Feldman, 'Josephus' Attitude toward the Samaritans: A Study in Ambivalence', in *idem, Studies in Hellenistic Judaism* (AGJU, 40; Leiden: E.J. Brill, 1996), pp. 114-36 (first published in M. Mor [ed.], *Jewish Sects, Religious Movements and Political Parties* [Studies in Jewish Civilization, 3; Omaha, NE: Creighton University Press, 1992], pp. 23-45). See also Hjelm, *Samaritans and Early Judaism*, pp. 104-15.

66. Cf. the return of Judah and Benjamin in the biblical books of Ezra and Nehemiah.

> But they alter their attitude, according to circumstance and, when they see
> the Jews prospering, call them their kinsmen, on the ground that they are
> descended from Joseph and are related to them through their origin from
> him, but when they see the Jews in trouble, they say that they have nothing
> whatever in common with them nor do these have any claim of friendship or
> race, and they declare themselves to be aliens of another race.

This problem of ethnicity forms the central core of Josephus' struggle with
the Judaean-Samaritan relationship. Although recognised as sharing belief
and tradition with the Jews of his own days, it is denied that the Samaritans belong to the patriarchal heritage. In an implicit reversal of Deuteronomistic History's claim for religious conduct rather than lineage, the
Samaritans are claimed not to be true Israelites, because of the ethnicity
ascribed to them (*Ant.* 9.277-91). In variants on this theme, Josephus
offers different origin narratives for the Samaritans at turning points in
Jewish history. At the return of Judah from the Babylonian exile he identifies the people of the land, the עם הארץ of biblical literature, with the
Samaritans (*Ant.* 11.1-119 [85]). In the time of Alexander's conquest of
Palestine, the Samaritans, he argues, are apostate priests from Jerusalem's
temple, mixed through marriage with Samaria's foreign population (*Ant.*
11.287-347 [341]). In a narrative placed in the time of Antiochus IV's
oppression of Jews and Samaritans, he accuses Samaritans of having
cowardly denied their ethnic ties with the Jews (*Ant.* 12.237-64 [257]).

3. Samaritan Identity

Against Josephus' first-century CE views on Samaritan origins, stands
Samaritan self-understanding: that they belong to Old Israel from the
lineage of Joseph, Ephraim and Manasseh, and that they have an unbroken
chain of high priests with a cultic continuation that has kept their heritage
unchanged since the time of the entrance into the Promised Land.[67] While

---

67. For general introductions to the Samaritan literature, see, for example,
J.A. Montgomery, *The Samaritans: The Earliest Jewish Sect: Their History, Theology
and Literature* (Philadelphia: John C. Winston, 1907 [reprint = New York: Ktav,
1968]); M. Gaster, *The Samaritans, Their History, Doctrines and Literature* (Oxford:
Oxford University Press, 1925); J. Macdonald, *Samaritan Chronicle No. II (or: Sepher
Ha-Yamim) From Joshua to Nebuchadnezzar* (Berlin: W. de Gruyter, 1969), pp. 3-14;
A.D. Crown, 'New Light on the Inter-Relationships of Samaritan Chronicles from
Some Manuscripts in The John Rylands Library', *BJRL* 54 (1972), pp. 282-313, and
BJRL 55 (1973), pp. 86-111; R.J. Coggins, *Samaritans and Jews: The Origins of
Samaritanism Reconsidered* (Growing Points in Theology; Oxford: Basil Blackwell,

Judaism argued for the necessity of a new beginning after the Babylonian exile, Samaritans insisted that the old tradition be maintained. As Abraham had left the godless world of Haran to go to Shechem, so in their post-exilic return, the Samaritans brought home their old tradition (kept in custody in Nineveh) from Haran. In both the biblical and the Samaritan tradition, Abraham raised his first altar in Shechem,[68] and in the Samaritan tradition, Joshua built a cult place on the summit of Mt Gerizim. The Samaritans claim a continuation of these cult places and especially of their holy mountain Gerizim. Put very simple, while Jewish tradition maintains the sovereignty of Jerusalem and the Davidic line of kingship, based on the Deuteronomistic and Chronistic Histories, Samaritan tradition maintains the sovereignty of Gerizim and its priesthood, on the basis of the authority of Moses and the Patriarchs. At the return from the Babylonian exile (*AF*, chs. 19–20, pp. 66-79 [see n. 62, above, for details about *AF*]), neither group would accept a compromise, and the split, which, according to Samaritan tradition, had begun in the eleventh century BCE when the

1975); J. Bowman, *Samaritan Documents Relating to their History, Religion and Life* (Pittsburgh: Pickwick Press, 1977); P. Stenhouse, 'Samaritan Chronicles', in A.D. Crown (ed.), *The Samaritans* (Tübingen: J.C.B. Mohr [Paul Siebeck], 1989), pp. 218-65; J. Zangenberg, *Samareia: Antike Quellen zur Geschichte und Kultur der Samaritaner in deutscher Übersetzung* (TANZ, 15; Tübingen: Francke Verlag, 1994), pp. 180-229; Hjelm, *Samaritans and Early Judaism*, pp. 76-103; F. Niessen, *Eine Samaritanische Version des Buches Yehošua' und die Šobak Erzählung: Die Samaritanische Chronik Nr. II, Handschrift 2: JR(G) 1168 = Ryl. Sam. MS 259, Folio 8b-53a* (Texte und Studien zur Orientalistik, 12; Hildesheim: Georg Olms, 2000), pp. 4-18; A.D. Crown, *Samaritan Scribes and Manuscripts* (Texts and Studies in Ancient Judaism, 80; Tübingen: J.C.B. Mohr [Paul Siebeck], 2001), pp. 1-39; B. Tsedaka, *The History of the Samaritans Due to Their Own Sources: From Joshua to the Year 2000 AD* (Holon: Institute of Samaritan Studies Press, forthcoming [2004] [Hebrew]). For earlier literature and references to text editions, see bibliographies in the works mentioned and in A.D. Crown, *A Bibliography of the Samaritans* (London: Scarecrow Press, 2nd edn, 1993 [1984]).

68. Not mentioned by Josephus, who demonstrably denigrates Shechem (and other cult places) in favour of Shiloh; cf. T.L. Thornton, 'Anti-Samaritan Exegesis Reflected in Josephus' Retelling of Deuteronomy, Joshua and Judges', *JTS* 47 (1996), pp. 125-30. For Josephus' polemical use of the terms Shechem and Sidon as a depreciatory gentilic for Samaritans, see Hjelm, *Samaritans and Early Judaism*, pp. 218-22. For an unconvincing positive appreciation of Josephus' objectiveness, see R. Egger, *Josephus Flavius und die Samaritaner: Eine terminologische Untersuchung zur Identitetserklärung der Samaritaner* (NTOA, 4; Fribourg: Vandenhoeck & Ruprecht, 1986).

priest Eli moved from Shechem to Shiloh to erect a temple and a cult independent of Gerizim, became manifest.[69]

With the biblical Prophets and Psalms, which supported Jerusalem's sovereignty, while, however, testifying to the Samaritan claim of priority as firstborn (e.g. Jer. 31.9, 20; Ezek. 37.16-28; Hos. 13.1; Ps. 78), the Samaritans had a good case. It is important to notice that the hostile attitude of the returning Jews towards the people of the land, and the claim for ethnic purity found in the Ezra–Nehemiah tradition, are not shared by the biblical prophets Isaiah, Jeremiah and Ezekiel. They all argue for a reconciliation between Ephraim and Judah in Jerusalem. In Isaiah, this is taken even further to include also the people outside the land, the foreigners who

---

69.   *AF* (= *Chronicle* IV), ch. 10, pp. 45-48; *Liber Josuae* (= *Chronicle* VI), chs. 44–45; the *Chronicle* has been published in Arabic and Latin with notes by T.W.J. Juynboll, *Chronicon samaritanum, arabice conscriptum, cui titulus est Liber Josuae* (London: S. & J. Luchtmans, 1848; English translation with notes by O.T. Crane, *The Samaritan Chronicle, or the Book of Joshua the Son of Nun* [New York: John B. Alden, 1890]); Macdonald, *Samaritan Chronicle No. II*, ST Judg. §LO*-T; ST 1 Sam. § BA'-F*. The manuscripts of *Chronicle* IV can be safely dated from the seventeenth century CE, but the writing of the chronicle (based on earlier sources) dates to the fourteenth century CE (1355). The manuscripts of *Chronicle* VI, covering the period until the arrival of Alexander the Great, date to the thirteenth century CE (1362), while matters, regarding the later period until the seventh century CE, are added in 1513 CE. Juynboll's edition is based on MS Or. 249, a manuscript acquired by J.J. Scaliger in 1584 and now in the library of the University of Leiden. The book is written in Arabic with Samaritan characters, which Juynboll transcribed into Arabic on the basis of other Samaritan manuscripts written in Arabic characters. The basic manuscript of *Chronicle* II, written in Hebrew, is by most scholars considered to be a compilation from 1908. Macdonald argued that the manuscript should be dated to 1616. Parts of another manuscript, similar to Macdonald's and referred to in his apparatus, have been dated to either pre-Christian times (M. Gaster, 'Das Buch Joshua in hebräisch samaritanischer Rezension. Entdeckt und zum ersten Male herausgegeben', *ZDMG* 62 [1908], pp. 209-79, 494-549), the fourteenth century CE (J.A. Cohen, *A Samaritan Chronicle: A Source-Critical Analysis of the Life and Times of the Great Samaritan Reformer Baba Rabbah* [SPB, 30; Leiden: E.J. Brill, 1981]) or the nineteenth–twentieth century (Niessen, *Eine Samaritanische Version des Buches Yehošua*). Another Hebrew variant from 1900 is Chronicle Adler or New Chronicle (= *Chronicle* VII), published by E.N. Adler and M. Séligsohn, 'Une nouvelle chronique samaritaine', *REJ* 44 (1902) pp. 188-222, *REJ* 45 (1902), pp. 70-98, 160, 223-54, and *REJ* 46 (1903), pp. 123-46. See further, Crown, *Samaritan Scribes and Manuscripts*, pp. 27-32; Hjelm, *Jerusalem's Rise to Sovereignty* (forthcoming), Chapter 4; *idem*, 'What Do Samaritans and Jews Have in Common? Recent Trends in Samaritan Studies', *Currents in Biblical Research* (forthcoming [2004]).

are invited to take part in the blessing given to Abraham as Yahweh's people. The Samaritan case, related to cult but highly influenced by policy, was politically lost to the Jewish struggle for independence and hegemony during the second-century BCE Maccabaean revolt against the Seleucids. Reiterating the religious and political reforms ascribed to the Jewish king Josiah from the sixth century BCE, the Maccabaean king John Hyrcanus is granted history's dubious honour of having destroyed the Samaritan temple on Gerizim in 128 BCE (Josephus, *Ant.* 13.254-78) and, further-more, of having destroyed the city of Samaria entirely (*Ant.* 13.281). In Samaritan tradition, the destruction and subsequent oppression of the Samaritans took place before Alexander the Great's arrival (*AF*, ch. 24, pp. 87-89). Confusion of names, which links the Jewish king Simon, men-tioned as responsible for the destruction with 'Arqīa (Hyrcanus) as his son,[70] usually leads to the conclusion that the chronology should be aligned with that of Josephus'. Similarly, in the talmudic tractate, *Megillat Ta'anit*, which places the destruction as a reaction to Samaritan attempts to destroy the Jewish temple in Jerusalem on Alexander's arrival, the king mentioned is called 'Simon the Just'. In Josephus' judgment of these acts, Hyrcanus took these steps because 'he hated the Samaritans as scoundrels because of the injuries which, in obedience to the kings of Syria [i.e. the Seleucids], they had done to the people of Marisa, who were colonists and allies of the Jews' (*Ant.* 13.275). In biblical material, a similar accusation of betrayal had been given as an explanation of the fall of Israel to the Assyrians in the eighth century BCE (Isa. 7.1-9; 9.7-20). The destruction increased religious and political antagonisms. Based on religious and political ideas of centrality, there was no room for competing cult centres in this newly won semi-independent Maccabaean state.[71] The centrality of Jerusalem's temple became the main issue, and increasingly so, after its destruction by the Romans in 70 CE.[72] In my book on Samaritans and Early Judaism, I claimed that 'Samaritans and Jews never formed a single state and that the only historical effort to establish such a state destroyed its basis'.[73] How-ever, Samaritans and Jews did form a single state after the Hasmonaean conquest of Samaria initiated by Jonathan (145 BCE) and completed by

70. Stenhouse, *The Kitab al Tarikh of Abu'l-Fath*, pp. 106-108.

71. D. Mendels, *The Rise and Fall of Jewish Nationalism* (New York: Doubleday, 1992), pp. 150-51.

72. Hjelm, *Samaritans and Early Judaism*, pp. 226-38, and, 'Cult Centralization as a Device of Cult Control', *SJOT* 13.2 (1999), pp. 298-309.

73. Hjelm, *Samaritans and Early Judaism*, p. 284.

John Hyrcanus and his sons Aristobolus I and Alexander Jannaeus (after 111 BCE). What I should have stressed is that they did not form a common state based on mutual agreements. The duration of the Maccabaean Israelite 'state', from around the mid-second century BCE until the Roman conquest in 63 BCE, corresponds fairly well with the duration of the 73 years of the Davidic–Solomonic Empire and the 70 years of exile. History does not repeat itself, even though historiography tends to make it appear so. It is the job of the scholar to judge between competing stories, which create a past from distorted and hidden realities, interpreted against the background of vivified traditions.

HOLY WAR AT THE CENTER OF BIBLICAL THEOLOGY:
SHALOM AND THE CLEANSING OF JERUSALEM

Thomas L. Thompson

'Holy War' in the Bible is war that is fought by Yahweh. It reflects a cosmic struggle barely suggested in the creation story of Genesis 1's opening enigma of God creating the world out of darkness and the cosmic desert of תוהו ובוהו, the nothingness of chaos' darkness and emptiness. The divine strength against such forces of non-being, which holds the world in existence under Yahweh's patronage, provides the mythological and transcendent context that supports a tradition of narrative and song about 'holy war' with its hallmark stories urging the extermination of indigenous peoples and xenophobic cleansing of a holy land of its foreigners. In the Bible, holy war comes to us, not as a fact of history, but as a discourse of literature. It forms not policy but philosophy.

Theologically, the biblical stories on the theme of holy war have long been seen as problematic. This is particularly the case within the historical-critical tradition of interpretation, with its orientation towards events as point of departure for the development of biblical tradition.[1] Such difficulties are not so obvious with the more romantic folktales of biblical lore such as Israel's war against the Valley of the Giants, as in Numbers 13; nor even with the great miracle stories of Joshua, as in the stories of Jericho's fall or the battle of Gibeon where the sun stood still. Such stories

---

1. There are also very important social and political goals at stake in the scholarly interpretation: issues which have been explored, for example, in M. Prior, *The Bible and Colonialism: A Moral Critique* (The Biblical Seminar, 48; Sheffield: Sheffield Academic Press, 1997); *idem*, 'The Moral Problems of the Land Traditions of the Bible', in *idem* (ed.), *Western Scholarship and the History of Palestine* (London: Melisende, 1998), pp. 41-81; R.M. Schwartz, *The Curse of Cain: The Violent Legacy of Monotheism* (Chicago: University of Chicago Press, 1997); I. Hjelm, *Jerusalem's Rise to Sovereignty in History and Tradition: Zion and Gerizim in Competition* (London: T&T Clark International, forthcoming [2004]).

taste so much of free-floating fantasy that they are washed of their grue. The problems are far greater with such a story as Saul's in which, as in 1 Samuel 15, the good general is rejected by his God because he had neglected to execute the king of the Amalekites and had not rid the land of its people: a story in which, after Saul's humiliation by Yahweh, the prophet Samuel takes Agag's sword and 'chops him in pieces before Yahweh in Gilgal' (1 Sam. 15.33). Such hatred of foreigners as is portrayed in this story of holy war, is an integral part of a continuous theme that begins already in Genesis and does not close until the final chapter of Revelations. Viewed historically, one must surely find it an odd religion which has a God who chooses an ever-worthless folk for his own, while viewing all the world's peoples with murderous enmity. While there are many different ways in which one can read and understand this very problematic theme in the Bible, I have chosen the particular thematic element of 'the stranger in the land of Israel' in an effort to explore a dominant literary function in the composition of biblical narrative, which I identify as 'thematic reiteration'.[2] In doing so, I intend to argue against historical readings of the Bible,[3] that the theme of holy war in this corpus, unlike its use in some ancient Near Eastern campaign inscriptions,[4] is self-consciously a product of a secondary literary tradition, which uses this theme with didactic purpose.[5]

---

2. This article continues themes of divine patronage, warfare and biblical theology centered in forms of reiterative history. See T.L. Thompson, *The Bible in History: How Writers Create a Past* (London: Jonathan Cape, 1999), pp. 267-92; *idem*, 'Historiography in the Pentateuch: 25 Years after Historicity', *SJOT* 13 (1999), pp. 258-83; *idem*, 'Kingship and the Wrath of God: Or Teaching Humility', *RB* 109 (2002), pp. 161-96; I. Hjelm and T.L. Thompson, 'The Victory Song of Merneptah, Israel and the People of Palestine', *JSOT* 27.1 (2002), pp. 3-18.

3. More than 60 years ago, Ernst Würthwein published a historical study of the use of the phrase 'people of the land' (עם הארץ), *Der 'amm ha-'arez im alten Testament* (BWANT, 17; Stuttgart: W. Kohlhammer, 1936), a study in which he examined the syntax of the various Old Testament stories that made use of the phrase. Würthwein's approach was to use the apparent historical context of each story in order to construct a chronology of the progressive development he perceived. While I have been unable to share the historiographical premise of this work, I am much indebted to this study in all that follows.

4. See especially M. Liverani, *Prestige and Interest: International Relations in the Near East ca. 1600–1100 CE* (Sargon: Padua, 1990), pp. 115-204.

5. In this, I continue the argument first presented in 'Kingship and the Wrath of God'.

1. *A New Israel and the People of the Land*

While there is much competition for the most brutal of holy war scenes, this theme also provides us with the most tristful in biblical literature: that which closes the book of Ezra, offering a reiteration of a synoptic tradition that is also found in Nehemiah and 1 Esdras. The sadness of the book of Ezra's rendition cannot be shaken even as it undermines the reader's expectations. The final shift to the third-person voice in Ezra 10 is brilliant. It is no longer Ezra who speaks with the voice of the text, but the author chooses to stand at a distance from the scene he paints. His dramatic gloss on Ezra's wish for purity touches directly the priest's prayer of shame and guilt over the pollution of 'the peoples of the land' (Ezra 9.11) which Israel's faithless remnant continues. The second half of the book in chs. 7–10 has brought the learned scribe and priest, Ezra, from exile. Commissioned by the Persian king Artaxerxes to rule Judah and Jerusalem in accord with God's law, the priest marks Israel's wives and children as 'foreign women' (נשׁים נכריות),[6] who belong to the 'peoples of the land' (Ezra 10.2). Such נכריות are, with linguistic appropriateness and rhetorical effect, to be 'cut off' by a covenant (ועתה נכרת ברית). The punning of נכריות with נכרת ברית, which excludes foreign women[7] by a covenant creating a new Israel, seems as harsh as it is tendentious.

The sadness of the text's voice seems to provoke an implicit debate: Does the covenant require obedience or compassion? Jonah, of course, has long been recognized as engaging a similar debate. Such central Torah texts as Deut. 10.19; 14.19, 29, and Lev. 19.18 emphatically support and protect the rights of the stranger within Israel. These are, moreover, texts which, as we will see below, have a complex discursive context dealing with themes that are central to the book of Ezra. Is the theme of the story that of the cleansing of Jerusalem, expressed by the surface plot's xenophobia and furthered by an implicit divine demand to complete a holy war neglected by 'old Israel', or is it rather the theme of understanding what Israel's covenant theology truly demands? The covenant texts which the priest Ezra evokes in his demand for ethnic cleansing, such as Deut. 6.4-5 and Joshua 24, stand within a wide spectrum of texts which the book of Ezra provocatively engages in a theological discourse.[8] As in the related

6.   Similar to the 'foreigners' of Gen. 17.12, 27 and the foreign gods of Deut. 32.12.
7.   Cf. Gen. 17.14.
8.   On the complexity of Ezra's text, see E. Nodet, *A Search for the Origins of Judaism: From Joshuah to the Mishnah* (JSOTSup, 248; Sheffield: Sheffield Academic

holy war story of 1 Samuel 15, the reader must engage his text in debate: the law requires obedience and compassion. Much is at stake: not least, the identity of the 'new Israel'.

In a final, dramatic scene, the priest Ezra's tears succeed in Israel's purification. In telling his story, our book's author has subtly separated himself from his character. The people, crying with their reformer, make their covenant in an effort to accomplish a goal that Yahweh himself had sought by the same means—through centuries of war—since he had first chosen Israel. By their own oath, the people agree to banish all the foreign women and their children, as Ezra and the righteous ('those that had trembled before God') demand. Yet, the author does not close with his new covenant, but chooses to reiterate the wilderness narrative of the first Israel. After three days, the people of the author's new Jerusalem murmur against their new Moses. They complain of the unreasonableness of Ezra's decree to cleanse the nation without delay. Their rebellious cry is used to close the story of Ezra's 'success' on a note of discord and sadness. Banishing their wives and children is too much in such a short time, *while standing in the rain* (Ezra 10.13).

The literary intrusion of the motif of rain is as disruptive as it is unsettling to the plot. Shaking from the awful demands of their own pact, as from the rain's coldness marking God's presence in the scene, the people complain with a loud voice. However this is a cry that goes unanswered; nor does the rain stop. The thematic element of rain, directly associated with divine wrath and violence, is a substantial, if infrequent element in holy war traditions: most notably in the traditions of the covenant after the great flood, as also in the story of Elijah's great contest with the prophets of Ba'al and Asherah in 1 Kings 18. It does not rain without God's command. In both of these rain stories, theodicy and irony are important aspects of the narrative function.[9] A note of discord which the cold winter rain of Ezra stresses is created by the inappropriateness of the motif in its

Press, 1997), p. 25. On a similar problem with a related text, see T.L. Thompson, 'Some Exegetical and Theological Implications of Understanding Exodus as a Collected Tradition', in N.P. Lemche and M. Müller (eds.), *Fra Dybet: Festskrift til John Strange* (Forum for Bibelsk Eksegese, 5; Copenhagen: Museum Tusculanum, 1996), pp. 233-42. Also discussing the same problem but oriented to the theme of identity, see *idem*, 'Hvorledes Jahve blev Gud: Exodus 3 og 6 og Pentateukens centrum', *DTT* 57 (1994), pp. 1-19.

    9.   See further Thompson, *The Bible in History*, pp. 59-61, and, 'Kingship and the Wrath of God'.

context. The rain is not like Jeremiah's righteous rain which falls at the right time (Jer. 5.24; see also Joel 2.23); nor is it like Ezekiel's rain of fertile blessing, bringing fruit in its season (Ezek. 34.26). Ezra's rain is a rain out of time. It is like Isaiah's rain, which, like God's word, does its work and fulfills his intentions (Isa. 55.10); though we need to think more of Ezekiel's use of a Genesis-like rain of the flood story, which brings an element of mortal danger and bears the mark of covenant and war (Ezek. 1.28). Ezra's is a cold winter rain that causes the people to shiver, offering subtle contrast to the 'fear of God' expressed in their covenant. The rain of Ezra 10 is precisely the rain that falls on Ezekiel's day of judgment when brother fights against brother: a rain to make men shake (Ezek. 38.21-22). The misery of the scene is unmitigated. After a long delay—created as much by the list of those who had married foreign wives as by the delay in obedience—the book closes with its sadness intact, as the people's 'new covenant' cuts them off from their loved ones forever (Ezra 10.44).

2. *Variants of Ezra 10*

Variants of the story of the ethnic cleansing of Jerusalem are presented in 1 Esdras 8–9 and in Nehemiah 9–10.[10] The story in 1 Esdras begins with the description of state affairs in 1 Esd. 8.1-24, within a description of perfect harmony between Ezra and Artaxerxes. Ezra's rule was to be for Jerusalem's benefit and its temple's wealth. Ezra himself, trained in the Torah, wields dictatorial powers. So complete is the identity of the laws of God and empire through the priest Ezra that one must wonder if Persian policy is not one of the work's surface targets. Might not the book of Ezra offer an implicitly polemical response to the narrative in 1 Esdras, in which 1 Esd. 8.25-90 offers an imitative memoir commenting on the seemingly positive state of affairs of Ezra's collusion with the Persians? After a list of this Quisling's companions (chs. 28–40), this variant briefly recounts Ezra's journey to Jerusalem and the grandeur and wealth for the temple that he brings (chs. 40–67). The high and pompous tone of Ezra's mem-oirs, with its attention on wealth and on Ezra's exalted position could be understood as entirely stylistic. The wish not to ask the Persians for troops, expressed in 8.50-52, while unsettling the pro-Persian grandeur of Ezra's rhetoric and the request for his young men to seek refuge in Yahweh

---

10. M. Noth, *Überlieferungsgeschichtliche Studien* (Tübingen: Max Niemeyer, 1943), p. 147; see, however, already, W. Rudolph, *Ezra und Nehemiah* (HAT; Tübingen: J.C.B. Mohr, 1949).

instead are fully in accord with the piety expressed (cf. Ps. 2.12c) and supports the contrasting emotional import of Jerusalem's lack of faithfulness to Yahweh. When Ezra arrives in Jerusalem, after the wealth is delivered to the temple, he is told that the people of Jerusalem and its leaders had not banished the foreigners from the land with their pollution. These he identifies by recounting a stereotypical list of nations: the Canaanites, Hittites, Perizzites, Jebusites, Moabites, Egyptians and Edomites, a variant of which appears in Ezra 9.1.

'The holy race has been mixed with foreign peoples of the land' (1 Esd. 8.68-70). Grief-stricken, Ezra prays because this sin—the cause of Jerusalem's destruction—has accumulated from the time of the fathers until today (8.76-77). He stresses once again the wonderful conditions granted to the city by the Persians in order to underline the corresponding thanklessness of Israel's guilt (8.82-90). Does 1 Esdras' author not distinguish between the Persian and the divine will? The voice of the text changes rather drastically by its shift in voice to the third person. The tones which had been used to support Ezra's distance and hauteur are now abandoned, as the people of Jerusalem gather around Ezra. Weeping, they lie down before the temple in their intense response to his prayer. They urge the taking of an oath to banish their wives with their children and to do all that is demanded of the temple. In this response and in 1 Esdras 9 generally,[11] only minor differences are to be noted. Rain becomes mere 'bad weather', but the marriage of foreign women is stressed, as is an increase in Israel's sin (9.6-7). As in Ezra and Nehemiah, the foreign wives are equated with the 'people of the land' (9.9) and they are banished with their children (9.36). 1 Esdras speaks of an oath rather than a new covenant. It lacks, however, the intentional discord of the murmuring motif that is found in the book of Ezra. The response of the people to Ezra is filled not with complaint, but with emotions of piety. The oath, harmonious with Ezra's prayer, commits a united people to both God and empire.

It is appropriate in the story as told by 1 Esdras, that it is only after the banishment scene that the people, returning from exile, first settle in Jerusalem and its countryside. Safely separated from the cleansing of Jerusalem scene, the return is celebrated by a solemn New Year's reading of the Torah (1 Esd. 9.37-55). It is a scene that is a puzzling mixture of joy and sadness, more reminiscent of Ezra 3 than of Ezra's closure. It ends abruptly, on an apparently unmotivated note of piety, with all rejoicing in

11. Whose text is unfortunately often used as an aid in translating the book of Ezra's closure (cf. 1 Esd. 9.36).

harmony: the very motif which the author of the book of Ezra has rejected so dramatically in his closure. The contrast between the solemn, if pompous, rejoicing in 1 Esdras and the sadness of Ezra can be explained by differences in dramatic function. The irony of Ezra's closure and the lack of irony in 1 Esdras mark a conflicting self-identity of their implied audiences. 1 Esdras compares the greatness and harmony of Persian cooperation with the priest Ezra against the inexcusable nature of Israel's guilt and impurity, in order to support the narrative's piety. In contrast, the author of Ezra has questions and doubts to raise about what might be understood as collusion with the Persians. He places the banishment scene dramatically at his closure, in order to mark the harshness rather than the piety of ethnic cleansing. Already in Ezra 3, he has prepared his audience for his sharp critique by undermining the celebration of Israel's unity, by marking it ironically with the conflicts in this 'new Jerusalem' with the 'people of the land' and with the Samaritans. Having planted the seed of doubt, he is able to use the closure in Ezra 10 to transform the story and establish common cause with Nehemiah 13 against 1 Esdras [12]

The third variant of the story of Jerusalem's cleansing, in Nehemiah 8–12, begins with the people's response to Ezra's reading of the Torah. The people confess their guilt and decide to separate Israel from all 'foreigners' because of the covenant Israel had established in the wilderness under Moses. In prayer, they praise God and joyfully celebrate a recitation of Yahweh's faithfulness to the covenant that had given them the land of the nations (the Canaanites, Hittites, Amorites, Perizites, Jebusites and Girgashites—Neh. 9.7-8), a covenant to which they had not been faithful. The people are now determined to send the 'people of the land' away decisively (Neh. 10.31-32). Tears are introduced only briefly—in Neh. 8.9-12—and are shed independently of the scene in which 'foreigners' are sent away. Nehemiah's people are 'as one' (8.1): 'men, women and all those who could understand; the ears of the whole people were listening to the book of the law' (8.2-3). The sorrow in Nehemiah hovers fleetingly, seemingly out of context. Nevertheless, the reader is not long

12. E. Nodet (*A Search for the Origins*, pp. 33-34), in his effort to use *Ezra* and *Nehemiah* to reconstruct the history of early Judaism, notes the 'deliberate...persistent haziness in the events recounted'. Noting that intermarriage continued even among priests, he cites Morton Smith's 'sweeping view' that opposition existed between a separatist party and assimilationists. Cf. M. Smith, *Palestinian Parties and Politics that Shaped the Old Testament* (Lectures on the History of Religion, NS 9; New York: Columbia University Press, 1971), pp. 148-92.

uncertain as to the cause of the tears. Rather than as a foreshadowing of the coming separation creating tears of grief as in Ezra 10, the thematic element of tears in Nehemiah 8 functions in a manner similar to the use of this element in the closely parallel scene of 'old men's tears', which come at the completion of the temple in Ezra 3.11-13 (see below). They lack, however, that scene's implicitly ironic commentary. In Nehemiah 8, tears are the sign of a united and pure heart with which the people respond to the renewal of the Torah. In biblical narrative, tears generally bear more than their weight in the plot development of a story; they epitomize the needed response of humility to the divine will, and they mark the repentant as righteous or as one who seeks refuge in Yahweh. In Nehemiah 8, such a traditional pattern seems to be introduced as the Levites admonish the people not to cry, but turn instead to a 'great rejoicing', coming from understanding,[13] clearly echoing the compassionate exhortation of Isa. 40.1: in Nehemiah's new Jerusalem, the tears of exile are over, and, accordingly, the Levites 'speak tenderly to Jerusalem' (Isa. 40.1-2).

Nehemiah's treatment of Jerusalem's separation from the 'people of the land' parallels 1 Esdra's story of banishing 'foreign women and their children' closely. The obligations for keeping Jerusalem clean are contractually set down in writing in ch. 10 by Nehemiah and all the people who were able to understand and who had separated themselves from foreigners in accordance with God's law. This is to give solemn witness to the founding of a new Israel of righteousness and faithful observance of Torah. The inauguration of a new creation is marked as the people offered great sacrifices 'on that day', sing and rejoice: 'for God made them rejoice with great joy' (Neh. 12.43). Nehemiah 12 closes its narrative by shifting from the first-person voice of Nehemiah's memoir. Addressing the audience in the third person, a new omniscient, authorial voice reiterates 'on that day' interpretively in order to draw a grand comparison of the cleansed and reformed 'new Jerusalem' of Zerubbabel and Nehemiah's days with the Jerusalem of the days of David and Solomon. As in the days of David and Asaph, so now, Jerusalem sings songs of praise and thanksgiving to God (Neh. 12.44-47). There can be little doubt where this author's sympathies lie.

---

13. The role of tears in Mesopotamian and Egyptian literature is dealt with in Thompson, 'Kingship and the Wrath of God'. A more detailed analysis of the biblical use of this thematic element is presented in *idem*, 'From the Mouth of Babes, Strength: Psalm 8 and the Book of Isaiah', *SJOT* 16 (2002), pp. 226-45.

In spite of its rhetoric, the book, however, does not close on this note. Whatever the history of composition may be, Nehemiah 13 marks critical distance from both the cleansing of Jerusalem and from its hero, Nehemiah. It stands even further from the omniscient voice of ch. 12's commentator. Nehemiah 13 opens by reiterating 'on that day'. The reader is taken back to the beginning of ch. 8. The voice is third person, and offers an alternative closure, similarly oriented towards interpretation. The narrative form of ch. 13 might best be described as an 'envelope structure' in three interrelated narratives.[14] First, a holy-war story is read from the Torah. It deals with the story of Numbers 22–24, in which the Ammonites and Moabites are banned for having hired Balaam to curse Israel. This curse Yahweh had turned to blessing (Neh. 13.1-2). The people respond to the story by separating themselves from 'everything foreign' from Israel. Dramatically engaging this reiteration of Nehemiah 8, a long section immediately follows which is given over to a doublet story, rendered in the first person of the memoir style. Nehemiah recounts his cleansing of the temple (Neh. 8.4-14) and Sabbath in Jerusalem (8.15-22), offering apt echoes of 2 Kings 18's and 23's reforms of Hezekiah and Josiah.[15] Each recitation closes with the prayer that God remember Nehemiah's piety. This confessional mime, picks up a thematic element of Neh. 5.19 and deftly establishes a leitmotif with which the chapter closes the book (13.31b). It is important to note that the first use of this motif had closed the social reforms of Nehemiah 5 in which Nehemiah, Moses-like, responds to the people's murmuring by defending a Joseph-like exploitation of famine (cf. Gen. 47.13-26). In this defense, he argues for a Jubilee on the basis of other Torah passages (implicitly citing such passages as Exod. 22.24 and esp. Lev. 25.47-49), where motifs of foreigners mistreating Israelites are central. A Torah discourse obviously underlies the narrative. In his third reform, Nehemiah directly addresses the theme of banning 'all that is foreign', the motif with which ch. 13 had originally opened the envelope: the immediacy of the whole people's response to the Balaam story. Nehemiah 13.23-29, finally, closes the envelope with a brief, final story in which the object of ethnic cleansing is progressively narrowed,

---

14. A classic example of an 'envelope structure' is the Jacob–Esau conflict narrative whose opening and closing scenes embrace a Jacob–Laban conflict narrative, which, in its turn, centers the whole in a contest between Rachel and Leah; see T.L. Thompson, 'Conflict Themes in the Jacob Narratives', *Semeia* 15 (1979), pp. 5-26.

15. And, of course, in its turn, becomes the basis for the New Testament reiteration in Mk 11.15-19.

until the enemies of Nehemiah's mission are identified. The epitomy of the
foreigner is, in fact, the uncleanness of the covenant of the priests and
Levites. A delightfully brawling scene of violence is sketched wherein
Nehemiah aggressively imposes banishment on the wives—not the wives
of all Israel or of Jerusalem—but the wives of the 'Judeans': Ashdodite,
Ammonite and Moabite, the 'half of whose children could not even speak
Judean'. Nehemiah is in rage in his efforts against 'all that is foreign'. He
interprets and 'improves' on the ban of Deut. 7.3. He scolds, curses and
beats the Judeans, tears out their hair and breathlessly commands them:
'You shall not give your daughters to their sons or take their daughters for
your sons *or for yourselves* [*sic*]' (אם תתנו בנתיכם לבניכם ואם תשאו
מבנתיהם לבניכם ולכם, Neh. 13.25).

The addition of ולכם ('or for yourselves') is instructive in its implications. Unlike Deuteronomy, which looks to the narrative's distant future
for its references to Israel's betrayal of the covenant, the mission of
Nehemiah looks to the heart of Jerusalem's contemporary uncleanness.
Not a yet future Samaria and Jerusalem, but Nehemiah's own wicked
'Judeans' are given over to the wrath evoked by his citation of Deuteronomy. While Deuteronomy's narrative had a more classic list for its
'nations in uproar against Yahweh' (cf. Ps. 1.2), Nehemiah 13 transposes
this to Ashdodites, Ammonites and Moabites to accord both with Balaam's
story and the Ashdodite allies of Sanballat in Neh. 4.1. These play the updated role which Sidonians, Ammonites and Moabites had played in being
a snare to Solomon (Neh. 13.26; cf. 1 Kgs 11.3-11 as interpreted by 2 Kgs
23.13!). In this way, Nehemiah identifies 'all that is foreign' with those
who have resisted him (cf. esp. Neh. 2.10, 19; 6.1). It is neither the women
of Jerusalem nor their children, which Nehemiah prays God will remember in his wrath. It is the priests. They are the ones who—with Sanballat—
made the covenant of priests and Levites unclean (Neh. 13.28-29). Nehemiah 13.30's new closure turns the ban of all that is foreign against those
who themselves are evil, an interpretation quite appropriate to the Torah.

3. Interpreting the Torah and the People of God

A similarly interpretive course is marked by Ezra 10.12's motif of murmuring against Ezra, Jerusalem's leader, echoing the Torah's stories of
murmuring against the first Moses. The people once again resist their
prophet's demand of unflinching obedience with complaint and delay. In
reiteration, however, Ezra's role as Moses *redivivus* has lost much of its

humor and persuasion. The reader has learned from the long story of Israel's fall from grace which has carried him to this scene before Jerusalem's walls. Rather than taking the easy closure in the joy of a purified and united Jerusalem, the author keeps his readers in mind, as those slowly disappearing wives and children become 'widows and orphans' before their mind's eye. The people's effort to replace a failed covenant of the past with a new one through the banishment of wives and children intimates expectations violently opposed to the surface plot.

We need to take a brief look at this discourse on the Torah. Psalm 146, the first of the five psalms which close the five books of the Psalter as an elaborate Torah of praise, announces the victory of those who set their hope in the God of Jacob, rather than in the great men of the world, who cannot save (Ps. 146.3, 5). This utopian peace closing the Psalter is marked by a classical eight-fold reversal of fortune, epitomizing the blessings of divine patronage realized. The best known Old Testament example of this trope is found in the song of Hanna, which opens the story of David (1 Sam. 2.4-8).[16] I have called this ubiquitous celebration of God's rule over the world the 'poor man's song'—an abiding literary element of holy war ideology common to the ancient Near East:[17] 'justice is created for the oppressed; bread is given to the hungry; prisoners are freed; the blind see; the crooked are made straight; the righteous are loved; *foreigners are protected and widows and orphans supported*, while the way of the godless is twisted (Ps. 146.7-9). Among the many biblical texts of this type which need consideration, Ps. 94.6 and Zech. 7.10 similarly link the fate of foreigners together with widows and orphans. Both these and Psalm 146 are linked to the interpretively pivotal narrative of Exod. 22.20-23, where it is prophesied that the mistreatment of foreigners, or of widows and orphans, will make widows and orphans of Israel's own wives and children, a prophecy fulfilled in the tragic irony of Ezra 10.

The classic reiteration of beatitudes and the fulfillment of divine promise captured by the 'poor-man's song' in ancient literature creates expectations in the reader: expectations that Ezra's author affronts. By dramatically setting the banishment of foreigners, wives and children in collision

---

16. The 'poor man's song' is also used with great effect in the New Testament, most notably in the Magnificat of Lk. 1.51-53; the Beatitudes of Mt. 5.3-12 and Lk. 6.20-26 and as a sign of the Messiah in Mt. 11.5 and the 'good news' to the poor in Lk. 4.18.

17. Thompson, 'Kingship and the Wrath of God'.

with this set literary pattern, the very foreigners, women and children whom Ezra had declared to be the cause of Jerusalem's corruption and uncleanness become transformed into victims of public righteousness. The reader is forced to rethink the entire story. Implicit expectations, struggling with the thematic requirement of a reversal of the fortunes of the oppressed, change suddenly this seductively simple closure into a 'never-ending story'. Old Israel, once again, has failed its test for the righteousness that had been Abraham's. A tragic reversal of their covenant's expected blessings is implicated by the author's subversive recasting of a stock tale. Begun as the fulfillment of one Jeremiah prophecy, it, in fact, fulfills the same prophet's vision of Jerusalem as moral wilderness. Hardly a new Jerusalem of upright piety, not a single righteous man can be found (Jer. 5.1-6).

An echo of Abraham is doubly evoked by the scene of banishment. The thematic reiteration of Abraham's obedience to both God and wife, in the story of Abraham and Sarah's ill-treatment of the slave-girl Hagar and Abraham's son Ishmael (Gen. 16.6 and 21.9-12, against, esp. Deut. 10.19), when Abraham sent away the heir of divine promise (so Gen. 16.10; 21.18, 20), is indicated.[18] It allows Ezra's author to enter a discourse that the prophet Hosea once held with Genesis. Abraham's reluctance to part with his firstborn is reiterated in the people's murmuring and tears as they too delay. Ezra's learned confidence in knowing God's will[19]—like the knowledge of Job's friends—is to be pitted in debate with Hosea's obedient, if comic, mime of Yahweh's relationship to his people. Having earlier rejected his wife and children, Hosea received them back with compassion (Hos. 2.23; cf. 1.10–2.1). Just so, had Abraham faced a divine demand to sacrifice his son, held his trust in God rather than himself (Gen. 22.8), and was rewarded with boundless and retributive fertility, *a blessing he is to share with the nations* (22.16-18). In this story world of biblical theology, the curse of the divine patron is distinguished from his blessing, precisely as wives and children are to be distinguished from widows and orphans; namely, by the specific text's purpose and function in the reiteration of Torah.

---

18. The figure of Sara is just perceptible in 1 Esd. 9.40-41, standing together with the 'men and women' who listen to Ezra reading of the law, once the 'foreign women' have been banished from the city.

19. For the sectarian quality of exclusion, see T.L. Thompson, 'Salmernes bogs "enten-eller" spørgsmål', in T. Jørgensen and P.K. Westergaard (ed.), *Teologien i samfundet: Festskrift til Jens Glebe-Møller* (Frederiksberg: Anis, 1998), pp. 289-308.

Is the debate about the Torah, which the book of Ezra provokes, also a debate about identity that underlies the obvious collision in Ezra between virtues of obedience and compassion?[20] We must also ask whether such a collision between the apparent and the true is already intrinsic in the Bible's discourse on holy war. In contrasting simplicity, the disobedience of a Jonah is simply falsified by divine compassion, even as a very similar contrast in opposing concepts of the divine governs Jonah's story as a whole, as it also does 1 Kings' more laconically ironic tale of Elijah and the prophets of Ba'al, which opens with a victory of Yahweh's great storm only to end with the silent voice of the God at Horeb.[21] The question about Torah interpretation is not idle, because it adds a layer of complexity to the more direct ironies of the Jonah and Elijah narratives. Nor is the debate over the Torah ever far from the text. Ezra, the great reformer's understanding of the law is, in fact, quite problematic and one must ask whether the description of his great learning identifies him more as target than voice of the text. We have already seen that, contrary to his demand that the law be obeyed, and that, accordingly, the people's wives and children be sent away, very central, epitomizing texts of the Torah support and protect the rights of 'foreigners' within Israel.[22] Ezra's learned application of the law cannot be taken at face value. No one who has read the Pentateuch, let alone 2 Kings, Jonah or Ruth would or should. Although a historical-critic's anachronistic assumption of national purpose in our texts may find the reformer's concern for the ethnic purity of Jerusalem obvious, the literary presentation, in which such ethnic purity is couched, introduces substantial doubts that the author is in agreement with his characters.

The priest Ezra's enactment of the law's demands for ethnic purity in Jerusalem and Judah is placed as a response to the situation he had found on his arrival. The 'people of Israel' had not separated themselves from the 'peoples of the lands', whose behavior is like that of the Canaanites, Hittites, Perizzites, Jebusites, Ammonites, Moabites, Egyptians and Amorites. The problem of impurity Ezra faces not only identifies the

20. On the complexity of Ezra's text, see Nodet, *A Search for the Origins of Judaism*, p. 25; on a similar problem with a related text, see Thompson, 'Some Exegetical and Theological Implications of Understanding'; also discussing the same problem but oriented to the theme of identity, see *idem*, 'Hvorledes Jahve blev Gud'.

21. Thompson, *The Bible in History* (= *The Mythic Past: Biblical Archaeology and the Myth of Israel* [New York: Basic Books, 1999]), pp. 57-59.

22. Esp. Deut. 10.19; 14.19, 29; Lev. 19.18, 34. See further below.

'peoples of the land' with the nations from whom Yahweh had originally taken the land, as in the song of Yahweh's covenant in Neh. 9.7-8, it presents the narrative of the cleansing of Jerusalem as a variation of an earlier story in Ezra 2–6. This had presented the 'people of the land' as Judah's and Benjamin's military *enemies* (Ezra 4.1-4).[23] The observation of a note of discord in our text, which is exposed in the people's murmuring acquiescence to the ethnic cleansing of Jerusalem, mixed with their shivering at the coldness of the rain, finds support also in the implicitly critical commentary on foreigners with which the book began. Cyrus' behavior established a model to be imitated by noting the universal support and care that the returning remnant of Israel is to receive because they had been foreigners in exile (Ezra 1.2-4). This motif so pointedly reiterates Exodus' story of the Israelites receiving gifts from the Egyptians when they left Egypt (Exod. 12.35-36), that we can see that the function of the Cyrus decree is to illustrate Lev. 19.34's retributive law to care for the foreigner in Israel, as Israel itself had once been (cared for as) a stranger in Egypt (and Babylon). This authorial critique of our synoptic tradition challenges its hero Ezra's competent grasp of Torah.

Our author's critique takes decisive shape in the temple-building story of Ezra 3–4. Alternative reasons are given for building an altar. The people follow the Torah of 'Moses, the man of God', but they also fear 'the peoples of the land' (Ezra 3.2-3). This thematic element, we will see below, undermines the purity of their 'fear of God'. It is this critique which seems to underlie the ironically confused tears and cheer of Israel's celebration of an invisible 'unity' when the foundations of the temple are laid (3.11-13). Thus unsettled, the reader is prepared for the further conflicts with the Samaritans and the peoples of the land, which mock any unity asserted. The returning remnant are offered support and help from the people of the land, who are identified as enemies of Judah and Benjamin, though they present themselves as fellow worshippers brought there by the Assyrians (4.1-5). But Zerubbabel and the elders of Israel refuse the support and cooperation offered, insisting that the temple will be built by themselves alone. This rejection is the opening of a brief conflict story of political intrigue to stop the building of the temple, which finally ends when Darius unequivocally supports the temple's completion (6.1-12). The motif of Persian support is again emphasized as Ezra is commissioned

---

23. צָרִי ('enemies') has messianic overtones as in Pss. 3.2 and 89.24, 43, and is similarly used for enemies of Yahweh in battle in Deut. 32.41, 43.

by Artaxerxes, a scene which opens ch. 7 and the story of Ezra's reform. However, that the craftsmen, who build the temple, are paid with money and include Sidonians and Tyrians, again undermines any certainty about the sympathies of the author for or against 'enemies' offering help, or indeed regarding the quality of this temple or the piety of a community, which is so-clearly a creature of the Persians.

The people's slogan, under which the temple is built, is quoted from the opening line of Psalm 106: 'Praise Yahweh for he is good; his steadfast love is eternal'.[24] This reiterates the singing and citing of the same song by Solomon and the people when the first temple had been dedicated in 2 Chron. 5.13 (see also 2 Chron. 7.3). The author of Ezra uses this theme-establishing citation to provide undermining commentary. When the people sing their song, they add a tendentious 'for Israel' to the text of the psalm: הודת ליהוה כי טוב כי לעולם חסדו על ישראל (Ezra 3.11). Adding על ישראל to the song of praise shifts the thematic weight of such praise significantly from God to an Israel that is now marked by hubris. It allows a Torah-conscious reader to hear this people define and limit Yahweh's explicitly infinite love to Israel's advantage. Such a small adjustment might be argued to be insignificant were it not for the Ezra-echoed themes that dominate Psalm 106; particularly the illustration of an old Israel's similar hubris through the use of the murmuring motif of Exodus as leitmotif (see esp. Ps. 106.6-7). It is just such complaint and fecklessness described in the psalm cited, which are explicitly reiterated in the presentation of the priest Ezra's new Israel and which are brought to bear with their full weight in our text's ironic closure. Citing this song's perversion at the temple's reconstruction allows the author to turn the Psalter's great shout by *all the people* about God's boundless grace into nostalgic, truth-telling *tears* of old men (cf. Ps. 8.3), who remember the temple that had been, and to bring this scene to close in discord, preparing the reader for the tragic irony of Ezra 10.

We can now ask: Is the book of Ezra an origin story of a new, repentant Israel that understands? Or is it a story of tragic failure, another downward cycle in the never-ending story of Israel past? Does the author have cheers or tears for the people of Jerusalem and for the Persian appointment of Ezra who—after so many delays and fears—finally completes the project decreed by the inspired King Cyrus in the opening of the book? The answer, I believe, lies implicit in the text. Cyrus' decree is supposed to

---

24. Also Ps. 78; cf. Pss. 100.5 and 118.1.

lead to the fulfillment of a prophecy of Jeremiah, with reference to Jer. 29.10-14. Israel's exile is over and God will fulfill his good news by bringing them back to Jerusalem. 'When you call to me and submit yourselves to me, I will hear you. You will search for me and find me, *if you seek me with all your heart*' (Jer. 29.12-13). Whether the contingency of Jeremiah's prediction is also prophetic seems to be the author's ever undermining question.

The book of Ezra is not a chapter in 'salvation history', recounting events as acts of God.[25] It is theological discourse. The condition Jeremiah has given for Yahweh's hearing the prayer of the people is a classic requirement of biblical theology. 'If you seek me with all your heart', provides the reader with the key to the author's subtext and functions as a leitmotif for the author's narrative-driven interrogation. Do we find the purity of heart demanded by the theme-bearing prophecy cited in the book's opening? At its closure, we watch the fulfillment of Abraham's covenant, his blessing of children, leave the city. Such a closure does invite the conclusion that the thematic issue, which this narrative strives for, challenges the theme of ethnicity that every conflict of the story underlines. No aspect of the text strays from this issue or its debate.[26] This debate is not only with the characters in our story, but engages a wide range of Old Testament texts, which speak of Israel as the people whom God chose. The 'law' that Ezra announces broken and which the story of Ezra engages to repair when the people of Jerusalem banish their wives and children from the city, is not a foundation for a society's racism and xenophobia, though it is often misunderstood to encourage both. The 'fear of God', which leads to the ethnic cleansing that Ezra and the people of Jerusalem engage in, relates to the commands implicit in the 'blessings and curses' of divine patronage. It relates not simply to an element of story and tradition or society, but to the intellectual world that implicitly governs their interrelationship: the 'symbol-system' supporting the relationships of early Judaism with its god.[27]

---

25. T.L. Thompson, *The Historicity of the Patriarchal Narratives* (BZAW, 133; Berlin: W. de Gruyter, 1974), pp. 326-30.

26. T.L. Thompson, 'The Problem of Ethnicity in the Bible', in Prior (ed.), *Western Scholarship*, pp. 23-39.

27. For this anthropological term, see C. Geertz, *The Interpretation of Cultures* (London: Hutchinson, 1973), pp. 91-99.

4. *Holy War in Genesis*[28]

It is clear that the Bible's use of holy war lies fully within a continuum of literary and mythic expression based on a shared social structure of patronage.[29] I limit myself to those elements which seem to be related directly to the book of Ezra's literary strategy and pedagogical intention, specifically to test the degree to which the biblical use of the theme of holy war supports or undermines the surface story's demand for ethnic cleansing. Everywhere it is used in the Bible, the formulaic list of nations which Ezra 9.1 identifies with 'the people of the land' implicitly epitomizes nations in uproar against Yahweh's patronage, much as in the opening of Psalm 2. This is not intended to suggest a specific literary relationship of Ezra with these texts other than a related participation in a literary discourse based on a common symbol-system. One of the variants of this list of nations occurs also in the central text of Deut. 7.1, which is a reiteration of the covenant. The expanding discussion on a 'Deuteronomistic' corpus of literature casts a heavy shadow on any effort to restrict this discussion of the implicit references in the books of Ezra and Nehemiah, particularly in regard to the demands of the covenant, which the reformer Ezra strives to resolve in his banishment of the wives and children in Ezra 9–10. Efforts to identify a specific literary corpus centered in Deuteronomy–Kings and the prose sermons of Jeremiah are particularly problematic in their dependence on the circular argument of Josiah's reform's historicity, which itself is based solely on texts that post-date an alleged reform.[30] Apart

28. For the following, the early work of C.H. Brekelmans, *De* חרם *in het Oude Testament* (Nijmegen: Centrale Drukkerij, 1959) has been particularly useful, as has O. Kaiser's *Die mythische Bedeutung des Meeres in Ägypten, Ugarit und Israel* (BZAW, 78; Berlin: W. de Gruyter, 1959); R. Smend, *Yahweh War and Tribal Confederation: Reflections on Israel's Earliest History* (Nashville: Abingdon Press, 1970); B.N. Wambacq, *Lépithéte divine Jahvé Seba'ôt: Étude philologique, historique et éxégétique* (Paris: Desclée de Brouwer, 1947).

29. See M. Liverani, 'The Ideology of the Assyrian Empire', in M.T. Larsen (ed.), *Power and Propaganda: A Symposium on Ancient Empires* (Mesopotamia, 7; Copenhagen: Akademisk Forlag, 1979), pp. 297-317; *idem, Prestige and Interest*, pp. 115-204; B. Oded, *War, Peace and Empire: Justifications for War in Assyrian Royal Inscriptions* (Wiesbaden: Reichert Verlag, 1992); and T.L. Thompson, 'The Messiah Epithet in the Hebrew Bible', *SJOT* 15 (2001), pp. 57-82.

30. See T.L. Thompson, 'Martin Noth and the History of Israel', in S.L. McKenzie and M.P. Graham (eds.), *The History of Israel's Traditions: The Heritage of Martin Noth* (JSOTSup, 182; Sheffield: Sheffield Academic Press, 1993), pp. 81-90.

from very specific reiterations of language, most metaphors that have been identified as particularly deuteronomistic are in fact commonplace among texts associated with the social system of patronage.[31]

While the theme of holy war in the Bible shows itself already in the creation story's motif of humanity created in God's image to rule the earth and play a defining role in the stories of the great flood and the destruction of Sodom, the narrower geographically oriented focus in the Table of Nations in Genesis 10 brings us closer to Ezra. Echoing the twelve kings united in conspiracy against Assur in Assyrian campaign texts,[32] Gen. 10.15-20 presents an eponymous list of twelve names representing the indigenous peoples of Palestine. After a threefold introduction: 'Canaan[33] begot Sidon,[34] his firstborn, and Heth',[35] nine nations are added: Jebusites,

31. For a catalogue of such traits, see N. Lohfink, 'Gab es eine deuteronomistische Bewegung', in Walter Gross (ed.), *Jeremia und die deuteronomistische Bewegung* (BBB, 98; Weinheim: Belz Athenäum, 1995), pp. 313-82; E. Ben Zvi, 'A Deuteronomistic Redaction in/among "The Twelve"', in L.S. Schearing and S.L. McKenzie (eds.), *Those Elusive Deuteronomists: The Phenomenon of Pan-Deuteronomism* (JSOTSup, 268; Sheffield: Sheffield Academic Press, 1999), pp. 232-61, as well as R.R. Wilson, 'Who Was the Deuteronomist? (Who Was Not the Deuteronomist?): Reflections on Pan-Deuteronomism', pp. 67-82, in the same volume. E.A. Knauf ('"L'Historiografie deutéronomiste [DTRG]" existe-t-elle?', in A. de Pury and T. Römer [eds.], *Israël construit son histoire: L'historiographie deutéronomiste à la lumière de recherches récentes* [MB, 34; Geneva: Labor et Fides, 1996], pp. 409-18) not only rejects the existence of a Deuteronomistic History, but also correctly identifies such common literary traits and theological ideas as drawn from Assyrian ideology.

32. On the influence of Assyrian texts related to war and patronage, generally, see Knauf, '"L'Historiografie deutéronomiste (DTRG)" existe-t-elle?'.

33. A geographic name for a very imprecise region in texts since the end of the third millennium and more precisely in the Late Bronze Age as an Egyptian province. In biblical tradition, Canaanites are used for the indigenous people of Palestine and as epitome of those to be eradicated by holy war. Canaanite also epitomizes the gods to which Israel, having failed to fulfill their eradication, gives its allegiance. See, especially, N.P. Lemche, *The Canaanites and their Land: The Tradition of the Canaanites* (JSOTSup, 110; Sheffield: Sheffield Academic Press, 1991).

34. A Phoenician town with harbor on Lebanon's coast. In the Assyrian period, Sidon is frequently listed in the coalitions of towns and the petty states of Palestine. Josephus often identifies the Samaritans as Sidonians much as he uses (like Ezra 4) the term 'people of the land' in an effort to dissociate them from Judaism. See I. Hjelm, *The Samaritans and Early Judaism: A Literary Analysis* (JSOTSup, 303; CIS, 7; Sheffield: Sheffield Academic Press, 2000), pp. 195-97, 218-22. In the Bible, the Sidonians are the objects of holy war and to be driven from the land, but Israel fails to carry this out (Josh. 13.6; Judg. 1.31).

Amorites and Girgashites, Hivites, Arkites and Sinites, Arvadites, Zemarites and Hematites. This is the first of many variations. The identical list occurs in the genealogy of 1 Chron. 1.13-16. References to the nations who fall under the ban of holy war can often occur with as few as two or three names as in Neh. 13.2, with reference to Ammonites and Moabites, and 13.23, where Ashdodites are added. The limitation of the list in this text seems to be determined by the particular explanatory gloss. A stereotypical list of six or seven is more commonly found, often including Canaanites and Hittites. While Arvadites are associated with Sidon in another context in Ezek. 27.8-10, the Sinites, Zemarites and Hematites occur only here and in the list's reiteration in 1 Chronicles. In Gen. 13.7, this list of nations finds a faint echo in a secondary but disturbing gloss that identifies the peoples of the land as 'Canaanites and Perizzites'. This is possibly attracted by the story context, in which Abraham separates himself from Lot, the ancestor of the Ammonites and Moabites, mentioned in Ezra 9.1's list. These two nations are placed under the ban of holy war in the wilderness story of Numbers 22–24, because of their attempt to use the prophet Balaam to curse Israel. Yahweh had turned this curse into blessing for Israel. The story of Balaam turns on the issue of patronage. Balaam, though a foreigner ('son of Beor in Pethor, which is on the Euphrates', Num. 22.5), is a true prophet, and therefore a servant under Yahweh's patronage. He answers Balak, king of Moab: 'I can do nothing, great or small, contrary to what Yahweh my God commands me to do'. When he does try to act on his own and accompany the Moabites, Yahweh uses Balaam's ass to correct him, much as the prophet Jonah is corrected whenever he attempts to decide matters for himself.

Supported by Yahweh's patronage oath to Abraham which had opened his journey to the land of Canaan (Gen. 12.3),[36] the Balaam story underlines the ironic logic of retribution that governs the reversal of destiny so favored by patronage justice: 'Blessed are they who bless you and banned are they who curse you'. In the Genesis story, the tale of Sodom's destruction, where only the righteous of Lot's house are saved, offers a classic

35. The eponymous ancester of the Hittites. Hatti is a name used in Assyrian texts for Palestine, and the Hittites in the Bible are among the original peoples of the land. They are among the nations set under ban in Exod. 23.23 to be eradicated, and in Ezek. 16.3 and 1 Kings is used as epitome for Solomon and Jerusalem's failure to hold itself pure from the nations.

36. This is reiterated in Isaac's blessing to Jacob in Gen. 27.29.

illustration of the blessings and curses with which the deity judges the world. The blessing and curses of the nations are also given an important and simpler variation: 'in you all the nations of the earth will be blessed'. This positive version forms a leitmotif in the stories that follow[37] and opens an implicit debate of considerable importance for our understanding Ezra.

One needs to ask whether the nations are to be blessed or cursed through Abraham. Are foreigners to be banished and dispossessed as the priest Ezra had understood? The Abraham story of Ishmael's banishment, however, suggests not a curse, but the leitmotif of blessing in the rescue in the wilderness scene. God hears Ishmael's tears and blesses him with Abraham's blessing (Gen. 21.17-21). This is only one example among many. In a chain of reiterating narrative, the patriarchal stories bring a repetition of blessings, peace and ties of covenant and patronage with foreigners. The chain begins with a peaceful agreement with Lot, the father of the Ammonites and Moabites (13.8-13). It continues with the blessing of Melchizedek, the priest of Jerusalem (14.18-20) and similar stories of the patriarchs with the Philistine Abimelek (Abraham in 20.17; 21.27; and Isaac in 26.28-31), with the Hittites and Ephron (23.3-20), with Bethuel and Laban in Aram-Naharaim (24.32-61), with the Aramean Laban (31.44–32.1), and with Esau, the father of the Edomites (33.3-11).

It is interesting, in light of the tendency in Ezra 3–4 to place Samaria among those who are not allowed to help in the rebuilding of the temple when the Jews returned from exile, that the most striking exception to Genesis' string of tales of the patriarchs making bonds of peace and friendship with the various nations in the land of Canaan, is the story of Shechem, Samaria's alter-ego (Gen. 34). This story about Simeon and Levi's breaking of their covenant with Shechem, of their slaughter of all the young men and of their plundering of the women and children of the city, hardly meets the author's approval. It is an ironic story of retribution. This story of revenge and a city's destruction closes with Jacob's echoing rebuke: they have caused the nations not to bless but to hate Israel.[38] Jacob's rebuke marks the bloody tale of Simeon and Levi as a story of

37. In Gen. 18.18; 22.18; 26.4; 28.14. We have a wholly negative variation of the curses and blessings of Yahweh's covenant in Exod. 23.20-26, where Moses is promised that if Israel does all that Yahweh commands, Yahweh will hate those who hate Israel. But this only sets the stage; it is not the point of the story.

38. The reference to the Canaanites and Perizzites ties the story closely to Gen. 13.7.

curse and betrayal of covenant, bearing a judgment that is retributive.[39] Like the Ammonites and Moabites of the Balaam story, Jacob's curse falls back upon Simeon and Levi, as Yahweh once again reverses the curses of men.[40] The greater story-chain of blessings has an emphatic and positive closure in the story of Joseph, where Joseph is blessed because his Egyptian master saw that Yahweh was with him (Gen. 39.3) and finally interprets the narrative as a whole for his brothers and for the reader: God has turned evil to good that 'many people' found life (Gen. 50.20).

5. *Holy War from the Wilderness to the Conquest*

It is in the extended narratives of the wilderness wanderings that the themes of Yahweh's patronage and holy war become dominant. Already in Yahweh's first appearance to Moses from the burning bush on the mountain of God, the narrative structure is set. Having heard the cry of his people in their suffering in Egypt, Yahweh calls Moses to free his people and bring them to the land of the Canaanites, Hittites, Amorites, Perusites, Hivites and Jebusites, a land 'flowing with milk and honey' (Exod. 3.7-10). Yahweh describes himself as Israel's patron; 'the God who will be with them' (Exod. 3.12).[41] This small literary element identifying Yahweh as the divine as he is with Israel defines the ironic leitmotif of the story of Israel as God's chosen people, a story which centers on the question of

---

39. I. Hjelm (*The Samaritans in Early Judaism*, p.151) in discussing the violence of the Levites in contrast to the peaceful Jacob, states: 'In this Jacob tradition of the old Israel, there is credited no promise of eternal priesthood. The Levites are those who, dispersed among the cities of Israel, are ranked lowest. From here sprouts reinterpretations of this tradition, which in *Testament of Levi*, *Jubilees* and parts of the Old Testament become paradigmatic for the zealous Israel, which in the Ezra–Nehemiah model denies *'am ha-aretz* any participation in the building of the temple; and which raises a fence, a wall around the city and the law. The historical reality that is reflected implies a rejection of the Shechemites/Samaritans, who, as *'am ha-aretz* in rabbinic tradition, keeps the old law written in Hebrew characters, while the new Israel is given the new law written in Aramaic by the hand of Ezra. This is the Judea/Jerusalem alone policy that, with the reform of Josiah, destroys the old cult places and does not invite people from the outside to participate in the celebration of the Passover (2 K 23, 21-23).'

40. In striking contrast, the story in Jubilees is rabidly anti-Shechemite (cf. *Jub.* 34).

41. T.L. Thompson, 'How Yahweh became God: Exodus 3 and 6 and the Heart of the Pentateuch', *JSOT* 68 (1995), pp. 57-74.

whether Israel will have Yahweh with them, begins in blessing and ends in curse.

In response to Israel's cry in suffering, Yahweh chooses Israel as his people; 'he will be with them'. He will take them out of their misery in the land of Egypt and give them a land of boundless fertility: the land of the twelve nations of chaos (Exod. 3.17). The price of Yahweh's patronage is always marked by a logic of retribution. As Yahweh had killed the firstborn of the Egyptians to effect Israel's rescue, the firstborn of Israel now belongs to Yahweh (13.15). The feast of Passover and Unleavened Bread are to remind them of this (13.1-16). While the narrative serves as an origin story, both for the origin of animal sacrifice (Lev. 27.26-27) and for the role of the Levites in the temple (Num. 3.13), it also prepares the reader for the story of punishment of a later Israel that has not been faithful. Jeremiah 4.31 similarly uses the suffering of a first birth to prophecy the destruction of Samaria and Jerusalem and their subsequent deportation.[42] The neglect of this feast becomes the mark of Israel's neglect of Yahweh in the story of Josiah's reform (2 Kgs 23.21-23). With even greater force, Jeremiah uses the Exodus story directly to explain why the Babylonians laid siege to Jerusalem. Yahweh, he argues, had freed Israel from Egypt…with a strong hand…and great 'terror'. Yahweh had given them a land flowing with milk and honey and they took it. Yet they never listened to him or followed the Torah. *Therefore*, disaster befell them (Jer. 32.21-25). Jeremiah describes how the justice of this God works: 'He is the great god, the warrior. Yahweh of the armies is his name. Large in purpose and great in what he does, *whose eyes observe all the ways of men, that he might pay each according to his way, according to the fruits of his actions* (Jer. 32.19). This principle of retribution—that God will deal with Israel as they themselves deal—sets the logic which the story requires. It is a message to the reader. 'Punishment fits the crime' or 'evil turns back upon itself'. It is this Torah message that Ezra in his story had not understood, but Ezra's author did.

The specific misunderstanding of the Torah that the book of Ezra deals with can be seen in the story of Yahweh's promise to send an angel to guide Moses and the Israelites in the future. If Israel defies this messenger, he will not forgive it. After he destroys the nations of Canaan, Israel must not worship their gods. If they worship Yahweh, however, blessings are

---

42. See further Thompson, *The Bible in History*, pp. 353-60. The transference of the metaphor of the firstborn to the whole of Israel in the context of covenant can be seen in the role of David in Ps. 89.28.

theirs (Exod. 23.20-26).[43] The implied prophecy of destruction to come is obvious to the reader who knows the story's ending in 2 Kings. The scene's reuse in Exod. 33.1-3 has Yahweh explain that he sends his angel out of mercy, because he fears that if he himself were present, his impatience would cause him to annihilate his people. The plot is delayed by an explanatory gloss to establish links to other, future tales. The angel becomes Yahweh's 'terror',[44] and then 'a swarm' (plague?) which Yahweh will send to drive the Hivites, Canaanites and Hittites from the land. Yet, he will not drive them out all at once, he explains, lest the land become a wilderness. He commands them not to make a covenant with them or with their gods. Nor must they allow them to remain in the land 'lest they be a snare for them' (Exod. 23.27-33). This considerable story chain in which Israel is lead by the angel, Yahweh's terror, finds close reiteration in Moses farewell speech from Mt Nebo (Deut. 7). All the same thematic elements are present: the demand of obedience, a promise of utopia, the covenant, the sending of Yahweh's terror and the *gradual* elimination of the nations. In Moses' farewell speech, the closing warning (Deut. 7.26) plays on the same theme of retributive justice: 'Do not bring what has been set under the ban into your house or you yourself will be put under the ban'.

The story purpose of the holy war theme is explained in the farewell speech of Joshua at the close of the stories of conquest (Josh. 23.9-16). 'All that Yahweh has promised is now fulfilled; not a single thing has he failed to accomplish' (Josh. 23.14). The threat of retribution is set as a theological principle: 'Just as every good thing that Yahweh has promised has been fulfilled, he could as well bring every evil thing, until he has removed you from the land he has given you'. Not only is the future of Israel predicted, but it is made clear that Yahweh controls that future. 'If you break the covenant, and serve other gods; then Yahweh's anger will burn against you and you will perish from the good land he has given you'. In this patron's absolute demand for loyalty from his client, the holy war theme is not used to argue that Israel should kill their enemies, let alone destroy the peaceful population of Palestine. Nor is this to be read too simply as a negative command to obey or else. It is not even a warning

43. Also reiterated in Exod. 34.10-16.
44. Note also that as the messenger is Yahweh's terror for the twelve nations of Canaan, in Josh. 24.12 he is just such a 'terror' against the twelve Amorites, whom Yahweh had conquered with his bow, the sign of his covenant with humankind (Gen. 9.12-13).

against worshipping foreigners' gods, though all of these ethnically competitive overtones are important elements of attraction,[45] helping to capture the story's audience. The story's audience does not live in the time of Joshua, and never had anything to do with such mythic peoples as the twelve nations of chaos. Nor does the author address any historical bloodshed except that of the real destruction of Samaria and Jerusalem past. The author already knows the end of his story, and nothing he or his audience could do would change it. He uses the story to instruct his own, not Joshua's, audience. It is they who need to understand what Joshua's audience had not.

The fictive world of Joshua's conquest—though separated from Ezra in the story chronology by a thousand years—lies very close to Ezra's point of departure. Within Joshua's plot, Israel is admonished that it should take care to love Yahweh. If, however, the people of Israel do what they have done in the story's future and intermarry with the remnant of these nations, Yahweh will refuse to drive these peoples out of the Promised Land. Foreigners 'will be a snare' (Josh. 23.11-13). The refusal to drive the people out sets the stage for just that alternative future. By the close of the conquest of Palestine (Judg. 2.2), the covenant made in Egypt has already been broken. Accordingly, Yahweh decides he will not drive the nations out. They will become a snare for Israel. The people in the book of Judges respond with tears of repentance. This brings forgiveness and sets the basis for serving Yahweh for that generation. In the generation following the conquest, Israel turns away from Yahweh and turns to the gods of the nations. A cycle of stories is established, illustrating the ways of virtue and vice, as Yahweh allows these nations to oppress Israel, only then to be moved by pity by their suffering (Judg. 2.1-19). Rather than driving the nations out, Yahweh chooses to test Israel (Judg. 2.21-22): 'to learn whether they would obey the commandments which Yahweh had given their ancestors under Moses' (Judg. 3.4). Stories of repentance and backsliding fill the plot's progress.[46] The logic of retributive justice implied in the command to love Yahweh drives the narrative and creates a debate of considerable irony. While this discourse plays primarily with the thematic opposition between Israel's love for God and their love for their foreign

45. On the function of elements of attraction in narrative, see T.L. Thompson, 'Conflict Themes in the Jacob Narratives', *Semeia* 15 (1979), pp. 5-26.

46. For example, see the thread continue in Judg. 8.27 and esp. 17.5-6, where it is linked to the chain of origin stories of the monarchy introduced by Judg. 18.1; 19.1; 21.25, etc.

wives (acting as 'a snare' to seduce them to love other gods), it is never far from the parallel thematic discussion in the prophets about Yahweh and his wives, representing Samaria and Jerusalem.[47]

Exodus 23's use of the thematic element of Yahweh's terror to drive the nations from the land, pitting both old Israel and the audience's 'fear of God' against their fear of the nations, has a related logic of retribution. If they have fear of God,[48] they need not be afraid of their enemies; if, however, they fear their enemies, then they will certainly need to be afraid of God.[49] It is within such a context of debate over the philosophical virtue of humility ('fear of God')[50] that Moses' gloss reintroducing Exodus' angel—now Yahweh's terror (Deut. 11.25-26)—finds its place. If Israel holds to its covenant with Yahweh, he will drive all the nations before them; he will bring 'fear and horror' over the whole land. This Yahweh embodies not only the 'horror of Isaac' (as epithet of Isaac's God), but also the 'fear and 'horror' that humankind has brought to animals since humans first began to eat meat after the flood story.[51]

This even violently ironic play on the virtue of 'the fear of God' finds ample illustration in the tragedy of Yahweh's first attempt to drive the nations from the land (Num. 13–14) in the story of the valley of Eshkol. This holy war story is introduced by two very short but important tales centered on the thematic elements of murmuring and meat. The first tale (Num. 11) begins with the people loudly complaining about the manna that God had given them for their food in the wilderness. The blandness of such food and their hunger for meat is such that they now want to go back to Egypt's famous flesh-pots. Yahweh gives them quail as his anger follows the logic of retribution. They will get so much meat that it will come out their noses. They will vomit it—a prediction which prepares the

47. See my discussion in *The Bible in History*, pp. 369-72.

48. The beginning of wisdom and source of life in Prov. 14.27 and 15.33.

49. The same narrative irony is found in Isaiah in the Akaz story, where the issue is whether Israel really wants God's presence (Isa. 7.1-17). For a different discussion, see P.E. Dion, 'The "Fear Not" Formula and Holy War', *CBQ* 32 (1970), pp. 565-70.

50. See my 'Kingship and the Wrath of God'.

51. In the thematically related covenant story of Gen. 9.1-7. Verse 4's reference to human flesh is clear from v. 5 which requires the life of any man or animal which kills a man. Genesis here should be read along with Exod. 21.28, which ends such a potential chain of blood revenge by arguing that the meat of an animal guilty of homicide cannot be eaten. On this same thematic element, see Hjelm, *Jerusalem's Rise to Sovereignty* (forthcoming).

reader for the story in Numbers 14.[52] The second story (Num. 12), in turn, give the reader the key for interpreting Yahweh's holy war against the nations and is helpful in understanding the story in Ezra. Miriam and Aaron murmur against Moses because he has married a foreigner. They claim that Yahweh speaks through them just as well as he does through Moses. However, in contrast to Miriam and Aaron's hubris, we are told that 'Moses was humble, more than any man on earth' (Num. 12.3). In anger at their claim to speak for God, Yahweh strikes Miriam with leprosy, 'like a dead-born child: its flesh eaten away'. While the referential key to the story is flesh, we are also warned against any who might claim to speak for God. In the final story of this chain,[53] the Israelites prepare to attack the נפילים in the valley of the giants by sending out spies. After 40 days, the scouts return with a giant cluster of grapes from a land that has rivers flowing with milk and honey. Kaleb is eager to take the land (Num. 13.30). The other spies, however, refuse, arguing that it is an evil land: a land which *eats* its inhabitants, where the men are giants. They saw the נפילים there (cf. Gen. 6.4). The people cry all night. It is not, however, a saving cry of humility expressive of their fear of God. It is a cry of murmuring and fear for the נפילים. Yahweh's demand that they fight giants endangers their wives and children (Num. 14.3). When they want to choose a new leader and return to Egypt, Moses and Aaron submit to their demands. Caleb and Joshua object, promising to reverse the very fate the people fear: 'Do not be afraid of the people of the land, for they will be *our* food. Their protection is false.[54] Yahweh is with us' (Num. 14.8-9). Israel refuses, and the entire generation are condemned to wander 40 years in the wilderness. Only the next generation, for whose sake they had been afraid to obey, will be the ones to be led by Caleb and Joshua and come to know the land that their father's fear had rejected (Num. 14.31-33). Hearing their fate, the people finally agree to attack. Without God, however, they are defeated. In contrast to this wilderness generation, David, in his battle

---

52. Ps. 78.26-33 similarly interprets the story of the quail in light of Num. 14.

53. For the significance of the third story of chain narratives, see T.L. Thompson, *The Origin Tradition of Ancient Israel* (JSOTSup, 55; Sheffield: JSOT Press, 1987).

54. Akkadian *sarru* ('shadows'): perhaps a polemical play on the Assyrian version of humanity as created in the divine image, in which humans are the shadows of kings and kings are the shadows of the gods. See J.-G. Heintz, 'Royal Traits and Messianic Figures: A Thematic and Iconographical Approach (Mesopotamian Elements)', in J.H. Charlesworth (ed.), *The Messiah: Developments in Earliest Judaism and Christianity* (Minneapolis: Fortress Press, 1987), pp. 52-66.

with a giant, did not fear Goliath's threat of having his flesh fed to birds, but feared God instead (1 Sam. 17.44). Numbers' message to the audience is not hatred of foreigners, whether נְפִילִים or Philistine. The moral points rather to the humility of Moses as example for virtue. It is submission to Yahweh's will that is demanded. Yahweh will have an Israel of Davids: ready to fight giants if he asks it of them.

The retributive logic of patronage's blessings and curses undermines the reader's certainty about who falls under the curse and whom will be blessed: Israel or the nations? None of the stories on holy war in Numbers, Deuteronomy or Joshua give any real hope that Israel will succeed in fulfilling the more than human demand that Yahweh has set them: to love God with a pure heart. Israel is doomed to failure from the start. The nations on their part survive, and they are still around in Solomon's day as a snare (1 Kgs 9.20-21). Their gods steal Solomon's love from Yahweh (1 Kgs 11.1-8), a betrayal that sets the stage for the long narrative chain recounting the failure of Israel's kings to hold with Yahweh's covenant, a chain which ends only in Jerusalem's destruction. The most striking irony of the Bible's use of holy war is that all such stories focus on the destruction of Israel and on the motives for Israel's failure. Samaria and Jerusalem are biblical holy war's primary victims and goal. Our critical question, regarding Yahweh's demand for ethnic cleansing, cannot be complete without brief reference to the story of Joshua's farewell speech (Josh. 23–24).

The narrative has a paraphrastic aim. It provides a key to reading the whole of Joshua. We are at the end of Joshua's career and his death is impending (Josh. 23.1; 23.14). The story is situated and structured compositionally in the same way as the closure of the Moses story and his death (Deut. 31.16-30; 32.48–33.1), as of David's (2 Sam. 22.1; 23.1a). While Moses and David each sing pairs of songs and Joshua gives two speeches, all three closures offer an interpretive summary of their narratives. The closure of Genesis also shows strong similarities with this paraphrastic technique, particularly in its presentation of the 'song of Israel' to interpret the fate of Jacob's sons, much as Deuteronomy 33's blessing of Moses interprets the fate of Israel's tribes. Genesis, however, has a double death to deal with and closes Joseph's life with a final, epitomizing tale, interpreting the transcendent moral significance of Joseph's legend (Gen. 50.20), similar to the way that the Song of Moses (Deut. 32.1-43) and David's 'last words' (2 Sam. 23.1-7) epitomize their stories.

In his first speech, Joshua explains the past. The conquest of Palestine has been Yahweh's. He has driven the nations out. It is also he who will drive out those who remain (Josh. 23.1-5). On their part, Israel must be faithful to Moses' teachings, *deviating from it neither to the left nor right*; and they must not mix with the remnant of the nations. Ever the soldier, Joshua points out that 'with God a single man can put a thousand to flight'. The people must take care to love God, rather than intermarry with the women and 'remnant of these nations' (Josh. 23.10-11). The narrator reiterates the contrast between love of Yahweh and love of wife and family to express the demand of Yahweh's Torah and of Israel's destiny as chosen. The parallel to this speech in Moses' farewell address, however, has already exposed Joshua's reader to the fate of his singular hero against a thousand. The logic of retribution owns the holy war theme as, in failure, Israel has its giant-killing future turned against itself. For Moses, the people are ever the hapless Israel of Isaiah's generation: not yet touched with the burning coal of an exile's suffering (Isa. 6.6-10). Because of its lack of understanding, Israel is destined to be a teacher's example of a nation with impure lips (cf. Zeph. 3.9): a senseless folk, without discern-ment. They are Joshua's thousand who flee a single enemy, the 10,000 who are chased by two (Deut. 32.28-30; cf. Isa. 30.15-17).

The logic of retribution and Israel's implicit identification with 'the people of the land' also sets the terms for future guilt. As Israel's refusal to go up against giants was out of fear for their women and children, so Joshua's story turns to Israel's marriages with the remnant of those nations to bring a new generation of Israel under the ban of holy war. A threefold narrative might be seen within the tradition's larger structures: Exodus to Joshua, in which Israel fails to fear God but fears rather the people of the land; Joshua to Solomon, in which Israel takes wives from the remnant of the people of the land, which then prepares for stories of reconstruction such as in the book of Ezra, where a repentant remnant face the remnant of the people of the land, *who are in fact themselves*.

Does Ezra's Jerusalem succeed in loving God as Joshua had long ago urged Israel, when they themselves banish their wives and children? The praise of Moses' humility when Miriam and Aaron had played Ezra's role to Moses' Cushite wife, contrasting strongly with the description of Ezra, provides a clue: a sign of contradiction. For the people of Jerusalem, as with Moses, the choice between one's wife and one's God is an impossible choice. With Abraham's climbing his Mt Moriah and with Israel before its valley of the giants, and, for that matter, with Job before Yahweh in the whirlwind, the Bible's impossible choice requires humility. The solution Ezra sought in a self-asserted covenant is one—like the covenant of Joshua 24—that bodes only disaster. Hardly a mark of success fit for rejoicing, the story of Jerusalem's cleansing belongs to Israel's chain of failure, demanding the tears of a new exile. We are dealing with reiterated tropes, where Israel in its impossible task of obedience to its infinite and transcendent God must fail most miserably, if it does not remember its humanity.[55]

That such failure is, in fact, intended is never far from the text itself. In the opening words of Joshua's second address, he describes the destiny to which the story's logic has brought its participants. All the good things that Yahweh has promised Israel have come true. But just so, Yahweh can as well bring every evil, until he has banished them from the land he has given (Num. 23.14-15). The story is not talking about what Israel should or should not do in the audience's distant past. Joshua recaps Israel's story from Abraham to the conquest of Canaan. Yahweh was the one who had fought the war, and, echoing the promises of the king of Assur of Isaiah 36, offers them land which they did not work, towns which they did not build, vineyards and olive groves they did not plant (Josh. 24.13; cf. Deut. 6.10-11). Like Moses (Deut. 6.12) and King Solomon (Eccl. 12.13), Joshua epitomizes Yahweh's claim on Israel: 'fear Yahweh and serve him with unflinching loyalty' (Josh. 24.14). The people are eager to serve Yahweh: 'he is our God' they shout (Josh. 24.16). The speech, however, takes a surprising dramatic turn, for Joshua is not happy with this response. He tells the people that they are not capable of fulfilling Yahweh's demands. He warns them of hubris and of the danger they put themselves in: Yahweh is a holy god. He is קנוא אל: a jealous God who will not forgive disloyalty. He will bring unhappiness and destroy them even as he has been good to them (Josh. 24.19-21). Even after this brutal analogy of the divine patron to a murderously jealous husband, the people are un-moved by Joshua's predictions. They repeat that it is their wish to serve Yahweh. Joshua's acquiescence marks the tragedy implicit in every word: 'You are witnesses against yourselves. By your own act, you have chosen to serve Yahweh' (Josh. 24.22). The scene closes with solemnity: Joshua, like Ezra, creates a covenant on the people's behalf for his new Israel. Also like Ezra, Joshua plays the role of a Moses by fixing statutes and ordinances, writing them in the book of God's Torah, after which he sets

---

55. Cf. the motif of tears in Thompson, 'Kingship and the Wrath of God', and especially 'From the Mouth of Babes'.

up a stone as a witness *against* them. It is such a covenant and closure that is reiterated for the book of Ezra.

6. Shalom *as the Goal of Holy War*

What then can be said about Ezra's story of Israel's returning remnant? On the surface of plot, neither Joshua nor Ezra's sad and ambiguous endings function as closures. The stories do not rest. They create discomfort. The endings of both stand at a distance, yet within their story's rhetoric, absorbed in the broader biblical discourse about fighting giants, a jealous God, foreigners and love. Can the people of Israel love God with its whole heart? Can the remnant of Israel love the remnant of the nations and Yahweh too? Can the reader? To fight giants, one risks the loss of the wives and children one loves, but in hating our wives and children, do we love God? Such are the questions the Bible presents in many variations.

In closing, let us return briefly to the Merneptah Stele,[56] the earliest text we have in which Israel is wed to Palestine. The goal of Merneptah against the 'nine bows': the classic designation for foreign nations under Egypt's patronage, the goal of the God Assur and the Assyrian king against Palestine's twelve kings in rebellion, and the goal of Yahweh against the twelve nations of Canaan in uproar (Ps. 2.1-12c) is the singular goal common to all holy war. This transcendent goal is not the extermination of enemy nations, but an eternal, universal peace: the rule of the divine patron over the whole world. War is the result of a divine curse determining human destiny, but it is the song of *shalom* (שלום), as in Merneptah's song, which expresses divine power to turn such curse to blessing. This is a song we find, for example, reiterated in Yahweh's victory song sung by the prophet Isaiah about Cyrus as messiah (Isa. 45.1-8). Isaiah also sings the good news of Yahweh as savior (Isa. 40.1-11). All three songs echo the herald's cry, announcing the birth of Ramses IV and the dawn of a new world:

> O Happy Day! Heaven and earth are in joy. They who had fled have returned to their homes; they who were hidden live openly. They who were hungry are filled and happy; they who were thirsty are drunken. They who were naked are clothed in fine linen; they who were dirty are dressed in white; they who were in prison are set free; they who were chained rejoice. The troubled of the land have found peace.[57]

56. Hjelm and Thompson, 'The Victory Song'
57. Cf. *ANET*, pp. 378-79.

The promise of such peace, evoking the kingdom of God, is illustrated in the שלום of Solomon's (= שלומו) kingdom and through Hezekiah's 14 years of peace in our day (1 Kgs 5; 2 Kgs 20.6). שלום is celebrated as a mythic banquet on the mountain of God in the wilderness story, as the 70 elders of Israel 'saw God, ate and drank', and is implicit in the metaphor of the table that Yahweh spreads for his flock in Ps. 23.5. A closure in such a peace is intrinsic to all of the Bible's 'holy war' themes.

Yahweh's war against the twelve nations of Canaan finds its שלום in a scene in Ezekiel that parallels the book of Ezra's story of the temple. Ezekiel recounts a vision from exile (Ezek. 40–48) and describes a new temple, a new Israel and a new Jerusalem. He draws a picture of a return to paradise and to the tree of life.[58] Water springs up from the temple platform (cf. Gen. 2.6, 10-14) and becomes a great stream, flowing into the Arabah, giving life to every living creature.[59] Fishermen stand on the banks of the Dead Sea, which is lined with trees whose leaves do not whither (cf. Ps. 1.3). Ezekiel's vision then divides the land for a new inheritance, reversing the disaster of Joshua 24's covenant. In doing so, it illustrates the Torah's great command to 'Love your neighbor as yourself' (Lev. 19.18), reminding us of Moses and his Cushite wife as well as of Boaz and Ruth, of Abraham, Ishmael, Esau and Joseph and their wives. Ezekiel's land is an inheritance to both Israel and the foreigners living among them with their children: 'The foreigner among you becomes as one of Israel's sons' to be given his share in the land where he lives (Ezek. 47.22-23).[60] The ironic critique accomplished by Ezra's recasting of

58. The theme of holy war, for example, also finds a similar closure in Revelations' decisive victory of heaven's army. The king is astride a white horse, judging and making war through righteousness. In the closing scenes of heaven's war, the 'nations' and 'kings of this world' are cast into an all-consuming lake of brimstone (Rev. 19.11-21). This victory allows Jerusalem to return to its role as paradise, even as the Bible's reiterative history's destructive destinies are reversed in a New Jerusalem (Rev. 22.1-5), which reiterates Ezekiel's vision: the streets of the city, where Jeremiah once found not a single righteous among its inhabitants (Jer. 5.1), becomes a universal source of living water, turning the Dead into a Living Sea (Ezek. 47.1-2). On each of its banks stands the Garden story's tree of life, bearing fruit at the right time (Ps. 1.3). Its leaves not only cover the garden story's hubris but also heal the nations. There is nothing that is cursed (Rev. 22.3).

59. As in Akhenaten's long hymn to the Aton. See J.H. Breasted, *The Dawn of Conscience* (New York: Charles Scribner's Sons, 1933), pp. 366-70; cf. also *ANET*, pp. 369-71.

60. See also the 'new song' (Ps. 149.1), which has been placed as a chiastic response to Ps. 2's war against the 'nations in uproar'. It is sung in the utopian context of

Ezekiel's vision of the temple, though unacknowledged, is implicated by the opening description of the book as a fulfillment of the prophecy of Jeremiah which is in fact a close parallel to Ezekiel's vision (i.e. Jer. 29–33).

The intertextual techniques binding these passages together are particularly marked. Ezra presents the decree of Cyrus, with which his book opens, as the fulfillment of the prophecy which Jeremiah had written in a letter to the exiles in Babylon announcing the exile's closure 'when Babylon's 70 years are over (Jer. 29.10). Whereas Ezekiel closed his vision and his book on the note that from that day his new Jerusalem will be named: 'Yahweh is there', Jeremiah's prophecy opens in a declaration, reiterating Deut. 4.29. When Israel, accordingly, calls and prays and seeks Yahweh, he will answer and hear and be found by them (Jer. 29.12-14). Jerusalem is under siege and is to be destroyed by the Babylonians as Jeremiah prophesies a new Jerusalem. He interprets the suffering of the people as a path to understanding. In the new Zion, they will be Yahweh's people and he will be there God (30.22, 31). Their destiny will be turned. They had once been scattered, but now they will be gathered: mourning will be turned to joy (31.10, 13). At the center of this 'poor-man's song' and prophecy of the new Jerusalem, come tears of suffering: first the mother's, weeping for the dead; then she is comforted; the suffering had purpose (Jer. 31.16). We have Ephraim's tears, successfully chastised. Yahweh will receive his prodigal child back in love (31.18, 20). Why? Not for any value in either Ephraim's or Rachel's children. Yahweh's love is eternal (31.3). Like his anger, it will fulfill its purpose (30.24).

An even closer variant to Ezekiel's vision is found in the closing songs of the prophet Isaiah (Isa. 64–66). This addresses directly holy war's שלום. Jerusalem's destiny is determined as Yahweh dissolves his curse of the city with the blessing that Ezra and his people implicitly sought in a new Jerusalem, where hatreds of the past are so forgotten that they are to be hidden even from God's eyes. A new earth and a new heaven are created (Isa. 65.16-17). The garden story's snake is eternally tamed (Isa. 65.25). As in Ezekiel and the book of Revelations, Isaiah gathers 'all the nations' (אֶת כּוֹל הַגּוֹיִם) into his new Jerusalem (Isa. 66.18-21). In

---

Jerusalem's resurrection (Ps. 147.2-6), where the 'nations' and the 'kings of the world', are bound and chained under a universal and divine patronage of blessing (cf. the Egyptian parallel in Hjelm and Thompson, 'The Victory Song': the pharaoh is 'lord of every land...for all distant countries he makes life' (text in *ANET*, pp. 376-78).

contrast, the book of Ezra does not celebrate a שלום. In banishing their wives and children, the people have banished themselves. The Jerusalem the priest Ezra and the remnant of Israel rebuild is not the new Jerusalem of Isaiah, Jeremiah and Ezekiel, but rather a reiteration of old Jerusalem past, trapped within a never-ending story.

In the closing songs of Isaiah, the author adds a significant motif that touches a central cord of the biblical discussion of holy war. Whereas Ezra 4 had identified the people from Samaria with the people of the land in excluding them from building the temple and the new Jerusalem,[61] Isaiah's recognizes Israel's House of Yahweh as an example for Jerusalem (Isa. 66.20). The command of the Torah to 'love your neighbor as yourself' (Lev. 19.18) is often closely linked to the Samaritans. In Lev. 19.34, the command of Lev. 19.18 is interpreted expansively, becoming love of the stranger within Israel, much as Ezek. 47.22-23 illustrates. Both strangers and their children are given the status, not of a גר but of an אזרח, who are allotted land equally with the Israelite, as, for example, in Exod. 12.19, 48, the story of Israel's sojourn in Egypt to which Leviticus explicitly refers. The discursive logic of Lev. 19.34's expansion ('because you were your-selves strangers in Egypt') is significant for interpretation, as it associates the love of the other within holy war's central concept of Israelite identity. In his illustration of the gathering of the nations in his New Jerusalem, Ezekiel resolves the seeming conflict of this law with holy war's command to 'love God with your whole heart', with tacit recognition of the legen-dary Samaritan association with the command of love of neighbor as reflected by the dedication of their temple to *Dios Xenios*, which, as an epithet of Yahweh, extols his mercy for the poor, foreigners and those seeking protection.[62]

Such an understanding is reflected in 2 Macc. 6.2, which understands the Hellenistic names of both Jerusalem's and Samaria's temples polemi-cally.[63] Deuteronomy 23.8-9 is in agreement with Lev. 19.34's expansion. The love of one's neighbor includes third-generation foreigners from

---

61. Compare this with the potentially supersessionist variant of the new Jerusalem in Jer. 31.5-6, 31; also 1 Esd. 9.26, 37-38. See further Hjelm, *The Samaritans and Early Judaism*, p. 280; *idem*, 'Tabte drømme og nye begyndelser: Bibelsk tradition som reiterativ diskurs', in G. Hallbäck and N.P. Lemche (eds.), *'Tiden' i bibelsk belysning* (Forum for Bibelsk Eksegese, 11; Copenhagen: Museum Tusculanum, 2001), pp. 48-64.

62. See further Hjelm, *The Samaritans and Early Judaism*, pp. 116-17.

63. Hjelm, *The Samaritans and Early Judaism*, pp. 210-11.

Edom and Egypt as part of Israel. With Leviticus, Egyptians are accepted because Israel had lived as foreigner in Egypt. A similar expansion of Lev. 19.18 is illustrated by Samaritan legends as in the story of 2 Kgs 6.8-23. In this story Israel is at war and Elisha, the great prophet, tells the Israelites all the secrets of the Aramean king's bedroom. When the Arameans learn of this, they go to the town of Dothan and capture Elisha, who, however, blinds them with a divine light, and, in disguise, leads the Arameans unwitting into the Israelite fortress of Samaria. Once helpless within the city, Elisha opens their eyes as they discover that they have been duped. Israel's king is eager to kill his enemies, but is rebuked by Elisha. Rather than kill your enemy, give them a great feast and let them return home! The story closes with the delightful pedagogical notice that the Arameans thereafter stopped invading Israel. The pedagogical—rather than historiographic—purpose is particularly clear by the placement of the tale, immediately preceding the story of the Aramean's siege of Samaria. This 'good Samaritan' story finds a close parallel in the legend found in 2 Chron. 28.8-15 in which the Samaritans again illustrate brotherly love. With strong echoes of the Cain and Abel story, this narrative of holy war as divine punishment protests strongly against Israel's deportation of 200,000 Judeans to Samaria (significantly for our story in Ezra 10: 'women, sons and daughters'). The prophet Oded sees this deportation as breaking the Torah prohibition against the enslavement of kinsmen and declares that the wrath of God which had been set against Judah is now turned against themselves. The chiefs of Ephraim also protest and the story creates a messianic peace out of this act of war. The naked are clothed and the captives, as in the story in Kings, are given food and drink and anointed with oil. The feeble are put on asses and are brought to their kin in Jericho, the city of palms. These stories of the good Samaritans compete well with their more famous New Testament descendent (Lk. 10.30-37) in offering a radical answer to Leviticus' discursive question about whom our neighbor is, a question which also emphatically informs the implicit polemic in the book of Ezra both in regard to the purported unity of the new Israel in ch. 3-4 and in the scene of the 'cleansing of Jerusalem' in ch. 10.

It is in a paired vision of the new Jerusalem, one that opens the book of Isaiah, that holy war finds closure and this paper must end. It addresses the theme of holy war by bringing us back to the stories of Abraham, in whom all nations will be blessed. With Ezekiel's vision, Isaiah presents a utopian Jerusalem, the end of war and a time of peace. Foreigners give the measure of the New Jerusalem's blessing. 'Jerusalem will stand strong and foreigners will pour into Jerusalem, seeking the truth of the Torah.'[64] It is not the priest Ezra's scorn[65] of Jerusalem's foreign wives and children, but Isaiah's universal view of the utopia of divine instruction, which comprises שלום in the Bible's holy war theme: the author of Ezra's message for Jerusalem and its priest is the humility of recognizing themselves in the children they have sent away.

64. 'They will hammer their swords into plowshares and their spears into pruning hooks; nation shall not take up sword against nation. They will never again know war' (Isa. 2.3-4).

65. Like the Jeremiah prophecy of the new Jerusalem, Isa. 2 identifies Israel's past betrayal as hubris (Isa. 2.5-22).

'NEXT YEAR IN JERUSALEM':
BIBLE, IDENTITY AND MYTH ON THE WEB

David M. Gunn

In May 2001, as many Israelis celebrated their 'Jerusalem Day', Prime Minister Ariel Sharon assured his audience that Israel would achieve peace without relinquishing control of east Jerusalem. 'Jerusalem', he stated, 'has been the capital of Israel for 3000 years, and the Temple Mount is the heart of the Jewish nation and its center, forever united and indivisible'.[1] In the United States it has become common to hear Jerusalem described by Israeli officials as 'the eternal and undivided capital of Israel', language that not only claims exclusive political possession but also implies divine ('eternal') sanction.

Why do Americans not question this claim about a modern state barely 50 years old? One reason is that it is sustained by a powerful 'foundation myth' or what Yael Zerubavel[2] calls a 'master commemorative narrative' about Israel which is linked to the Bible. By reciting a story that reaches back into the past, master narratives of this kind provide legitimation for present institutions and practices.[3] In this particular case the narrative draws authority not only from its constant recitation as official history but also from its association with the Bible, a major 'authorizing' text in the United States where large numbers of people hold the Bible to be Holy Scripture.

Over the past 500 years European colonists developed a stock of language for legitimating their encroachment on the land of others. By the end of the nineteenth century and throughout the twentieth century, Zionists shared this repertoire of legitimating language, including, for example, the

1. Associated Press report, 5 May 2001.
2. Y. Zerubavel, *Recovered Roots: Collective Memory and the Making of Israeli National Tradition* (Chicago: University of Chicago Press, 1995).
3. H.-P. Müller, 'History-Oriented Foundation Myths in Israel and its Environment', in J.W. van Henten and A. Houtepen (eds.), *Religious Identity and the Invention of Tradition* (Assen: Van Gorcum, 2001), pp. 156-68 (156).

claim that they were transforming a 'wilderness' and 'making the desert bloom' (a claim with overtones from biblical passages such as Isa. 35). Zionist rhetoric, however, includes one claim that is highly unusual in colonization—namely, the claim to 'return'. If the Jewish settlers are making the 'wilderness' into a 'garden' they are doing so in accordance with their role in a larger story. In this story, this 'master narrative', the settlers are not really colonists at all but rather returnees. In this story they are the true indigenous people of the land; they have always possessed the land; the land is their destiny, a gift from God.

In one form or another this settlers' story—this 'myth' or 'master narrative'—runs as follows. The story starts by telling of the ancient presence of the Jewish people/nation in the land (*Eretz Yisrael*); in this land the people along with their religion and culture have been born; this land (the 'Promised Land'), so runs the story, has been given them by God. From this basic situation the plot develops through a complication: the Jewish people are forcibly removed by the Romans and exiled from the land. The story now enters into a new phase, an episode, which tells of a long period of exile: The people endure vicissitudes in far lands (oppression, but also sometimes prosperity). In this episode, so the story goes, the people look always with yearning to their lost land. Then, after long centuries, the plot takes another turn, this time towards resolution, as the Zionist movement begins to forge for the people a return, an 'ingathering of exiles', to their ancestral homeland. The end of the story comes with the people's return in order to 'redeem' Israel/the land, establish law, and exercise justice and equity.[4]

This narrative sounds very 'biblical'. The first biblical story of exile and return is found in Genesis–Judges. This story tells of Israel's ancestors leaving the 'Promised Land' of Canaan under threat of famine and going to Egypt where they become enslaved. Eventually, however, under the leadership of Moses and at God's direction, the people leave Egypt in a great 'exodus'. They return to the 'Promised Land' and take possession of it. A second story of exile and return is told in the biblical books of Kings, Chronicles and Ezra–Nehemiah. This time, many generations after the first return, the people of Judah (called also 'Israel') are driven into exile in Babylon at the hands of the Babylonian army. The years pass and the Babylonians are displaced by the Persians. Once more the people of Judah return from exile and take possession of the land.

---

4. Israel Information Center, *Facts about Israel* (Jerusalem: Israel Information Center/Hamakor Press, 1996).

As Niels Peter Lemche observes,[5] both these stories had become foundations myths for Jewish communities by the end of the first millennium BCE at the time the Bible was beginning to take its present shape and rabbinic Judaism to emerge. With the Zionist narrative, therefore, we have a third, post-biblical story of exile and return to take possession of the land. It is a story that borrows authority from the Bible not only by claiming that the Jewish settlers are 'returning' to their 'Promised Land', the land of Israel of the Bible, but also by imitating the very structure of the biblical stories of exile and return. The present return is to be compared with the exodus from Egypt and the return from Babylonian captivity.

What the Zionist story suppresses, however, is the unstable nature of the biblical stories that are lending it authority. As told above, each story ends with return. However, when the stories in the Bible are read not separately but consecutively, as one ongoing story, the nature of the ending becomes less clear. A biblical story of exile and return followed by exile and return raises the distinct possibility that return is always subject to the possibility of further exile. That is why some Jewish writers have urged that the Zionist story cannot end until there is an establishment of justice and equity in the land. On this understanding of the Bible, return and possession of the land is always a provisional, never a certain, end. Exile is potentially only an injustice away.

As an entry point into the present discussion I go to the Israeli Ministry of Foreign Affairs website on the Internet. This site offers an 'official' voice on the subject of exile and return seeking widespread circulation in the Anglophone world (see Fig. 1).[6]

I find the Zionist story of exile and return repeated often. Indeed, one notable rendition of the narrative, to which others on the website make allusion constantly and which may itself be found on the website[7] is the 'Declaration of the Establishment of the State of Israel' (14 May 1948) (see Fig. 2).

---

5.   N.P. Lemche, *The Israelites in History and Tradition* (London: SPCK; Louisville, KY: Westminster/John Knox Press, 1998), pp. 86-97.

6.   Much of the material I cite is also available in a Ministry publication called *Facts About Israel* (1996). The URL is: <www.mfa.gov.il/mfa/go.asp?MFAH00080>. Hereafter I shall cite only the last part of the web address, beginning MFA, which is the only part of the address that changes.

7.   <MFAH00k90>.

Figure 1. *Israeli Ministry of Foreign Affairs website*
<www.mfa.gov.il/mfa/go.asp?MFA00080>

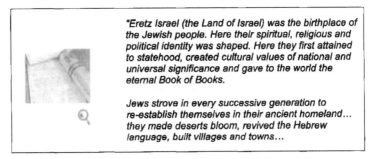

Figure 2. *From 'Declaration of the Establishment of the State of Israel'*
<www.mfa.gov.il/mfa/go.asp?MFAH00k90>

Quotations from the Bible are set out at the top of pages like religious proof texts, lending the authority of the Bible to the story being recounted. For example, the web page 'Jerusalem: The Capital of Israel'[8] begins with a quotation from the book of Kings about King David reigning in Jerusalem. The page claims that since that time 'Jerusalem has stood at the center of the Jewish people's national and spiritual life', and, after speaking of the city as capital of Israel, but of no other political entity through centuries of exile, ends with Jerusalem 're-integrated' as the nation's capital in 1967 (see Fig. 3 [next page]).

8.   <MFAH00w40>.

Figure 3. *Jerusalem, 'The Capital of Israel'*
<www.mfa.gov.il/mfa/go.asp?MFAH00w40>

Likewise, the web page 'Jerusalem: Through the Centuries'[9] begins with David and an expression of yearning in the biblical Psalm 137: 'If I forget thee, O Jerusalem...' and ends with the 'reuniting' of the city in June 1967. Here, just as in the Bible and often in Jewish and Christian thought, the city Jerusalem (or Zion) is understood as representing the whole land, so that Jerusalem's story represents the larger story of return to the land (see Fig. 4).

9.   <MFAH00w50>.

▶ JERUSALEM

JERUSALEM CAPITAL HISTORY HOLY CITY ARCHEOLOGY WITHIN THE WALLS ARCHITECTURE MODERN CITY

THROUGH THE CENTURIES

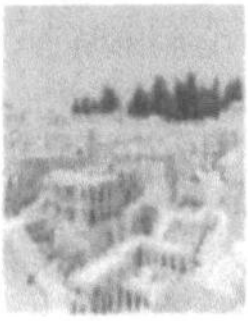

If I forget thee, O Jerusalem,
may my right hand forget its cunning.
May my tongue cleave to the roof of my mouth,
if I do not set Jerusalem above my highest joy.
(Psalms 137:5-6)

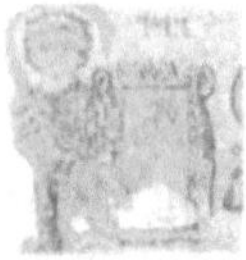

King David made Jerusalem the capital of his kingdom, as well as the religious centre of the Jewish people, in 1003 BCE. Some forty year later, his son Solomon built the Temple (the religious and national center of the people of Israel) and transformed the city into the prosperous capital of an empire extending from the Euphrates to Egypt.

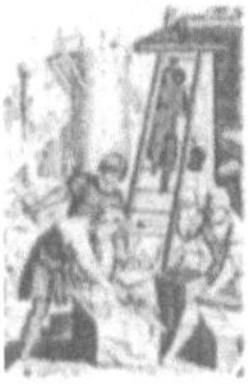

The Babylonian king Nebuchadnezzar conquered Jerusalem in 586 BCE, destroyed the Temple, and exiled the people. Fifty years later, when Babylon was conquored by the Persians, King Cyrus allowed the Jews to return to their homeland and granted them autonomy. They built a Second Temple on the site o the First, and rebuilt the city and its walls.

Figure 4. *Jerusalem, 'Through the Centuries'*
<www.mfa.gov.il/mfa/go.asp?MFAH00w50>

Jerusalem is also a key element in the narrative because it provides the motivation for return from exile. The 'Holy City' web page[10] tells us: 'The many Jews who had been exiled after the Roman conquest and scattered throughout the world never forgot Jerusalem. Year after year they repeated "Next year in Jerusalem". Jerusalem became the symbol [of] the desire of Jews everywhere to return to their land.' So the ancient liturgical phrase, 'Next year in Jerusalem', expresses 'yearning for Jerusalem', which in turn expresses 'yearning to return to the land' (see Fig. 5 [next page]).

10. <MFAH00w60>.

The Jewish bond to Jerusalem was never broken. For three millennia, Jerusalem has been the center of the Jewish faith, retaining its symbolic value throughout the generations. The many Jews who had been exiled after the Roman conquest and scattered throughout the world never forgot Jerusalem. Year after year they repeated "Next year in Jerusalem." Jerusalem became the symbol of the desire of Jews everywhere to return to their land. It was invoked by the prophets, enshrined in daily prayer, and sung by Hebrew poets in far-flung lands.

Figure 5. *'Next Year in Jerusalem'*
<www.mfa.gov.il/mfa/go.asp?MFAH00w60>

In addition to Psalm 137, accounts of Jewish yearning for Israel usually also include reference to the words of the medieval Spanish-Hebrew poet Yehuda Halevi writing of Jerusalem: 'Could I but kiss thy dust / so would I fain expire. / As sweet as honey then, / My longing and desire'.[11]

Such accounts of Jewish yearning in exile are common in Jewish writing about Israel[12] and are often impassioned. Meron Benvenisti writes that Jews for 2000 years vowed 'Next year in Jerusalem'; time 'did not diminish their yearning, and it burst forth with irresistible force when the political conditions necessary for its fulfillment were attained'. Amos Elon cites again 'If I forget thee, O Jerusalem...' and 'Next year in Jerusalem' as the cries of the wandering exiles over the centuries as they recalled 'their great Capital of Memory', and, like many other writers, Elon invokes the words of Yehuda Halevi (c. 1075–1141) to confirm 'this devotion' to the city.

In the Zionist narrative, then, this language of yearning for Jerusalem appears as an integral part of the story's episode recounting exile. Jerusalem is the object of the people's desire; but the exigencies of exile in far

11. J. Halevi, *Selected Poems of Jehudah Halevi* (trans. N. Salaman, chiefly from the critical text edited by H. Brody; Philadelphia: Jewish Publication Society of America, 1924).

12. M. Benvenisti, *City of Stone: The Hidden History of Jerusalem* (trans. M. Kaufman Nunn; Berkeley: University of California Press; 1996), p. 145, or A. Elon, *Jerusalem: Battlegrounds of Memory* (New York: Kodansha International, 1995 [first published Jerusalem: City of Mirrors, 1989]), pp. 33-34.

lands prevent that desire from being attained. The story demands an end where the obstacle, exile, is overcome and desire is no longer thwarted.

Here we come to the crux of the matter. Such a story has great appeal to an American audience. Who is not going to be swayed by the expression of such deep and longstanding desire coming to fulfilment? 'Yearning' not only drives the plot of return and rebuilding. At the same time, to an audience schooled in popular Romance, it validates the outcome—namely, possession of the yearned for, the beloved. Jerusalem is a woman, waiting for her lover's embrace (the metaphor has a long rhetorical history).

The master narrative of exile and return arose in Europe in the context of nineteenth-century romantic nationalism. Seeking a national literature, Zionists preferred the Bible over the Talmud, which had been central to Jewish identity since medieval times. The Talmud tells no glorious story of a nation, has no warriors and heroes, and no 'geography which arouses longing in the reader or a sense of connection to an ancient home'.[13] The Bible, on the other hand, could be understood in the terms of romantic nationalism as a national drama focused on possession and loss of the land of Israel. Zionists linked the biblical stories to Jewish traditions of longing to return to the ancient homeland (e.g. 'Next year in Jerusalem') and assumed that 'an inherent bond between the Jewish people and their ancient land was a necessary condition for the development of Jewish nationhood'.[14] Hence the traditional language of longing was (and still is) understood by Zionism as the innate desire of an exiled people to become a fully-fledged nation state. 'Longing' became the motive power for a geopolitical venture in Palestine (*Eretz Yisrael*) by those who, irrespective of their prosperity or oppression, construed themselves as 'exiles'.

The medieval poet Yehuda Halevi is often invoked as evidence of an ancient desire by Jews to possess the land/Jerusalem which has found its fulfilment in the romance of Zionist settlement and state-building. But Halevi is writing in a quite other vein of Romance, typical of twelfth-century Spain. He is as adept at penning love poetry for his imagined lovers as for any far-off holy city, perhaps rather more so. He is writing of yearning itself, and not simply of its object.

The language of yearning has a peculiar power that it draws from being situated in the time and space between desire and attainment, between passion (suffering) and consummation. That space 'between', where desire

---

13. M. Halbertal, *People of the Book: Canon, Meaning, and Authority* (Cambridge, MA: Harvard University Press, 1997), p. 131.

14. Zerubavel, *Recovered Roots*, p. 15.

can flourish as longing, is also the condition of much religious yearning. Indeed the language of romantic love and religion often change places: the yearning lover 'adores' and 'worships' the beloved, while in the Middle Ages the yearning lover of the Song of Songs was understood to be the soul seeking the divine, or Israel yearning for God. When Halevi writes of yearning for Jerusalem he is writing in this literary context.

He did in fact set off on pilgrimage to Palestine. We do not know if he arrived. If he reached the physical place, Jerusalem, did he find his yearning gone? Or did he find it simply displaced? Without yearning, what would have become of him, this poet of yearning? Whatever happened, his poetry lived because its admirers found that they could easily relate it to their own emotional and spiritual lives.

Many Jews (and Christians) through the centuries have understood 'Jerusalem' metaphorically as a transcendent object of spiritual longing. Many Jews (and indeed many Christians) have regularly, over the centuries, understood 'Jerusalem' metaphorically as a transcendent object of spiritual longing. Halevi himself was a master at constructing religious sensibility out of such conceits, as witness his beautiful poem on the Sabbath as beloved. The Zionist co-option of his language into a geo-political program envisioning the conquest and physical rebuilding of Jerusalem by Jews is then a remarkable one. Indeed, by the end of the nineteenth century the apparent abandonment of traditional spiritual, metaphysical or messianic meanings of exilic longing in favor of geo-political/historical constructions prompted strong opposition to Zionism from Orthodox Jews.[15]

The liturgical phrase, 'Next year in Jerusalem', is as problematic a witness to the Zionist understanding of traditional Jewish yearning as Halevi's poetry. There are many ways of understanding the phrase, from its simply performing the end of the Passover service to indicating that it is time to book a passage on a ship. Given, however, that few of those who recited the phrase over many centuries ever did attempt to travel to Jerusalem, it is reasonable to conclude, at the very least, that a literal meaning was uncommon.

---

15. B. Evron, *Jewish State or Israeli Nation?* (Bloomington: Indiana University Press, 1995 [Hebrew original = Tel Aviv: Dvir, 1988), pp. 54-55; Zerubavel, *Recovered Roots*, pp. 14-16; and see further M. Prior, *The Bible and Colonialism: A Moral Critique* (The Biblical Seminar, 48; (Sheffield: Sheffield Academic Press, 1997), pp. 152-56, 200-208, for a broader account of this transposition of religion and politics.

More likely the phrase has been used to locate the speakers within a distinctive ritual space and time. 'Next year' ritually constitutes the present as being in the not-yet-there time; 'Jerusalem' ritually constitutes the present as being in the not-yet-there place. Paradoxically the ritual places a value upon one's present time/place both as liminal, the in-between time, the not-yet-arrived-at place and at the same time as the place and time to which one really belongs. 'Now and not-then' and 'here and not-there' is what one repeats. Such a ritualized understanding of 'where one is' may become a fundamental matter of identity. Attainment or possession of 'Jerusalem', then, entails serious risk to Jewish identity, as many Jewish thinkers well understood and argued in relation to Zionism in the years before the Holocaust radically shifted the grounds of the debate.

As the Ministry of Foreign Affairs website's epigraphs and texts make clear, it is of the essence of the foundation myth that it is biblically warranted. A few clicks take us to a brief article in the journal *Ariel* on longings for Jerusalem in Jewish folk art of Eastern Europe. Zusia Efron, too, is eager to claim this biblical stamp of approval.[16] No less than 1000 times are longings for Jerusalem expressed in the Bible as well as in the Talmud, the writer tells us. But in fact the Bible's expression of such sentiments is sparse, to say the least. We have already mentioned most of them, since most appear on the website. Psalm 137 tops the list and Lamentations is frequently invoked. The latter part of Isaiah is full of calls to return (from the Babylonian exile) but curiously little 'longing'. In the event, it is becoming clear that relatively few did return. Perhaps others decided to stay where they were and get on with their lives, all the while learning to 'yearn' as a ritual condition of their identity as 'exilic' people, people of the God of Israel.

Both Psalm 137 and Lamentations are themselves witness to the complexity of 'longing' as a literary construct since in neither case is it certain that they are the direct product of 'exile'. But whatever the case on that score, there is an obvious difference between the modern context (for example, the website) and the ancient literary context of the passages. These 'longing' passages do not obviously specify political independence or sovereign 'nationality' as objects of desire, whether past or future. But neither, for the most part, do the biblical texts to which they belong. Indeed, it is notable that the literature, which touches most the theme of

16. Z. Efron, '"If I Forget Thee...": Longings for Jerusalem in the Jewish Folk Art of Eastern Europe' (trans. J.M. Green), available online at < MFAH01xx0> (= *Ariel: The Israel Review of Arts and Letters* 102 [1992]).

political sovereignty, the accounts of the Maccabean revolt in the second century BCE, is not accorded canonical status within early Judaism.

Hence, at least in this specific regard, 'Hatikva',[17] the Zionist rallying song, does not recapitulate the biblical expression of yearning as transparently as one might at first suppose: 'As long as deep in the heart, / the soul of a Jew yearns, / and towards the East / an eye looks to Zion, / our hope is not yet lost, / the hope of two thousand years, / to be a free people in our land, / the land of Zion and Jerusalem'. As 'the Hope' would have it, to be a 'free people' in the land is the summation of desire. That is a concept certainly not explicit in the oft-cited biblical passages of yearning. Certainly, too, the orthodox community of Jerusalem at the end of the nineteenth century did not look kindly on such a conceit. Nor do many of their spiritual descendants today. Where, they would ask, is the singing of God's song? (See Fig. 6.)

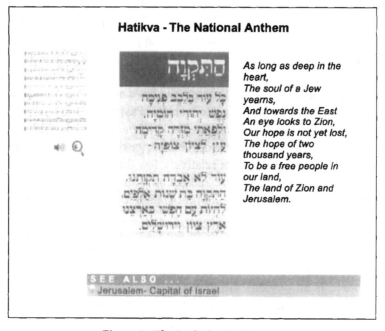

Hatikva - The National Anthem

As long as deep in the heart,
The soul of a Jew yearns,
And towards the East
An eye looks to Zion,
Our hope is not yet lost,
The hope of two thousand years,
To be a free people in our land,
The land of Zion and Jerusalem.

SEE ALSO . . .
Jerusalem- Capital of Israel

Figure 6. *'The Soul of a Jew Yearns'*
<www.mfa.gov.il/mfa/go.asp?MFAH00k90>

17. <MFAH00k90>.

Myths, master narratives, often mask structural social and ideological tensions. Many commentators share Boas Evron's analysis of a secularist vs. religionist divide at the heart of Israeli society, his sense of deep fractures in Jewish identity. I would argue that the myth of exile, yearning and return attempts to mask this ongoing and bitter struggle over Jewish identity.

Let me go back to the web pages and ask: Who is the subject of yearnng in this particular master narrative of exile and return? Who yearns? The answer, of course, is 'the Jewish people'. So yearning not only motivates the plot's transition from exile to return, it also constructs the narrative's subject or main character. Without 'yearning' the singularity and continuity of the subject would be less apparent.

As Zerubavel and others have argued, from its beginnings in the nineeenth century the Zionist myth has tended to make strenuous efforts to collapse all experience of exile into the (unquestionably pervasive) negaive of persecution and suffering. But it has proved difficult to erase from memory the manifold positive dimensions of Jewish life over many centuries. As seen in more recent, post-State, versions of the narrative (like the website), the pressure of alternative memories of flourishing comunities, distinctive ethnic customs and rich cultural contributions has begun to make inroads into the myth, straining the Zionist characterization of exile as only disaster. Under the strain, the singularity of the subject—the 'Jewish people who suffer in exile'—begins to break down. Yearning, on the other hand, unlike suffering, is an affect that unites the subject across all periods and places, and through the rough and the smooth. No matter what was happening, the myth could confidently assert, 'the Jewish people' continually 'yearned'.

Not that yearning has been wholly immune from contradiction. The Zionist movement has always had to struggle to persuade people to go to Palestine; most, even in the face of persecution, would rather have gone somewhere else, the United States most notably. Fifty years after the foundation of the State, however, this unitary, yearning (and/or suffering) subject is under even greater stress: as the website is forced to acknowledge, most of 'the Jewish People' continue to live 'in exile' or in 'Diaspora' or, as Zionist vocabulary would have it, in 'voluntary exile'.

So the story of yearning presents the 'Jewish people' as a unitary subject. But the very website that recounts the myth of unity displays through text and pictures another story, one of vast diversity.[18] As I view the (ultra-orthodox) men in black hats and dark suits 'mingling with people wearing the spectrum of modern fashion', as one of the web pages puts it, I see southwest Asian space being reconstituted as eighteenth- or nineteenth-century eastern Europe. I see late twentieth-century western Europe or North America; or Russia or Ethiopia. The 'Jewish people' is in reality a collective of myriad disparities—religious, ethnic, political, and cultural—sharing little in common. According to the master narrative, however, the members of this people share a name, a suffering, and, of course, a yearning. Yearning restores the people as it restores the national romance.

The rhetoric of yearning is powerful and slippery. Yearning's passionate imaginings may indeed empower, yet blind the yearning subject to another subject's very existence.

The great ethical thinker Emmanuel Levinas pondered deeply on the indispensable place of the 'other' person in our moral lives. Yet I find him writing in 1951 of the religious genius of the Jewish people coming to flower in the foundation of the State of Israel. He wrote: 'The Jewish people...craved their own land and their own State not because of the abstract independence which they desired, but because they could then finally begin the work of their lives...a difficult and erudite work of justice... The masterpiece has now finally come.'[19] Nowhere does he mention the dispossession of the Arab people of the land.

Likewise with the website: it both hides and reveals these participants in the story. 'Yearning' plays its part in the hiding. Indeed, in my view, it has overwhelmed Levinas's sense of justice.

A narrative of yearning which ends with fulfillment, possession, may sustain its tellers and hearers for generations. But arrival always risks dissipating the power that the 'longing' generates. Ironically, the master commemorative narrative of Zion, the more it becomes the narrative of the 'eternal and undivided capital of Israel'—that is, the eternal political possession—the more it risks emptying traditional Jewish 'yearning' of meaning. As it seeks to shore up Jewish identity it is at the same time subverting it.

18. See, e.g., 'Culture' (<MFAH00L90>) or 'Society' (<MFAH00ky0>); cf., on Jerusalem, Benvenisti, *City of Stone*, pp. 169-84.

19. E. Levinas, 'The State of Israel and the Religion of Israel', in *idem, Difficult Freedom: Essays on Judaism* (trans. S. Hand; Baltimore: The Johns Hopkins University Press, 1990), pp. 216-20 (218) (first published in *Evidences* 20 [1951]).

I return to the website.[20] In 1967 Amos Oz, born and raised as a child in Jerusalem, found himself walking through the newly captured streets of the city:

> Their eyes hate me. They wish me dead. Accursed stranger...
>
> I tried my hardest to feel in East Jerusalem like a man who had driven out his enemies and returned to his ancestral inheritance. The Bible came back to life for me: kings, prophets, the Temple Mount, Absalom's Pillar, the Mount of Olives... I wanted to belong, I wanted to share in the general celebrations.
>
> But I couldn't, because of the people.
>
> I saw resentment and hostility, hypocrisy, bewilderment, obsequiousness, fear, humiliation and new plots being hatched. I walked the streets of East Jerusalem like a man who has broken into a forbidden city. City of my birth. City of my dreams. City of aspirations of my ancestors and my people. And here I was, stalking its streets clutching a sub-machine-gun, like a figure in one of my childhood nightmares: an alien man in an alien city.[21]

Amos Oz, armed with his identity and an Uzi, had realized his people's ancient yearning, had returned and taken possession of the 'eternal and undivided capital'. Amos Oz had arrived.

20. <MFAH01y10> (= *Ariel* 102).
21. A. Oz, 'An Alien City' (trans. N. de Lange), <MFAH01y10> (= *Ariel* 102).

Imagining Jerusalem

Keith W. Whitelam

Introduction

The sense of pain and loss in being exiled from Jerusalem is captured in the words of the psalmist: 'If I forget you, O Jerusalem, let my right hand wither! Let my tongue cleave to the roof of my mouth, if I do not remember you, if I do not set Jerusalem above my highest joy!' (Ps. 137.5-6). The words reverberate across the centuries and serve as a paradigm of grieving for those exiled from the land and the city. As with the adaptability of all great literature, these words express the pain of those recently separated from the city and denied any right of return. This is poignantly captured in the childhood reminiscences of Serene Husseini Shahid in her *Jerusalem Memories*. This moving story of childhood and adolescence in Jerusalem invokes an earlier, and now lost, world of tranquility and Palestinian family life which became ever more fractured, dangerous and tragic. Her separation from the city, just as for the psalmist, causes an overwhelming sense of sadness: 'the past is heavy on the heart sometimes. But I often go back to it, and remember', she says.[1] The revival of these memories, as Jean Said Makdisi notes,[2] arouses a 'strong sense of loss, so poignantly woven into the fabric of these pictures as a kind of narrative counter-point'. However, the stories of Serene Husseini Shahid, and the many more like hers, have been ignored all too often in favour of a much more exclusivist claim that Jerusalem is the sovereign capital of Israel that is deeply rooted in Western imagination and its view of the past and the immediate present. Their right of belonging and return is either denied or ignored by an unthinking acceptance of the exclusivist claim to and history of the city. Yet the counter-stories of Serene Husseini Shahid, and many

1. S.H. Shahid, *Jerusalem Memories* (ed. J.S. Makdisi; Beirut: Naufal Group, 2000), p. 278.
2. Jean Said Makdisi, 'Editor's Note', in Shahid, *Jerusalem Memories*, p. v.

Palestinians like her, illustrate that the real and imagined are ever subject to contest, particularly in the case of Jerusalem.[3]

The declaration of 'Jerusalem 3000', and the many sites on the internet devoted to its celebrations, take no account of the memories of Serene Husseini Shahid or her contemporaries in the Palestinian community of Jerusalem. Benvenisti notes[4] that during the official 'Jerusalem 3000' celebrations that took place on 4 September 1995, the programme informed guests that

> no other people designated Jerusalem as its capital in such an absolute and binding manner—Jerusalem is the concrete historical expression of the Jewish religion and its heritage on the one hand and of the independence and sovereignty of the Jewish people on the other. Jerusalem's identity as a spiritual and national symbol at one and the same time has forged the unique and eternal bond between this city and the Jewish people, a bond that has no parallel in the annals of nations. Israel's rule over the united city has allowed her to bloom and prosper, and despite the problems between the communities within her, she has not enjoyed such centrality and importance since her days as the capital of the Kingdom of Israel.

This proclamation invokes and draws on a story and a past that has been central to Western imagination. Crucially, the claims explicit in the proclamation are an attempt to make real an image of the city that is deeply rooted in the ways in which Western tourists, travelers and scholars have imagined Jerusalem. Here we see the persuasive power of the 'rhetoric of memory', so powerful that it admits of no alternative image of the city or conception of its past.

The exhibition of maps and images of Jerusalem chosen to accompany the Jerusalem 3000 celebrations helps to illustrate the different ways in which Jerusalem has been imagined and idealized throughout the centuries. The various maps and views of Jerusalem are introduced in the following way:

> The Land of Israel and its capital city, Jerusalem, boast the longest unbroken succession of maps of any country in the world. Through a choice selection of maps, this exhibition presents the cartographic history of the city which King David established as his capital 3000 years ago. The exhibition

---

3.   R. Friedland and R. Hecht, *To Rule Jerusalem* (Cambridge: Cambridge University Press, 1996), p. xii.

4.   M. Benvenisti, *City of Stone: The Hidden History of Jerusalem* (Berkeley: University of California Press, 1996), pp. 1-2.

comprises maps and views of both the city itself and the land of which it constitutes the heart and the soul.[5]

There is no mention that Jerusalem has a history stretching back centuries to the early Bronze Age (c. 3000 BCE), two millennia before the period when David is supposed to have made it his capital. The view of history projected in the official program of the 'Jerusalem 3000' celebrations, or the statement above, leave no room for any counter-narrative. Furthermore, the clear implication is that the control of Jerusalem guarantees control of the land of which it is said to be 'the heart and the soul'. The important role of Western imagination in idealizing Jerusalem is emphasized by the fact that most early maps of the land and the city were produced by European cartographers and artists, who had never visited either. The European style architecture of a number of these images are a striking illustration of the ways in which the Orient was constructed and imagined. This has been continued in the idealization of Jerusalem over the centuries as seen in the 1913 model of Solomon's Temple, constructed by the New York firm of architects Helme and Corbett, with its reflection of the skyscraper design of contemporary New York. It was Harvey Corbett, of course, who later designed the Rockefeller Center in New York.

The claim that Jerusalem was founded as the capital of Israel by King David and so is the 'eternal capital' of Israel is so frequently repeated that it has become deeply ingrained in the popular and political imagination and accepted as self-evident. The power of this image is vividly illustrated in numerous sites on the internet. One Canadian site,[6] entitled 'Whose Jerusalem?' and maintained by 'Christian Action for Israel', shows how the exclusive claims on the city inform the ways in which significant numbers of people view Jerusalem's past and present. The words of Psalm 137 are placed next to an appeal, which urges its readers to 'show your stand for an undivided Jerusalem under the sovereignty of the State of Israel'. It then advertises 'The Jerusalem Covenant' presented to the Israeli government on the 19 May 1993, claiming that 'Jerusalem, unified and whole, is the Capital of Israel' and again citing the words of the Psalm 137. This claim is given added force by a series of 'timeless quotes'.[7]

---

5. Available online at <http://www.israel-mfa.gov.il/mfa/go.asp?MFAH00jb0>. The website is a selection of the exhibition produced by the Public Affairs Division of the Israel Ministry of Foreign Affairs for the 'Jerusalem 3000' celebrations.
6. Available online at <http://www.cdn-friends-icej.ca/whosjeru.html>.
7. Available online at <http://www.cdn-friends-icej.ca/whose.html>.

These include the words of Winston Churchill in 1938 claiming that, 'You (the Jews) have prayed for Jerusalem for 2000 years, and you shall have it', followed by a statement by Reverend Douglas Young to Evangelical Christians in 1971 that 'Jerusalem has never been the capital of any people except the Jewish people. The unity of Jerusalem must be preserved. Internationalization is an idea that has never worked in history.' The view of history and the image of the city projected through this site and countless others, as well as through many popular books, has no place for the alternative memory of Serene Husseini Shahid as a counterpoint to the exclusive claim of Israeli sovereignty. What is significant about the power of the imagery projected through such sites and publications is that it is precisely this image which informs the thinking of many within the current American administration.

Such a view of the past and the present as expressed in the Jerusalem 3000 celebrations, reiterated constantly in Israeli government pronouncements and repeated in countless news reports, is made visible for tourists who visit the so-called Tower of David Museum of the History of Jerusalem. Nadia Abu el-Haj[8] points out that the reconstruction of the new Jewish Quarter of the Old City after 1967 was part of the claim that the reunification of the city was the fulfillment of Israel's historical claim to the city. She cites the assertion of the former mayor Teddy Kollek that 'there is a certain desire on our part to re-create, for sentimental reasons, an atmosphere which will recall the Quarter when it was the only center of Jewish life'.[9] But, as she notes, this drew on an ideal image of the ancient city rather than any understanding of the city before 1948. She highlights the way in which the history is presented in order to justify a claim to the city:

> The first exhibition room displays the First Temple period, telling the story of David's conquest of the city and his transformation of Jerusalem into the spiritual and national capital of the Jewish people. It is the telling and display of Jewish history in Jerusalem and Jewish longing for the city that forms the thread of continuity that weaves together each subsequent exhibition room and each succeeding epoch: the Babylonian exile or Second Temple period, Byzantium or early Islam.[10]

8.   N. Abu el-Haj, *Facts on the Ground: Archaeological Practice and Territorial Self-Fashioning in Israeli Society* (Chicago: University of Chicago Press, 2001), p. 169.

9.   Minutes of the Jerusalem Committee 1969, p. 40; cited by Abu el-Haj, *Facts on the Ground*, p. 170.

10.   Abu el-Haj, *Facts on the Ground*, pp. 174-75.

She also noted two photographs at the exit of the final room which depict the divided city before 1967. One of the placards reads, 'Jerusalem is an inseparable part of the State of Israel and its eternal capital'.[11] But the archaeological remains around the tower illustrate that for most of its history Jerusalem was not a Jewish city but one integrated into larger empires and inhabited, primarily, by 'other' communities. Although it is acknowledged in official publications and information supplied to tourists that the tower does not date to the time of David, but is much later, the continued use of the name only reinforces the collective memory that the history of the city is tied indelibly to David. The fact that the exhibit does not begin with the earlier history of the city but reiterates the claim that it is David who founds the city illustrates how memory is shaped. As Abu el-Haj expresses it so aptly, 'this is an embodied story of national origins and continuities, one with early-Israelite beginnings and contemporary Israeli endings'.[12]

It has become increasingly clear in recent years, following the innovative work of Maurice Halbwachs,[13] that the formation of collective memory is critical in shaping the way in which people view the past and so the present. Becker[14] has pointed out that 'whether the general run of people read history books or not, they inevitably picture the past in some fashion or other, and this picture, however little it corresponds to real past, helps to determine their ideas about politics and society'. The idea that Jerusalem's history only begins with David or that the roots of Israeli sovereignty lie deep in the past are significant in legitimizing current attempts to make real such an exclusivist claim to the city by the ever increasing pace of the 'Judaization' of Jerusalem. But it is a view of the past which is deliberately selective and which is often at odds with current understandings of the history of Jerusalem. Yet although Halbwachs drew a distinction between scholarly constructions of the past and collective memory which is continually transformed in response to the changing needs of society,[15]

---

11. Abu el-Haj, *Facts on the Ground*, p. 175.

12. Abu el-Haj, *Facts on the Ground*, p. 190.

13. M. Halbwachs, *The Collective Memory* (New York: Harper & Row, 1980).

14. C.L. Becker, 'What are Historical Facts?', in P. Snyder (ed.), *Detachment and the Writing of History: Essays and Letters of Carl L. Becker* (Ithaca, NY: Cornell University Press, 1958), p. 61, as cited in Y. Zerubavel, *Recovered Roots: Collective Memory and the Making of Israeli National Tradition* (Chicago: University of Chicago Press, 1995), p. 3.

15. See Zerubavel, *Recovered Roots*, p. 4.

the dominant image of Jerusalem in Western and Israeli memory illustrates how scholarship and collective memory are intimately entwined. As
Zerubavel shows, 'in fact, historians may not only share the basic premises
of collective memory but also help to shape them through their work, as
the history of national movements has shown'.[16] The Zionist construction
of history has drawn upon biblical scholarship for its own ends, but
abandoned that scholarship when it is no longer useful or necessary for the
legitimization of its control of Jerusalem. It is a view of the past which
draws upon the Western imagination in order to make it a lived reality. It
is a selective exploitation of the past, which increasingly blurs the lines
between the real and the imagined so that the present reality of the city
becomes self-evident and no longer subject to contest or alternative memory.

1. *Longing for Jerusalem*

The Western fascination with Jerusalem, stirred by reading the Bible, has
an astounding longevity and hold which has inspired Christian pilgrims
from the Middle Ages onwards, provided the foundations for the appeals
of Urban II and St Bernard of Clairvaux in preaching the necessity of the
Crusades, and has inspired great works of art from the Middle Ages
onwards. Invariably, the images that inspired great self-sacrifice in facing
the hardship and dangers of travel, the cruelty of the Crusaders or the
artistic imagination of painters and poets was a longing for an ideal
Jerusalem. Inevitably, such images ignored the realities of Jerusalem and
its inhabitants. It was to such an imaginary Jerusalem that Thomas Cook
appealed in advertising his tours to the Holy Land in the nineteenth
century:

> It will be joyous event to see the 'mountains round about Jerusalem;' but its
> culminating glory would be to look beyond those mountain ranges to the
> 'Jerusalem above;' and if a tour to famed attractions of Palestine should
> inspire all who accompany us to seek the 'better land', a rich reward crowns
> our labours.[17]

---

16. Zerubavel, *Recovered Roots*, p. 5.
17. Cited in R. Kark, 'From Pilgrimage to Budding Tourism: The Role of Thomas
Cook in the Rediscovery of the Holy Land in the Nineteenth Century', available online
at <http.//learn.snunit.k12.il/huji/mskark>; Kark's article is to appear in Sarah Searight
and Malcolm Wagstaff (eds.), *Travellers to the Near East* (London: Libri Books), from
Thomas Cook, 'Personal', *Cook's Excursionist* Supplement 25 (November 1867), p. 2.

Visitors to Jerusalem were being actively encouraged to replace the reality they found with the Jerusalem of their own imaginations and longings. Western visitors who came on tours, such as those led by Thomas Cook, imposed on Palestine and Jerusalem their own 'sacred geography' which ignored many of the lived realities of inhabitants they encountered. In the words of Shandler and Wenger,[18] 'they portrayed contemporary Palestine sometimes as a living embodiment of the ancient past, other times as the fallen remnant of a once-great culture. Zionists depicted the land as the site of a modernist utopia in the making.' Such travelers, apart from a few notable exceptions, remained ignorant of real lives of local notables, merchants, peasants and nomads, or their deep attachment to the land. Just as now, the alternative memories of those such as Serene Husseini Shahid were ignored in the Western idealization of Jerusalem.

In the United States, this imagination was fed by the so-called American Holy Land tours as described by Burke Long in a series of studies.[19] Such was the fascination with Jerusalem that the World's Fair in St Louis in 1904 included a full-scale replica of Ottoman Jerusalem covering 11 acres. Thousands of visitors, who had never set foot in Jerusalem, were able to experience the 'reality' of the city for themselves. But it was a reconstruction that ignored and silenced the realities of Ottoman Jerusalem. Those unable to visit Jerusalem and Palestine, or the Jerusalem of the World's Fair or the numerous Holy Land projects throughout the United States, were provided with other means of experiencing Jerusalem. 'Large-scale panoramic paintings of Holy Land vistas, especially views of Jerusalem, attempted to simulate the pilgrim's experience, so that spectators might feel that they had actually "stood in her gates"'.[20] Kent and Hulburt's *Palestine through the Stereoscope* offered those who purchased it in the early years of the twentieth century a set of 200 photographs, a viewing device that enhanced the illusion of three dimensional scenes, and a 300 page commentary.[21]

18. J. Shandler and B.S. Wenger, *Encounters with the 'Holy Land': Place, Past and Future in American Jewish Culture* (Hanover, NE: National Museum of American Jewish History, 1998), p. 21.

19. B. Long, 'Parlor Tours of the Holy Land: Fantasy and Ideology in Stereo-graphic Photographs of Palestine', *Religious Studies News* 13.4 (1998), pp. 9-10, 'Lakeside at Chautauqua's Holy Land', *JSOT* 92 (2001), pp. 29-53, 'Scenery of Eternity: William Foxwell Albright and the Notions of "Holy Land"', available online at <http://www.cwru.edu/affil/GAIR/papers/96papers/Constructs/long/Blong.htm>.

20. Shandler and Wenger, *Encounters with the 'Holy Land'*, p. 21.

21. Long, 'Parlor Tours', p. 9.

The parlor tour offered rewards assumed to derive from intimate experience of the holy land: affective support for believing the Bible's historical accounts and religious claims; enhanced commitment to Christianity felt to be challenged by modern sceptics and historians; renewed fervor for Christian missions; heightened sense of possessing the Bible and, by right, penetrating and dominating the land of its origin.[22]

The way in which present claims were ignored or erased is evident from the instructions to the viewers of the stereoscopic slides: in experiencing Palestine, viewers were warned that they must 'go back in imagination from the ignoble present of this land into its mighty past'[23], and, on viewing a slide of the port of Jaffa, biblical Joppa, the viewer was told to ignore 'the few people in semi-European dress—combining Paris with Baghdad fashions' and 'easily imagine that we have been transported back a couple of thousand years and that we are looking on a Joppa as the Apostle Peter saw it... We are in a Bible landscape, among people clad in biblical garments.' The reality of the present was forgotten in appealing to a collective memory of an idealized 'Holy Land'.

It is a tradition that is continued today in the so-called Holy Land Experience, a $16 million theme park, which opened in Orlando, Florida, on the 5 February 2001. The site has been developed by Zion's Hope, an evangelical Christian organization. Its president, Marvin J. Rosenthal, was the editor of *Israel, My Glory* and is the editor of *Zion's Fire*, which focuses on the study of 'the Bible, Israel, and the Scriptures'. He was also the director of *Friends of Israel*, 'a world-wide Bible-teaching ministry'. Its website[24] describes how visitors enter the Jerusalem gate into a street market of the first century CE. It is marketed as a 'living, biblical history museum'. But it is one in which an exclusivist view of history is imposed and in which the lived realities of the inhabitants of Jerusalem are erased. This is illustrated, unwittingly, in the advertising claim that the Oasis Palms Café offers 'a wide variety of American and Middle Eastern food items—many of which are themed to the historical and geographical setting, including the "Thirsty Camel Cooler" and "Goliath Burger"'. It is

22. It should also be remembered that in the 1920s Kent co-authored with Bailey the standard academic textbook on ancient Israelite history, *History of the Hebrew Commonwealth* (New York: Charles Scribner's Sons, 1920), and was responsible for a number of influential works in biblical studies at the beginning of the twentieth century.

23. Cited in L.I. Vogel, *To See a Promised Land: Americans and the Holy Land in the Nineteenth Century* (Pennsylvania: Pennsylvania State University, 1993), p. 11.

24. Available online at <http://www.theholylandexperience.com>.

the construction of the Orient as fantasy; a world sanitized of any real inhabitants or indigenous culture. Vogel notes[25] that in the minds of nineteenth-century Americans, 'the Holy Land had been a classic geographical image, a far-off place of both real and imagined features peopled by groups about whom the Americans already had well-formed preconceived notions'. Sites such as the Holy Land Experience help to perpetuate this image and at the same time offer both implicit and explicit support for exclusivist claims upon Jerusalem which ignore the alternative memories of the Palestinian population.

2. *Biblical Scholarship and the Imagination of Jerusalem*

Long has demonstrated the complex ways in which biblical scholarship was intimately linked in the development of popular conceptions about Palestine and Jerusalem. The ways in which American biblical scholars in the late nineteenth and early twentieth centuries imagined Palestine and Jerusalem as objects of fantasy and desire informed popular and political opinions. Furthermore, biblical scholarship was often enlisted in the service of the Zionist movement's campaign for a Jewish homeland as illustrated by the publication in 1917 of Samuel Hillel Isaacs' *The True Boundaries of the Holy Land*.[26] In the Foreword to the second edition, his daughter, Jeanette Isaacs Davis, claims that she published her father's work because 'he foresaw the great events that were transpiring during the closing years of his life and felt that the time had come to bring into the foreground the extent of Israel's inherited territory'.[27] The work, which was begun after the first Hague Peace Convention, was designed to influence the discussions at the time of the Balfour Declaration in favour of Israel's claims to the land. Her Foreword to the second edition in 1919 goes further in stating that the book had been 'received in authoritative circles with high appreciation' at a time when momentous events were taking place. However, she adds, 'it seems necessary to bring to the attention of our readers and to emphasize the fact that the boundaries herein laid down by our author are those of Numbers XXXIV: 1-12 and do

25. Vogel, *To See a Promised Land*, p. xiv.

26. S.H. Isaacs, *The True Boundaries of the Holy Land as described in Numbers XXXIV: 1-12: Solving the Many Diversified Theories as to their Location* (Chicago: n.p., 1917).

27. J.I. Davis, 'Foreword', in S.H. Isaacs, *The True Boundaries of the Holy Land as described in Numbers XXXIV: 1-12: Solving the Many Diversified Theories as to their Location* (Chicago: n.p., 2nd edn, 1919), p. 7.

not include all of the Scriptural allotments mentioned in other Biblical passages'.[28] Clearly, the intention now was to influence political and popular opinion in favor of a claim to a greater area on the grounds that Num. 34.1-12 represented only 'a *reduced* grant'. She then adds that 'but this does not mean that his request for a Homeland must be confined to these boundaries' since the 'Biblical, traditional, and historic boundaries' include a much larger area than is generally conceded to the Jewish nation. Shemuel Yeivin, director of the Israeli Department of Antiquities from 1948 to 1961, described the primary aim of the Israel Exploration Society as to provide 'concrete documentation of the continuity of a historical thread that remained unbroken from the time of Joshua Bin Nun until the days of the conquerors of the Negev in our generation'.[29]

The relationships between biblical scholarship and the popular and political imaginations are extremely complex. Biblical scholarship has been at times shaped by popular and political expectations about Palestine and Jerusalem, while at other times the popular and political imaginations have been reinforced by the direction of biblical studies. Although on occasions biblical scholarship has been enlisted directly in the support of Zionist claims for Jerusalem, as seen in the work of Samuel Isaacs, more frequently the findings of such scholarship have been appropriated on a very selective basis in order to support an exclusivist claim to Jerusalem. This selective appropriation can be seen in the ways in which the scholarly understanding of Jerusalem at the time of David has been represented and appropriated.

Theodore Robinson in his first volume of *A History of Israel*, written with W.O.E. Oesterley in the 1930s during the period of the British Mandate,[30] describes David's capture of the Jebusite city. This he describes as 'one of the strongest places in Palestine'.[31] He stresses that this showed the 'highest qualities of statesmanship'. Jerusalem, he says, 'stood at the head of the best of all passes into the hill country, and any power which would be absolute in the land must hold it'. Its capture is seen as an act of tactical and political genius in bringing together the Southern and Northern Kingdoms on 'neutral' ground. Robinson likens it to the roles of Washington

28. Davis, 'Foreword to the Second Edition' (1919), pp. 8a-8b.

29. S. Yeivin, *Eretz Israel* 3 (1954), p. 210, as cited in J. Blenkinsopp, 'The Bible, Archaeology and Politics' (unpublished paper).

30. T. Robinson, *A History of Israel*. I. *From Exodus to the Fall of Jerusalem, 586 B.C.* (Oxford: Clarendon Press, 1932).

31. Robinson, *A History of Israel*, p. 214.

and Canberra free from the claims of any one state. The transfer of the Ark is seen as the one single action that confirmed Jerusalem as 'the center of national life'.[32] Interestingly, the 'Jerusalem 3000' celebrations, or the political claims of Israeli spokespersons on the status of Jerusalem in contemporary negotiations make no mention of the pre-Israelite history of the city or the idea that it was chosen as a neutral site to bring together two separate kingdoms. It is only the claim that it is the eternal foundation of David, which is seen to be relevant and worthy of mention.

The presentation of David's capture of Jerusalem did not change very significantly over the rest of the twentieth century. However, the selectivity of the political use of this scholarship is striking. John Bright, writing in the 1960s in his classic work on the history of Israel, claims that David's seizure of Jebusite Jerusalem 'both eliminated a Canaanite enclave from the center of the land and gained a capital from which he could rule a national state'.[33] He stresses the same two elements as Robinson, that David chose Jerusalem because of its strategic location and that the transfer of the Ark confirmed Jerusalem as the political and spiritual capital as a masterstroke. Similarly, Martin Noth,[34] in the other classic statement on Israel's history which emerged in the middle of the twentieth century, stresses Jerusalem represented neutral soil between the two kingdoms. He emphasizes that although it is mentioned in the Egyptian Execration texts and the Amarna tablets, 'it had not been one of the really important cities of the land'. He then adds:

> It was in no sense the obvious centre of the land and the natural features of its position did not mark it out as the capital. What it became under David, and what it has meant in the history right up to our own day, it owes not to nature but to the will and insight of a man who, disregarding the natural conditions, made a decision that was right in a particular historical situation.[35]

Notice how the language used by Noth mirrors political claims of the present. The emphasis is upon the special status of Jerusalem and that it owes its significance to David. Biblical scholarship, however unwittingly, seemingly provides legitimation for the exclusivist claim advanced by Israeli government spokespersons. But most interestingly, Noth claims

32. Robinson, *A History of Israel*, p. 218.

33. J. Bright, *A History of Israel* (Louisville, KY: Westminster/John Knox Press, 4th edn, 2000), p. 200.

34. M. Noth, *The History of Israel* (London: A. & C. Black, 1960), p. 187.

35. Noth, *The History of Israel*, p. 190.

that Jerusalem did not become part of Israel or Judah but remained a separate city-state inhabited by its previous inhabitants who were joined by David and his entourage. Notice that he then claims that 'all these made up a considerable body of people, however, corresponding to the size of the political organization that was now ruled from here'.[36] Furthermore, Noth insists that the transfer of the Ark confirmed the centrality of Jerusalem. However, most interestingly, he claims that 'the ancient Israelite shrine now stood in a Canaanite place of worship in a Canaanite city which, though it was now David's royal city, had hitherto known no Israelite traditions of any kind'.[37] The link with Jebusite/Canaanite history is ignored in the political appropriation of this scholarship. The history of Israel produced by Siegfried Hermann later in the century[38] emphasizes that 'Jerusalem was not part of either kingdom but was David's city, an independent city state which belonged to him alone'. He notes that Jebusites still lived in it and that Jerusalem retained the character of an 'international' city whose population was composed of its former Jebusite inhabitants along with new elements. 'It was a city', he claims, 'that belonged neither to Judah nor to Israel, but was almost an alien body within the new state'.[39] But this recurrent theme of the status of Jerusalem and its former history is never mentioned in the contemporary Israeli claim over Jerusalem. The construction of a collective memory is a selective process that draws together historical scholarship and popular conceptions. The official memory projected during the 'Jerusalem 3000' celebrations and echoed in the political rhetoric of the present is a selective memory that ignores alternative voices and memories, whether popular or academic.

However, perhaps the most striking aspect of these academic accounts of David's capture of Jerusalem is that there is no acknowledgment that this an act of dispossession of the indigenous population. It is seen as a natural act of conquest that required no comment. In the same way, biblical scholarship until recently only emphasized the liberation themes of the Exodus traditions and ignored the dispossession and wholesale slaughter of the inhabitants of the land.[40] The status of Jerusalem as it has

---

36. Noth, *The History of Israel*, p. 191.

37. Noth, *The History of Israel*, p. 191.

38. S. Herrmann, *A History of Israel in Old Testament Times* (London: SCM Press, 1975), p. 149.

39. Herrmann, *A History of Israel*, p. 160.

40. See the essays in R.S. Sugirtharajah, *Voices from the Margin: Interpreting the Bible in the Third World* (London: SPCK, 1991) and the discussion in M. Prior, *The*

been represented in biblical scholarship throughout much of the twentieth century has been appropriated and used to bolster the exclusivist claim to Jerusalem. The loss of an indigenous Canaanite or Jebusite voice in the past is paralleled by the loss of the indigenous Palestinian voice in the present.

Robinson, Noth and Bright, of course, were writing before the Israeli annexation of east Jerusalem in 1967 and the subsequent series of Israeli excavations of the city which focused on the Iron Age through the Second Temple period, the period from David's supposed capture of Jerusalem and its loss to the Romans in 70 CE. These excavations were seen by many as offering the possibility of confirming the historical picture as it had been painted by numerous biblical scholars and thereby confirming the imagined Jerusalem of collective memory. The large-scale excavations by Mazar (1968–77), Avigad (1969–78), and Shiloh (1978–85) added significantly to the history of the city in the Iron Age, the Herodian, Roman, Byzantine and early Islamic periods, although the Iron Age was of particular interest. However, as Abu el-Haj points out:

> That Iron Age city, of course, represented the culmination of the Israelite conquest: the settlement, expansion, and establishment of Jerusalem as the capital of an ancient Israelite state. The nation's origin myth—a history that begins in the process of Israelite settlement and *culminates* in Israelite 'sovereignty'—had been substantiated in empirical form.[41]

Yet the excavations failed to confirm either the academic or popular images of Jerusalem associated with David. What was missing, most strikingly, was any evidence about the size and nature of the Jerusalem during the time of David, when according to collective memory and the picture painted by biblical historians it was supposed to be the capital of a significant ancient Israelite state. The contemporary political claim to sovereignty over Jerusalem has frequently appealed to this notion of continuity from the time of David's supposed conquest of the city and its foundation as the capital of Israel. The silence in the archaeological record was matched for a long time by a silence in the scholarly literature and, of course, the political rhetoric. The imagined Jerusalem of collective memory remained unchallenged until a number of dissenting scholarly voices began to question this picture towards the end of the twentieth century.

Bible and Colonialism: A Moral Critique (The Biblical Seminar, 48; Sheffield: Sheffield Academic Press, 1997), for attempts to read the Exodus and Conquest narratives 'through Canaanite eyes'.

41 Abu el-Haj, *Facts on the Ground*, p. 139.

A number of scholars began to take seriously the silence in the archaeological record and began to question the very notion that Jerusalem in the tenth century BCE, the time of David, was the capital of a significant ancient state. Increasingly it began to appear that Jerusalem, supposedly the capital of an Israelite state in the early tenth century under David according to biblically based reconstructions, was little more than a small isolated town at this time, reflecting the lack of population in the immediate vicinity. Ze'ev Herzog, in his now famous letter to *Ha'aretz* (29 October 1999), says that, despite excavations in Jerusalem over 150 years, the digs have turned up impressive remains from the Middle Bronze Age and the Iron II periods, but no remains of buildings from the time of David or Solomon: only a few pottery sherds. He concludes that the silence is significant and that given the remains from earlier and later periods, Jerusalem at the time of David and Solomon was a small city, possibly the center of a chiefdom but not an empire. 'Perhaps even harder to swallow', he says, 'is the fact that the united kingdom of David and Solomon, described in the Bible as a regional power, was at most a small tribal kingdom'. Similarly, Israel Finkelstein and Niel Silberman[42] take seriously the fact that these excavations not only failed to reveal any monumental architecture from this period but uncovered very few pottery sherds which are abundant at other sites in the tenth century. This fact combined with the discovery of impressive remains from earlier and later periods suggests to them that 'the most optimistic assessment of this negative evidence is that tenth century Jerusalem was rather limited in extent, perhaps not more than a typical hill country village'.

The inconvenient fact of the silence of the archaeological record on tenth-century Jerusalem has been dealt with in a number of ways in order to try to maintain the imagined Jerusalem of collective memory and to deny any alternative memory of the past. At first, as we have seen, it was ignored: traditional presentations of the history of Jerusalem continued to stress the importance of the period of David. However, in recent years, it has not been possible to ignore the growing challenge to the imagined Jerusalem of collective memory as the clamour of voices from Western scholars, such as those of Davies, Jamieson-Drake, Lemche, Thompson, Whitelam and others, as well as mainstream Israeli archaeologists such as Herzog and Finkelstein, has become ever greater. More recently, the

---

42. I. Finkelstein and N. Silberman, *The Bible Unearthed: Archaeology's New Vision of Ancient Israel and the Origin of its Sacred Texts* (New York: Free Press, 2001), p. 133.

silence in the archaeological record has been dismissed as being of no significance. Dever claims that the argument against Jerusalem as a state capital before the seventh century is 'entirely an argument from silence'.[43] He claims that 'few 10th century archaeological levels have been *exposed* in the deeply stratified and largely inaccessible ruins of ancient Jerusalem, so the paucity of finds means nothing. Yet there is growing evidence of extensive occupation.' However, he is unable or unwilling to state what the evidence for this supposed 'extensive occupation' might be.[44]

Increasingly, scholars who challenge the collective memory are dismissed as ideologically motivated, are vilified personally, have their scholarship and integrity questioned, and are accused of being anti-Israel and anti-semitic. Dever's recent work *What Did the Biblical Writers Know and When Did they Know It?* is only the latest in a series of attacks upon scholars who dare to question the standard presentation of Jerusalem's history. It is part of a defense of an exclusivist reading of the past, which seeks to deny any reality to alternative memories of the past. It also mirrors attempts to intimidate and silence journalists who dare to question the policies and actions of the Israeli government by claiming that any such criticism is anti-semitic. Such personal vilification, attacks and charges of anti-semitism only serve to reveal just how politically important the understanding of the past is for the legitimization of contemporary claims to exclusive sovereignty. Significantly, the political appropriation of this narrative of the past has failed to acknowledge the changing perspective on the size and nature of Jerusalem in the tenth century BCE. It is a view of the past, which undermines the constant claim to sovereignty based upon a continuum with the past. Furthermore, it shows that Jerusalem of the tenth century was little different from the Canaanite city-states of the Middle and Late Bronze Age, suggesting a much greater continuity in the history of ancient Palestine rather than some radical break. The time of David did not represent the development of a nation-state, along the lines of the

43. W.G. Dever, *What Did the Biblical Writers Know and When Did they Know It?* (Winona Lake, IN: Eerdmans, 2001), pp. 130-31.

44. He cites the work of N. Na'aman, 'Cow Town or Royal Capital? Evidence for Iron Age Jerusalem', *BARev* 23.4 (1997), pp. 43-47, 67; *idem*, 'It is There: Ancient Texts Prove It', *BARev* 24.4 (1998), pp. 42-44; J. Cahill, 'It is There: Archaeological Evidence Proves It', *BARev* 24.4 (1998), pp. 34-41, 63, against the view of M. Steiner, 'Redating the Terraces of Jerusalem', *IEJ* 44 (1994), pp. 13-20; G. Auld and M. Steiner, *Jerusalem I: From the Bronze Age to the Maccabees* (Cambridge: Lutterworth, 1996).

modern nation-state. It was little different from the preceding Bronze Age with a number of towns controlling their own hinterland in order to supply agricultural produce to support the population. An integrated history of Palestine offers a profound challenge to the exclusivist reading of history and the political claims to sovereignty which wish to deny any alternative memory of the past and of attachment to Jerusalem in particular. The warning offered in *Cook's Tourist's Handbook for Palestine and Syria*[45] to prospective visitors to the city at the end of the nineteenth century might stand as an epitaph to the enterprise undertaken by biblical scholars and archaeologists to construct ancient Jerusalem of the time of David: 'its magnitude is so much less than the imagination had pictured'.[46]

Conclusion

Imagination and memory have played a crucial role in shaping the present reality of Jerusalem. The image of the city which has inspired Western imagination and longing has helped to underpin the political claim to sovereignty encapsulated in the Jerusalem 3000 celebrations. The power-ful force of this projection can be seen in the way it has obscured the disparity between the idealization of the city and its lived reality, both in the past and in the present. Edward Said has highlighted this disparity in recent times with the imposed changes in Jerusalem which have converted it from a multi-cultural and multi-religious city to a primarily Jewish one, with sovereignty controlled exclusively by Israel:

> What it did was to project an idea of the city that not only contradicted the city's history, but also its very lived actuality, and turned it into what appeared to be a unified, 'eternally' central reality in the life principally of Jews the world over. Only by doing so first in projections and information could it then proceed to do what it has done on the ground during the last eight or nine years, that is, to massively undertake the architectural, demo-graphic and political metamorphoses that would then correspond to the images and projections.[47]

He describes this as

45. T. Cook, *Cook's Tourist's Handbook for Palestine and Syria* (London: Thomas Cook & Son, 1876), p. 112.

46. Cited in Shandler and Wenger, *Encounters with the 'Holy Land'*, p. 17.

47. E. Said, 'Keynote Essay', in G. Karmi (ed.), *Jerusalem Today: What Future for the Peace Process?* (Reading: Ithaca Press, 1996), pp. 1-21 (3).

an assault not only on geography, but also on culture, history, and religion. Whatever else it may be, historical Palestine is a seamless amalgam of cultures and religions, engaged like members of the same family, on the same plot of land, in which all has become entwined with all. Yet, so powerful and, in my opinion, so socially rejectionist is the Zionist vision, that it has seized the land, the past, and the living actuality of interrelated cultures in order to sever, carve out and unilaterally possess a territory and a place that it believed to be uniquely its own.[48]

The rich and complex history of the city over many centuries, from the Bronze and Iron ages through the Persian, Hellenistic, Roman, Byzantine and Islamic periods to the present are all part of the seamless history of Palestine. Yet much of this has been marginalized in the political rhetoric which claims a direct continuum from the time of David to the present. The continuous reiteration of this theme in official government statements, from the Declaration of Independence to the Jerusalem 3000 celebrations, or on countless official and unofficial websites which project an imagined Jerusalem as the capital of a kingdom under David and therefore the 'eternal' capital of Israel has no room for the alternative memories and lived realities of its 10,000 year old history. Zerubavel's comment,[49] although said of the way in which a national collective Israeli memory has been constructed, provides an apt comment on the power of such political rhetoric as embodied in the Jerusalem 3000 celebrations: 'the commemoration of historical events is not only a powerful means of reinforcing social solidarity but also an arena of struggle over power and control'. Her study, among other things, highlights how the disputes within the Jewish community over particular events 'demonstrate how the past is invoked to promote present political agendas and the emergence of competing interpretations of 'history' versus 'memory' in Israeli discourse'.[50] This is particularly true of disputes over the interpretation of historical events and the way in which the stories about David and Jerusalem have been appropriated to legitimize the Israeli claim over Jerusalem and the construction of facts on the ground which make this a lived reality. As Noam Chomsky noted,[51] the development of Givat Ze'ev Bloc northwest of Jerusalem, after the signing of the Wye Memorandum in 1998, cut off what was left

48. Said, 'Keynote Essay', pp. 7-8.

49. Zerubavel, *Recovered Roots*, p. xix.

50. Zerubavel, *Recovered Roots*, p. xix.

51. N. Chomsky, *Fateful Triangle: The United States, Israel, and the Palestinians* (London: Pluto Press, updated edn, 1999), p. xvii.

to the Palestinians from the region around Jerusalem from the territory to the south. The building projects in recent years have constructed 'facts on the ground' in order to realize the imagined Jerusalem as the sovereign and eternal capital of Israel thereby changing the lived reality.[52] The political appropriation of collective memory and the narratives of the past, particularly those constructed by biblical historians, has been selective. It has conveniently ignored those aspects of the narrative which suggest a much more multicultural past or, more recently, where scholars have questioned the legitimacy of the construction of the past. However, once the reality has been created, as with the present building projects in Jerusalem, the memory is no longer as important and can be given up since it is no longer relied upon for political and popular legitimation. The creation of 'facts on the ground' create the new lived reality and its own justification. All that is left to those who contest this reality is the pain of remembrance. Yet the testimony of individuals such as Serene Husseini Shahid becomes vital in remembering and making real an alternative memory of Jerusalem. Equally, it is vital that historians continue to question and probe the way in which the history of the city is constructed, presented and appropriated in political rhetoric. Those alternative voices of the past, both popular and academic, provide the basis for an alternative collective memory which stresses a rich and complex history of the city made up of the many threads of its inhabitants over thousands of years. It is a vital part of the integrated history of Palestine from deep in the past to the present and a counter-voice to the exclusivist reading of history, which currently dominates the way in which Jerusalem is imagined.

52. Geoffrey Aronson's bimonthly *Report on Israeli Settlement in the Occupied Territories* (available online at <http://www.fmep.org/reports/2002/v12n2.html>) provides detailed information on building activities in Jerusalem and elsewhere.

INDEXES

INDEX OF REFERENCES

OLD TESTAMENT

Genesis		14.12-16	182	21.27	242
1–11	23	14.15	185	22	113, 200
1	179, 223	14.18-20	182, 183,	22.8	234
2.6	253		242	22.16-18	234
2.10-14	253	14.18-19	200	22.18	242
6.4	248	14.18	152	23.3-20	242
9.1-7	247	14.21-24	182	24	200
9.4	247	14.22	183	24.32-61	242
9.12-13	245	14.22 LXX	183	25.1-6	200, 201
10	240	14.22-24	183	25.12-18	200, 201
10.15-20	240	15.2	199	25.22-23	201
11.1-9	13	15.3-5	199	25.23	201
11.27-32	198	15.13	204	25.28	201
11.30-31	199	15.19-21	155	25.32	201
12	200	15.20	157	26.4	242
12.1-3	199	16	200	26.28-31	242
12.3	241	16.2	199	27–35	208
12.5	199	16.6	199, 234	27	201
12.6-9	208	16.7-14	199	27.27-29	206
12.6	156	16.10	234	27.28	201
13.6	202	17	200	27.29	241
13.7	241, 242	17.12	225	27.39-40	201
13.8-13	242	17.18-21	200	27.43	202
13.8-9	199	17.18	200	27.44	202
13.14-17	199	17.20	200	28.8-9	202
13.18	208	17.27	225	28.14	242
14	151, 152,	18.18	242	29.35	205
	178, 181,	20	200	30.22	204
	183-85,	20.17	242	30.24	206
	188	21.9-12	234	31.44–32.1	242
14.1-11	182	21.17-21	242	32.4	202
14.5	157	21.18	200, 234	32.39	4
14.8	185	21.20	234	33.3-11	242
14.10	185	21.22-33	208	33.9	202

33.16	202	33.1-3	245	7.26	245
33.18–35.29	202	33.2	155, 204	9.1-5	28
34	242	34.10-16	245	10.19	225, 234,
35.16–19.24	205	34.11	204		235
35.23	205			11.8-9	28
36	202, 204	*Leviticus*		11.23	28
36.3	202	19.18	225, 235,	11.25-26	247
36.6	202		253, 255,	11.31-32	28
36.7-8	202		256	12	180
37.5-11	204	19.34	235, 236,	14.19	225, 235
39.3	243		255	14.22-23	192
45.7	204	25.47-49	231	14.29	225, 235
45.11	204	27.26-27	244	16.21	140
46.12	205			20.16-18	28
46.19	206	*Numbers*		23.8-9	255
47.12	204	3.13	244	31.16-30	249
47.13-26	231	11	247	32.1-43	249
47.27–48.4	206	12	248	32.12	225
49	4	12.3	248	32.28-30	250
49.8	205	13–14	247	32.41	236
49.22-26	206	13.25-29	204	32.43	236
49.22	206	13.30	248	32.48–33.1	249
50.15-21	204	14	248	33	249
50.20	243, 249	14.3	248	33.2	202
50.21	204	14.8-9	248	33.13-17	206
		14.31-33	248	34.1-3	28
Exodus		22–24	231, 241	34.4-12	28
3	27	22.5	241		
3.7-10	243	23.14-15	251	*Joshua*	
3.7-8	27	34.1-12	280, 281	2.1–12.24	28
3.8	27, 155			3.10	155, 204
3.12	243	*Deuteronomy*		9.1	204
3.17	204, 244	1.4	157	9.10	157
6.2-3	183	2.11	157	9.21-27	29
12.19	255	2.20	157	9.23	159
12.35-36	236	2.33-34	28	9.27	159
12.48	255	3.3	28	10	184, 185,
13.1-16	244	3.10-11	157		188
13.15	244	3.11	157	10.3-5	185
21.28	247	3.13	157	10.9	185
22.20-23	233	4.29	254	10.12-13	11
22.24	231	6.4-5	225	10.16-18	185
23	247	6.10-11	251	10.28	29
23.20-26	242, 245	6.12	251	10.29-39	29
23.23-24	28	7	245	10.40-43	29
23.23	155, 204,	7.1-11	28	11.1-23	29
	241	7.1	204, 239	12	185
23.27-33	245	7.3	232	12.4	157

12.10	185	18	47	11.3-11	232
13.6	240	18.1	246	11.36	180
13.12	157	19.1	246	12	48, 205,
15.63	152, 162,	19.10	153, 162,		206
	185, 188		185	12.24	205
18.28	153	21.25	246	15.13	139
21.43-45	29			15.34	207
22.19-24	4	*1 Samuel*		16.19	207
23–24	249	2.4-8	233	16.26	207
23.1-5	250	5.9	186	16.29 LXX	207
23.1	249	15	224, 226	16.30-32	207
23.9-16	245	15.33	224	16.31	207
23.10-11	250	17.44	249	18	226
23.11-13	246	17.54	186	19.10	188
23.14	245, 249			22.53	207
24	205, 225,	*2 Samuel*			
	251, 253	1.11	154	*2 Kings*	
24.11	204	5	175, 186,	2.12	208
24.12	245		187	3.3	207
24.13	251	5.6-9	153, 162	6.8-23	256
24.14	205, 251	5.6-8	186	10.29	207
24.16	251	5.6	186	10.31	207
24.19-21	251	5.7	187	13.2	207
24.21-24	215	5.8	186	13.11	207
24.22	251	7.5	180	14.24	207
24.25-28	205	7.11	180	15.9	207
		11.3	154	15.18	207
Judges		12.28	176	15.24	207
1	184, 185,	22.1	249	15.28	207
	188	23.1-7	249	16	128
1.4-8	153	23.1	249	16.5.10	129
1.8	185	24	188	17	216
1.21	153, 162,	24.15-25	180	17.7-24	215
	185, 188	24.16-25	153, 162	17.7-23	207, 215
1.31	240	24.23	153	17.22	207
2.1-19	246	26.6	154	17.24-41	212, 214
2.2	246			17.24	207
2.21-22	246	*1 Kings*		17.26-28	215
3.4	246	3.12	135	17.28	215
5.4	202	5	253	17.29	214
6–7	183	5.4-5	206, 213	17.30	216
6.25	140	8.10-11	180	17.34-41	215
8.22-23	205	8.16	181	17.35	215
8.27	246	9.3	180	17.36-38	215
9	205	9.20-21	249	17.37	215
9.4	205	9.20	155	17.38	215
13–16	4	11.1-8	249	17.41	215
17.5-6	246	11.1	206	18–20	11, 12

18–19	132	35.4	213	2.19	232
18	231	35.18	213	4	189
18.5	208	36.21	208	4.1	232
18.12	207			5	231
18.13	207	*Ezra*		5.13	191
18.17–20.19	207, 214	1.2-4	236	5.19	231
18.31-32	213	2–6	236	6.1	232
19.15	208	2.36-58	159	8–12	229
19.20	208	3–4	236, 242,	8–9	189, 196
19.29-31	213		256	8	190, 230,
20.6	253	3	228, 229		231
21.7	139	3.2-3	236	8.1	229
22	196	3.11-13	230, 236	8.2-3	229
22.3-20	208	3.11	237	8.4-14	231
22.15	208	3.12	190	8.9-12	229
22.18	208	4	240, 255	8.15-22	231
23	213, 231	4.1-5	236	9–10	227
23.4-20	207, 208	4.1-4	236	9.7-8	229, 236
23.11	142	4.2	216	9.8	155, 157
23.13	232	4.4	158	10	230
23.15	206, 207	4.9-10	158	10.29	158
23.21-23	243, 244	4.10	216	10.31-32	229
23.22	207	4.17	158	10.31	158
23.25	135	6.1-12	236	11	159
23.30	135	7–10	225	12	230, 231
23.31-35	135	7	237	12.43	230
24.10-17	136	8.15-20	159	12.44-47	230
25	137, 208	9–10	158, 190,	13	190, 229,
30	128		239		231, 232
		9	204	13.1-2	231
1 Chronicles		9.1	155, 157,	13.2	241
1.13-16	241		158, 239,	13.23-29	231
5.1-3	198		241	13.23-27	158
11	186	9.11	158, 225	13.23	159, 241
11.7	186	10	225, 227,	13.25	232
11.15-19	187		229, 230,	13.26	232
17.4	180		233, 237,	13.28-29	232
21	188		256	13.30	232
21.18–22.1	180	10.2	158, 225	13.31	231
		10.11	158		
2 Chronicles		10.12	232	*Job*	
3.1	113	10.13	226	26.5	157
5.13	237	10.44	227		
7.3	237	28–40	227	*Psalms*	
28.8-15	256	40–67	227	1.2	232
30	215			1.3	253
34.3-7	208	*Nehemiah*		2	239, 253
34.9	213	1–6	159	2.12	228
34.21	213	2.10	232	3.2	236

8.3	237	7	128	31.5-6	255
21.1-12	252	7.1-17	247	31.9	220
23.5	253	7.1-9	221	31.10	254
48	185	8.23	145	31.13	254
76.3	182	9.7-20	221	31.16	254
78	220, 237	26.14	157	31.18	254
78.26-33	248	26.19	157	31.20	220, 254
78.54-55	29	27.3	136	31.31	255
78.69	179	30.15-17	250	32.19	244
80.8	29	35	259	32.21-25	244
88.11-13	157	36–39	207, 214		
89.24	236	36	251	*Ezekiel*	
89.28	244	37.31-32	204	1.28	227
89.43	236	37.35-38	11	14.22	204
94.6	233	39	12	16.3	241
100.5	237	40.1-11	252	27.8-10	241
105.44	29	40.1-2	230	34.26	227
106	237	40.1	230	37.16-28	220
106.6-7	237	45.1-8	252	38.12	179
110.4	182	46.3	204	38.21-22	227
118.1	237	55.10	227	40–49	192
137	262, 264,	60.3-13	179	40–48	173, 253
	267, 274	64–66	254	47.1-2	253
137.5-6	263, 272	65.16-17	254	47.22-23	253, 255
146	233	65.25	254		
146.3	233	66.18-21	254	*Hosea*	
146.5	233	66.20	255	1.10–2.1	234
146.7-9	233			2.23	234
147.2-6	254	*Jeremiah*		13.1	220
149.1	253	4.23-26	13		
		4.31	244	*Joel*	
Proverbs		5.1-6	234	2.23	227
9.18	157	5.1	12, 253		
14.27	247	5.24	227	*Micah*	
15.33	247	25.11	208	4.7	204
		29–33	254		
Ecclesiastes		29.10-14	238	*Zephaniah*	
12.13	251	29.10	254	3.9	250
		29.12-14	254		
Isaiah		29.12-13	238	*Zechariah*	
2	257	30.22	254	7.10	233
2.3-4	257	30.24	254		
2.5-22	257	30.31	254		
6.6-10	250	31.3	254		

OTHER ANCIENT REFERENCES

Apocrypha and		7.24	80	*Mark*	
Deutero-Canonical		7.25	90	11.15-19	231
1 Esdras		8.17-18	90		
8–9	227	8.31-32	90	*Luke*	
8.1-24	227	9.1-22	89	1.51-53	233
8.25-90	227	9.31	91	4.16-30	27
8.50-52	227	9.43-49	92	4.18	233
8.68-70	228	9.73	92	6.20-26	233
8.76-77	228	10.1-6	92	10.30-37	256
8.82-90	228	10.15-20	92	19.28-47	178
9	228	10.18-21	92	21.5-6	165
9.6-7	228	10.22-46	92		
9.9	228	10.62-66	92	*John*	
9.26	255	10.68-69	93	2.13-25	178
9.36	228	11.20-53	160	2.20-22	165
9.37-55	228	11.33-37	93		
9.37-38	255	12.3	93	*Hebrews*	
9.40-41	234	12.35-36	160	1.1-3	20
		13.1-9	93		
Sirach		13.41	93	*Revelation*	
49.13	189	13.49-52	160	19.11-21	253
		15.2-9	84	21.9-27	173
1 Maccabees		15.26-31	94	22.1-5	253
1.10	86			22.3	253
1.11-16	87	*2 Maccabees*			
1.29	94	1	189	Pseudepigrapha	
1.33-36	80	2	196	*Jubilees*	
1.41-64	105	3.3	83	12.12	199
1.41-51	87	4	160	12.15	199
1.41-50	87	4.7-10	80, 82	12.22-27	199
2.16	87	4.7-9	82	15.28-32	201
2.18	87	4.7	82	15.32	201
2.31	160	4.9	104	34	243
2.65	87	4.13-15	82		
3.3-9	87	4.23	83	Qumran	
4.59	87	6.2	255	*1Qap Gen^{ar}*	
6.17	83	13.4	88	22.13	182
6.18-27	87				
6.23	88	New Testament		Talmuds	
6.58-61	88	*Matthew*		*b. Qid.*	
7.6	89	5–7	16	75a-76a	217
7.8-11	90	5.3-12	233		
7.9	88, 90	11.5	233	*Masseket Kutim*	
7.12-13	90	26.61	165	27	217
7.14	88				

Josephus
Antiquities
1–20	207
2.5.2-3	161
5.121-24	185
9.265	215
9.277-91	218
9.279	215
9.280	217
9.288	216
9.290	217
9.291	217
10.184-85	217
10.37-38	215
11.7	109
11.1-119	218
11.287-347	218
11.3.3	104
11.325-39	178
11.325	184
11.329-35	184
11.336	184
12.1.1	81
12.10.1	89
12.10.2	89
12.10.6	85, 90, 91
12.11.2	85
12.237-64	218
12.3.1	81
12.3.3	83
12.5.1	82, 83
12.5.2	87
12.5.3	87
12.5.4	87
12.6.5	87
12.9.3	87, 88
12.9.6	88
12.9.7	88
13.1.1	91
13.1.5	92
13.1.6	92
13.10.1	84, 95
13.11.1	84
13.11.2	109
13.13.5	86
13.15.1	84
13.152	83
13.16.2	85

13.2.1	92
13.2.2	85, 92
13.2.3	92
13.254-78	221
13.275	221
13.281	221
13.3.9	93
13.4.2	92
13.4.3	93
13.4.9	93
13.5.10	93
13.5.11	93
13.5.4	93
13.5.8	85, 93
13.6.3	93
13.6.4	93
13.6.7	85, 93, 94
13.7.2	85, 94
13.7.3	85, 94
13.8.1	85, 86
13.8.2-3	94
13.8.3	86
13.9.1	160
13.9.2	85, 95
13.9.3	84
14.1.2	95
14.1.3-2.1	95
14.10.22	86
14.13.9	101
14.2.3	95, 96
14.3.1-3	96
14.3.2-3	96
14.3.2	96
14.4.4	96
14.5.4	85
15.10.3	107
15.11.1	111
15.8.1	109
15.8.5	109
15.9.3	109
17.10.2	109
18.4.3	109

Life
153	96

War
1–7	207

1.4.7	84
1.7.2	104
2.5.2-3	161
2.5.3	161
2.17.3	104
2.344	109
4.4.1–6.1	161
4.9.11	161
5.108	109
5.156-83	109
5.238-46	109
5.507	109

Classical
Appian
Historia Romana
46-47	89

Aristotle
Politics
1253a	171

Diodorus Siculus
40.3.1-7	160

Dionysius of
Hallicarnassus
Roman History
1.53-71	195
1.72-73	194
1.72	194
1.89	195
2.2	195

Herodotus
Histories
1.84	187

Homer
Iliad
21.446-47	178

Livy
1.1-2	195
1.3-6	175
33.30.1-2	82
33.32.5	82
33.33.5-7	82

34.41.3 82
39.37.10 82
45.12.3-8 87
45.18 94

Plutarch
Alexander
42 187

Polybius
18.44.2 82
18.46.5 82
29.27.1-10 87
31.11.1–15.12 89
31.11.4-12 89
31.2.1-7 89
31.33.1-5 89
32.2.1–3.13 89

Strabo
15.2.34 161
16.2.40 84

Virgil
Aeneid
1.272 195

Inscriptions
Mesha Stele
7-8 58

Tel Dan
A.1-13 51, 55-57
A.8–9 57
A.8 58, 62, 63
A.9-10 56
A.9 46, 58, 66
A.12 59
B.1-8 51

El-Amarna Texts
EA
280 150
284 146
285 147

286 147
287 148
288 148
289 126, 149
290 149
366 150

Ugaritic Texts
KTU
1.21 157
1.108 157
1.161 157

INDEX OF AUTHORS

Abu el-Haj, N. 275, 276, 284
Abu-Sitta, S.H. 35
Adler, E.N. 220
Ahlström, G.W. 3, 67, 117, 213
Albright, W.F. 41
Anderson, F. 182
Anver, U. 140
Aronson, G. 289
Athas, G. 53, 67
Auld, G. 286
Avigad, N. 103

Baltzer, K. 182
Bar-Kochva, B. 80, 160
Barghouti, A.N. 101
Barnett, A.D. 79
Barrick, W.B. 213
Barstad, H. 13, 158, 211
Becker, C.L. 276
Becking, B. 57, 67, 207
Bellia, G. 177
Ben Zvi, E. 180, 240
Benvenisti, M. 264, 270, 273
Berger, P. 171, 175
Bickerman, E. 184
Bigger, S. 182, 183
Biran, A. 46, 48, 49, 67
Blenkinsopp, J. 159, 281
Bolin, T. 177, 181, 183, 190, 192, 193
Borges, J. 174
Botha, J. 40
Bowman, J. 219
Breasted, J.H. 253
Brekelmans, C.H. 239
Brett, M.G. 145
Bright, J. 282
Brueggemann, W. 32
Buccellati, G. 156

Burke, K. 19
Burrows, M.S. 42
Busink, A. 112
Busse, H. 173

Cahill, J. 71, 286
Callaway, J. 117
Carter, H. 78
Charlesworth, J.H. 168
Chomsky, N. 288
Coggins, R.J. 218
Cohen, J.A. 220
Cohen, S.J.D. 161
Cook, T. 277, 287
Coote, R.B. 117, 118
Cornelius, F. 156
Crane, O.T. 220
Cross, F.M., Jr 153
Crown, A.D. 218-20
Cryer, F.H. 52, 54, 67

Davies, J.K. 80
Davies, P.R. 118, 167, 180
Davies, W.D. 31, 32
Davis, J.I. 280, 281
Deist, F.E. 29
Dever, W.G. 286
Dion, P.E. 247
Donlan, W. 194, 195
Donner, H. 54

Edzard, D.O. 216
Efron, Z. 267
Egger, R. 219
Ellacuría, I. 18
Ellis, M.H. 26
Elnes, E. 183
Elon, A. 264

Emerton, J. 182
Enslin, M.S. 44
Evron, B. 266

Feldman, L. 217
Finkelstein, I. 6, 8, 116, 117, 121, 123-
    25, 127, 130, 132, 133, 137, 142,
    154, 209-13, 285
Fitzmyer, J. 182
Foster, B. 173, 174, 183
Franken, H.J. 71
Friedland, R. 273

Gabba, E. 194, 195
Gafni, I. 191, 193, 194
Galil, G. 57, 67
Gallery, M. 216
Garbini, G. 60, 67, 117, 189, 212, 213
Garrow Duncan, J. 73
Gaster, M. 218, 220
Geertz, C. 238
George, A. 171-73
Ginsberg, H.L. 141
Gmirkin, R. 61, 67
Gottwald, N.K. 154
Grabbe, L.L. 1, 154, 155, 158, 160, 161,
    189, 193
Graf, D. 99
Graham, A. 176
Gruen, E.S. 90, 99
Gurney, O.R. 156

Halbertal, M. 265
Halbwachs, M. 276
Halevi, J. 264
Handy, L.K. 155
Hansen, M.H. 99
Hauer, C.E. 153
Hayes, J.H. 80
Hecht, R. 273
Heintz, J.-G. 248
Hengel, M. 98
Herrmann, S. 283
Hestrin, R. 140
Hjelm, I. 4, 9, 11, 12, 14, 202, 203, 205,
    212, 214, 216, 217, 219-21, 223,
    224, 240, 243, 247, 252, 255
Holm-Nielsen, S. 187

Hoppe, L. 172, 173
Horn, S.H. 136

Irvin, D. 202
Irvine, S. 8
Isaacs, S.H. 280
Ishida, T. 156

Jacobsen, T. 173
Jacobson, D.N. 105
Jamieson-Drake, D. 72
Juynboll, T.W.J. 220

Kaiser, O. 239
Kark, R. 277
Kenyon, K.M. 68, 104, 114, 119, 121,
    125, 132, 137, 142
King, P. 181
Kleven, T. 188
Knauf, E.A. 6, 181, 240
Knoppers, G.N. 210, 212
Koester, H. 176
Kretschmar, G. 173
Kuhrt, A. 179

Labat, R. 216
Lamadrid, A.G. 30
Lemaire, A. 78, 140
Lemche, N.P. 10, 59, 67, 117, 147, 154,
    155, 211, 214, 240, 260
Levenson, J. 180, 185
Levinas, E. 270
Lichtheim, M. 174, 175
Liverani, M. 5, 177, 224, 239
Livingstone, A. 217
Lohfink, N. 33, 240
Long, B. 278
Luckenbill, D.D. 207, 211
Luckman, T. 171
Luz, U. 42

Maani, S. 6
Macalister, R.A.S. 73
Macdonald, J. 218, 220
Maier, J. 167
Makdisi, J.S. 272
Mandell, S.R. 80, 82, 89, 91
March, W.E. 32

Mazar, A. 72
Mazar, B. 73, 74
Mazar, E. 73, 74
McCarter, P. 186-88
McNamara, M. 182
Meissner, B. 216
Mendels, D. 191, 221
Meshel, Z. 140
Miano, P.J. 43
Miller, P. 183
Momigliani, A. 105
Montgomery, J.A. 217, 218
Moran, W. 146
Mulchrone, K. 21
Müller, H.-P. 258

Na'aman, N. 126, 146, 150, 213, 214, 286
Naveh, J. 46, 48, 49, 67
Neugebauer, O. 112
Newsom, C.A. 168
Nielsen, I. 109
Niessen, F. 219, 220
Nodet, E. 14, 225, 229, 235
Noth, M. 181, 192, 227, 282, 283

Oded, B. 8, 211, 239
Ofer, A. 74, 123
Oppenheim, A.L. 127, 129, 132, 134, 136
Oz, A. 271

Patai, R. 139
Postgate, J.N. 174
Prior, M. 15, 20, 26, 27, 30, 33-37, 39, 45, 223, 266, 283
Pritchard, J.B. 112
Pury, A. de 181

Rad, G. von 31
Räisänen, H. 38, 43
Reed, S. 186
Rendsburg, G. 184, 188
Richardson, P. 107, 109, 110, 161
Riches, J. 44
Robinson, T. 281, 282
Rollefson, G.O. 3
Röllig, W. 54

Römer, T. 181
Rorem, P. 42
Rose, M. 203
Rosenthal, F. 128
Rowland, C. 164
Rowley, H.H. 153
Rudolph, W. 227

Saggs, H.W. 8
Said, E. 287, 288
Sarna, N.M. 117
Sawah, F. 117
Schalit, A. 109
Schechter, S. 168
Schüssler Fiorenza, E. 40, 43, 44
Schwartz, D. 193
Schwartz, R.M. 15, 199, 202, 203, 223
Scott, R.B.Y. 76
Séligsohn, M. 220
Shahid, S.H. 272
Shandler, J. 278, 287
Shiloh, Y. 73, 74, 76, 187
Shoham, J. 76
Silberman, N. 8, 209-13, 285
Simons, J. 68
Singer, C. 112
Smend, R. 239
Smith, M. 229
Sobrino, J. 19, 27
Soggin, J. 184
Sparks, K.L. 201
Spieckermann, H. 216
Steiner, M.L. 7, 71, 73, 123, 126, 146, 286
Stenhouse, P. 216, 219, 221
Stern, E. 140
Stern, M. 190, 191
Stieberg, J.R. 122
Stone, B.J. 101
Strange, J. 98, 101, 102, 104, 106, 108, 110, 111
Sugirtharajah, R.S. 17, 283

Tamez, E. 17
Tarler, D. 71
Tatum, L. 77
Taylor, J.G. 140, 142

Taylor, W. 27
Thompson, T.L. 4, 6-10, 14, 59, 67, 72,
    117-20, 122, 124, 156, 181, 193,
    200-202, 209, 211, 224, 226, 230,
    231, 233-35, 238, 239, 243, 244,
    246-48, 251, 252
Thornton, T.L. 219
Tropper, J. 54, 67
Tsedaka, B. 219
Tushingham, D. 103, 109

Vaage, L.E. 18
Van Dijk, J. 174
Van Seters, J. 116, 172, 203, 205, 210
VanderKam, J.C. 83, 85
Vilmar, E. 216
Vogel, L.I. 279, 280

Wambacq, B.N. 239
Wenger, B.S. 278, 287
Wesselius, J.-W. 56, 67

Westermann, C. 152, 182, 183
Whitelam, K.W. 10, 41, 117, 210
Whybray, N. 151
Wilken, R. 173
Wilkinson, J. 109, 110
William, H. 122
Wilson, J.A. 125, 126
Wilson, R.R. 240
Wilson, W. 189
Wright, G.E. 41

Yadin, Y. 167
Yeivin, S. 281
Yoffee, N. 171
Younger, K. 177, 185

Zangenberg, J. 219
Zerubavel, Y. 258, 265, 266, 276, 277,
    288
Zobel, H.J. 152

JOURNAL FOR THE STUDY OF THE OLD TESTAMENT
SUPPLEMENT SERIES

260 A.R. Pete Diamond, Kathleen M. O'Connor and Louis Stulman (eds.), *Troubling Jeremiah*

261 Othmar Keel, *Goddesses and Trees, New Moon and Yahweh: Ancient Near Eastern Art and the Hebrew Bible*

262 Victor H. Matthews, Bernard M. Levinson and Tikva Frymer-Kensky (eds.), *Gender and Law in the Hebrew Bible and the Ancient Near East*

263 M. Patrick Graham and Steven L. McKenzie, *The Chronicler as Author: Studies in Text and Texture*

264 Donald F. Murray, *Divine Prerogative and Royal Pretension: Pragmatics, Poetics, and Polemics in a Narrative Sequence about David (2 Samuel 5.17–7.29)*

265 John Day, *Yahweh and the Gods and Goddesses of Canaan*

266 J. Cheryl Exum and Stephen D. Moore (eds.), *Biblical Studies/Cultural Studies: The Third Sheffield Colloquium*

267 Patrick D. Miller, Jr, *Israelite Religion and Biblical Theology: Collected Essays*

268 Linda S. Schearing and Steven L. McKenzie (eds.), *Those Elusive Deuteronomists: 'Pandeuteronomism' and Scholarship in the Nineties*

269 David J.A. Clines and Stephen D. Moore (eds.), *Auguries: The Jubilee Volume of the Sheffield Department of Biblical Studies*

270 John Day (ed.), *King and Messiah in Israel and the Ancient Near East: Proceedings of the Oxford Old Testament Seminar*

271 Wonsuk Ma, *Until the Spirit Comes: The Spirit of God in the Book of Isaiah*

272 James Richard Linville, *Israel in the Book of Kings: The Past as a Project of Social Identity*

273 Meir Lubetski, Claire Gottlieb and Sharon Keller (eds.), *Boundaries of the Ancient Near Eastern World: A Tribute to Cyrus H. Gordon*

274 Martin J. Buss, *Biblical Form Criticism in its Context*

275 William Johnstone, *Chronicles and Exodus: An Analogy and its Application*

276 Raz Kletter, *Economic Keystones: The Weight System of the Kingdom of Judah*

277 Augustine Pagolu, *The Religion of the Patriarchs*

278 Lester L. Grabbe (ed.), *Leading Captivity Captive: 'The Exile' as History and Ideology*

279 Kari Latvus, *God, Anger and Ideology: The Anger of God in Joshua and Judges in Relation to Deuteronomy and the Priestly Writings*

280 Eric S. Christianson, *A Time to Tell: Narrative Strategies in Ecclesiastes*

281 Peter D. Miscall, *Isaiah 34–35: A Nightmare/A Dream*

282 Joan E. Cook, *Hannah's Desire, God's Design: Early Interpretations in the Story of Hannah*

283 Kelvin Friebel, *Jeremiah's and Ezekiel's Sign-Acts: Rhetorical Nonverbal Communication*

284 M. Patrick Graham, Rick R. Marrs and Steven L. McKenzie (eds.), *Worship and the Hebrew Bible: Essays in Honor of John T. Willis*

285 Paolo Sacchi, *History of the Second Temple*

286 Wesley J. Bergen, *Elisha and the End of Prophetism*

287 Anne Fitzpatrick-McKinley, *The Transformation of Torah from Scribal Advice to Law*

288 Diana Lipton, *Revisions of the Night: Politics and Promises in the Patriarchal Dreams of Genesis*

289 Jože Krašovec (ed.), *The Interpretation of the Bible: The International Symposium in Slovenia*

290 Frederick H. Cryer and Thomas L. Thompson (eds.), *Qumran between the Old and New Testaments*

291 Christine Schams, *Jewish Scribes in the Second-Temple Period*

292 David J.A. Clines, *On the Way to the Postmodern: Old Testament Essays, 1967–1998 Volume 1*

293 David J.A. Clines, *On the Way to the Postmodern: Old Testament Essays, 1967–1998 Volume 2*

294 Charles E. Carter, *The Emergence of Yehud in the Persian Period: A Social and Demographic Study*

295 Jean-Marc Heimerdinger, *Topic, Focus and Foreground in Ancient Hebrew Narratives*

296 Mark Cameron Love, *The Evasive Text: Zechariah 1–8 and the Frustrated Reader*

297 Paul S. Ash, *David, Solomon and Egypt: A Reassessment*

298 John D. Baildam, *Paradisal Love: Johann Gottfried Herder and the Song of Songs*

299 M. Daniel Carroll R., *Rethinking Contexts, Rereading Texts: Contributions from the Social Sciences to Biblical Interpretation*

300 Edward Ball (ed.), *In Search of True Wisdom: Essays in Old Testament Interpretation in Honour of Ronald E. Clements*

301 Carolyn S. Leeb, *Away from the Father's House: The Social Location of na'ar and na'arah in Ancient Israel*

302 Xuan Huong Thi Pham, *Mourning in the Ancient Near East and the Hebrew Bible*

303 Ingrid Hjelm, *The Samaritans and Early Judaism: A Literary Analysis*

304 Wolter H. Rose, *Zemah and Zerubbabel: Messianic Expectations in the Early Postexilic Period*

305 Jo Bailey Wells, *God's Holy People: A Theme in Biblical Theology*

306 Albert de Pury, Thomas Römer and Jean-Daniel Macchi (eds.), *Israel Constructs its History: Deuteronomistic Historiography in Recent Research*

307 Robert L. Cole, *The Shape and Message of Book III (Psalms 73–89)*

308 Yiu-Wing Fung, *Victim and Victimizer: Joseph's Interpretation of his Destiny*

309 George Aichele (ed.), *Culture, Entertainment and the Bible*

310 Esther Fuchs, *Sexual Politics in the Biblical Narrative: Reading the Hebrew Bible as a Woman*

311 Gregory Glazov, *The Bridling of the Tongue and the Opening of the Mouth in Biblical Prophecy*

312 Francis Landy, *Beauty and the Enigma: And Other Essays on the Hebrew Bible*

313 Martin O'Kane (ed.), *Borders, Boundaries and the Bible*

314 Bernard S. Jackson, *Studies in the Semiotics of Biblical Law*

315 Paul R. Williamson, *Abraham, Israel and the Nations: The Patriarchal Promise and its Covenantal Development in Genesis*

316 Dominic Rudman, *Determinism in the Book of Ecclesiastes*

317 Lester L. Grabbe (ed.), *Did Moses Speak Attic? Jewish Historiography and Scripture in the Hellenistic Period*

318 David A. Baer, *When We All Go Home: Translation and Theology in LXX 56–66*

319 Henning Graf Reventlow and Yair Hoffman (eds.), *Creation in Jewish and Christian Tradition*

320 Claudia V. Camp, *Wise, Strange and Holy: The Strange Woman and the Making of the Bible*

321 Varese Layzer, *Signs of Weakness: Juxtaposing Irish Tales and the Bible*

322 Mignon R. Jacobs, *The Conceptual Coherence of the Book of Micah*

323 Martin Ravndal Hauge, *The Descent from the Mountain: Narrative Patterns in Exodus 19–40*

324 P.M. Michèle Daviau, John W. Wevers and Michael Weigl (eds.), *The World of the Aramaeans: Studies in Honour of Paul-Eugène Dion*, Volume 1

325 P.M. Michèle Daviau, John W. Wevers and Michael Weigl (eds.), *The World of the Aramaeans: Studies in Honour of Paul-Eugène Dion*, Volume 2

326 P.M. Michèle Daviau, John W. Wevers and Michael Weigl (eds.), *The World of the Aramaeans: Studies in Honour of Paul-Eugène Dion*, Volume 3

327 Gary D. Salyer, *Vain Rhetoric: Private Insight and Public Debate in Ecclesiastes*

328 James M. Trotter, *Reading Hosea in Achaemenid Yehud*

329 Wolfgang Bluedorn, *Yahweh Verus Baalism: A Theological Reading of the Gideon-Abimelech Narrative*

330 Lester L. Grabbe and Robert D. Haak (eds.), *'Every City shall be Forsaken': Urbanism and Prophecy in Ancient Israel and the Near East*

331 Amihai Mazar (ed.), with the assistance of Ginny Mathias, *Studies in the Archaeology of the Iron Age in Israel and Jordan*

332 Robert J.V. Hiebert, Claude E. Cox and Peter J. Gentry (eds.), *The Old Greek Psalter: Studies in Honour of Albert Pietersma*

333 Ada Rapoport-Albert and Gillian Greenberg (eds.), *Biblical Hebrew, Biblical Texts: Essays in Memory of Michael P. Weitzman*

334 Ken Stone (ed.), *Queer Commentary and the Hebrew Bible*

335 James K. Bruckner, *Implied Law in the Abrahamic Narrative: A Literary and Theological Analysis*

336 Stephen L. Cook, Corrine L. Patton and James W. Watts (eds.), *The Whirlwind: Essays on Job, Hermeneutics and Theology in Memory of Jane Morse*

337 Joyce Rilett Wood, *Amos in Song and Book Culture*

338 Alice A. Keefe, *Woman's Body and the Social Body in Hosea 1–2*

339 Sarah Nicholson, *Three Faces of Saul: An Intertextual Approach to Biblical*

   Tragedy

340 Philip R. Davies and John M. Halligan (eds.), *Second Temple Studies III: Studies in Politics, Class and Material Culture*

341 Mark W. Chavalas and K. Lawson Younger Jr (eds.), *Mesopotamia and the Bible*

343 J. Andrew Dearman and M. Patrick Graham (eds.), *The Land that I Will Show You: Essays on the History and Archaeology of the Ancient Near East in Honor of J. Maxwell Miller*

345 Jan-Wim Wesselius, *The Origin of the History of Israel: Herodotus' Histories as Blueprint for the First Books of the Bible*

346 Johanna Stiebert, *The Construction of Shame in the Hebrew Bible: The Prophetic Contribution*

347 Andrew G. Shead, *The Open Book and the Sealed Book: Jeremiah 32 in its Hebrew and Greek Recensions*

348 Alastair G. Hunter and Phillip R. Davies, *Sense and Sensitivity: Essays on Reading the Bible in Memory of Robert Carroll*

350 David Janzen, *Witch-hunts, Purity and Social Boundaries: The Expulsion of the Foreign Women in Ezra 9–10*

351 Roland Boer (ed.), *Tracking the 'Tribes of Yahweh': On the Trail of a Classic*

352 William John Lyons, *Canon and Exegesis: Canonical Praxis and the Sodom Narrative*

353 Athalya Brenner and Jan Willem van Henten (eds.), *Bible Translation on the Threshold of the Twenty-First Century: Authority, Reception, Culture and Religion*

354 Susan Gillingham, *The Image, the Depths and the Surface: Multivalent Approaches to Biblical Study*

356 Carole Fontaine, *Smooth Words: Women, Proverbs and Performance in Biblical Wisdom*

357 Carleen Mandolfo, *God in the Dock: Dialogic Tension in the Psalms of Lament*

359 David M. Gunn and Paula N. McNutt, *'Imagining' Biblical Worlds: Studies in Spatial, Social and Historical Constructs in Honor of James W. Flanagan*

361 Franz V. Greifenhagen, *Egypt on the Pentateuch's Ideological Map: Constructing Biblical Israel's Identity*

364 Jonathan P. Burnside, *The Signs of Sin: Seriousness of Offence in Biblical Law*

369 Ian Young (ed.), *Biblical Hebrew: Studies in Chronology and Typology*

371 M. Patrick Graham, Steven L. McKenzie and Gary N. Knoppers (eds.), *The Chronicler as Theologian: Essays in Honor of Ralph W. Klein*

372 Karl Möller, *A Prophet in Debate: The Rhetoric of Persuasion in the Book of Amos*

374 Silvia Schroer and Sophia Bietenhard (eds.), *Feminist Interpretation of the Bible and the Hermeneutics of Liberation*

379 Mark W. Bartusch, *Understanding Dan: An Exegetical Study of a Biblical City, Tribe and Ancestor*

380 Sidnie White Crawford and Leonard J. Greenspoon (eds.), *The Book of Esther in Modern Research*

381 Thomas L. Thompson (ed.), *Jerusalem in Ancient History and Tradition*

Made in United States
Troutdale, OR
10/02/2024

23359130R00186